The Heart of Altruism

The Heart of Altruism

PERCEPTIONS OF A COMMON HUMANITY

Kristen Renwick Monroe

PRINCETON UNIVERSITY PRESS

PRINCETON, NEW JERSEY

Library of Congress Cataloging-in-Publication Data

Monroe, Kristen R., 1946–
The heart of altruism : perceptions of
a common humanity / Kristen Renwick Monroe.
   p. cm.
Includes bibliographical references and index.
ISBN 0-691-04355-8 (alk. paper)
1. Altruism. I. Title.
BJ1474.M74   1996
171'.8—dc20   95-39585
CIP

This book has been composed in Berkeley Book

Princeton University Press books are printed on
acid-free paper and meet the guidelines for permanence
and durability of the Committee on Production Guidelines for
Book Longevity of the Council on Library Resources

Printed in the United States of America
by Princeton Academic Press

10 9 8 7 6 5 4 3 2

To my beloved family
Chloe, Nicholas, Alexander,
Wil, and Trudi

Contents

The Human Face of Altruism   ix

Acknowledgments   xvii

PART I: *The Importance of Altruism*

Introduction   3

CHAPTER 1
The Puzzle of Altruism   6

PART II: *Narratives: From Self-Interest to Altruism*

CHAPTER 2
The Entrepreneur   27

CHAPTER 3
The Philanthropist   41

CHAPTER 4
The Heroine   63

CHAPTER 5
Rescuers of Jews in Nazi Europe   91

PART III: *Traditional Explanations for Altruism*

CHAPTER 6
Sociocultural Attributes of Altruism   121

CHAPTER 7
Economic Approaches to Altruism   137

CHAPTER 8
Explanations from Evolutionary Biology   161

CHAPTER 9
Psychological Discussions of Altruism   179

PART IV: *The Altruistic Perspective*

CHAPTER 10
The Altruistic Perspective: Perceptions of a Shared Humanity   197

CHAPTER 11
Perspective and Ethical Political Acts: Initial Thoughts   217

Conclusion   233

Notes   239

Bibliography   271

Index   285

The Human Face of Altruism

I LIKED Otto Springer. I liked him immediately.

I had been given Otto's name as someone I should contact about his wartime experiences. Otto was an ethnic German who lived in Prague during World War II. As such, he was entitled, under Nazi law, to privileged status and special favors. Otto relinquished these benefits by serving as the Aryan head of a Jewish firm, working in the Austrian underground, officially and openly marrying (and thereby protecting) a Jewish woman, pulling Jews off transports for concentration camps, forging documents, and bribing numerous Gestapo officials and concentration camp guards. His efforts cost Otto his German citizenship and, when he was finally arrested and sent to a concentration camp himself, his freedom. Even then, however, Otto continued his activities on behalf of others, saving over one hundred Jews from imprisonment and death.

I wrote to Otto at his home in San Anselmo, California, asking if he would be willing to speak with me in connection with my work on altruism. I soon received a short, handwritten note, informing me that he would be delighted to talk and adding that many things needed to be told about the Nazi era. He gave me a phone number and invited me to contact him at my convenience.

When I called Otto, I was immediately struck by the forcefulness in his voice. There was a buoyancy and spirit that reached across the phone lines, a Germanic precision, even a slight formality, to his answers.

"Is this Otto Springer?"

"Correct!" Otto would boom out, rather than employing a weaker form of affirmation. I felt the presence of the man behind the voice. And I liked him immediately.

When we met, Otto readily acknowledged that he had saved many Jewish lives; but he insisted that the value of his acts was overestimated, that others had done much more. He even suggested that what he had done was not really altruistic.

> I don't know whether I'd consider what I did altruistic. Now, if you want an example of altruism, I know an absolutely clear case. A friend of mine. A very, very intelligent gentleman. He was a bachelor. He was German himself. But when the Germans took over, he was so mad about what the Nazis were doing that he said, "Now I am Czech." And he didn't register as German at all.
>
> Now, you may remember that for the Czechs, the Nuremberg laws came much later. The Nuremberg laws, these were the laws that made it a

crime against the race to marry a Jew. But at the beginning of the war, if you were a Czech Aryan, it might be a protection for a Jew if you were married to her. My friend Kari knew this and said, "Where is a Jew that I can marry?"

And there was one. She had fled Prague and lost, in Vienna, already her husband. She was left alone with two daughters. She and Kari didn't know each other. It was very funny, because when we introduced them, you know how it is in German, you use "thou" when you get intimate. You call each other "thou" instead of "you." Usually it happens that when you are alone, you call each other by the more intimate form than when you are in company. But with them, it was just the opposite. In company, they used the intimate form of address; but when they were alone, they were formal.

Now, I say that this man was a true altruist. Why? Not just because it was his idea to marry her. It is true that this marriage was motivated only because Kari knew at that time that this marriage would still give her protection. But it was more than that. Let me tell you.

For a while Mrs. Kari was safe. But then the Gestapo came and arrested Kari's new wife, due to a stupid mix-up of names. They came at a time when one daughter was at home, so they grabbed her too. The second daughter, the ten-year-old child, was with friends [that day]. Kari took the little girl who remained with him and hid her in the country somewhere. Mrs. Kari— Kari Mayer was his name—Mrs. Mayer was sent already to Auschwitz with her older daughter.

Now, sometime after this, everyone married to a Jew gets a summons to get divorced from their Jewish wives. If you refuse, you go to prison, since such a marriage is now a crime against the race. People told Kari, "Look. You don't help your wife at all because she is already in Auschwitz. To get a divorce is just a signature for you. So why don't you do it? It's ridiculous. You help nobody. And, of course, if you refuse, you risk being arrested yourself."

But Kari said, "No. Germans are sticklers. Sticklers with all kinds of procedures and rules and forms." He said, "When I get a divorce, they could look up the files and could find that they had arrested only one child. And then they could figure that the other one must be somewhere. If there is only a small risk that they will find this child, it is my duty to go on to whatever end results."

He went to the concentration camp even though his wife had already been arrested, just in order to avoid the slight possibility that the child would be discovered. *That* is a clear case of altruism.

How do we explain people like Kari? People like Otto? As I came to know him well, I realized Otto simply did not fit into any of the easy categories we social scientists like to employ to explain away actions by which individuals risk their own welfare, perhaps even their lives, to help others.

Otto was not religious; he described himself as some combination of agnostic, Kantian, and pantheist. Otto did not consider himself a particularly virtuous man, joking that his morals were only slightly better than those of an average American congressman. As a German national and proud supporter of the Hapsburg monarchy, he was politically in tune with, and would have benefited greatly from, a political movement that promised to restore the status quo ante. And even beyond the protected status insured him within the Third Reich by his German ethnicity, Otto's company had offered him the chance to transfer to a similar position within the company in India, where he could easily have expected to sit out the entire war in safety.

So why did he do it? Why did he risk his life for others? "One thing is important," Otto told me. "I had no choice. I never made a moral decision to rescue Jews. I just got mad. I felt I had to do it. I came across many things that demanded my compassion."

This theme repeated itself throughout my many conversations with Otto. He had to do it. He had no choice. It was impossible not to feel compassion at the sight of such brutality. I believed Otto. I listened to him long enough to trust that he was sincere. Yet both he and I knew full well that there *was* another choice. Indeed, had not another option existed, were Jews not condemned by the state and turned in by their neighbors in the first place, there would have been no need for Otto to save them. Otto claimed that he had no choice and that his actions were only normal. "No big deal. Nobody could stand by and do nothing when the Nazis came." Yet at a deeper level, both Otto and I knew that most people did precisely that: nothing. If everyone had been normal in the way Otto defined the term, then the Holocaust would not have occurred. Clearly, understanding Otto and figuring out what made him different from other people was not going to be easy.

Getting to know Otto, however, was a pleasure. It was also exciting and emotionally painful. Some of the excitement came simply from being so close to history, and I listened, fascinated, as Otto told me private details about critical events. I was often struck less by the historical significance of what Otto was saying, however, than by what I could hear between the lines about how Otto treated other people, the remarkable integrity of person that permeated Otto's relations with others, without his even being aware of it. One instance was particularly touching.

The Czech underground had been "rolled up" in 1942, decimated by the Germans in retaliation for the killing of Reinhard Heydrich, the German administrator of Czechoslovakia. The Czech option now closed to him, Otto's Hapsburg loyalties came into play, and he contacted the Austrian resistance groups. He worked with them for a year before he learned he was actually working for the British Secret Service. His work with the O-5 resistance group gave Otto a tangential relationship with the von Stauffenberg plot in 1944 to kill Adolf Hitler.

Shortly after the coup failed and the Nazis began their mass arrests of the plotters and their families, Otto was sent to Vienna. His immediate superior in the resistance was in danger and hid out in Otto's hotel room. In one of those rare twists of fate, the man had a heart attack. Thinking that he was dying, and knowing that in any case he was being pursued by the Nazis, the man unburdened himself to Otto, telling Otto that he was the one who had manned the radio transmitter that conveyed messages between the Stauffenberg plotters and the British Secret Service. The final message, which von Stauffenberg had insisted on receiving before he agreed to attempt the assassination, was a British guarantee that the unconditional surrender terms would be dropped and that Germany would not be partitioned after the war. According to Otto's boss, Churchill had agreed to this demand, and his agreement was taken to von Stauffenberg by another member of the O-5 resistance movement, a woman code-named Mafalda.

Otto had met Mafalda only once, but he remembered that she was very beautiful and had been accompanied by a lady-in-waiting throughout their meeting. Now Otto learned that Mafalda was the sister of the heir to the Portuguese throne.

Otto told me this story because he wanted history to know that the British had agreed to certain conditions for ending the war, conditions that von Stauffenberg insisted upon before setting the coup in motion, conditions that Winston Churchill had always insisted he had never agreed to grant the German opposition to Hitler. Otto was particularly pleased because he had recently tracked down Mafalda and thus could now verify everything he was telling me.

Since my boss is now dead, that leaves Mafalda and me as the only surviving eyewitnesses. She is the only one who knows the actual wording of a message of Winston Churchill to Count Stauffenberg at the end of June 1944. Mafalda is classified as Top Secret in order to protect what is a falsification of history. Her secrecy agreement will expire only in 1995. But I have signed no such agreement. And this that I am telling you now is part of history. It should be known.

Churchill even gave his word of honor to Stalin that he would never contact the German Resistance. But he did. And that's why it is still secret. It will be secret for fifty years.

But I have discovered where the woman is who was our connection! I have just learned this since the last time we spoke. I found her! I had trouble tracking her down, because of the secrecy. Count Thurn und Taxis, who was also a member of the Austrian O-5 Resistance, helped me do it. So this is very exciting.

Otto went on to tell me more about Mafalda, where she now lives and how he had tried to contact her through her family, who apparently were not pleased to have a Mata Hari in their midst. As Otto talked, he was so excited that he could hardly catch his breath. The main point of the story for Otto was that he would now be able to document all he claimed had happened, that he had finally found the only other living person who could verify his statements and correct a falsification of history. But what was striking to me was Otto's treatment of Mafalda. Despite the fact that Otto felt this was one last thing he had to do before he died, he displayed a touching reluctance to divulge information that might violate Mafalda's privacy. He insisted that I have all the information in case something should happen to him, making sure I took it all down in copious detail, but he also made me promise not to reveal it until Mafalda's fifty-year secrecy agreement had expired. The thought that he might gain public attention or fame by divulging this information simply did not occur to him, because he did not want to intrude on the privacy of another person.

If Otto touched important historical events, if he epitomized altruism, he also provided a specific instance of how a sensitive man lives his own life with integrity and dignity even in the midst of monstrous barbarity and unbearable suffering. One interview was particularly difficult, as Otto told of the last days of the war, after he had been sent to a concentration camp in October 1944.

On May 9 the Russians took Prague. But on May 5 already there was street fighting in Prague, and our camp was liquidated. The inmates were forced to march about thirty miles to a camp named Graeditz. For six weeks, the camp was near absolute starvation. I had been elected speaker of the camp and had to negotiate about the prisoners' transportation into the interior as the Russians came closer. I walked with the camp physician to a little town named Schweidenitz to negotiate with the "Organization Todt," the enforced labor section. Then we marched back.

Suddenly, the roads were blocked by military police and only ammunition transports could get through. There was a transport of heavy grenades, and I approached the German lieutenant and told him, "Look here. We have to march eight miles. Would you look the other way if we hopped on your truck carrying the grenades?" The lieutenant told me, "I could do that, but I warn you. You will see the most terrible things you can imagine. Absolutely beastly."

He was apparently no Nazi. And so we went on his truck. And coming toward us, going in the other direction, there was a death march. The Germans were trying to hide the inmates of the concentration camps from the approaching Allies. This was the death march of Gross Rosen camp. It skirted all the villages and went only through fields and forests. In the beginning there were four thousand people, and in Dachau, where it stopped, there were less than two hundred left. The people simply collapsed on the road. And the guards killed them, some in front of me. They just kept shooting them. Any stragglers who leaned against a tree were shot. And amongst these in the death transport is a very good friend of mine, who came to Auschwitz as a boy and was in this kind of death march and survived it. He's now a professor in Sonoma University, a sociologist. John S——— is his name. . . . I might have seen him.

This conversation took place over the telephone and I had listened quietly as Otto spoke. Only as he finished, did I realize Otto was crying. I quickly suggested we stop talking for the day. "No, no," he said. "Just give me a few minutes and I'll be all right." I insisted we stop and said I would call him later that afternoon, but only to make sure he was okay, not to continue the interview. There was a long silence. "Thank you," Otto said quietly, and we hung up.

Usually after such an interview, I went home to talk with my husband, to hug my children, to call my mother. But that day my husband was on the East Coast, the children were at friends, and my mother was not at home. I went upstairs and threw myself down on the bed. I lay there, just staring at the ceiling for a long time. I thought of the old man with such laughter in his voice, the forcefulness and precision in his answers, boomed out with great confidence and authority. I remembered the funny stories, the incidents that revealed Otto's joy in life. The time the heir to the Austrian throne visited Otto's grandfather, got drunk, and poured an entire bottle of cognac into the grand piano. I remembered Otto's description of a fairy-tale childhood in the fin de siècle Austro-Hungarian empire. Of his sitting in the cafés of prewar Prague, drinking strong coffee and discussing Kafka and Freud and Kant. Of Otto's stubborn refusal to believe that Jews were bad and all that followed because of this refusal, followed simply because he would not deny the humanity of the Jews for Adolf Hitler any more than he would, in the America of the 1950s, deny the humanity of blacks or will now deny the humanity of the Palestinians. I thought of Otto's spying for the British and escaping from the Russians after the war and still trying, at the age of eighty-two, to track down the woman Mafalda, a woman who was Otto's link to a moment in history. I remembered the excitement in his voice as he told me that he had finally found Mafalda and his touching reluctance to reveal her name or whereabouts, even now, out of respect for her privacy. I heard Otto's voice as he told me of witnessing the death march and seeing Jews being killed, of his horror at hearing the guns, shooting more and more stragglers, and his revulsion at his own helplessness as he turned his face to the truck's wall to vomit, even though he had nothing left in his stomach with which to be sick. I heard Otto's voice, his strong, buoyant, laughing voice, catch and break as he told how he later discovered one of his childhood friends had survived this march.

"I might have seen him," Otto said. And only then had I realized the old man was crying.

I thought of Otto and all that he had seen and felt and carried with him all these years. I knew I was in the presence of something extraordinary, something I had never before witnessed in such intensity and purity. I thought it was altruism. I knew it was real. I did not know if I could understand it myself, let alone explain it satisfactorily to others.

In this book I will try.

Acknowledgments

THERE IS A STORY told by Robert Graves that goes something like this. Graves was researching a book on the White Goddess, a mercurial, primitive deity once worshiped by people in the Mediterranean. According to myth, the Goddess was fiercely passionate, quick to reward her friends and equally prompt in punishing her enemies. As Graves became immersed in his research, he became so entranced with the Goddess that he sometimes almost felt her unseen presence.

Graves mailed off the book manuscript to several publishers. The American editor who rejected the manuscript soon lost his job and all his money in the stock market and committed suicide. The English editor who rejected the manuscript was killed in a car accident shortly thereafter. T. S. Eliot, who accepted the manuscript, went on to receive the Nobel Prize for literature. After that, Graves claimed he never again doubted the existence of the White Goddess.

No goddess hovered over my shoulder as I wrote this book, but I did experience something analogous. I have been most fortunate in receiving extraordinary assistance from many good people. In both my interviews and my work with colleagues, any small act of generosity on my part came back tenfold, so much so that I almost wonder, as Graves did, if the research project has not directed me rather than I it.

Certainly, in one sense, I do not feel this is my work. It belongs to the kind people who so willingly made themselves vulnerable to a stranger asking difficult personal questions. These are their stories, their lives. I have tried to be a faithful scribe, and I hope they will forgive me for the inevitable retreat into the scholarly analysis of what were also cherished exchanges with people I came to like. Although many of these people were willing to have their full names used in the book, and although I would like to thank them publicly, my first obligation must be to protect their privacy. In most cases, therefore, I employ pseudonyms or first names and have changed minor details to protect the people with whom I spoke. I regret that I may not publicly thank these people, or the friends who originally supplied their names. My gratitude is heartfelt, nonetheless.

I was equally fortunate in receiving generous assistance from many colleagues and students who worked on this project: Michael Barton, Connie Epperson, Katharine Gilan-Farr, Silla Kim, Ute Klingemann, Lara Legge, Deborah Leete, Kristen Maher, Lori Parker, Anne Saddington, Mark Sellick, Martin Young, and Marissa Wadsworth. Dan Batson, Bob Grafstein, Howard

Margolis, Sam and Pearl Oliner, and Etel Solingen provided generous assistance, read drafts of my work, and engaged in extensive friendly dialogue. Even when we disagree over conceptualizations, methodological approaches, or the merits of specific findings, I value their advice. Ellen Land-Weber sent an advance copy of her own manuscript on rescuers, and Phillip Alexander showed me his interviews with Bert. Eva Fogelman provided names and addresses of rescuers living in this country.

I have benefited further from extremely helpful comments from Gabriel Almond, J. Budziszewski, Joseph Cropsey, Jane Mansbridge, Trudi Miller, William Riker, Stergios Skaperdas, and Stephen Weatherford and from comments received when I presented seminars at the University of Pittsburgh, Carnegie-Mellon University, and Northwestern University. Articles in the *Journal of Politics*, the *American Journal of Political Science*, *Political Psychology*, *Ethics*, and chapter 13 in *The Economic Approach to Politics* presented some of my preliminary findings on altruism.*

Part of the book was written while I was on leave at Princeton University as a Laurance S. Rockefeller Fellow in the University Center for Human Values, as a Fellow in the Woodrow Wilson School at the Center for Domestic and Comparative Policy Studies, or as a participant in the weekly seminars at the School of Social Science at the Institute for Advanced Study. I appreciate the valuable comments and institutional support from colleagues at Princeton, especially Nancy Bermeo, Luc Botanski, John DiIulio, Mike Danielson, Rebecca French, Elizabetta Galeotti, Amy Gutmann, George Kateb, Helen Nissenbaum, Alan Ryan, and Michael Walzer. Special thanks to Jennifer Hochschild and Albert Hirschman.

Ross Quillian, while chair of the Department of Politics and Society, and William Schonfeld, dean of the School of Social Sciences at the University of California, were most helpful in granting generous leave time and in arranging my teaching to accommodate my interview schedule and writing needs. Their support and the receptive atmosphere they create for a scholar are greatly appreciated. David Easton, Harry Eckstein, Bernie Grofman, Mark Petracca, and Shawn Rosenberg were especially helpful in commenting on early drafts of the manuscript. Kim Campbell, Lynda Erickson, Jennifer Hochschild, Jane Mansbridge, Gertrude Monroe, Marie Provine, Janusz Reykowski, Laura J. Scalia, and Dorie Solinger were kind enough to read the entire manuscript and provided comments that were extremely helpful in my attempts to refocus my presentation in a more coherent fashion.

Jeanne Hawthorne assisted in technical preparation of the manuscript. Susan Lee transcribed many of the English interviews. German interviews were translated and transcribed by A. Dallendorfer, Michelle Mueller, and Ute

---

* Certain quotations may appear in slightly different form in these articles.

Klingemann. Mary Murrell provided valuable substantive comments and proved a most sympathetic editor, directing a superb staff at Princeton University Press. Special thanks to Victoria Wilson-Schwartz and Beth Gianfagna.

Finally, my thanks to the Earhart Foundation for their generous financial assistance, Fay and Nani for their friendship, my mother for her sense of decency, my children for their forbearance and their laughter, and my husband for being both my most stringent critic and my most encouraging and constant supporter.

PART I

The Importance of Altruism

Introduction

MOST SOCIAL and political theory since Hobbes is constructed on the norm of self-interest. As a guiding principle, self-interest informs many public policies and directs our daily lives. Yet even in the most vicious of Darwinian worlds, altruism and selfless behavior continue to exist. Why? In the following pages I try to answer this question, to consider the various influences that produce or encourage altruism and to examine the critical differences between rational actors and altruists. I will argue that altruists simply have a different way of seeing things. Where the rest of us see a stranger, altruists see a fellow human being. While many disparate factors may contribute to the existence and development of what I will identify as an altruistic perspective, it is the perspective itself that constitutes the heart of altruism. To understand what makes one person act out of concern for others, instead of pursuing individual self-interest, we need to ask how that individual's perspective sets and delineates the range of options the individual finds available, both empirically and morally.

Beyond explaining altruism as an empirical phenomenon, however, I have a second purpose in writing this book. I treat altruism as an analytical tool that can yield insight into the strengths and limitations of the dominant theoretical structures underlying many public policies and academic disciplines that assume normal human behavior consists of the pursuit of individual self-interest. This assumption exists in disciplines as diverse as economics, evolutionary biology, and psychology; it permeates much of social science through rational choice theory. The assumption that self-interest is an intrinsic part of human nature lends an aura of scientific inevitability to self-interested behavior. Altruism challenges the inescapability and the universality of that assumption. I will argue here that although self-interest forms a useful starting point for explicating human behavior, it leaves many important forms of human action unexplained. Altruism is but one example. By understanding how theories based on self-interest fail to offer adequate explanations for altruism, we may learn something about the limitations of these theories themselves. This theoretical aspect of the analysis led me to develop my own theory of ethical political behavior. Although incomplete and flawed, this theory is offered at the end of the book in the hope that it will stimulate the debate necessary to advance the development of theoretical tools useful in both understanding altruism and more fully explicating other forms of ethical political behavior.

The preface tells the story of one altruist, an ethnic German who risked his life to rescue over one hundred Jews during World War II. Otto's story gives a human face to altruism; it provides a specific example of what I mean by altruistic behavior. I hope it supplies the dramatic and emotional contact with altruism necessary to break through the somewhat blasé analytical barriers often constructed to explain away acts that challenge the usual pattern of self-interested behavior in which most of us engage every day. By concentrating on personal stories, told by Otto and other altruists in their own words, I hope to convince the reader immediately that altruism does exist. I then can move on to the main task of explicating altruism.

Part I begins the actual analysis of altruism and immediately involves us in several tangles. What is altruism? Who is an altruist? How do we know that the altruistic act was what it seems and not just a clever attempt to gain praise while feigning modesty? Similarly, might not the true altruist be reluctant to talk about the altruistic act, shying away from attention and praise? I confront some of these questions directly by stating clearly my own definition of altruism: action designed to benefit another, even at the risk of significant harm to the actor's own well-being. While this reflects the way altruism is commonly used, both in everyday discourse and among scholars, accepting any simple definition of such a complex phenomenon, with no further discussion, must leave the analyst dissatisfied. One practical solution to such conceptual difficulties can be reached by locating a group of individuals who most of us would agree provide unusual exemplars of altruism. This I have done through concentrating my analysis of altruism on three different groups: philanthropists, heroes, and rescuers of Jews in Nazi-occupied Europe. Part I explains the methodological and conceptual aspects of this approach. Here I situate my work within the broader context of earlier research on altruism and helping behavior. I then make clear what I mean by perspective and discuss why it is important to focus analysis on perspective rather than on the more traditional predictors of altruism so frequently emphasized in the literature. In constructing this argument, I consider the difficulties involved in attempting to gain insight on something as nebulous and subtle as perspective. I then describe how I constructed my survey questionnaire and located my sample of rational actors and altruists, how I dealt with problems of verification and selective memory, and the process by which I came to realize that traditional survey research will not adequately reveal either altruism or the cognitive orientations of human beings.

Part I thus contains much of the methodological and conceptual discussions that will interest scholars. I have constructed my argument, however, so that readers less concerned with these questions may move directly to part II, in which I introduce the people interviewed in this book. To avoid confusing the reader with too many different speakers, I present archetypes, actual individuals who are representative of the people in each of the four groups on which I focus analysis. In doing so, I have drawn heavily on transcribed interviews, which I edited into narratives. These narratives provide the details of the speakers' life stories and focus on the speakers' perspectives. These narratives provide impressionistic but firsthand knowledge of the differences between altruists and rational actors.

In part III, I present a systematic examination of the traditional explanations of altruism. I do this by using the narratives to construct an interpretive analysis of the different explanations offered by economics, evolutionary biology, and psychology. These are all disciplines that assume normal human behavior is self-interested and therefore have difficulty explaining altruism within the confines of their paradigms. The particular approaches under scrutiny range from the sociocultural, which explains altruism through the altruist's religious or educational background, to more elaborate theoretical concepts, such as kin or group selection in evolutionary biology, role models and social learning in psychology, and reciprocal altruism and psychic utility in economics. My analysis suggests that none of these traditional explanations adequately and fully accounts for altruism, and I conclude that most of them are misleading or incomplete. They explain behavior by rational actors but not by altruists.

In part IV, I offer my own explanation, one stressing a particular perspective in which altruists see themselves as bound to all mankind through a common humanity. I will argue that this is the critical component of altruism and that earlier works which attempt to explain altruism through other factors actually identify the trigger mechanisms that precipitate this critical altruistic perspective. I then step back from the specifics of the empirical examination of altruism and ask what this analysis can suggest about general theories of behavior and about ethical political behavior in particular. I use my knowledge of how existing theories fail to offer adequate explanations for altruism to develop my own theory of ethical political action, one that emphasizes perspective. After sketching the outlines of this theory, I offer further examples of important political acts for which this theory of perspective might prove useful. I take the opportunity in my concluding remarks to comment briefly on what a study of altruism reveals about moral choice and about what it means to be a human being.

CHAPTER 1

The Puzzle of Altruism

WHAT IS ALTRUISM, and why is it important? Altruism's significance comes not from its empirical frequency, which is relatively rare, but because its very existence challenges the widespread and dominant belief that it is natural for people to pursue individual self-interest.[1] Indeed, much important social and political theory suggests altruism should not exist at all. It thus becomes important to consider altruism not just to understand and explain the phenomenon itself but also to determine what its continuing existence reveals about limitations in the Western intellectual canon, limitations evident in politics and economics since Machiavelli and Hobbes, in biology since Darwin, and in psychology since Freud.[2]

In constructing my empirical analysis, I intend to present a theoretical framework within which altruism can be explained more fully, and I hope that this explanation will in turn lead to major revisions in the dominant self-interest paradigm within social science. The implications for general theory and for the social policies based on the self-interest paradigm can hardly be overstated.[3]

A careful review of the voluminous and wide-ranging literature on altruism reveals a remarkable lack of agreement over what is meant by the term. As a result, we find widespread confusion in discussions of altruism, with altruism often used interchangeably with giving, sharing, cooperating, helping, and different forms of other-directed or prosocial behavior. I define altruism as behavior intended to benefit another, even when this risks possible sacrifice to the welfare of the actor. There are several critical points in this definition. (1) Altruism must entail action. It cannot merely be good intentions or well-meaning thoughts.[4] (2) The action must be goal-directed, although this may be either conscious or reflexive.[5] (3) The goal of the act must be to further the welfare of another. If another's welfare is treated as an unintended or secondary consequence of behavior designed primarily to further my own welfare, the act is not altruistic. (4) Intentions count more than consequences. If I try to do something nice for you, and it ends up badly or with long-term negative consequences for you, this does not diminish the altruism of my initial action. Most analysts now consider motivation and intent critical, even though motives and intent are difficult to establish, observe, and measure objectively.[6] (5) The act must carry some possibility of diminution in my own welfare.[7] An act that improves both my own welfare and that of another person would not be altruistic but would fall instead into the category of collective welfare. (6) Altruism sets no conditions; its purpose is to further the welfare of another person or group, without anticipation of reward for the altruist.

Without much difficulty, we can think of various conceptual subtleties to introduce into this basic definition. This definition, for example, does not distinguish among various targets of the altruistic act, assuming that the act itself is altruistic regardless of the recipient. A contrasting approach could focus on group distinctions; we could then refer to what I have defined above as pure altruism and distinguish it from what we might call particularistic altruism, defined as altruism limited to particular people or groups deemed worthy because of special characteristics, such as shared ethnicity or family membership.

I decided to eschew terminological complexity in favor of one single definition.[8] The problem then became to recognize and allow for the subtle variations in altruism while retaining the simplicity of the single term. To solve this problem, I refer to acts which exhibit some but not all of the defining characteristics of altruism as quasi-altruistic behavior. This distinction allows us to differentiate between the many acts frequently confused with altruism (such as sharing or giving) without having to lump these significant deviations from self-interest into a catch-all category of altruism.[9] I further conceptualize behavior as running along a continuum, with pure self-interest and pure altruism as the two poles and modal or normal behavior, including quasi-altruistic acts, distributed between them.[10] This approach avoids the problem of dichotomizing behavior into only altruistic or self-interested acts. It minimizes the confusion resulting from excessive terminological intricacies. Yet it retains the advantage of allowing us to discuss quasi-altruistic acts or limited versions of altruism (such as the particularistic altruism discussed above) that would be provided for by more complex definitional terminology.[11]

TRADITIONAL APPROACHES TO ALTRUISM

What causes altruism? Analysts offer a wide range of explanations, from innate predispositions to socialization and tangible rewards. The best analyses of altruism consider more than one explanatory variable, and many of the underlying influences on altruism are frequently referred to by different names, depending on the discipline or the analyst. Thomas Hobbes, for example, suggested an explanation for altruism that emanates not from genuine concern for the needy person but rather from the so-called altruist's personal discomfort at seeing someone else in pain. Economists designate such altruism a form of psychic utility;[12] psychologists identify the same general phenomenon but refer to it as aversive personal distress created by arousal.[13] Any cross-disciplinary overview that seeks to summarize a vast literature thus must deal with two problems. (1) Analysts refer to the same—or to vastly similar—concepts using quite different terminology. These terminological differences vary, more or less systematically, from discipline to discipline; in any given analysis, they may reflect deliberate choices based on important philosophical orientations toward understanding behavior or, conversely, may merely be conventionally and uncritically adopted. (2) For purposes of analysis we need to separate predictors of altruism into distinct components in order to clarify and understand their relative influences. But in reality, these various influences often blend together and are far less distinct than our analysis suggests. To deal with these two problems, I save detailed discussion of specific findings on altruism for part III, where they can be discussed within the more general context of each discipline.

To situate my own approach within the extensive literature on altruism, however, I need at this point to provide a general overview of the differences among these various approaches. Explanations tend to cluster into four analytical categories: sociocultural, economic, biological, and psychological.

Sociocultural explanations focus on the individual demographic correlates of altruism that occur immediately to most of us. These range from religion, gender, and family background to wealth, occupation, education, or political views.[14] The basic assumption underlying sociocultural explanations is that belonging to a particular sector of the population will predispose one toward altruism. It might be argued, for example, that membership in a religious community encourages altruism.[15]

Economic explanations tend to consider altruism a good. Economists then stress the importance of rewards for altruism, rewards that may be material (e.g., money) or psychological (e.g., feeling good about oneself). Economists usually contend that altruism results from a basic economic calculus that figures individual costs and benefits. This leads to explanations in which altruism becomes a short-term strategy designed to obtain later goods for the altruist, either through reciprocated benevolent behavior or the alleviation of guilt.[16]

Explanations from evolutionary biology and psychology draw on many of the same concepts utilized by economists, and reflect an overall lack of interdisciplinary communication, despite occasional cross-fertilization. Biologists tend to stress explanations that favor kin or group selection. Such analyses rely heavily on in-group/out-group distinctions and on the importance of clusters or networks of altruists who are tolerated and even protected, not for themselves but rather because their altruism benefits the group that contains them. Community size and birth order are typical of biological explanations of human altruism.[17]

Psychologists offer the richest and most varied explanations of altruism. They frequently consider developmental factors, such as socialization or child-rearing practices and the level of sociocognitive development. Unlike economists and biologists, psychologists allow directly for norms, usually by

assuming that these are values internalized through socialization and development and are at least partially cognitive in construction. Culture is an important influence insofar as these values and norms are reinforced by the society at large, but psychologists also allow for more personal construction of values by the individual. Psychologists frequently include some of the same factors considered by other analysts, such as reciprocity (the exchange of benefits), and often build these values into complex systems of moral judgment.[18] Characteristics of the specific situation, including the identity of the recipient, the anonymity of the helper, and the number and identity of observers, also play a part in the emergence of altruistic behavior.[19]

Psychological discussions, and their counterparts in philosophy, touch on the category of explanation I find the most promising. These works emphasize empathy, views of oneself and of the world, expectations, and identity. They include the cognitive and emotional bases of altruism and introduce the impact of culture via the psychological process of reasoning that leads to altruism. When these factors come together in a particular way, they constitute what I refer to as an altruistic perspective.

PERSPECTIVE

From the Latin for "seen through," perspective as a general term refers both to the vista of space spread out before the eye and to the range of ideas or facts known to one in a meaningful relationship. It includes the faculty of seeing certain data in a particular context and suggests the idea of a mental view or prospect. As I develop and use this general term in my own analysis it includes five concepts of critical importance for altruism: cognition, world view, canonical expectations, empathy/sympathy, and views of self. Let me discuss each of these in detail.

Cognitive Frameworks and Processing. Cognition[20] is an important concept in psychology, where it grew out of two[21] separate intellectual trajectories.[22] The first is the developmental, where cognition is discussed in the early works in developmental psychology[23] and in later work on the development of moral reasoning.[24] These works suggest the way in which information is received and processed affects the likelihood of altruism occurring. The nondevelopmental origin of the concept of cognition comes from both theoretical work, such as that of William James, and experimental studies of consciousness and cognition, such as Bartlett's in the 1920s.[25] Works in this second trajectory assume that there is a given process by which humans process information, regardless of culture or social structures. It focuses on explaining this process rather than tracing its development and can be found in contemporary work in psychology by Simon and by Kahnemann, Tversky, and Slovic.[26] The later, more technical work on cognition assesses how the mind processes and frames its understanding of reality.[27] These studies do not deal explicitly with altruism, however, and the more general philosophical works that address altruism in terms of differences in world views are few.[28]

In my own work, I refer to cognition as the general process by which individuals come to know about and make sense of the world. This definition moves away from the popular tendency in cognitive psychology to focus on computational forms of processing information and moves into the more interpretive approach to cognition that examines how people construct meaning in their lives.[29] In my conceptualization of cognition, I make several assumptions. First, intentionality and agency exist. Second, individuals have both a biological self and a cultural self that is created in interactions with others. Finally, the biological substrate—often called human nature or the universals of human nature—does exist and must be allowed for, but I view it more as a constraint on behavior than as a determinant. In terms of the self-interest paradigm that underpins so much social theory, I would argue that any biological drive toward self-preservation no more *causes* us to act in certain ways than a biological need to reproduce can be said to determine our choice of marriage partner, or even our choice to marry at all, since marriage is a cultural construct and not a biological inevitability.

This conceptualization of cognition accepts the anthropologist's idea of the constitutive role of culture[30] and posits a transactional or intersubjectively constituted model of mind in preference to the isolating individualistic one of Anglo-American philosophy, illustrated by both state of nature and rational choice theory. I assume that cognition is influenced by norms and culture. This occurs through the process by which norms are internalized through socialization; this cultural component of socialization is then reflected in the actor's particular cognitive constructions. Culture thus helps to shape the human mind and gives meaning to action. The particular way in which this occurs for an individual will be refracted through the patterns embedded in the culture's symbolic systems, in its language and discourse modes, and in the forms of logical and narrative explication. The interpretation of a person's narrative thus becomes a powerful tool for understanding the different ways in which culture influences behavior. This tool must be used with care, however, as I shall discuss later in the chapter.

My interest in cognition and the process by which an individual structures and processes information arises in part from a desire to understand how cultural influences affect altruism. I hope to present a somewhat subtler argument than what frequently passes for a cultural explanation of behavior; for example, the idea that there are national or group characters that promote or discourage certain styles of conduct ("Germans are naturally aggressive" or "Religious people are more altruistic"). Cognition in my conceptualization reflects a culture's way of valuing particular behaviors as well as its way of knowing. Cognition thus includes both awareness of something and a judgment about it based on more general ideas about the natural occurrence of events.[31] I then employ the term cognitive-perceptual frameworks to refer to the particular part of an individual's beliefs about how the world works that is used to organize and make sense of reality for the individual at that particular time.[32] We may note, for example, that it is snowing (awareness) and that such snow is unusual in July in southern California (judgment).[33] Such judgment carries the idea of normality, of what usually happens, but it is not normative in the sense of prescribing what should happen. To allow for these normative influences on altruism we must include other components in our conceptualization of perspective.

Canonical Expectations. The expectation of what is normal and ordinary constitutes an extremely powerful influence on altruism.[34] This influence can be explained in part merely by introducing the concept of expectations into our analysis.[35] But the concept of expectations alone is insufficient, since we are interested not just in understanding what people expect but also in how particular expectations lead them to help others.[36] Any analysis of altruism thus needs to include a normative content supplied by the actor's opinions, stereotypes, and beliefs related to the object and the situation. To allow for this, I develop what I refer to as canonical expectations.[37] I intend this concept to suggest that an individual's actions—altruistic or egocentric—will be critically influenced not just by the actor's perceptions of the situation and its participants[38] but also by the actor's expectations about what should occur in the normal course of human behavior and by his or her sense that such normal behavior is right and proper.[39] We expect our parents to love us, for example, and are hurt when they do not, feeling that such love should occur naturally and that something is wrong when it is not forthcoming in the manner we expect.[40]

The expectation about what is ordinary and right and proper translates into the idea that such behavior requires no explanation. When quizzed about it by analysts, people are often puzzled; when pressed further, they often explain it through a quantifier ("Everybody does it") or through reference to a deontic model ("That's what you're supposed to do"). I found precisely this kind of response when I spoke with people who had rescued Jews from the Nazis. When I asked what made them risk their lives for strangers, they usually looked at me with some surprise and replied, "But what else could I do?" Their behavior was ordinary to them, although it seemed exceptional to me and was certainly exceptional statistically during the war.

Canonical expectations thus have a normative quality: it is "good" when the world operates in the expected way. To understand altruism, then, we must ask what the altruist expects will and should occur under ordinary circumstances. These expectations should differ in significant ways from those of nonaltruists.

World View. The idea of different modes of mentality and behavior, even different kinds of society, remains a perennial category of social thought.[41] Tönnies's work (1887/1955) is but one detailed discussion of the behavioral consequences of different world views. Using broad archetypes, Tönnies describes a *Gemeinschaft* world, exemplified by the medieval peasant rooted in his soil, in which behavior emanates from community ties or intrinsic moral values (*Wesenwille*). This archetype is juxtaposed to the *Gesellschaft* world of the merchant, where behavior reflects a goal-oriented rationality (*Kurwille*). In the *Gesellschaft* world, groups or relationships can be willed because those involved want to use the group or relationship to attain specific ends and "are willing to join hands for this purpose, even though indifference or even antipathy may exist on other levels."[42] In contrast, the *Gemeinschaft* world view is associated with groups based on friendship, neighborhood, and blood relationship; such groups view the relationship between members as an end in itself rather than as a means to an end.

A vast contemporary literature in psychology stresses the importance of group memberships,[43] and much normative political theory discusses the behavioral importance of communitarian versus liberal or contractarian world views.[44] I found the idea of mental concepts or constructs compelling and originally thought altruism would be more evident among those with communitarian world views than among those individuals who see life as a dog-eat-dog world in which every man is out for himself.[45] I did find world view a significant influence on altruism but not as I had anticipated. What seemed more important in predicting differences in treatment of others was the extent to which world views provide a sense of connectedness to others.[46]

Empathy.[47]   Unlike the three concepts discussed above, which are primarily cognitive, empathy is both a cognitive and an affective response. As a cognitive process, it provides the ability to understand what another person is feeling and to discriminate among various behavioral cues in order to assess the other person's emotional state. (An altruist, for example, would assume the perspective of the needy person in an attempt to understand that person's thoughts and intentions.) Previous cognitive analyses of empathy often argued that this cognitive ability provided a connecting bond that encourages more humane and compassionate treatment toward the other.[48] Indeed, early cognitive explanations of moral action were rooted in an actor's ability to empathize, to shift the actor's central perception from him or herself to that of another person or to members of a particular group. Particularly relevant examples include Hume's work on empathy and ethical development (1751/ 1902) and Smith's on sympathy (1759/1853).[49]

As we think about empathy and altruism, however, we soon realize that mere cognitive understanding is not enough, for such knowledge could be used to harm or manipulate the other person. We also need to conceptualize empathy as an affective reaction in which the altruist is emotionally aroused by the feelings of others in a way that is favorable to the satisfaction of their needs.[50]

Assuming we include both affective and cognitive factors in the concept of empathy, how might we expect empathy to relate to altruism? The cognitive aspect of empathy could enter through the structures of knowledge that form an expectation of a coherent sequence of actions and events in a given situation.[51] These are stored in an actor's memory and used as a guide for behavior. Such scripts and schemas would explain habitual altruism that is nonconscious or reflexive in origin, such as automatically helping the weak. Altruism would then manifest itself as a habit of caring, for example, or a reflexive jump to save someone from drowning, rather than as acts arrived at through a conscious calculus.[52]

Empathic motivation thus includes both affective and cognitive components and introduces many of the personality factors that result from socialization or developmental processes. Empathic motivation would allow for influences from the altruist's learned values and desires to help others, such as those arising from traditional religions or systems of morality and from socialization. These influences could operate either nonconsciously or consciously.[53]

View of Self.   Identity and our perceptions of who we are constitute important determinants of behavior.[54] Scholars concerned with altruism and identity often focus on the actor's view of him or herself, posing questions such as whether people try to act in ways that are consistent with their self-images.[55] The process by which identity might influence altruism is not clearly established, however: different analysts find conflicting and nonintuitive patterns of influence.[56] Because of these conflicting findings in the literature, I felt it was crucial to allow for the importance of self-image in my own approach. I also wondered if important cultural influences might not indirectly favor or discourage altruism through their effect on an actor's view of him or herself. Transactional contextualism would suggest that human action cannot be fully accounted for only by reference to intrapsychic traits, dispositions, and motives. The self is situated; it exists in a cultural world. This means that the realities speakers construct are social realities and permeate all the transactions an individual has over a lifetime.[57]

One problem was immediately evident: How could I learn about the speaker's sense of self without letting my preconceptions shape the conversation? The narrative format supplied a partial solution here. Beginning an interview by asking the speaker to tell me about him or herself seemed the best way to learn about the speaker's central self-image without intruding any of my own views into the conversation.

My initial interviews with altruists suggested that their altruism often did emanate from their concepts of themselves. These early interviews thus seemed to confirm previous findings by other scholars.[58] As my research progressed, however, I realized that explaining altruism through the sense of self was defining the influence too narrowly. I also needed to consider the altruists' views of others and the way altruists perceive linkages among different individuals. In particular, I needed to consider how other people were perceived in relation to the altruist. The narrative format of the interviews again proved extremely useful in this regard, allowing me to listen closely as the speaker wandered over the past, describing and reconstructing events and other people. What I heard did not fall into any of the preset categorizations I found in existing work in the field—an important development that I will discuss later in this chapter.

Importance of Perspective. To describe my approach in a summary form, I turned to the idea of perspective, a concept I find useful in several ways. Perspective conveys the visual idea of locating oneself in a cognitive map, much as one locates oneself in a landscape. It contains the idea that we each have a view of the world, a view of ourselves, a view of others, and a view of ourselves in relation to others. This captures what interests me about the importance of world view and identity for altruism. But I also use perspective to imply that each actor has a particular way of seeing the world and constructs this view much as a painter creates a painting. I presume that the perspectives of altruists will resemble each other and that they will differ in significant and consistent ways from the perspectives of nonaltruists.

Perspective incorporates our world views and our identities, since these affect the cognitive frameworks we use to process new information, make sense of reality, and give meaning to our actions. Our behavior exists in a context of relationships that allows for cultural influences through socialization and the development of values that both define us and influence our cognitive processes.

The idea of canonical expectations, of what seems normal and right to us, also can be subsumed to the concept of perspective. We look at a picture and expect objects to fall into a certain spatial construction that corresponds to our perception of reality. We are surprised when the artist has not aligned the objects in a manner that corresponds to our expectations and speak of an artist's perspective as being "off" or unusual. (Much of the power of certain Picasso paintings comes from his rearrangement of facial planes, for example.) So it is with our expectations of behavior. Since perspective also implies the idea of different viewpoints, of different ways of seeing reality and making sense of that reality, the term allows for a differentiation between the self and others and introduces a concern for how we connect and forge ties with "the other."

In a similar vein but at a more affective level, the term perspective also implies the possibility of adopting a new perspective, of putting oneself in someone else's vantage point, taking their side and feeling what they are feeling because we see what they see, much as we move our position to examine a painting from a different angle or to consider it in a different light. This shift in perspective should capture the idea of empathy, of the sympathy and compassion for others that can come by shifting our perspective and adopting the other's point of view, much as we suspend our own views and judgments and try to enter into the artist's way of seeing the world in order to understand what the artist wants to convey through his or her painting.

Although the way I have just conceptualized perspective is my own, a related concept appears in some theories of prosocial behavior, where it is more often referred to as role taking.[59] Unfortunately, research utilizing the concept of perspective has focused on prosocial behavior (such as helping) rather than on altruism, and the findings—as described by two of the best writers in the field—are "woefully inconclusive" (Krebs and Russell 1981: 137). Beyond this, the studies are usually conducted on children. Moreover, they frequently deal with hypothetical situations presented in experimental laboratory settings, not with actual behavior, and the results are widely acknowledged as being highly dependent on subtle changes in the wording of questions.[60] The general importance of perspective as I have defined it thus constitutes a rich but underexamined area in the research on altruism, and I refer to my approach as "perspectival."[61]

RESEARCH DESIGN

Can perspective explain altruism? To test the significance of perspective, I designed my research around behavioral archetypes, with self-interest and altruism at opposite poles of the conceptual continuum rather than as dichotomous phenomena. I then selected several groups of interview subjects to serve as behavioral archetypes representing different points on the continuum, beginning with groups of individuals who most frequently engage in self-interested acts, moving on to those whose actions are more mixed, and ending with people whose actions are more consistently altruistic. The perspectival differences between the different groups provide the kind of comparison that can determine whether altruists have a fundamentally different way of seeing themselves in relation to others. This design also allows us to ascertain whether there are consistent correlations between individuals' behaviors and their perspectives. Analyzing archetypical groups also makes it possible to test alternative explanations of altruism from the current literature, to explore which other factors correlate with behaviors at different points on the continuum.

Conceptual Continuum and Archetypes. I have already suggested why it is important to analyze altruism as one of several types of behavior along a conceptual continuum. The continuum also helps move from the theoretical definition of altruism to behavior by specific altruists. To suggest how this occurs, I need to discuss briefly both the continuum and my use of archetypes.

The conceptual continuum allows us to view self-interest and altruism as the two poles between which human behavior oscillates, rather than as separate, distinct, and inversely related phenomena. It contains one dimension for behavior and another for what I have defined as perspective. By considering altruism on this kind of continuum, I hope to be able to detect subtle differences in an array of behaviors labeled altruistic, from individuals who fit only the narrower definition adopted by economists to the kinds of self-sacrificial altruists who interest evolutionary biologists. With self-interested actors located on the left of the continuum, altruists on the right, and individuals whose actions were of mixed type distributed in between, the critical question becomes: Is there a correspondence between the points where these individuals are located in terms of their behavior and the points where they are located in terms of perspective? To answer this question, I focused on four distinct groups of individuals: entrepreneurs, philanthropists, heroes and heroines, and rescuers of Jews in Nazi Europe.

Why locate these particular groups at these points on the continuum?[62] At the left of the continuum lies the quintessential rational actor, whose behavior appears to follow perceived self-interest. Contemporary social theory, be it in economics, evolutionary biology, politics, or psychology, suggests that most individuals cluster around this point on the continuum.[63] These are the individuals most frequently said to represent the majority of humankind. They thus approximate baseline data. To find such individuals, I turned to the entrepreneurs and interviewed five who had achieved significant financial success. All were self-made millionaires; one was a billionaire. I treated the entrepreneurial type as the paradigmatic self-interested rational actor, since the entrepreneur does have the material resources to give to others but instead seeks to maximize individual self-interest, subject to information and opportunity costs.[64] The entrepreneur probably engages in limited other-directed behavior, such as charitable giving or occasional volunteer activity; but such giving would primarily be to causes or institutions with which the entrepreneur has a personal connection, such as his or her alma mater.[65] I would expect the entrepreneur's limited quasi-altruistic activity to be most easily explained by existing theories of altruism that emphasize conscious calculus of benefits to the giver, anticipation of praise, or deferred reciprocal altruism. Such explanations, developed using theories that assume self-interest as the norm of human behavior, interpret limited deviations from this norm within an individualistic paradigm rooted in self-interest.

Further to the right on the continuum are five philanthropists, those who give away significant amounts of the money they inherited or earned themselves.[66] Their actions are conscious. Their philanthropy lessens but does not destroy their individual well-being. Indeed, it is not clear that philanthropists seek *only* to maximize their individual self-interest. They may well enjoy the kinds of psychic rewards from their altruism that the economists emphasize. But they do engage in more altruistic activities than the entrepreneurs. The mere fact that we designate as "philanthropists" those wealthy people who give away large quantities of money reminds us that *most* wealthy people do not. I assume this terminological distinction constitutes evidence that there are critical differences between philanthropists and other rich people.

Philanthropists are particularly interesting to consider in terms of the self-interest paradigm, because philanthropy diverges from the norm of self-interest but still allows for clear distinctions between the individual philanthropist's welfare and the well-being of others. Because they give much of their material goods to others but usually retain enough to live quite comfortably, their philanthropy results in little harm to their own welfare. Insofar as philanthropists deviate slightly from the individualistic continuum assumed by economists, evolutionary biologists, and many psychologists, I would expect philanthropists to be the kinds of altruists whose behavior will be captured at least partially by some, but not all, of the explanations existing in the current literature on altruism.

The next group consists of heroes. These five individuals were identified by the Carnegie Hero Fund Commission and are defined by the commission as ordinary individuals who risk their lives to save others.[67] This group differs from philanthropists insofar as the heroic act (as defined and operationalized by the Carnegie Commission) carries a significant risk of death. In fact, approximately one-fourth of the Carnegie Hero awards are made posthumously. This means an examination of heroes moves analysis into the conceptual area of altruism that involves possible self-sacrifice and we might expect biological explanations of altruism to work best for this group. It is important to note that the Carnegie definition of hero excludes individuals (such as firemen and policemen) whose jobs are defined as protecting or saving others. The heroes recognized by the Carnegie Commission do not *have* to risk their lives for others as part of their job.[68] The fact that they do risk their lives sets them apart from philanthropists, whose donations may lessen their individual welfare but rarely to the point of serious economic harm or endangerment of life.

I thus locate heroes to the right of philanthropists but to the left of the last group analyzed, people who rescued Jews in Nazi Europe during World War II. I chose this location for rescuers for several reasons. (1) The length of the altruistic act was shorter for heroes than for rescuers. Many rescuers had Jews in their homes for many months, even years in some cases. Saving Jews from the Nazis thus could entail more extensive time commitment than a heroic act such as jumping into a lake to save someone from drowning or pulling someone from a burning vehicle. (2) The altruistic action of heroes usually evokes praise from the immediate society, and the hero generally knows this in advance. But the rescuers of Jews in Nazi Europe could expect not merely social ostracism but punishment from the political authorities if their deeds became known. (3) The altruistic act carried no cost to the physical safety of the hero's family or associates. In contrast, people who rescued Jews knew that if they were caught both they and their family members, including small children and elderly parents, would be killed.

In all these regards, then, altruistic activity carried the harshest potential penalties for the last category of people interviewed, people who rescued Jews in Nazi Europe. The rescuers risked their lives and those of their families to save Jews, many of whom were strangers to them. Instead of praise for their selfless actions, rescuers received scorn, vituperation, torture, imprisonment, or even death both from their own communities and from the poltical authorities. While some evidence suggests that rescuers' initial decisions were often spontaneous,[69] the continuing nature of rescue efforts entailed conscious reexamination and elaborate logistics.[70] For all of these reasons, I thought rescuers came closest to approaching pure altruism. Partly because of their theoretical significance, partly because these people were old and their stories, which have great historical value, need to be recorded now, and partly, perhaps, simply because I found myself closely drawn to these people, I interviewed ten rescuers of Jews.[71]

METHODOLOGY

In addition to the conceptual continuum and the behavioral archetypes discussed above, my empirical examination of altruism was designed around two further research tools: (1) the interpretation of narrative interviews and (2) a traditional survey questionnaire, designed to augment the narrative and administered after the narrative was completed.

The Narrative. In all of the twenty-five interviews, the speakers were invited to tell me their life stories. I wish I had been clever enough to understand the value of a narrative when I began the research, but the truth is that the narrative evolved less as a formal principle of research design and more out of personal concerns. I tried not to interrupt while people told me their stories, for example, as much to be polite as to avoid letting my questions steer the account in a direction it would not otherwise take.[72] I wanted to avoid imposing my own views on others through asking predesigned questions. I wanted to move empirical analysis away from an unexamined a priori attachment to a conceptual world in which actors are implicitly assumed to be both individualistic and self-interested in their orientation. And I was uncomfortable conducting interviews that felt mechanistic and impersonal; it seemed more natural to engage in a conversation with the individuals I interviewed, treating each as I would a new friend rather than as a subject. I thus found myself beginning interviews by suggesting that we get to know each other by the speakers telling me something about themselves and how they became entrepreneurs, philanthropists, heroes, or rescuers. What began as a matter of instinct and personal comfort, however, ended as a critical component of research.[73]

In this, I was extremely fortunate, for the narrative is one of the most widespread and powerful forms of discourse in human communication. It differs from other modes of discourse and other modes or organizing experience in several important ways. First, it requires agency: it involves human beings as characters or actors who have a place in the plot, in the story. When it emphasizes human action that is directed toward goals, a narrative provides insight on how different people organize, process, and interpret information and how they move toward achieving their goals. Second, it suggests the speakers' view of what is canonical. What is ordinary and right is discussed as the matter-of-fact. The unusual and the exceptional are what is remarked upon. Narrative thus provides "data" for analysis, not only in spoken responses but also in the spaces and silences. Third, narrative requires some sequential ordering of events, but the events themselves need not be real. The story that is constructed is indifferent to extralinguistic reality; it is the sequence of the sentences, the way events are structured, rather than the truth or falsity of any of the particular sentences or the events recounted, that reveals the mode of mental organization of the speaker. How the speaker organizes events to give meaning to them is what becomes important, for it is the process of organization that reveals much about the speaker's mind and perspective. This was particularly important in dealing with elderly speakers talking of troubled times.[74] Finally, narrative requires the narrator's perspective. It cannot be voiceless. It thus moves beyond mere reporting; it suggests how the speaker makes sense of what occurs. It suggests how the speaker organizes experience and reveals the distinctions people make in their everyday lives.[75] (We will soon discover, for example, that where most of us distinguish between how we treat strangers and friends, altruists do not.) The speaker essentially creates the context for the analyst by drawing in what the speaker finds are relevant cultural influences. This makes the narrative contextually thick and hence provides a sense of the speakers' "maps" of themselves in relation to others in the very particular contexts in which their behavior has occurred.

This is especially useful in revealing the speaker's concept of self, for it is the self which is located at the center of the narrative, whether as active agent, passive experiencer, or tool of destiny. All of the narratives in this book are autobiographies, accounts given by the narrator in the present about a protagonist, bearing the same name, who existed in the past and who blends into the present speaker as the story ends. The story explains and justifies why the life went a particular way, not just causally but, at some level, morally. The narrator uses the past self to point to and explain the future, as when one of the rescuers (chapter 5) describes how being ridiculed as a child for wearing a sailor suit made him realize he should not care what other people thought of him. He immediately related this incident to his life as a rescuer, when he was condemned to death for helping Jews and had to live underground and on the run for most of World War II.

While I interpret the narratives told to me, I do not perform the kind of linguistic analysis of narrative that a cognitive scientist or linguistic scholar would, focusing on lexical and grammatical usages or counting types of structures.[76] My interest in interpretation focuses primarily on understanding how people conceive of themselves and of themselves in relation to others. The narrative provided an especially important tool for this, one underutilized in analyses of altruism, where respondents are frequently expected to answer questions in the categorical form required in formal exchanges rather than in the narratives of natural conversation.[77]

Reliance on an interpretive narrative is rarely done by economists or biologists, but it does have precedents in cognitive psychology,[78] particularly in research utilizing schemas or scripts.[79] Researchers in anthropology, linguistics, and psychotherapy are making increasing use of these ordinary discourse materials (such as natural conversations) to discover the self-schema in naturalistic situations, that is, situations that occur outside the controlled, experimental laboratory.[80] This naturalistic aspect of the research seemed particularly important, since many of the best works on altruism and cognition came from hypothetical dilemmas or problems posed in laboratory settings, often to children.[81] When we deal with accounts of actual behavior by adults—as my narratives do—the findings may differ in significant ways. While many scholars who deal with narratives[82] develop intricate diagrammatic maps of self-schemas or employ various psychological tests,[83] I have not attempted this here.[84] My approach thus rests somewhere between the technical diagrammatic mapping of schema theory and the more anthropological or linguistic interpretations of narratives and stories that construct reality for people.[85]

Combining the Narrative with a Survey Questionnaire. To knit together these various theoretical concepts into an empirical examination of earlier ideas about altruism, I followed the narrative interviews with a survey questionnaire. This questionnaire addressed specific hypotheses about altruism but was not administered as a traditional survey because of my concerns about possible limitations of survey research.[86] To avoid these possible pitfalls, I began with the narrative and only then proceeded to ask questions from a more traditional fourteen-page questionnaire. This survey questionnaire, designed to test systematically the findings on altruism by scholars from Hume to Trivers, clustered into ten specific categories of topics: (1) family background, (2) political views, (3) group ties, (4) situational factors, (5) views on human nature, (6) concepts of duty, (7) view of self, (8) expectations, (9) costs, and (10) empathy. The questionnaire was intended to supplement the initial, more free-flowing part of the interview and to pinpoint critical information. I also tried to ask the same question in several ways and at different times during the interview, to determine whether the phrasing of the question or the context in which it was posed influenced the response.

The interpretation of narrative data is as much an art as a science. Because the concepts that interested me are so abstract and so finely differentiated, I had to phrase questions carefully and listen to how the speakers actually perceived their own actions or made the subtle distinctions between similar concepts, such as empathy and identity. Reliance on such an interpretive analysis necessitates quoting extensively from interviews and making data available to other scholars—which I will do upon request—who can correct my errors of judgment.

Subject Selection. Names of heroes were furnished, as already mentioned, by the Carnegie Hero Commission. Rescuers' names came from Yad Vashem, an Israeli agency established to honor Holocaust victims and their rescuers. All of the entrepreneurs and two of the philanthropists were identified through personal connections.[87] The other three philanthropists were contacted by writing to them care of the philanthropic foundations they headed or on whose boards they served. All subjects were older than fifty, to approach age comparability with the rescuers. Beyond this, I tried to match entrepreneurs with philanthropists on critical background characteristics, such as initial socioeconomic situation, education, religion, and so forth. The entrepreneur and the philanthropist described in chapters 2 and 3, for example, are approximately the same age and moved to California during high school after spending their early childhoods elsewhere. I recognize that this matching can only be approximate at best.

Interviews with all these people were taped with audio equipment. Except in rare instances, the interviews were transcribed.[88] Once transcribed, they were offered to the respondents for approval. (Some people said they did not want to see the transcript, in which case I did not send a copy.) Any material the respondent felt was too private, or simply wanted deleted for any reason, was excised from the transcript. My concern here was simply to respect the privacy of people who might open up in a conversation and then feel they had revealed too much.

To my surprise, few people ever asked to have substantive material excised from the transcript, and their choice of what to excise was revealing. A Dutch rescuer named Bert, for example, was shown both his interview and a draft of an article in which I analyzed his transcript. In the article, I had used the commonly employed term for the last year of the war in Holland, referring to it as the "Hunger Winter." I said this winter was particularly cold and harsh and that many people in Holland died as a result. Bert wrote back approving the use of the material but added a touching note to assure me that no one was ever cold or went hungry in his home.

As the research progressed, I found it best to modify the general technique described above in several minor ways. (1) The entrepreneurs liked seeing the questionnaires in advance. The heroes and the rescuers were intimidated or put off by the detail and formality of a long questionnaire, and it was therefore wisest *not* to show it to them in advance. Philanthropists appeared to evidence no clear preference. (2) The use of several short (i.e., forty-five to sixty minute) interviews appeared to elicit better information than long interviews. Knowing there was a definite time limit seemed to encourage subjects to raise important points, often just at the end of a session. Longer sessions also both tired the subject and made me less sensitive as a listener. I therefore eventually began to conduct short interviews, interspersed with breaks, even when the interviews were conducted in person. (In only a few cases, usually with entrepreneurs, did the person being interviewed object to this, preferring instead to push on and complete the interview in one or two sessions.) (3) Conducting several interviews over an extended time period allowed the subjects to develop trust in the interviewer. Long-term trust was also increased by not pushing the subject on emotionally painful issues, by automatically reaching to turn off the tape recorder whenever the subject recounted something that appeared to be upsetting, and simply by expressing concern not to tire interviewees by subjecting them to a lengthy session. The ordinary thoughtfulness of human interaction was repaid ten-fold. This was especially significant with the rescuers, many of whom offered to show me memoirs or short stories they had written about their war experiences—but usually only after we came to know each other.

Most of the interviews were conducted between March of 1988 and the fall of 1992, either by telephone or in person. During the summer of 1990 I also conducted interviews with six rescuers on videotape. My intent here was both to have videotaped interviews to use later for a possible documentary and to determine whether or not the difference in medium affected the substance of the interview material in any significant way. As far as I can tell, there was no significant difference. Despite my initial concerns about their impersonal nature, the telephone interviews actually turned out to offer the advantage of increased anonymity and, I believe, an increased comfort level for the subject as a result. In addition to this, in part perhaps *because* of this, utilizing the telephone meant I could conduct an extended series of shorter interviews (approximately forty minutes each). This increased trust and meant that people could re-raise an issue or remember that they had wanted to tell me about something not discussed before.[89]

In editing the transcripts, I try to present stories that flow naturally and carry the reader, while still retaining the basic integrity of the narrative as data. In doing so, I have occasionally condensed sentences or rephrased questions of mine to integrate them into the flow of the narrative. I tried to err on the side of verisimilitude and to remember that these narratives do constitute original data,[90] of use for others as well as the foundation of my own analysis.[91]

CONCLUSION

In this chapter I define altruism and situate my empirical analysis in the general body of literature on altruism. I outline the philosophical underpinnings of my research design and suggest why I believe an overlooked area in the literature on altruism concerns the importance of what I call perspective. I describe the kinds of individuals interviewed and suggest how and why I structured and interpreted narrative interviews with these particular individuals. To give body to this sketch of the research design, let us now turn to the edited interviews with individuals from each of these groups.

PART II

Narratives: From Self-Interest to Altruism

CHAPTER 2

The Entrepreneur

ENTREPRENEURS—classically defined as those who take an idea and turn it to personal profit—are well illustrated by Billy, a self-made man who amassed his millions through casting parts for cars.[1] I began by asking Billy to tell me something about himself and, in particular, how he became an entrepreneur. Like most entrepreneurs, for whom time is money, Billy was succinct and direct in telling his story.

> I was born in Alabama and grew up my first seven or eight years in Alabama. Then we moved to California. My father was in the foundry business, which I went into eventually. He was the type of person who has always been in demand, a very intelligent man and a good engineer, and I grew up in that atmosphere. He always worked seven days a week because he loved it, and he never had the thought of making money. That was never in his makeup. If he had wanted to make some money, he could have made some money, but he liked creating things. So I was always in that atmosphere. He invented a lot of things, but he never patented any of the ideas, because that wasn't important to him. Money didn't matter. Although we didn't have a lot of money, we always were an average family. But that influence was a real influence on me: the influence of someone who enjoyed inventing things, and the idea that money wasn't important, that it would be there if you needed it.
>
> My mother was mostly Irish and a hard-charger. She worked and had her own hair salon. It was a small operation, but she always worked. My mom has always been the aggressive one, and I think I'm kind of in between the two. My dad's personality is such that he never says anything, but he always gives you that air of knowing; even if he doesn't know, you think he does, because he listens. He's a great listener. My mom's a terrible listener. She's a very aggressive lady. She makes snap decisions. She just won't listen to anyone. When she was a young woman, she was a very good business-woman, much better at business than my dad. Maybe you could say I got my basic personality from my dad but my business sense from my mom. That's about the way it worked out.

Billy's ambition and drive were evident throughout his narrative. He knew what he wanted and went after it with determined enthusiasm, whether playing football or acquiring the good things in life that only money can buy.

I went to school in California after leaving Alabama, sometime around the fourth grade, and my whole ambition in life was to play sports. So when I went to high school, I didn't really care about learning anything. All I wanted to do was play football. That's the only thing that mattered to me. Football is almost the most important thing in the world to people back [in Alabama]. So I go down to Compton Junior College to play football. But now I started wanting these things, things like cars and some money in my pocket.

I had been working at the foundries in the evening—my dad was in the foundry business—so I started working for him in the evening, and on Saturdays and Sundays. Dad had a partner, who was my uncle. He and I never saw eye-to-eye, just because I was a pretty aggressive kid. Next thing you know, I'm making more money than the average guy working in the foundry, because it was all incentive-type work. And my uncle started saying, "No, this can't be." Because the older men are getting upset that I'm getting paid so much. I look back now and know he was correct.

So I finally quit, and Dad and I rented a little building in South Gate and started making some pattern plates. It's a special little item in foundries, a very simple thing to make. I thought, "Well, I could work nights and go to school and play ball and do what I want to do." Now, pattern plates come in maybe fifty different sizes. We start making patterns so that we can make the full line. No one did that before. One foundry would make the small sizes, another would make the intermediate, another would make the large ones. So when we got started, we made the real popular models, naturally. All the supply houses said, "We'll buy that one from you, but we'll buy the other ones from someone else." I took a hard line. "No, you buy them all from us or you don't buy anything." So, to make a long story short, eventually we pretty well captured that business. So I'm going along, doing well, buying me new cars. I have some money in my pocket. Chasing girls and all the good things in life. I'm twenty years old and playing ball and life is wonderful.

But the Korean War was going on then. And I get drafted. Which is bad. Here I'm going into the army. What am I going to do with this little business? My dad had meanwhile invented a machine, and his business had gone to pot just because he put all his time into this invention, because he loved it. So he closed his foundry, and he and I were partners. He would run the foundry while I'm in the army. "That's great," I said. So I go in the army. By that time things are pretty tough at home, so I'm sending some of my money home. Of course, in those days you didn't make much money. Ninety-six dollars a month, something like that. But I was fortunate and got special service and I just played a couple of years of football in the army. I didn't get shot up or anything.

I come home still with the idea that I wanted to play football. I hadn't got that out of my system yet. And the business was just about where it was when I left.

I said to myself, "You know, the foundry is a dirty, hot, smelly business. It's a rough way of life. People that work in foundries are not generally very well educated, and it's not a sophisticated type of business. I'll hang around in this foundry until I'm out of school, then I'm going to go do something else."

I worked in the foundry at night, and my dad works in the daytime so I could go to school and play ball. When I do graduate, I'm thinking that this foundry is not the way to go. So I said, "If I'm going to stay in this business, I'm going to make a lot of money or I'm going to go do something else." Because what I really wanted to do with my life was to coach football. But realizing that there is no money in coaching, just a lot of pleasure in it, I guess I was too greedy and I wanted too many materialistic things to do that.

Like many entrepreneurs, Billy found a way to combine one of his passions—a love of cars—with making money.

I've always been fascinated with cars and engines, like most young guys. I started going after what at that time was called the hot rod industry and got involved with the hot rod king of southern California. He liked me personally, and I did a good job for him. That was a big boost.

By this time I decide that it's time to get married, and I did. This was about 1957. Off we go to Detroit, which wasn't a very glamorous place, and I'm knocking on the doors at Ford Motor Company. Well, a young fellow knocking on the doors at Ford trying to get business was almost a joke. But I ran into the engineer at Ford who had come to California, and they're still having problems with that one program. I tell him, "Why don't I make that for you?" "Fine," he says. "I'll bring it out. I need a vacation anyway." So he comes back to California, and we make a hundred manifolds. Then we make another hundred, then a thousand. Then 50,000, and 150,000. It was just like a dream come true. But we did a good job for them. Now we probably make most of the aluminum intakes in the world, really just because we specialized in that. But it was a hard struggle. I used to spend 25 percent of my time in Detroit. Ford gave me an office in their plant, I was such an integral part of their racing program. It was my little cubicle there cause I was there so much.

So we go along. Everything's fine. I'm married. I'm having a couple of kids. I'm living in a nice house. And one day I wake up and I say, "You know, this is no fun for me any more. I really don't enjoy it." I used to absolutely thrive on it. It was always six days a week and on Sunday go over and do some paperwork-type thing. Then my daughter comes along, and I said, "I don't want to grow up not spending some time with my kids." So I said, "I'm going to sell the business."

I'm in Detroit, at a function. And I run into the chairman of the board of American Motors. I then was doing a little work for American Motors, and he said, "I understand that you'd like to sell ———." "Yeah, I think so. I just don't want to do that any more." "Well," he said, "I buy a few companies, and I'm interested."

Three months later, he shows up in Los Angeles. We make a deal, shake hands, and it's done. I sell the business and sign on as a consultant, mainly to keep me out of the foundry business. I signed a five-year contract for $100,000 a year, plus an expense account and an automobile. They just renewed this deal last year at $200,000 for ten more years. So it was a very lucrative thing for me.

Although Billy is no longer in the business, he has kept his hand in lots of smaller, quite profitable business deals. He went into partnership with several family members and, in the process, has made several of them millionaires. He now concentrates his time on his family and on these other business deals, most of which, at the time I interviewed him, involved real estate in southern California. Billy is a happy man, not someone driven always to achieve more, and he does not ignore other aspects of his life. But as the following excerpt from his interview suggests, Billy's family and his business interests remain the twin poles of his existence, even after he has achieved financial success. In this he illustrates a difference between entrepreneurs and similar self-made millionaires who become philanthropists: philanthropists often walk away from the business game in ways that entrepreneurs do not.

I just love my life now. My life goes in spells: a certain amount for business and a certain amount for family. In the morning, I like to always get my run in, or to take whatever kind of exercise I'm going to do. By 10:00 normally, I'm ready to get out and face the world. In the summer time, for instance, I keep myself flexible so if we decide to go to the beach or the lake, then I can do it with the family. Those are my priorities. But if that's not going on, if the family isn't doing anything in particular, then my priorities are to get out and check out some real estate.

I seem to have found myself a little niche there in that people come to me. There's always a deal. People are always coming to me. "Billy, do you want to venture this? Would you like to do this?" they ask. Honestly, there's a hundred deals today I could go do if I want to put the effort in and check them out.

Listening to Billy talk revealed more about how he sees the world. He is full of optimism and energy, cautious and careful in his business deals. He values honesty just as much as many of the altruists in my sample and values family above all else in his life.

Honesty often formed as central a part of the ethical system for entrepreneurs as it did for altruists. This corresponds with other evidence suggesting that there are no substantive differences in the ethical systems of rational actors and those of altruists. I was first struck by Billy's honesty in recognizing the extent to which his current happiness is a reflection of his having achieved his goals. Billy was equally forthright in recognizing that he had neglected his family while making his fortune.

I'm a very easygoing person. I can accept things very easily. As I've gotten older now, everything doesn't have to be my way. My wife and I have been married a long time, and we probably have had a half a dozen arguments in our lives. My son and daughter, I don't think there's anyone who has a better relationship than we have. We all just like each other. But it's easy to be a good guy if you're financially sound and you've got good health. It's hard if you've got to get up every morning, listen to the boss yell at you, and do a job you don't like. Then it's hard to come home and have a smile on your face.

That kind of thing has an awful lot to do with it. I think back to when I was working at the foundry, to when I'm up at 4:15 every morning, and by 5:15 I'd leave the house and usually not get home till 7 or 8. I'm sure people have heard this story before, but that's the way life was, and I accepted it because I wanted to do something. I don't know if it's greed or what it was; but I saw the good things that you could have in life, that money could buy for you, and I think along in there when I first married, I lost sight of family and marriage more than anything. My wife was not very happy in those days, because I was never home. We got married on Friday. We went to the local mountains Friday night, stayed at some friend's cabin, and came home. Sunday morning, I went to work. That's the way it had to be. I even took her to Detroit for our honeymoon. But that was not unusual, because in those days I never took a weekend off.

The shift in Billy's feelings began after his daughter nearly died at birth. He then began to think more about what his family meant to him and less about how much he loved business.

We almost lost our daughter at birth. She had a heart defect, and they had to do a heart catheter. That changed my life. I started thinking, "Wait a minute now. This little girl here, if I'm going to get the chance to enjoy her, I've got to start taking some time."

The kids came along a little bit later in life, when financially we're kind of getting over the hump. That was an absolute plus. So I started having some time with the kids. And since the kids, I started taking a lot of time off.

It was interesting that while others might have seen his daughter's illness as a sign from on high, Billy fitted it into his general view on life: that one takes decisive action after recognizing a problem, given that one has the luck necessary to be in the right position (financially and therefore emotionally) to recognize the problem in the first place.

> Luckily enough she outgrew the heart problem, and everything's great. A lot of people tell me I was wise enough to see the signals, and that a lot of people don't. But I think you've got to be fortunate, too. You've got to be at the right place at the right time; on the other hand, I'm also a real believer that things don't happen, you make them happen.

Entrepreneurs differ from philanthropists in their abiding love of the game, their tremendous joy in taking an idea and turning it into a financial success. Convincing his wife to take their honeymoon in Detroit so he could cinch a business deal with General Motors was only one indication of Billy's drive, his determination to both build a better mousetrap and then make darn sure the world beat a path to his door to buy the mousetrap!

> And it's fun. If it's not fun, I really don't want to do it. I'm very fortunate financially right now that I can walk away from deals that aren't any fun. But years ago, I would tackle anything. I've mellowed with age.

In background characteristics, Billy typifies the entrepreneurs I interviewed. His self-image typifies those of other entrepreneurs and, interestingly enough, many philanthropists I interviewed. Billy saw himself as a decent, honest man who relies on himself and works hard.

> If I wanted to buy a new car—and I always wanted those kind of things—I wasn't afraid to work for it. Like, I wanted a new Thunderbird; I wanted a new Corvette. I was young and I couldn't afford those things, but I worked. I put in the extra time and effort so that I could have that new Corvette, so I could have that new Thunderbird. I guess basically, during those periods, when I really wanted something, I basically relied on myself, not on somebody else to take care of me.

The main difference in the self-images of entrepreneurs and philanthropists lies in the entrepreneurs' concern with an opportunity to make a profit. But Billy resembles many altruists in seeing himself as someone who takes charge of a situation and cares for those around him.[2]

> I'm someone who takes charge of things, and I do it in an easy manner. When I was younger, I was overly aggressive. But people generally like me. Maybe they didn't like what they saw in me, because I was too aggressive. As I've gotten older, I'm more secure. I don't have to make every deal work. Every deal doesn't have to be perfect.

Before, when I said I was fortunate, that's true, but I am not what you'd call really privileged by birth in any way. I guess, too, that I'm a tolerant person, very much so for the most part. And pretty hardworking. When I get involved in something, I'm involved. I don't do anything halfway. I have a fair bit of self-confidence. Yeah, I think I have the confidence.

Billy described himself as someone who takes on responsibility, who sees a problem and figures he'll do something about it. "I don't go out looking for problems," Billy told me, "but I'm not afraid of a problem." Although he sees himself as someone who "takes the initiative to make things happen in life," he recognizes that he is able to do this because he has been blessed. He mentioned good health several times. "Health has so much to do with it. People who truly feel good, physically and mentally, if you're fortunate enough to really feel good, it's easier to excel." Remarkably, Billy does not see himself as some kind of financial genius but as someone willing to work hard to get "the good things in life."

I don't know if I have such a good financial head. I think the key to that type of thing is to listen. If you think you know it all, you're never going to learn. But I think I'm pretty open-minded, and I don't do anything too radical.

It was interesting to compare entrepreneurs' and philanthropists' views on helping people financially, specifically, their beliefs about the effect of such charity on the recipient. Some—but not all—philanthropists resemble Billy and other entrepreneurs in their concern to structure aid so it does not inhibit the independence of the recipient. This attitude was evident in Billy's discussions of his charitable giving: he keeps strings attached to his gifts. He gives primarily to local causes or to people he knows personally and usually structures his gifts on a repay or loan basis. This was illustrated by his experience with his son's football team.

When my son was to the age that he was playing sports, I wanted to get involved. I loved sports, so I started coaching Pop Warner football and Little League baseball. The Pop Warner football team had a lot of success for the local kids here. When we got to my son's last year of high school, the kids had won the San Diego Championship and were invited to go to Hawaii and play the Hawaiian champions. That was a real project, to go out and raise the money to go to Hawaii, which we did.

Billy could easily have written out a check for the team to go to Hawaii, but this was not in his character. Instead he found a typically entrepreneurial way to get the team to Hawaii while at the same time teaching them the value of money and hard work: he lent them the money to build a house.

I took that project on, and what we did was we built a house. We had all the kids work on it. We had all the local people come in and donate their time, the plumbers and electricians and so forth. We went to the supply houses, and most of the material was donated. And we built the house. Every kid worked extra hours on the house. We sold the house. We got our sixty-five thousand dollars. We took all the kids to Hawaii, spent a week over there, and had the greatest vacation that any of us had ever had. We played the game, and we won the game, which is important.

This was important in my life. I kind of got to be a football coach after all. Although really what I did is I went down and put some front money up for the lot for the house and then went to the bank and guaranteed everything so that we could have them get the money to do what we had to do to build it. It really wasn't my idea on the house, it was another fellow's. It was just a great idea. So I took it from there.

Billy took a firm line on raising money this way, making sure that only those who worked would benefit from the project.

Every kid had to put in x number of hours. One kid, a black kid who was a real good athlete, he never put his hours in. When it came time to get the reservations for all the kids to go to Hawaii, his name wasn't on the list. We had three days before we were ready to go, and he lacks something like twenty hours to qualify. We told him that if your name isn't on the list, you're not going. He realized then it was serious, and he worked. One night he worked until midnight on that house, scraping floors, just doing anything at all to get his hours in. So I think it was great for the kids.

The above quote illustrates a particularly entrepreneurial way of looking at a situation: taking a good idea, even if it's not yours originally, figuring out what needs to be done, and doing it—but doing it in such a way that nobody reaps the benefits without making a contribution.

Billy's attitude toward his children reflects some ambivalence. He appears to alternate between trying to make them independent and trying to make them extremely wealthy through the companies he has created.

My son and I, my daughter and I, we have very close relationships. I spent a lot of time with the kids growing up. "You know, kids," I'd say, "you're going to get some flack in your life from other kids. They'll tell you, 'Oh sure, you can do this because your dad financially can help you.'" I told my kids, "That's true. And I intend to help you financially. This means you got a little head start. So do better! You got a head start, so you should be higher. And do it and accept it that way."

Even as Billy tried to teach his children old-fashioned values of hard work and perseverance, he also set them up in businesses that provided them with rather extraordinary financial opportunities.

My daughter does my books for me here at the house and works for me one day a week, sometimes two days. We're right now trying to get into the import business. It's something I would like her to do.

I also started a company called after my son. In that company, what I do is I take $100,000 of my commissions in my company and run it through his company, and in turn I take a little bit of money out of that and we have to do all of our play stuff out of that.

We have another company called after my wife. I get $100,000 (also from my main company), run through that, and then I also get 4 percent of their profits, which I run through that, and I run my commissions and things through that company. But out of that company, I really live out of that. I take a pretty good salary out of it. I'm able to set up a pension plan which I'm able to defer a lot of taxes through, and I also have my son and my daughter on that company. It's been able to put them through school and gives them their income out of that.

Billy has done the same thing for his parents, making his mother the secretary for his son's company and amassing a fortune of between $2 or $3 million for his father, the man who has no interest in money.

If Billy wants to help his family but not cripple them by doing too much, no similar vacillation extends beyond the family circle. Drawing strong distinctions between family and the rest of the world was a typical pattern for all the entrepreneurs I interviewed. Members of one's family can expect some degree of special help, but all others should help themselves; charity harms the recipient and gets in the way of normal relations between people.

This view was reflected behaviorally in the way Billy structured his charitable contributions. Here Billy expressed a view shared with the philanthropists. The first stage of the thought process concerns responsibility: "If you're fortunate enough to take something from the community—take something in a business opportunity, say, or a good school that has educated your kids—then you should give something back to them." The second stage concerns the entrepreneurial belief in the crippling effect of charity.

Q. How do you do this [give something back] in your community?

A. Well, I put a lot of time into the athletic program. I'm the guy they call when they got a problem with a kid. Particularly athletes, because I'm so involved in athletics. They say, "Billy, so-and-so is really having a problem at home. He doesn't have a place to live. Can you talk to him?" I've done that many times for the school. I've intervened with the kids. I've helped some financially. I've helped four or five kids go to college. If they need a place to stay or if they need to go talk to someone or they're fooling with some drugs, anything like that, I'm available. They know I'm available.

Periodically they call me and use me in that way. So I think I've helped the school.

I've also taken particular programs on at the school. For example, I had the new turf put in the stadium by raising money and getting the kids involved. We put new lights in the stadium. We helped build up the baseball area and put up new fences. Generally, I am involved financially. Maybe I've not always spearheaded the effort, but I have been one of the leaders in getting these things done for the school.

Q. You said you've helped several kids go to college. Did you do that the same way you handled the house, in that you gave them money and they paid you back, or some arrangement like that?

A. Yeah. I've helped kids that truly want to go to school. I've either helped them with the tuition or their books or room and board. There's one kid I helped. He went up to Chico. He was going to pay me back. I didn't hear anything from him. But then a short while ago he called me.

"Billy," he said, "I hadn't forgotten this. I can only pay you one thousand dollars." That was so nice. It wasn't the thousand dollars. It was the idea that this kid never forgot. He was that kind of kid. I'd kind of lost a little faith in him, briefly. And it was so rewarding to have him call me and send me a few dollars. He told me, "I'll take care of the rest when I can." I say, "Great. Pay me a dollar a year."

Most of the other kids have responded that way. They've remembered what I did and kept contact and gave the money back. A couple of them did not. In fact, it's hard just to give without making them earn it, because what happens is that when it comes to payback time, they avoid you, and you sometimes lose contact. You lose the friendship just by helping them. So I think you have to be pretty careful about that. It can put a barrier between you. It does. It puts a strain.

Q. Let me be sure I understand what you're saying. Is what I'm hearing you say is that if somebody gives money to people it can put a barrier there, but if it's done as almost a business deal—alright, I'll give you this money, and I'm investing in your future, and you give back to me or somebody else—that's a different kind of thing for you. Is that right?

A. I don't always live by that, but down deep I know that's true.

Q. Have you been involved in other volunteer activities? It sounds as if you're very active in the local schools. Has that been the main volunteer activity?

A. Yeah, it really has.

In discussing his other volunteer or charitable activities, I found that what money Billy does give is usually directed to causes with which Billy establishes some bond.

Q. *How about other philanthropic activities? Would you call yourself a philanthropist in any way?*

A. No, I don't think so.

Q. *What kinds of causes do you give to?*

A. I'm a believer in the Special Olympics. Abused children, I get emotional when I see things like that. I've been very generous that way, mostly just financially, not in time.

Q. *What amounts do you give, roughly? What percentage does this represent from your income?*

A. I probably give, I'd say, an average of maybe $15,000 a year to different charities, and income-wise, my income is normally $500,000 a year. On a financial statement my financial worth is conservatively $7–8 million, maybe as high as $10 million.

Responsibility and the crippling effect of charity. Hard work and self-reliance as a way to build character. These themes were evident when Billy discussed his treatment of his children, his limited volunteer activities, and his political views, particularly concerning charity, governmental aid, poverty, and welfare.

Q. *Let me ask you just a few questions about your politics. Don't answer if there's anything too personal. Do you have any particular political affiliations?*

A. I'm a true Republican. What that means to me is that I just don't like government interference. I think the Republican philosophy is to get the government out of our everyday lives.

I was born into a family from the South. They were true Democrats. You know, the good solid South. When I was growing up, everyone was a Democrat or you didn't belong in the state of Alabama. But my mom and dad, after they moved to California, or very shortly afterwards, changed over. They were the kind of people who were do-it-for-yourself types. They didn't want anyone dictating your policy to you. So that was my main philosophy: I didn't want the government involved in my life.

Q. *What about government activities with poor people? You've given some of your own money to people, usually in kind of a business arrangement. What responsibility do you think the state has? Or does the state have a responsibility?*

A. I think I'm almost a redneck. I really am. Because I believe that the majority of the people who are on welfare, the homeless, I think they want to be there. Maybe they don't want to be there, but they won't put the effort to get off those rolls. There's always a job out there. I think that, generally, there's too much welfare. I realize it's hard to separate those people who truly do need help; it overlaps, so it ends up that to help the few that really do need help, you help a lot of them that really don't. There's too much welfare going on in the country.

Q. *Is this the reason you've structured your giving the way you have, because you don't want the giving to be taken for granted and cripple people? You want to help them but not take care of them? Does that distinction make sense to you?*

A. I never thought of it in those terms. I think I'm the kind of person who, if you need something, truly need something, I'll help you. Everyone wants a new car. Everyone wants a new home. Everyone wants to have season tickets to the Chargers. But a want doesn't mean that you deserve the things.

Billy was not merely voicing idle opinions; he acted on these beliefs, as is evident in the following story about giving a friend money, a transaction structured, in typical Billy-fashion, as a loan to be repaid.

Q. *So when people give money, what kind of effect does it have? Is the overall effect positive? Or can it be negative? How does it affect everyone that's involved when you give money to them?*

A. At that moment it usually is a positive thing, because now they have the money to do what they want to do. But sometimes the effect can be very negative, because now it's time to pay it back. Even if they can afford to pay it back, everyone always has a place to put the money rather than pay back a debt. Then, the next thing you know, it could be a negative, because they don't want to face you, simply because they should have paid you back, because they said they were going to pay you back.

To give you a little example, I had a friend of mine, a man who's a builder. Like all builders, they're up and down. He has a brand new Lincoln Limo. He paid $60,000 cash for it. And all of a sudden, he gets in some trouble and he has to borrow $30,000. This was eight months ago. I said, "I'll loan you $30,000, but what about security? This is a business deal. Let's don't get personal relationships and business mixed up." He says, "Well, I'll put my limo up as security. Here's the pink slip. If I don't pay you back, you can take the limo."

I don't want the limo. I'm not the kind of guy in my cut-off pants and tennis shoes to be driving around in a limo. But the time comes to pay me back and he doesn't pay me back. So, what happens now? He called me the other night, and he said he wanted to go to the ball game. I said, "Where's my thirty grand?" He says, "Well, I don't really have it." "Good," I said, "Park the limo over here."

I'm not the kind of guy that could take his toy. The guy, he's down and out. He doesn't have thirty grand. He shouldn't even have the car. I could not, in good conscience, go take his toy away from him. But the negative part of it is, I lost a little bit of respect for him, and I wished I hadn't seen that side of him.

Q. *Let me be sure I understand this. I think what I'm hearing you say is that it disappoints you. If you give things to people, you try to help them, and then when they don't appreciate it or don't pay it back, at least in some token sum, you feel they've let you down, because you wouldn't have done that.*

A. That's what I feel with him. Sure, the guy's down and out, and I don't need the car. I don't need the money. Oh, sure, if I had it I'd do something with it, naturally. But the whole thing makes me think there's a flaw there in his character.

Billy's attitude toward the friend who owed him money and did not make even a token attempt to repay the debt was reflected in his attitude toward charity in general. The recipients' response and whether or not they are trying to improve themselves is very important to Billy.

Q. *What do you do in a situation like the one with the friend you mentioned? Once you've been disappointed by someone, will you help them out again?*

A. That's a hard question. Him, I would, because I like him personally. But this experience made me see a side of him that I didn't think he had. I thought he would say, "Hey, Billy. I can't do this. Take the car." Or, "I can pay you so much." But what it did is he avoids me now. And I just didn't like to see that side of him.

Q. *But that's somebody you knew. Most of these people you've given money to are people you've known. What about a situation that involves somebody you don't personally know? Consider this example. Somebody tells you, or you read something in the paper, about some welfare mother who's had a real hard time, and you give her some money. Then they don't appreciate it very much. Would you give them money again?*

A. Probably not. I honestly don't think I'm the person that—If you help someone, I'd rather for it not to be known. I like to think that I'd help them because they need the help, and I feel real good about it. I don't have to have someone pat me on the back. I never really have needed that, because I always have felt that if I did a good thing or did a good job, or I did the right thing, I didn't have to have someone tell me. I knew it. And that was always the important thing in my life. Don't pat me on the back; it's not necessary.

I found this answer significant. Billy did not want praise for his help, but he did want to feel that the money was being used wisely. And he resembled many philanthropists in preferring to give anonymously.[3] In this case, however, Billy's words are hard to reconcile with the fact that he gives primarily to people he knows and that he structures his gifts as loans to be repaid. None of this fits into the idea of anonymous giving.[4]

Finally, I asked Billy about his general view of life. Questions like, Were people good or bad? Were they born alone or into communities with ties? I found that Billy did not fit the standard Darwinian portrait of an entrepreneur. He did not see the world as a tough place in which one had to fight to survive. Nor did he see a division between being an individual rational actor and a member of a group. Although such dichotomies or polarizations may serve as useful classificatory categories for social scientists, they did not ring a bell for Billy. And—perhaps of greater relevance for the present study—there were in general no systematic differences on this point between entrepreneurs and philanthropists.

In the following response, for example, Billy seems to have a very positive view of human nature. His answer would be what most of us tend to associate more with an altruist than with a tough, shrewd entrepreneur.

Q. *Let me ask you a couple of questions about your view of man, about basic human nature. How do you view human beings? Do you think they're basically good or bad? Or can you make that kind of distinction?*

A. I think that when I look at everyone, I see the good in them. I really do. I don't see the bad. My philosophy is always, if you don't expect something, you get nothing. You expect a lot of someone, you get a lot. I think with the kids, that's probably the most important thing in kids, to expect a lot of them. Not to the point where there's pressure on them. But if you expect a lot, you'll get a lot.

Overall, Billy typified the entrepreneurs I interviewed, both in his complexity, his love of family, and his sheer delight in the entrepreneurial game that turns an idea into profit. Like other entrepreneurs, Billy's ethics seemed remarkably similar to the ethical systems held by many altruists, with honesty being stressed as the primary virtue. His attitudes toward the poor resemble those of the stereotypical Reagan Republican. He believes in hard work, self-reliance, repaying debts, and making donations sparingly and in such a way that they do not encourage dependence in the recipients. Billy was comfortable with himself and happy with his life. He seemed remarkably free of any need to prove himself by making yet more money or by pulling off any more winning deals. Nor is he a high roller, a big risk taker who lives for the thrills. He is simply a man who enjoys the fun of making an idea profitable and who works hard to get the good things that money can buy for him and for his family. These characteristics were typical of all the entrepreneurs I interviewed.

CHAPTER 3

The Philanthropist

WHAT IS IT LIKE to work very hard, see a business grow from nothing into a source of great wealth, and then give away much of this hard-earned money, with no strings attached? Melissa spoke graciously and openly about this, as about even more personal matters. Her narrative illustrates success and joy in sharing good fortune with others and captures the critical perspectival characteristics I found among all the philanthropists I interviewed.

Like Billy, Melissa was born into a small town and modest circumstances.

> I'll just start by saying I'm sixty-one years old and was born in Missouri in a little farm town in 1926, August 20. It was during the depression time, which was a very difficult time for many people, particularly those of us on the farm.
>
> I guess you'd have to call our own situation pretty depressed. When I was a child, we lived in a lesser way than my mother did in her youth on the farm. For example, we didn't have bathrooms; we had outdoor toilets. We didn't have any electricity; we had kerosene lamps. None of my present friends has ever lived that way.
>
> I was from a small town close to Carrolton, Missouri, which was then the county seat of Carrol County. At that time the farming communities were very neighborly. Neighbors helped neighbors. A major force in my life was my grandfather, and that was the way that he would help. Gosh, he helped us! He helped his family. The world was organized around church, neighbors, and family, because it was more of a closed community thing then, the way they lived.

Some of Melissa's drive comes from this period. While her feelings about her early life might suggest that Melissa would be more concerned about money than is Billy, we find later that this is not the case.

> My mother's brothers were pretty successful. My dad's brothers were successful. We were always the poor ones in the family. I think both my brother and I felt that oppression because we were always looked down upon. We wore all the cousins' clothes. That type of thing. My daughters talk about why or where we got such pride. Both my brother and I talk about that now. We didn't like to be in a lowly position. Even the small community that we lived in, we were still the poorest ones. I guess it makes a difference, just wanting to strive for something, to improve your situation.

Melissa's attitude toward helping others developed early in her life. Melissa finds it painful emotionally to be the one who takes, perhaps because that indicates vulnerability and need. She also learned early in life to take on responsibility, when her mother became ill.

Q. *It is easier for you to give than it is to take?*

A. Much, oh definitely. You can ask any one of my family. It's hard to take because I'd much rather give. I have much more pleasure in that than in receiving.

Q. *I wonder why that is. Do you have any ideas?*

A. I don't know. Maybe it comes from that very young age when I assumed the responsibility for my brother and my father and the house when my mother was ill. Maybe it was when I was taking over that I found a certain sense of responsibility and achievement in that. I don't really know.

Like many others of that period, Melissa's family left the Midwest and went to California, to find a better life. This move was difficult for Melissa, who was a shy girl.

I've lived in California long enough now that I consider Orange County my home. But when I was a child, leaving Missouri and coming out here was difficult, because I was shy and we were coming from the country. In elementary school I skipped a grade. I went from first grade to third grade. It was a little elementary school out in the country, so I was younger than my classmates. Then we came to California, when I was in the second half of my freshman year. Well, I wore knee socks, and I had an accent, and I came from a school that had six hundred pupils in high school to one that had twenty-four hundred! So that was difficult. Very difficult.

Melissa's response to trying times, such as moving to a new town at an awkward age, was to deal with it alone. This pattern repeated itself throughout her life during times of stress.

Q. *Was there anybody that helped you out during this rough period?*

A. No. My mother went to work because of our financial situation, and I had to figure it out for myself. I felt so shy and lost. I thought there'd be one way that I could really dig in, and that would be to make really good grades.

Melissa's grandfather served as an important role model for her, not just in her attitude toward and treatment of her own family but also in her philanthropy. Her grandfather taught Melissa the importance of family, hard work, and self-reliance—all typical Midwestern farm values that corresponded closely to Billy's.[1]

Grandfather was a very dedicated man, a very honest man, hardworking, diligent, devoted totally to his family, very loyal, and the work ethic was important to him. He felt family should take care of each other. He was adamant about that. Even so many years ago, when he became eligible for social security, he didn't believe he should take it. He thought he should be able to take care of himself. So I suppose the main thing he taught us was independence, taking care of ourselves.

Of course, he did have very definite ideas about what was right and wrong. We learned that early from him. It wasn't that he disciplined us harshly in any way. It was just that we knew how he felt, and we wanted to please him because we respected him so much. He would talk to us. He'd never talk *at* us; he'd just talk *to* us. That means so much. If we would do something wrong, he would make us look him straight in the eye and tell him what we thought we'd done wrong. That was worse than a spanking or anything could ever have been. It was your conscience working, I suppose.

The fact that Melissa's grandfather dealt with life on his own terms, without taking help from anyone, also colored Melissa's views on how people deal with adversity and on the structural problems of poverty.

Grandfather wasn't an educated man. He educated himself. He helped his father on the farm and grew up in a large family. And this always interested me, because you'll see someone—not that they were a ghetto type or in that particular field—but how one will persevere and come out of difficult living standards to make themselves stronger and grow, when the other brothers and sisters don't. Grandfather somehow had that desire very early. He could not go to school, because he had to help his father; but he would read and take advantage of what little education he could get. He always tried to further himself that way. He always encouraged us in education. To him, that was the most important thing that we could do. Of course, my father always discouraged us, because he wanted us to work to help the family pool.

Q. *Why do you think that you followed your grandfather's lead rather than your father's?*

A. Because he was very definitely a leader. And in the small town that we lived in, he was respected by all people, in all walks of life. I knew that even as a child. I was always proud to be his granddaughter. I didn't feel that same kind of pride with my dad. I can't say that I was close to my father. He never disciplined me, and he never was harsh with me in any way. But there was just no guidance there. We were just left on our own. Whatever you wanted to do, you could do, all the way through. And as we grew older and into our families, my brother and I, my father leaned on us. It was just a different type thing. I guess what I'm saying is that my grandfather was simply a stronger individual, and I realized that. So he was the main one when I was growing up that I felt real close to. There wasn't anybody else I was close to who helped others, either through giving money or volunteer work or other types of good deeds, other than my grandfather.

While still quite young, Melissa recognized her parents' limitations and moved quickly to deal with that reality.

Our parents were very immature. My mother and father were both the youngest of three children, and they never grew up. I said to my brother, "Well, we were just like four kids growing up." "Yeah," he said, "but you and I really grew up. Our parents never did."

And that's how they were. There was always my grandfather, my mother's father. He was a very strong individual. He more or less took care of them up until the time that my husband took over. Then my husband and I took care of them. My parents worked, but they just didn't know how to manage, or to initiate, or put things together. We love them dearly. We're very close. But they were definitely not leaders.

Q. *So in some ways you acted as the parents for your mother and father?*

A. Right. It was reverse roles. Definitely.

When Melissa was thirteen, she began a new stage in her life.

When I was thirteen years old, my mother and father and brother and I moved to Huntington Park, California, where my father found a minimum amount of employment. My mother went to work, and my brother and I entered high school there. It was during that time that the Second World War evolved. I met my future husband in high school in Huntington Park. He was a senior and I was a junior. He graduated and went into the Army Engineers. I graduated the following year and went to work for a navy supply depot in Vernon, California. When my husband went into the service and into basic training, he was away for about nine months, and when he returned for a leave of absence before going to the South Pacific, we eloped. Young people did at that time. I was seventeen and he was nineteen. We were both under legal age, and our parents would not have permitted [us to get married], so we ran away to Quartzite, Arizona. We were gone one day, and the following day Will shipped out for the South Pacific and was gone for two years. During that time, I continued to work at the navy supply depot, and Will saw heavy action in the South Pacific. He received a Purple Heart and the Bronze Star. He hated to follow orders, and I think that is what gave him initially his entrepreneurial spirit when he came home from the service. He did return after two years, and we had a little church wedding, which made me feel much better, because our parents and families were in attendance.

After struggling, trying to find "his place"—it was difficult—Will started working for a young man who had moved here from New York and was in the meat business in Vernon, California. Will worked as a salesman for him and acquired customers for restaurants for this meat-vending plant. He became very interested in it. I became pregnant with our first daughter at about the same time we found out that the gentleman—no, not gentleman, the man my husband was working for—was selling horse meat illegally. It was a difficult time for us. Will was not aware he was selling horse meat. The man was sent to prison, but Will's customers believed in his innocence. He loved the business so that he continued on in the business on his own. He bought a little panel truck, and we put an old freezer in my father's garage. I was Will's secretary at that time, while I was pregnant and even after the birth of our daughter.

As their family and business grew, Melissa and Will became more involved in their community, and, eventually, Melissa began her philanthropic activities. At first these resembled the kinds of volunteerism in which most of us engage: local school activities, hospital bazaars, and neighborhood causes.[2] But when her third daughter was born, Melissa's life changed, and her philanthropy took a new direction.

We worked that way for about five years, with the business growing. We had a second daughter. I was invited to become a member of the Huntington Park's Woman's Club. I think that's probably where I started becoming interested in philanthropic work because, aside from helping with the business and my two little babies, I found such an interest in this club. We were doing little benefits, chili suppers and what have you, and the profits would go to dental clinics, to helping children in different ways.

Then following that, we grew enough in our business to enable us to build a home and move to Whittier, and then on to Fullerton, California. During that time, my husband's business became involved with McDonald's. Mr. Ray Kroc, who was the founder of McDonald's, moved to California and opened two or three McDonald's restaurants in the Los Angeles area, which my husband supplied with meat patties. Will and Ray became very close friends, and through the years my husband's company grew right behind McDonald's as a food distributor to the McDonald's restaurants across the United States and in Canada and Hawaii. That's how it all began.

During this time, during the first five years after we moved to Fullerton, our third little girl was born. She was born with brain damage. It was not really apparent in the beginning, only to me because I had two others to compare her with. They were so young, all were just under five years, the three little girls, and so I knew the pattern of development. The doctor didn't recognize this because I would take Cristy once a month, and for the first two or three months he just thought her progress was slow. I knew something was more severe than that. As it turned out, I think she was nine months old when we took her to a specialist, and he decided—I didn't agree with his analysis—that she would be a vegetable. I couldn't agree with that because I could see that her development, although slow, was beginning. I started working with her personally, just on a daily, hourly basis, and I guess at that time I promised myself, I promised her, I promised God, I promised the world that if this little baby could grow up to have a some-what normal life, I would give my life to helping her and other children along the way.

And that's how my interest turned to philanthropic causes; it was just the natural way that things happened. Consequently I was involved with phil-anthropic groups, and each of them had special interests for children and disabled people, particularly an establishment called RIO, located in Or-ange. I started working there.

Even before Melissa and Will had much money, Melissa gave much of her time to causes for disabled children. As the family's financial situation im-proved, however, Melissa was able to give more. At the time of our conversa-tions, she had given more than $6 million in the preceding five years.

At first we didn't have the monetary funds to help. It was by volunteer work that I would go. I would help children with cerebral palsy maybe two or three days a week, or in the summer time at RIO I would take Cristy with me and we would work there with children in the therapeutic pool, or we would take them with their wheelchairs to Sea World and things like that for daily outings. I am still totally involved with RIO, and that was twenty years ago, so it has just been an ongoing thing. To see the growth of that place and what it is doing today is just remarkable.

At that time, when I was involved in my volunteer work, we had our fourth little girl. Our business was growing; we were able to move into a home that was large enough to give parties for benefits. We would have parties through the Assistance League or through the National Charity League, and the proceeds or profits of these parties would go to various charitable endeavors.

My husband was such a generous man. As his business was growing, he was helping other young men get started in different areas, such as McDonald's franchises, and we as a family gave a scholarship endowment fund for Stephens College students. As our company grew, we were able to help more people in other ways. Will and I were very much in tune with giving. Call it sharing, I like to say.

Sharing is an apt term for Melissa's philanthropy, which she views as giving back something to the people who helped her and her family prosper.[3]

Melissa's world of family, work, and giving was suddenly disrupted in 1975 when her first husband was diagnosed with cancer.

> The most tragic thing came when we knew Will had cancer in 1975. For three and a half years he suffered terribly, through four major surgeries. After the fourth surgery, he had a cardiac arrest. Although his heart was revived, he was in a coma for three and a half months. In 1978, he passed away.
>
> That was without a doubt the most devastating experience in my life. Following Will's death, I dedicated a building for the study of immunology in Duarte for the City of Hope, where Will was a patient during all that time. Hopefully, someday the researchers will find a cure for cancer.

After Will died, Melissa rebuilt her life, devoting herself to her daughters and to her charitable interests.

> I sold our business two years after Will's death, which was his wish. He did not believe in having his family involved in the business. Will was very strong on nepotism. He would help the children, sure. But he thought that each person should follow his or her own dream, his own interests. So consequently, the business was sold.
>
> That's when I entered college as a freshman, because I got married at seventeen and had never attended college. Returning to college saved my life, virtually, because it gave me something of my own interest, something to think about, and something to study. At the same time, I was very involved with RIO. Also, at about the same time, I had a little granddaughter who was born handicapped. We took her to RIO, where she was helped. It just seemed that I became more and more a sponsor in philanthropic causes because of personal reasons, because of many reasons. Partly, I was much more able, monetarily, to help now. Will and I set up a trust, before he passed away, for our daughters. Our feeling was not to give them a whole lot, but we wanted them to be secure, especially Cristy, the third little girl.
>
> I kept my interest in RIO going. It now has a vocational center, named after me, and a Marias Center, which houses senior citizens. They have all kinds of social activities going on there for disabled people. Young couples get married there. It's just a beautiful building. It serves so many, many people. I also became interested in the Performing Arts Center in Costa Mesa. There again, I went down to visit. I toured it while it was under construction. And I found that they were putting in special work for wheelchairs for disabled people, putting in audio equipment for those with hearing impairments. This is a requirement at most places now, but it wasn't

then. And my interest in helping them monetarily came because they helped disabled people.

Last fall I traveled with my family to Chicago, where we became involved in the Ronald McDonald Children's Charities. There is a new Ronald McDonald House being built in Orange next to the Children's Hospital. The Ronald McDonald House is a home that gives care for the parents and families of children who are probably terminally ill, and they have no place to stay. They want to be with their child, so it enables them to stay close during the child's illness and to be with them at that time. They are now internationally based, the Ronald McDonald Houses. So by giving money to this organization, I accomplished two purposes: it was a way to help my community to help the Ronald McDonald House become a reality in Orange, and a way to say thank you to McDonald's for the opportunity they had afforded my husband during his years of growth in the meat industry. So that's been a really neat thing.

The idea of building a better world through one's charity, and at the same time thanking people for your own success, seems to be the conception that guides and inspires Melissa's philanthropy.

Despite her gentle manner, Melissa is a tough lady. This strength was evident in discussions of her determination to keep her family together after her first husband died. The discussion of her husband's death flowed naturally into a discussion of how Melissa saw life. Her world view was intricate: sometimes she pictured people as alone in a harsh world in which they have to fend for themselves; at other times she expressed the feeling that family was the ultimate source of strength. In this respect she typified the philanthropists I interviewed. As Billy's and Melissa's comments attest, one need not have a monochromatic view of human nature and the human condition to be either an entrepreneur or a philanthropist. I found it especially interesting that in comparison with philanthropists, entrepreneurs did not more frequently articulate the view that life is tough and people are out to get you. In fact, Billy seemed more trusting and, in terms of the views he expressed, more altruistic than Melissa. His behavior did not reflect this difference, however.

Q. You've gone through so much, I'm interested in your views of life. Do you believe that man is essentially alone in the world?

A. Well, I believe that people need people. But essentially I do believe that you are alone, simply because of some of the experiences I've had. I feel that my family was very close and helped me so much, but that only I could really help me after Will died. After having a full, busy life, with all these people in my home, I was alone. I had to handle that myself.

Q. How would you describe man's basic human nature? Do you think people are essentially good, or bad? Are people more self-interested, or other-regarding?

A. That's an interesting question. I went over the questionnaire you sent, and I noticed that question. I'm kind of ambivalent about it, because I think they're both good and bad. Basically I think people are pretty much self-interested, but there are so many exceptions. I'm thinking of instances when tragedies happen, like a child is ill or something, and people just seem to flock to help. But then, on the other hand, I guess I've been hurt a lot; because of being a widow and in the monetary situation I was in, a lot of people did try to abuse that in ways. Even through my church, which really hurt me. But you can't ever get bitter about that. As my husband used to say, "If you're going to be a fool, be a quiet one." So I learned by those things not to be so trusting. But overall, I think it's very wrong to become bitter about things like that.

But to go back to your question, I suppose I'd say, first of all, I do think people are more self-interested than not.

Q. *How did people respond when Cristy was born and you realized you had problems with her development?*

A. I had a lot of support. But people didn't understand then. Now, I think, they have become much more understanding. But back then, if someone was a little different or a little slow, I think people were a little afraid of it. Maybe they'd be more standoffish. Or they'd act more like they were thinking, "Thank God, that didn't happen to me, or to anybody in our family."

There again, I was hurt a lot. I find to this day that people in my mother's era, for example, have a thing about anyone they call "different." Anyone who's "different" you shy away from. I don't know if it's because you're afraid of it, that you don't understand it, or if it's repellent to you. I don't know.

Q. *Did you have the same kind of experience when your husband had cancer?*

A. For quite a long time, we tried to keep it quiet, because of our company. These were reasons that were Will's. Our company was public. He was a very vital and strong figure in that company. We were responsible to a lot of people who were our shareholders. And we kept feeling that we were going to overcome it, the cancer. Therefore we tried to keep it within ourselves, which was very difficult. Will had a feeling that when people found out he had cancer, that they'd stay away or keep a distance. Cancer is not a thing that one can catch; it is not a sexually transmitted disease. It's a virus that affects the cells. I do think that there's even an established genetic causality. But people were afraid they'd catch it.

The adversity in Melissa's life seems to have made her more sensitive to the perniciousness of treating people as "different." Her own difficulties appear to have heightened her empathy for others, to have increased her ability to put herself into another's place. I did not find this same tendency among the entrepreneurs. Although many entrepreneurs see themselves as sources of strength and nurturance for others, the factor of empathy is less stressed.[4]

Q. *You never seemed to run away from problems.*

A. Well, no. I have a tremendous compassion for others. I don't mean that to sound self-serving, but I have a thing of putting myself in someone else's place. Even when I was really young, I think I was like that. I guess my mother was ill a lot when I was eight to ten. I helped to care for her, so therefore I kind of became a caretaker, I guess you'd call it, at a young age. But I used to think, "Boy, if that was me, how would I feel?" I always thought about that, about how if I had cancer or were old, if I had AIDS, if I were retarded, I'd still have feelings, just like you have, regardless. I wouldn't want to be looked on in a different way just because I'm different in some way.

Since I was very interested in understanding how people drew boundaries between themselves and others, I asked Melissa about the extent to which she differentiated between her own needs and individuality and those of other people and about how her philanthropy affected her children's welfare and whether that had an effect on her giving.

Q. *What if helping someone else endangers or hurts people you love? One of the other groups of people I've been talking with are people who lived in Nazi Europe and rescued Jews during that period. The penalty for rescuing people was death. I always wonder how they did it, because I have small children myself, and I don't know if I would be able to risk my children's lives for some stranger.*

A. I had the same reaction when I looked at that question [on the questionnaire you sent me], and I thought you could relate to it many different ways. If it's an emergency, and you're helping someone, you do it. You don't think. You just help people. If I had the time to think about it, I could put myself in jeopardy, but I would have a difficult time putting my family in jeopardy. If it was something monetary, like denying them some luxuries that they might otherwise have, I wouldn't have a problem with it. But if it was a question of their life or death, I'd have a great problem.

Q. *Of course, as a philanthropist, you are in one sense denying your children some of the money that you've earned.*

A. I've thought about that. We've talked about it, the children and I. In the trusts that my husband and I prepared for them, they will be financially strong enough so if something really vital happens to their health, [they'll be taken care of]. Otherwise, both my husband and I had the feeling that to give too much is to spoil, and therefore, whether they realize it or not, it denies them happiness. It denies them the right to make it for themselves. So I don't believe in leaving too much. I also am selfish, because I'm enjoying seeing people share it while I'm here.

I pushed Melissa a little on this topic, probing to determine where she drew the line between her own welfare and that of others.

Q. *Before you began philanthropic activity, did you ever feel guilty for not giving away money when you had it? Or if you didn't give money away now, would you feel guilty not doing it?*

A. I think so. It's surprising, because you think you should be earning with the money. Of course, I do that, too. I think I'm actually rather shrewd in how I invest. My family—and I do believe in the old saying my grandfather used to say, "Charity begins at home"—the idea that you need to take care of yourself and your family, their needs, if you can or are in the position, because otherwise they'll have to have help from others if they are disabled. I think help should start at home. I think you should do that first, and once that's basically covered, then I really think the important thing is to share what you have with others.

Q. *So you would feel that you first have to take care of people around you.*

A. Yes. As I helped my brother, who helped us so much as a family when we were young. I helped my deceased husband's mother and stepfather and my own mother. I helped all of those people because that's a responsibility that's mine. And I don't want to deny my children the sense of achievement [by giving them things too easily]. I'm thinking, "Am I saving this like Scrooge—saving, saving, saving—to die and leave it all to them?" I don't think that's doing them any favor. And it also promotes selfishness. I like to see it shared as we go along.

For both entrepreneurs like Billy and philanthropists like Melissa, "charity begins at home." For Melissa, however, after family is taken care of, one has the duty, not just the opportunity, to help others.

Q. *How important is duty in all of this? Do you think you have a duty to help people who are in distress?*

A. Yes, I think so. I think we all do. I think we all should. If we are in a position to be able to do so, I think it's very definitely a duty. I always remember Mr. Ray Kroc, who founded McDonald's; one of his sayings was that what we take out of a community, we should put back in.

Q. *What if doing so endangers or harms your own welfare?*

A. Well, there again, if it was an emergency-type thing where someone was in total distress, I would do it.

I also wanted to know how Melissa saw herself, how she saw herself in relation to others, and whether her perspective was related to her philanthropy.

Q. *Can you tell me how you view yourself? How would you describe yourself? How would you like to be remembered, if someone were to describe you after you've passed away?*

A. As someone that cared about other people. I hope to leave a legacy that I cared. Maybe that I left behind an attitude, a positive attitude, that life can be good, it can be shared, and you can get a lot of pleasure out of that. I guess I look at life as though the glass is always half full.

When I read through a list of adjectives, asking Melissa which ones characterized her, I found that both she and Billy described themselves in much the same terms.

I'm someone who's willing to take responsibility. Yes, that I am. In fact, I sometimes think I overdo it with some family. And I'd probably characterize myself as self-confident. I have to work on that sometimes. When I was giving the speech in Chicago before the First Lady, I was scared to death. But you just go do it.

I definitely think I'm tolerant. I also have been privileged. It was through hard work, but nevertheless a lot of people work hard and never are able to get there. They never get in the right position, or the timing isn't right, or something keeps them from achieving monetarily what my husband and I did. And we were blessed with a large family, which I'm very close to, to this day. So yes, I would say I was both privileged and fortunate, even with all the other things that have happened.

I'm both a leader and a follower. I can organize things and get things together that way, and so I would be a leader. My friends, other people, and my family consider me a leader. But I have a very difficult time delegating responsibility to other people, and I think a good leader has to do that. So, I couldn't say I'm a real leader.

I think I feel pretty secure in who I am and what I am. I think I'm an individualist but not necessarily a rugged one. I'm definitely an optimistic person about life. Yes. And gosh, I'm active. I'm running and going all the time. If a time goes by and something isn't happening, I'll create something.

Q. *Do you think people can control their own fate in life?*

A. To a certain degree. Not over the things that we've talked about. You certainly cannot control death or illness or birth defects or things like disease. And if that be your fate, as this was my husband's, well, that was certainly not controllable. But I think, yes, as far as other things go, we can, through our attitude, affect things. And your attitude affects your health, and your health affects your activities. So in that way I think you can control your own fate. I take a lot of initiative to try to control what's happening around me.

Q. *Do you have any kind of personal ethical credo that guides your life in any way?*

A. I certainly do, and it's one that I think probably many use. In all of my homes—I'm fortunate enough to have three homes—I have on my side of my bed the same little creed. It says, "God grant me the serenity to accept the things I cannot change, the courage to change the things I can, and the wisdom to know the difference." It's hard to do sometimes. Boy, is it ever! That's why I go back and look at it lots of times.

I wanted to know how Melissa's philanthropy makes her feel about herself.[5] Melissa's answer typified those I heard from all the philanthropists I interviewed. Most philanthropists say that giving makes them feel good (though not necessarily good about themselves) but that this feeling is an unexpected consequence of the giving and *not* the cause. The important emotion is knowing that others now can partake of your good fortune.

Melissa also spoke of how rich people can be taken for granted by those who treat them as bottomless bank accounts rather than human beings, and how money can separate you from other people, erecting barriers that limit communication and caring. Like other philanthropists I interviewed, Melissa related incidents in which her giving had resulted in her being hurt by others.

When I became a widow, it was very difficult because some of the people I trusted the most became the most aggressive in wanting funds for the ministry house, which I did help to fund. But the way I was approached really hurt me. They didn't come to see if I was alright, to see if I was grieving, if I was sad about my husband's death, if they could help me. They came for monetary purposes. And I'm very hurt about that.

A new minister was coming to the church and they asked me to contribute to the purchase of his home, which was quite a large sum. I said, "There are so many others in the church. I'd be glad to give this sum, and then couldn't we all contribute?" And they told me, "Well, before we do that, there's another widow who's quite 'well-to-do,' and we'll ask her too." I thought to myself, "This is how you do it?"

Then there was a lady in the church whose children had been in my youth group. She was in the process of getting a divorce and called to say that she was destitute, she needed cash. My daughter was there the night she called. I told the woman I'd give her a certain amount and that I would send it to her on Sunday. But she said, "No, I'll pick it up now." Well, it was just uncanny to me. We lived in a little gate-guarded area then. So I left it at the guard gate, and I never heard from her again. Not a thank-you note. Not a thank-you call. Nothing.

But then again, to repeat my husband's statement, if you're going to be a fool, be a quiet one. Don't give expecting anything in return. Give because you want to, because if you expect it, you're going to be very hurt.

This was just one example Melissa cited of how you have to give because you want to, that giving is not a loan or a quid pro quo in any sense. "You basically have to give because you want to." In this, Melissa's attitude differed considerably from Billy's attitudes toward giving. Altruists attach no strings to their gifts.

This also became clear during our discussions of an afterlife, discussions analyzed more systematically in chapter 6. But Melissa's attitude is typical of the general lack of connection I found between religion and philanthropy.

Q. Do you believe in any kind of an afterlife?

A. I thought about that a lot. I used to, but the kind of afterlife I believe in is what lives in the hearts of the people, the loved ones, the family and the friends, and the people left behind. The spirit of the person lives on in the hearts of others. That's the kind I believe in.

Q. A lot of people have said that many philanthropists give money because they feel this will buy them a better place in paradise. Is this so?

A. [*Laughing*] No, I don't believe that. Basically, you have to give without a reason, or a kickback, if you will. You can't be giving for the wrong reason.

Melissa characterized her giving as having arisen naturally, spontaneously. This spontaneous aspect of giving is typical of other philanthropists. But there is usually a personal connection with the recipient of the charity, for philanthropists as well as for entrepreneurs. This personal connection to the recipient becomes less important the more closely we approach pure altruism on our continuum.

If I do think about it, the philanthropy or the groups or the organizations that I've given to do have a thread in common, with the exception of the Performing Arts Center. Although, there again, in my mind I tied it into the general theme that it would be arts for the handicapped and the disabled. The disabled and the children—it always goes to that core somehow. That's always who I feel I want to be a part of or to help, the children and the disabled. That's probably basically because of my daughter, because with her I found and met so many others that were so charming and loving, people who needed that help or that support, whether it was emotional or monetary.

Q. Do you feel that you are trying in some sense to repay people who helped you when you had a child in this situation? Or is it more that you can just empathize?

A. I can empathize. It's an empathy for anyone who has a problem. I know it's harder, and I know that they have a lot of hurt inside. I know it takes them a lot more to do what we just normally take for granted, so therefore I really appreciate the effort that they make.

Q. *Some people I've spoken to say they give money because it's a way to get social and business or even family contacts. I don't think I'm hearing you say that. Correct me if I'm wrong.*

A. The only thing that might be close to that is that social contacts have come out of the giving, but that wasn't the first priority. In different instances I've met so many wonderful people through my giving, but it wasn't done for that reason. I guess that's the way to put it. It was more a by-product.

Q. *How about tax incentives? Does that affect your decision to give? People frequently talk about this.*

A. Oh, I know. You'd be surprised how many people think that's the only reason you do anything. But I have never considered doing it because of that, the tax advantage. Maybe it's nice, when you give, to be able to say, "I want it to go in this direction," rather than knowing that when the money goes in a big lump sum to the U.S. government, they determine what happens to it. You have a little bit of control over where you would like it to go when you give it away yourself.

For Melissa, the "benefits" that analysts often identify as reasons for altruism are seen more as unintended results than as motives.

Does Melissa consciously make a cost/benefit calculus when she gives away her money? Not at all. The following excerpt illustrates this, and in it we also find the glimmering of a distinction that will later emerge more clearly in the more life-threatening forms of altruism: a distinction between a spontaneous and nonconscious desire to give and a well-planned decision over *how* to give.

Q. *When you sit down to give money, do you consciously engage in any kind of deliberation with yourself over whether to give? Is there any kind of weighing the alternatives, considering the cost for you or your family, things like that?*

A. Not really. The strangest things are the times when I've made the large gifts. It all just kind of came to me, the timing I mean. I thought, "This is what I want to do. This is what I'd like to do." Then I would talk to my business manager and I would talk to my children and it just happened. There really wasn't a whole lot of thought put into any kind of deliberation. I always discussed it with my family. But no, as far as deliberating over whether it was right or wrong, or which charity to give to, it wasn't that. It was just that the time would come when this thing seemed to be the right thing to do.

Q. *So when you give, you just do it because you think it's the right thing to do?*

A. Yes. It's more spontaneous than deliberate, I suppose.

Q. *You've talked about empathy before. I know that a person's motives are very mixed. I'm just trying to sort them out a little bit. I'm not trying to pigeonhole you; I know some reasons can't be sorted out. But can you say how important empathy is, the feeling that you're actually identifying with the people to whom you're giving money, as opposed to feeling duty, that it's the right thing to do, that you have money, you have an obligation to give. Can you distinguish in any way between those two factors?*

A. Between empathy and duty? I suppose maybe there's a little bit of both. Maybe you feel that because you've been fortunate—not on any grand scale, but in a very comfortable situation, so that you're able to share that fortune—then probably I feel some duty to put back something that has come to me. But mostly I think it's empathy for people who really are in distress, or that it would just make their lives a little more comfortable in a lot of ways.

Finally, I wanted to determine how Melissa viewed poverty, in light of her own political views and her views of herself in relation to others. Melissa described herself as generally apolitical but conservative in her views. Her opinions reflected Billy's in certain regards and yet differed significantly from his in others. In general, Melissa seemed less adamant in her opinions, more willing to see variations among the poor. While both she and Billy are concerned not to make people dependent by giving them too much, Melissa seems gentler in her treatment of people who fail to live up to this goal.

My political views are, I would say, on the conservative side. Mostly, politics are not real important to me. I find so much rhetoric in politics. It's just talk. Just talk, talk, talk.

Q. *How would you explain why some people are poor and others are wealthy? Do you think it reflects their character in any way?*

A. I think so. I don't know that you ever say, "I want to be wealthy some day." I think you say, "I want something better than what I have now." So therefore I have the desire. It starts with the desire. You have to desire something, and then you have to have the ambition to work for it. I think the most important thing is perseverance. You have to just keep at it. It can be so difficult and so discouraging, whatever it is you're striving for. But just persevere.

Q. *What about people who are poor? Is it basically their fault do you think, because they just aren't trying hard enough? Does poverty reflect a lack of character?*

A. Probably, or lack of guidance from parents or grandparents or some person who takes the responsibility. You'll read so many times that it's an outside person who takes an interest, a teacher who takes an interest in that child who shows some promise and some desire, and works with them. But for the most part, it's awfully difficult for an entire poor family or a poor community to bring itself up without some outside help or without someone. They just seem to get in a rut, I guess, and stay there. Then that repeats itself the next generation. The most basic, the most important thing is education. But it takes generations—one or two or three—to get that started.

Q. *Are you saying that poverty is largely structural then?*

A. I think so.

Q. *Does society have a responsibility to take care of poor people?*

A. I think they have—not a responsibility to take care of them—I think they have a responsibility to help them. But I think the most devastating thing they do, which is a lot of time happening now, is to take care of them, and that's why they stay that way. We have to offer them education but not give them too much [in frivolous material things]. Offer them the opportunity to help themselves. And private charity is important.

As I said earlier, I didn't deliberate as far as when or whom I'm giving to. But I will tell you that there are ones that I would not give to, because I feel like the money that you give, so little of it goes to the purpose or the people that you're trying to help. Some of the telethons and so forth, so much will go into P.R. and overhead.

Q. *How about the concept of the deserving poor? Are there some people you feel are more deserving of your help than others? And if people didn't appreciate it or do something with it when you gave money, would you not give to that group anymore?*

A. I don't know if it's appreciation. If they didn't do anything with it to help their situation, I wouldn't. There again it depends on how much and the people that it's given to, but I think it has a great deal of impact. If it's something that could enable them to help themselves, that to me is always basically number one. Don't give too much. Give them enough to help. Let them have the pleasure of achieving themselves.

This goes right straight to disabled people. They can do incredible things, but they do need help. They need support morally. They need monetary support. It's been proven over and over. We have it right down at RIO, where they're living independently, working independently, and becoming achievers in the community. It's a sense of pride with them. That just makes you feel good to think that you've been able to help them achieve that, in that degree. It's a very good feeling to think you had a part if they become successful, in whatever degree they're able to. You've been able to help them do that. It's a great feeling.

Q. *What effect on society does philanthropy have? Do you see any effect?*

A. Yes, I think that it has a great effect. It enables scholarships. It enables young people, who never had the opportunity, to go to college. And all the people at RIO, the things given to them have helped them learn to get jobs. I see some employers that now will take disabled or handicapped people into their businesses. They find these people make the best employees in the world once they learn that job. So I think it has a great effect upon society.

Melissa's belief that it is important to give enough to help people but not so much that you encourage them to stay in their poverty put her closer to some of the entrepreneurs than to other philanthropists I interviewed. In this regard, I found philanthropists a varied group, expressing views ranging from Melissa's to the more typically liberal attitude toward poverty. Where Melissa was more fully representative of the philanthropists as a group was in her delineation of her own needs versus those of others.

Q. *If you can think back a moment to when you started giving money, did you wait until you'd taken care of your own basic economic needs and those of your family before you began your own charitable activities?*

A. Yes, and that's important, because you really need to take care of yourself. Otherwise you can't take care of anybody else.

Q. *Do you have any fears about your own financial security, particularly as you get older, and does that affect any of your charitable activities?*

A. No, because I am making sure that even if my health wavers, I certainly will be able to provide for myself. So no, I wouldn't give beyond that. I've also taken care of my daughters. We made a trust fund where they get interest only until the youngest daughter is thirty-five. Then the principal will be distributed among them. We set it up this way so we wouldn't cripple their own achievements. We wanted the girls to be able to take care of themselves.

Q. *Do you think philanthropists are better people than similarly wealthy people who may make only occasional or small charitable contributions?*

A. I don't know. I guess it depends upon your reason for doing it. If you're being the philanthropist for business contacts or political reasons, if those are the reasons, I don't think that you're a better person, no.

Q. *Let me turn the question around a little bit: are wealthy people who do not give money to charity failing to discharge their obligation to society in some way?*

A. I think so. I think that to have gained wealth you had to have done so through the help of other people. It had to come from other people helping in the background. You just don't do this all by yourself. It has to be through the efforts of many people. Whether it's an inheritance or whether you've made it yourself, other people helped you. So therefore you have the obligation to turn it around, to pass it on if you will.

In this, Melissa echoed Billy's view that it's appropriate to put something back into the community which gave you so much. Melissa's attitude toward these gifts, however, differed in a significant way from the entrepreneur's. Billy gave money to needy people on a loan basis. His quasi-altruistic acts were conditional: he expected at least partial repayment. In contrast, while Melissa also seems concerned that the gift be used constructively, she expects no repayment. Her giving has no strings attached.[6]

Q. *How would you feel if your generosity were not sufficiently appreciated? Would you still share it?*

A. Well, if the gift wasn't used in a constructive way, I wouldn't give it. But to be concerned with their response to me, that's not philanthropy. That's making a loan, even though it still comes under the same heading of helping other people.

Melissa articulates a critical point here. When entrepreneurs like Billy give money via loans or outright gifts, they are indeed "helping other people." But altruism with no strings attached is something else again. This is a crucial distinction: not all modes of helping other people are equally altruistic.

I found Melissa's explanation of why she ceased making anonymous gifts quite interesting. It suggested to me that the publicity was at least in part a negative for her; it was a burden she bore because it might help others. This, of course, is exactly the opposite from what economic theories of altruism suggest.

Q. *Did you expect to have any notoriety from this?*

A. Oh gosh, no! They made me see that it was necessary, what I was doing, but that what they needed was for other people to help too. And they convinced me that if I really wanted to help, that I had to let it be known what I was doing. I didn't go public with my gifts for notoriety or publicity or anything like that. I really detest that. But it was a way to encourage other people to give money. And I can see that it has helped a great deal. Many friends of mine, as well as other people whom I didn't know, became involved because of the publicity over my gifts.

When I first gave, I gave anonymously. I didn't want any particular benefits as a result of my gift. The Performing Arts Center, for example, that was a million-dollar gift. They asked me to give the money, and I said, "Fine, but I would prefer to be anonymous." In a month or so they called me. They were into a campaign for fund-raising. They said, "If you would just allow us to let this be known, you'd be surprised at what would happen. Other people will see this, and it will encourage them to give."

So, reluctantly, I did. Well, it was amazing! I had notes and letters from people who were with my husband at McDonald's many years ago. They all came forth. It was very surprising. I never expected anything like this to happen. I wanted to be anonymous because I didn't want any attention. I just didn't want to talk about it. I don't think a lot of my close friends knew the monetary situation I was in. It wasn't any tremendous thing, but it was certainly sizeable. That's one of the reasons I didn't want publicity, because I didn't want that barrier. And oftentimes it does create a barrier. It makes people feel awkward. Maybe because they're not in a position to do something comparable, they're not comfortable with you any more. I certainly don't want that.

So it would be easier for me to give it anonymously. But if it helps the causes more if you go through the suffering in the public eye, then you do it.

Melissa's attitude toward anonymous giving and her attitude toward receiving thanks also suggest that praise is not foremost in her mind.

Q. *Most people, knowing what you do, would think that the recipients should be grateful to you for your aid. Is this usually the case?*

A. Oh, I think so. I think one of the most pleasant experiences I've had, more than large amounts that I've given, was at Christmas time at the vocational center down at RIO. The director of the Center said to me, just in passing, that they needed a forklift. So my Christmas gift to the Center was a red forklift, a big red forklift. The executive director said, "Please, don't just send it. Bring it. It will mean so much to the clients."

That was one of the most rewarding times and one of the best things that I've ever done. I took it myself. I had learned to drive it myself, and I drove it up to the dock! All the clients [the handicapped people] in the vocational center were there. They were clapping and smiling, and then they got on it to drive it. That was probably one of the neatest things that I ever have experienced.

It just makes me feel wonderful, absolutely wonderful, when things like that happen. That was the Christmas spirit, both ways! You come home and you feel like you've done something so neat. Not for a pat on the back for yourself, but that you've hit the perfect present for somebody else. It's like when I give one of my grandchildren a specific gift, and it's just right! You just love it. That's the kind of reward that you want for giving.

It is the pleasure in finding "the perfect present for somebody else" and not the "pat on the back for yourself" that is more important to Melissa. This seems quite different from giving in order to get praise.

Finally, we turned to questions about how Melissa sees the world and her own identity. Here again, Melissa's boundaries in terms of delineation of self, family, and others fell somewhere between the entrepreneurs and the altruists who rescued Jews in Nazi Europe.

Q. *I'm trying to understand the way you view the world.*

A. I have a very strong sense of family. I believe it starts there, and then that goes into the community and thereafter into the country, and then from our country into the world. But the core is within the family. That's where it starts.

Q. *So your basic identity, how would you characterize it? Do you see a distinction between yourself and members of the family? Or would you see yourself as part of a whole group?*

A. My identity? I haven't really thought about it. My friend calls me the matriarch of the family. I don't really think of myself in that way. That's kind of difficult to say about yourself. Someone else who knows me could probably answer that better than I can.

Q. *Well, I'm just curious. Certain scholars have talked about different concepts of the individual's relationship with society. They juxtapose a concept that's organic, where people live in a body politic, a community, in the same way that the heart and the lungs and the different organs live within the body. They are distinct within the body, but they live within the body and they're not really separate: the one can't function without the other. Then that view's often held in distinction to a view where people are separate individuals who don't have to have any relationships with each other at all; where we're all existing in a society, and if we want to relate to each other, we can, but it's all done through volition. It's an act that has to be consciously made; it's not something that is a requirement. Does any of this ring true for you? Would you view yourself as fitting into one of these world views more than the other?*

A. Oh, I would see it as definitely a part of the whole, as far as a part of the community or a part of the people. I may have said earlier that I feel that we are alone, in a way. And I do believe that, when it comes down to it. But then how we act and interact with other people is very important. I definitely enjoy interacting and relating to other people.

Q. *Let me ask you one last question. If we wanted to have more people like you in the world, how would you suggest we go about doing that?*

A. I don't think that there need to be any more people like me!

Q. But just assume that we might.

A. Assuming we might, I'd just say living by example, not talking about all these things you're doing. I find the deepest people are usually silent. Maybe "humble" is the word I'm searching for. Others around you know by the way you live, the way you conduct yourself, I suppose; so I'd just say by living, by trying to be an example that you'd be proud to have your grandchildren follow.

I have a lot of faults. My gosh, I couldn't even begin to add them! But for the philanthropic things and the caring for others, I think that you have to do it. Teach them as you go along. Make them a part of it. That's how I was.

I encountered this same quietness and modesty of altruism in many other altruists I interviewed. Most altruists insisted that they had not done anything remarkable, that they were merely ordinary people. But this does not mean altruists cannot be extremely colorful individuals who perform larger-than-life deeds, as is amply demonstrated in the next two chapters.

CHAPTER 4

The Heroine

A MOST UNLIKELY HEROINE, Lucille is a frail grandmother with a heart condition and braces on both her leg and back. Nor does her occupation—poetry editor for a local newspaper—seem the obvious training for someone who would swear like a marine while beating the proverbial out of a large rapist. But that is exactly what happened. Furthermore, Lucille was involved in the southern civil rights movement of the 1950s; this also makes her well qualified as a heroine. Because of her history, and because she was a real character—feisty and vulnerable, emphatically and deliberately opinionated, yet touchingly insecure, delightfully and richly human—I chose Lucille to illustrate the heroes.

On July 29—I'll have to double-check that, but I think it's the twenty-ninth—I was working at my desk. I'm poetry editor for the *Gazette*, and I was trying to figure out a poem, whether it was right or not, when I heard some terrible screaming. "God, help me! Oh, Jesus, help me! You're hurting me! God help me!" I looked out and saw this man grabbing this young girl. It was my neighbor, washing her car. I did not know her personally, but I knew she was living with her sister there. He pulled her across the car. He had parked his car by hers. She had on shorts, decent shorts. She had on a nice little T-shirt with sleeves, and he had grabbed her ponytail and had dragged her over the car. He threw her onto the pavement of the driveway.

At this time, I knew that something had to be done and done now, and no time could be wasted. There was nobody in our neighborhood. They all work. I'm very crippled. I wear a back brace and a leg brace, and I had just gotten out of the hospital, where they told me I needed a bypass surgery and I refused it. This was just a few days before.

But I stepped out. I grabbed my cane. I use a cane to walk with, sometimes crutches, and I went out and I said, "God help me. How am I gonna run down two flights of stairs and get across two city lots over to that house? I just prayed, and I literally leaped four steps at a time and then I started running toward them, toward the rapist and the young lady.

Well, by then he had pulled her blouse off, ripped it off, and was biting her tits and biting her other places. I thought, "God, tell me something to do. This man is huge! He must be six, two."

Well, I felt then that I was almost lifted and carried over there, because when I got up [to them] I started screaming. Just when I went up to them, before I called to him, I heard him say to her—even though it was obvious she had lost consciousness by then, since she was purple—he said, "I'm gonna kill you, and then I'm gonna give you the best fuck you ever had."

That's when I told him, "No, you're not, you son of a bitch. You're gonna die." I swore, 'cause I thought, I can't sound like some little old gray-haired woman, so I tried to sound as fierce and as mean as possible. I called him a goddamn son of a bitch and told him if he didn't get off her, I would kill him. And I screamed it viciously.

He didn't pay any attention to me. He kept choking her. He was choking her all this time. Her face was purple. He had his penis out, and I got up to him and I told him again to get off of her. Well, he kind of turned his head and looked at me, and then he went back to her. I hauled off and hit him across the neck and the head with my cane. *This* caused him to get up. He started toward me. I said, "Come on, I'm gonna kill you. Just come on. I'm not foolin' with you." And I yelled ta the girl, "You get in the house and lock the door, and don't even let me in. I don't care who comes; just don't let 'em in."

People said, "Were you afraid?" Yes, I was. I kind of felt this was it for me, because he was so vicious-looking. I thought this was a death-to-death fight: I'm gonna kill him or he will kill me. Because he was hurting another human being, an innocent human being. I just can't take that. I wasn't trained that way.

He struck out at me and hit me in the shoulder. I hit him again with the cane. I beat at him and he stood there, and he was swinging at me and I wouldn't step back. I yelled again to the girl, "Go ahead and get in the house."

When she did get in the house, I realized that if I didn't catch him, he'd be another case where they'd say, "Well, you don't have any evidence." So I thought, I've started; I'm gonna finish it. I started just whaling out with the cane, and he told me he was gonna kill me. "You bitch," he said. "I'll kill you right here." "Alright, come on," I told him. "Let's do it." And finally he turned and ran to his car. I ran after him, and then he put his foot in to get into his car. I slammed the door on him and I thought, This'll hold him. "Somebody call the police! For heaven's sake, somebody get somebody over here!" I was screamin' and hollerin'.

Well, he got out of the car, and he came over and hit me. So I hit him again. I hit him in the crotch with my cane. He went back to the car, realizing by now surely somebody had called the police, as which I had thought, too. But I slammed the door on him again when he tried to get in the car. He got out of the car then and started running around to the next street, which is Thayer Street.

The only thing I know to do is to tackle him. I was running and swinging my cane, and my heart was just killing me. You know, I was feeling it; it was really hell.

I thought, Lord, forgive me. I hope the pope won't excommunicate me, but I gotta get this man. So I was getting ready to tackle him and try to hit him in the nerve of the neck, but a man ran up and he said, "What's happened?!" I said, "That man raped a beautiful young girl right back there on the other side of that house." He said, "You go on. I'll get him." So I turned around and went back to the house.

The young girl who had been raped was standing in the garage—it's a garage that's closed in, kind of like a studio—and she was looking out front. I called to her, "Will you let me in now?" She was just screaming, "I've been raped! I've been raped! Please help us!" I could hear a voice saying [on the phone], "Where are you? Where are you?" Finally, I went over and just started beating the door, and she opened it and I went in. I took the phone from her and told the operator where we were.

In the meantime, the young man who came to our aid had chased the rapist down Thayer Street. Two painters on a house saw them fighting. They came down, and it took all three of them to hold him [the rapist] till the police got there. Then the police got him and took him off. They didn't know about us. But after I gave the operator the address, they arrived so fast! I never saw so many policemen and ambulances in my life. I was hurt a little, and they asked about that. I hurt a lot more the rest of the week. But when you're that mad, you don't feel pain so much. So I was mostly just trying to calm down the young girl and tell her it was alright.

You know, I've said to many people, "These men [the rapists] are cowards. If you'll scream as loud as you can, it might make a difference. I went to a rape bureau, to a seminar on rape, and learned a lot of things there. There are a lot of things that people can do. Little things, like just getting acquainted with the neighbors. You don't have to be a busybody. You can just say to people, "Look, if you ever hear anything happening, start screaming out your window or call me on the phone. I'll be there." Everyone must know this. Each neighbor can do this. And then each neighbor must also call the police and the other neighbors, and then they all can raise the window and start screaming. The ones that have the courage to go down— and I don't say that the others are wrong in not doing anything. I hate the word courage, because it's not that. It's really not a matter of courage. Well, it is and it isn't. It's that you care enough about someone, about the human person, that you feel that you have to help no matter what.

So that was that. The young girl still lives near me. She stayed. I never did know her really, you know. She was young, and I'm sixty-six. But I knew her to see her; and I'd say, "Hi," and she'd say, "Hi." That was the only time we ever spoke.

She's doing better now. Her mother came down to the door once. She knocked, and when I opened the door, she just stood there bawling. "Oh, Miz B———, you saved my baby daughter." So she came in, crying and everything. They were very nice to me. They have written me and thanked me, just saying all kinds of lovely things.

Other repercussions from the rape were less pleasant for Lucille.

I assume, but I can't prove it, that the rapist sent people to get me after the rape. There was a problem with a knife. I've had my windows broken. I've had my file drawers all turned upside down. All this, because of this rape. You see, humanity's funny. Some people—I have no way to prove it—but I wonder if the people who are calling me are from his family. I know his family is very, very bitter, even though he beat up his wife's retarded sister and apparently beat his wife all the time. He was a vicious man. But I get the most disgusting calls. I thought I knew every word in the English language. Well, I do now! Particularly words about the sexual being, the physical being. They've called me everything. They described in great detail what they're going to do to me when they catch me. They're still phoning me. For a while it got so bad I finally had to get an unlisted number; but then I couldn't afford that. These people are hurt and obsessed. And a lot of people need something to excite them, to get mad at somebody, because this releases them. But when they call me and say, "I just saw you come in," then I'm scared silly, you know? Because I don't wanna have to fight anymore. I'm tired.

I talked to the police about it. They were wonderful. Gosh, we have the best police force here you ever saw. They are compassionate and kind, and they're good to everybody. But there's not much they can do. It's like people saying to me, "Well, where were the police when all this happened?" And I always say, "How could they be there if they didn't know what was going on? Where were you? Did you call?" Really! They want the police to be at everything happening, and how can they? So it's kind of ironic.

Lucille's compassion is tempered by her outrage at injustice and her desire not to be pushed around by others. This gives her a feistiness that borders on braggadocio and a determination to work together with others to make the world better.

Most of these bullies are cowards. I'm 5'7" and weigh about 130. I couldn't kill a fly. But they let me scare 'em. That's typical of people. So if people will quit being cowed and will start screaming [it might help]. If they can't go down and physically get involved, then at least pick the phone up and then get in the windows. We've got to watch out. We've gotta start doing something. Are we gonna lie around and let people misuse us all the rest of our lives?

I asked Lucille why she thought she had been the one to break up the rape, when so many other people would not have had the courage or simply would not have thought to try.

I have thought about that. My grandmother and my mother taught me that you always help somebody. They did. I came home one night and told them about some little girl that this kid had jumped on, teasing and pulling her piggy tails. Mother said, "Next time he does that, just get over there and throw him on the ground and tell him that you don't want to see him do that again."

So they taught me to defend people and myself, but mostly to fight against any injustice that was being done. If I was there, I was responsible. They taught me to love all humanity.

The idea of defending others, fighting against injustice, taking personal responsibility for others, and loving all humanity ran like leitmotifs throughout Lucille's narrative. Lucille also linked these feelings to the racial problems in the South.

We had a tremendous race problem down here, but my family, we took care and tried to help take care of the black people and see that they got home safely, because there were terrible things that went on in those days. I just was raised that way. Mother said, "If you really feel like somebody's mistreating somebody, and you feel like you can stop it, then step in, and I'll back you all the way." So I think that had a lot to do with it.

The idea that she should take responsibility for others formed a central component of Lucille's self-image and was evident both in her attitudes toward race and in her disruption of the rape.

I just don't know what's gonna happen to the world. I really am frightened, because so many of the people say to me [about the rape], "Well, that was great, but you were a damn fool," or "That was courageous, but she probably asked for it." *That's* when I want to knock their heads off! You know, that's really when I want to knock their heads off! "But she didn't have on a decent outfit," they say. "I bet she had a little bikini on." "So what? She was in her own yard tending to her business. You think that's okay that somebody can rape her for that?!" I know what would end it all. If all the women would stand out on the streets and when men went running by with these jockey shorts on, if we all jumped on 'em and raped 'em! It'd put a stop to rape! I mean, really!

People said to me that I went over there [to break up the rape] on a gamble. Well, you can call it whatever you want to. But I went over there because someone needed help.

Lucille's grandmother appears as the dominant force in Lucille's life. For example, when I asked Lucille why she felt she had developed her ideas of responsibility for others and her love for humanity, she immediately referred to her grandmother.

My grandmother was important [in making me feel this way]. She always told us we were not allowed to destroy anything in nature *unless* it was hurting something else. We were not even allowed to step on a bug or a spider. In fact, my grandmother had a snake live under her stove all the time, because he was cold and he wanted to live under there. She never hurt him. If a scorpion or something got in the house, she'd pick it up and scold it and put it outside. Scorpions aren't as bad as everybody makes out, you know. They *can* hurt you. But it hurts for them to sting. They like to come in, especially during the winter. They like to get into warm places.

In describing the values her grandmother taught, Lucille articulated a view of herself in relation to others that was remarkably close to that described by other altruists: the view that we are all one, all dependent on each other, and that what helps one helps all.

Grandmother taught me that everything is dependent on everything else; and if we wipe out any one of the other, we're going to lose that much more in the nature of things. And that we had no right to make a choice who or what would die.

Lucille started putting her grandmother's lessons into practice at a very young age.

Once a little black child got on the streetcar, with a chicken in her hands. It was close to Easter, I think. That's probably why she had the chicken. The streetcar driver said, "Hey, nigger. We don't let niggers on here with chickens."

They used to throw 'em off the streetcar all the time. This is in the thirties and forties that I'm talking about.

So I went up to the little girl and asked what was the matter. I went up and I saw that he [the conductor] had grabbed the little girl. He was getting ready to throw her off the bus. I said, "Just a minute." I told the little girl, "Here's a nickel. Give me your chicken." She gave me her chicken, and I said, "Go back and sit by that white lady you see back there. She's my grandmother." Then I turned to the conductor and said, "You gonna let me on with a chicken or not?" Oh, he started cussing and everything! But he let me stay.

I went back there with my grandma and the little girl, and I sat down with the chicken. Then Grandma and I both got off where the little girl got off, and we walked her home. We were afraid somebody would hurt her. I wasn't too old when this happened, just in grammar school. But I remember.

Lucille's grandmother imparted to her both a consciousness of the condition of American blacks and a willingness to fight for greater rights for them, as for all those who needed help.

My grandmother was important to me; she certainly was. I would say that she made my life.

She thought every city should have a museum. So she started one, the Arkansas Natural History Museum, in an old theater. At that time blacks could not walk through MacArthur Park; that was the law. They could not walk to get to their houses, really not very far from there. They had to go all the way around, about seven blocks. Grandmother wanted the black children to see the museum, so she would call the teachers and tell 'em she would meet them in the streetcar line, bring 'em in the museum and spend the day talking to 'em about all the wonderful things and where all these things came from.

It was hundreds of little things like that she did for people. She found an old lady who didn't have a home anymore. So Grandma hid her and let her sleep in the back of the museum at nights. Grandma'd sneak food into her, and then when Grandma'd come the next morning, the lady'd get up and go on back out on the streets. She was just a generous, beautifully educated, beautifully compassionate woman, my grandmother.

Lucille inherited some of her feistiness from her grandmother, who was a well-known author of children's stories, a suffragette, and a temperance worker.

She wiped out bars. She hated whiskey. She and Carrie Nation—Carrie Nation used to live in Eureka Springs—and she and my grandma, they'd go wipe out bars together, with a baseball bat. [*Chuckles*]

She went to New York once, when the women at that time started striking because they were being mistreated: they were only getting something like eight cents an hour. They went on strike and walked [a picket line]. The police came on great big horses. Grandmother went up there to look into it, because she wanted to write about it and see what she could do about it. Once, while she was watching a girl, a pregnant girl, a horseman ran up, a policeman. He told her to get back, and then he hit her with his billy club, right across the stomach. Then he pushed her down. Well, my grandmother went flying through the air, jumped up as high as she could, grabbed a hold of him and jerked him off his horse and threw him on the ground.

She got arrested for this. This was in the early twenties, I'd guess. But she couldn't stand it. Injustice to her was as horrible as hate or anything. She just thought people ought to stand up and stop it. She went [to] night court, and the judge said, "Are you Bernie B——?" So she told him, "Yes, I am." He said, "Come into my chambers." He knew her and knew her books. He told her, "Now, Bernie, you get on this damn train and you go home. We don't want you up here! Don't come causing any more trouble. We already got enough." But Grandma told him, "I want to see that policeman. Something happened out there that was wrong, and he had no right to do that."

I don't know what happened to the policeman. But the authorities put my grandmother on the train and sent her home.

Lucille sees herself as part of a long line of independent and crusading women who stand up for injustice and will not be intimidated.

My grandmother wasn't the only one in my family like this. All the women in my family are very strong women who feel very deeply about social justice and are willing to take a lot of personal risks. We do. All of the women in our family—I can't tell you as for all the men—but all the women in the family were the fighters. Bernie [Lucille's grandmother] had children: three daughters and two sons. And all of the women were far ahead of their time and were very knowledgeable and caring about people. We lived on the words love, compassion, hearing, and acting.

Lucille's feminism was deeply felt and complex. When I first asked her if she would characterize herself as a feminist, she wanted to know what I meant by the term. I replied that she sounded like a strong believer in equal rights for women. Lucille hastened to correct my slightly erroneous impression: "I'm for equal rights of all living creatures, including all humanity," she replied. This attitude, instilled by her suffragette grandmother, was important in forming Lucille's attitudes toward life as well as toward those who abuse living things.

We were raised to love animals, and I let in many at night and the evening. We didn't have indoor toilets or anything, and the water, we had to go get it out of the spring. I'd lay there, and the crawdads were walking all around. I talked to them, and it just gave me a feeling that that's what life is. It's everything; life is everything. Now, there's good and bad, but [when] the bad is bothering the underdog, then you act. So I used to get into fights for black people on the streetcars.

It is this world view that links Lucille's particular brand of feminism with her civil rights activities and her heroism in stopping the rape.

I think women are tougher than men. I do. Women have more feelings of social responsibility. Definitely. I know I have a really strong sense of social responsibility. I marched through the integration period and got beaten and stabbed and shot one time. That was during the integration period in Little

Rock, and I kept my theater open. I organized a theater here [in Little Rock]. The governor called me and told me to close it down. The Ku Klux Klan and the White Citizens Council also went after me. I just told 'em to go to hell! They bombed my car, blew the wiring out and set the car on fire. They put a cross in my yard. Oh, there's just lots of things that I could tell you. But I fought on for the blacks, because who else is going to? If whites can't help 'em, who else is going to? Most people [say], "Oh, well, that's a nigger. Let 'em be." We were told never to use that word. I remember one time, I said to my grandmother, "If I was a nigger, I'd do so and so." Well! My grandmother jerked me up and she said, "Don't *ever* say nigger!" "Why?! Viola [a black friend] called him nigger; she called him her nigger," I protested. This is true. The black woman will call a black man a nigger, but not with the same meaning that the white has. But we were never allowed to curse or use that word.

Lucille further linked this world view to what she was taught and how she was treated as a child.

We were never punished. Not one child in our family was punished physically. We were never whipped. We were never slapped. Never. Nothing. We were talked to. And then they'd say, "Now how do you feel about what you did?" And then the punishment came with, "Well, I can't just let this go by. We're gonna have to go apologize to the person involved or you don't get your pony this week," or something else that I wanted. We knew we would never be whipped or hurt in any way. It would not be allowed in our family. I think that instilled a kind of respect for human life in me. I think that had everything in the world to do with it.

Lucille's early childhood, then, was dominated by strong women who believed they should take care of others and fight against injustice. The idea that one should love all living things, and that this includes blacks, does not seem radical now, but it unfortunately was not the norm during Lucille's childhood.

Anyway, looking back, I wouldn't want to do it any different. I ran, I played with the black people. I'd go to their houses, and I heard *wonderful* stories. They were just beautiful people, who had so much in their culture to tell.

This one woman was a sorceress. I was just fascinated with her. She boiled a pot and she called out and got answers—that kind of thing. But she always loved me. She asked me one night, she said, "Look up on that hill. You see that big white horse up there?" I looked. I didn't see any white horse, but I didn't say so. I said, "Yes'm, I see it." "That's the horse of death," she said. "There's somebody going to die tonight." Four people died that night in the community.

I was fascinated with this. I was totally fascinated with this woman. I used to spend my time down at the black folks' house, where I ate opossum and everything. My mother near to died. But if it was something that I might learn from or that wasn't really wrong, she let me do it.

Lucille also felt great affection and respect for her mother.

My mother worked for the Welfare Department. I don't like telling this [next part]. Oh, I guess I don't care. She worked an extra night cleaning places so we'd have enough money for food. Then she got to be state hospitalization director, which was still like only one hundred dollars a month, so that wasn't anything much. She was a fabulous woman. She walked eight miles to work every morning and eight miles back.

For her father, on the other hand, Lucille reported only negative feelings.

My dad, I don't talk about. I hate him. I won't mention him, and I'm not even gonna tell you his name. He left my mother when my mother had two little children. He just up and left. I was just a baby, and he left all of us: me, my mother, and my older brother.

They weren't together long after I was born; I musta been about four to five months old when my father left. I never heard from him after that. I didn't want to and never cared. But he's dead now, I think. I don't care. In fact, I went to court and had my name changed, because I didn't want to carry his name.

Mother lost the Tyler Street house because of lack of money after my father left. So my grandmother moved us out. She had found a huge barn on a nice piece of land. She named the place Broadview, because there was a hill that overlooked Little Rock. She told my mother, "Francine, bring the kids out and we're gonna live out here. I'm gonna build you a house, and we're gonna live out here where it's Mother Nature and all the good things. I'll watch after everything."

So we did. We lived with Grandmother. She built the house, which was about three or four hundred feet away from her house, and we lived there. We grew up there, clear up to our teens. In fact, I lived there until I went into the army. My grandmother really helped out after my mother lost the home. My Aunt Lucille, who lived about a thousand feet from our house at Broadview, also helped. So it really didn't bother me to lose the house and move. Whether it bothered Mother or not, I never knew, 'cause I never saw her cry and I never saw her complain. I just don't know. Mother had a very interesting attitude toward crying. In fact, I was never allowed to cry. She always said nothing was worth crying over, and so we didn't cry or anything. We just did the best we could with what we had.

Grandmother never had any money. If she did, she gave it away. Everything she got, she gave away. My mother never had money until she married Dr. C———. He was a very rich man. She didn't know that when they got married, because he kept his money hidden. But then he died very soon after the marriage. Three years, I think. So she had quite a bit of money. He had no kinfolks so Mother got left with quite a bit of money and was well-to-do. That was the first time, I guess, in my life when any of us had any money.

Lucille was full of surprises, such as her army service during World War II and the fact that Eleanor Roosevelt had suggested that Lucille enlist.

I had gotten married back in 1941. It didn't last. I wasn't even married a year or two, I'm sorry to say. He was a delightful person, just very lovely, and I have an adopted daughter. But I was spoiled rotten and he was spoiled rotten, and neither one of us had an ounce of sense. I just left. I went up to work for Mrs. Roosevelt. Grandmother called her and said that I was gettin' a divorce and I needed a job, needed to get away from things in Little Rock, so Mrs. Roosevelt gave me a job at the Pentagon building. I was nothing important, just a clerk. Eleanor Roosevelt was a great admirer of my grandmother's. She had read all her books, and she used to call and talk to Grandmother. Then she often had Grandmother up to Washington, for a visit. Mrs. Roosevelt had a little radio show, and she had Grandmother on that often.

I meant to tell you all this the other day. I think this is probably in a way a philosophy. Miz Roosevelt said to Grandmother, "Well, you've been through so much, and you've survived and put out such wonderful things. Do you give all this credit to God?" And Grandmother told her, "Yes. But the trouble is, we ask too much of God. God gave us the blackberries, but he didn't give us the jam. We had to figure that out. And that's what life is about."

I think that's important to remember. Anyway, that's how I got into the army. Mrs. Roosevelt talked to me. She always used to eat with the employees. She wouldn't eat with the big executives at the Pentagon building. She'd usually eat lunch at the table with a lot of the other workers, whenever she was there. And one day she said, "Lucy, why don't you go into the army? You love the United States. But if you do enlist, go home, so your state'll get credit for it." She gave me the money and put me on a train and sent me home, and I went right down and got in the army.

Although Lucille was patriotic and loved serving her country, her experiences with the army were not entirely pleasant.

I love the flag and I love my nation. I joined the army for four years. I was in Italy and Egypt during World War II. You talk about scared! I'd never been that far away from my family.

I got a ruptured appendix, and the operation was done on the boat, in the middle of the ocean. Then, later, I was wounded in Italy. My company didn't actually do any fighting, but we were in the fighting area. I was in the ambulance when a bomb hit and threw the ambulance over. It broke my vertebrae and disc. But I kept on going 'cause I didn't wanna be sent home. I finally got fixed up and got back with my company. I went to Egypt with my company. When I got there, I drove a truck, kinda like an East Texas Motor Freight. I picked up stuff at Alexandria and Cairo; supplies, mostly. We used to pick up frozen beef halves. I mean the whole half, everything, and load it; and we'd count, and then we say "Three" and scoot it down the truck.

One day the colonel, who hated us, 'cause we were women—he said we were all a bunch of whores and lesbians, and that's the way he treated us—well, I was up there, and he said to the man, "Let go of that! If she wants to do a man's work, let her do it." When he let go [of the beef], it pulled all the muscles in my back, because then all the weight of the cow was on me. But I was so mean and stubborn, although I hurt and cried at night, I wanted to go on. I wanted to finish the war, whatever it was.

After this captain dropped the meat on me, I didn't wanna go to an army hospital, so I went to a private doctor. I found out I had four ruptured vertebrae, plus one was crushed. He fixed those up, but now one leg has a half-inch shortage. I wear braces, body braces and leg braces, just as a result of the army.

After I came home, at least at first, I really hated the army. Not the United States Army per se but the kind of people that were allowed to run things in the army. They hated women. It was very hard on the women in those days. They treated us like dirt and scum. I just said, Well, I'm gonna go ahead and get my honorable discharge.

After Lucille received her discharge, she returned to Little Rock. She attended college on the GI bill and then pursued a career in theater.

I was there for about a year, and then I decided I wanted to be an actress. So I applied and went to the Pasadena Playhouse in California, which is a professional theater school. But then, after being there maybe eight months, I didn't like the way it was run. All the professional people were doing the parts, and we were just gettin' 'em on and off stage if they were drunk or forgot about the curtain time and were still sittin' around at home, or whatever.

So I applied at the American Theater Wing in New York City. I went there, auditioned, and was accepted. I was in New York on the stage and then in touring shows. I was in New York on and off from the 1940s through the 1970s. Not all the time, just on and off. I didn't leave New York until—oh, dear me—well, let's see, my grandmother died in '62. I was still in New York then. It wasn't long after that when I had cancer of the uterus, and I had to have a massive operation. I went home to do it. My mother had married a doctor in the meantime, and he recommended somebody. So I did what he suggested. Then I got up and went back to New York, because I was doing some shows. But then I got cancer of the breast, and my back was bothering me. So I came home. I would say this was about 1963. I never did go back to New York. I've been in Little Rock ever since.

Lucille converted to Roman Catholicism as an adult, a decision that caused a temporary estrangement from her mother.

I think I told you I'm Catholic. I became a Roman Catholic in 1977. I was disinherited. My mother actually did disinherit me. And my brother took all the money. She had a lot of money from her second husband, the doctor. Then she had a stroke, and I had her for ten years, nursing her and caring for her. My brother didn't even pay her insurance. I had all that to do, but that's immaterial. Later, just before she died, she asked me, "Will you ever forgive me?" "For what?" I asked her.

I guess she felt bad about it [disapproving of the conversion] 'cause she knew if I was that determined, then that's what I needed. That's the only time she ever told me not to do anything, or that she could not approve of what I did. But it's been a grace for me, and it's calmed me down a lot. It's made a better woman out of me in many respects.

I love my religion. It's hard, the way I believe. I go to church everyday. But I don't go to confession and things like that; oh, no. Because God already knows what I've done. If he's gonna do anything, he was gonna whack me. I don't have to wait for the priest to do it. [Laughs] No, I think confession is a psychological thing. I think it's a wonderful release for those who want it, and a lot of people do get a release from it. I'm sure a lot of them bore the priests to tears hearing the same thing. Maybe it's the drama in me, but when I go into church, I become just almost radiant with love. I'm saying I feel this in myself; I feel a closeness to God. The ritual, the drama of it, makes me very conscious of the goodness of spirituality, no matter what church it is.

When I first called Lucille, I did not know about her participation in the civil rights movement in Arkansas, activity that made her even more interesting for purposes of my study. Fighting for the rights of blacks in the South, unlike the kind of heroism she displayed in the rape incident, required an ongoing commitment in the face of widespread social disapproval. On the continuum from pure self-interest to pure altruism, Lucille perhaps stood somewhere between the heroes and the rescuers of Jews.

I was actually in the civil rights [movement] for a while. I'd founded a little theater in the fifties, when all the integration was just starting. I'd use students from Philander Smith, which was a black college here. I allowed blacks to come to the theater, and I took my productions over to Philander College to do them over there, too.

Well, the White Citizens Council and the Ku Klux Klan called me. They warned me that I would die if I didn't get rid of all the niggers in my theater. I just hung up on 'em. Then the governor called, Governor Faubus. He had asked every art group to not let the blacks come into their buildings, including the auditorium, when a show came to town. They all agreed except me. So they called me and told me to shut my theater. I said, "I'll not shut it down. It'll have to be by force."

So they started calling me on the phone, the Ku Klux Klan and the White Citizens Council. They said who they were. They didn't make any two ways about it: they said that they were going to kill me, and I was gonna be bombed. And everyday they would also call the newspaper and call me and say, "There's somebody coming in, and you're gonna be bombed and killed within a few minutes." So here would come all the police, and I'd just have to tell 'em to go on back. Nothing was happening.

But one funny thing did happen. I had a back room in my theater. Somebody called one day and they said, "We're gonna bomb your theater." Well, by then I was not getting afraid, but I was tense and tired. Just in back of my theater there was a black movie house, so I thought, "Well, I'll go over to see a movie." Somebody paged me in the movie: "Lucille B—— is wanted on the phone."

I thought, "Lordie! Something has happened to my mother." So I went to the phone, and this voice said, "Do you know how Dillinger died?" "Dillinger who?" "Dillinger the gangster." "No, I don't think so." I couldn't figure out what they were talking about. "He was shot down when he came out of the theater. And that's gonna happen to you just soon as you come out, so you can't stay in there forever."

I went back in, sat down in the theater, and I thought, "To hell with 'em." I just sat down in the theater and continued to watch the show. Then all the lights come up, and the policemen are storming down the aisles, and one of 'em grabs me up and snatches me out and takes me off. They got the call at the same time, and they believed it! So that's the kind of thing I got used to.

These were not just idle threats designed to intimidate Lucille, however, for she actually was accosted on more than one occasion.

One time I got stabbed. I was coming home late one night and a woman waved. It was a black lady. I stopped my car, and she told me her husband was having a heart attack. I ran over and went around to the other side of the car, because the man was slumped over the steering wheel. I crawled in on my knee to get a grip on him so I could pull him out and lie him down. He raised up his hand and stabbed me. He said, "You get out of this nigger business and you get out of the state, or you'll be dead."

We finally called the FBI; at least, my mother did. They told Mother they can't protect me because I'm not on government property. "You'll have to hire a bodyguard," they said. After other things like that happened, Mother finally got me a policeman.

But in the meantime, somebody in Oklahoma called me and wanted to give me an award for contributing to the integration movement, for my standing up and keeping my theater open. I flew over there to get it, and while I was gone, they scared the heck out of everybody in my theater. All my members of my theater voted to oust me and keep me out of the theater. Then they padlocked the theater, and that was that.

It was hard for me when people dropped me because of this. We had a board meeting when I got back. I told them, "I'm sorry. I know how you feel. I know what you're sayin', [even though] I can't feel it myself. But I've gotta stand up for what this is. This is not just a little individual thing. I will not have any theater where certain people can't come." I told them, "I'm gonna keep the theater goin' even if I have to do monologues."

The black people in the theater were frightened. They were scared, but they stayed with me. We always had them taken home. Some of the men in the group always took them to their doors after the theater was over.

I didn't have any friends during this period. [*Laughs self-consciously*] Well, I did, but they quickly dropped me. They were against what I was doing. This was 1956 or 1957. I remember, 'cause the State Guard marched right past our house when they went down to the Central High School and kept those nine kids from entering school. Well, maybe it was in the early 1960s; I don't remember the dates exactly. But I do remember that Mother supported me during all this. She said, "If you get killed, why, that's your concern. You gotta stand up for what you think's right." But they burned the cross in her yard, and I got afraid for her. So when they closed the theater, at first I was gonna open another one. But I was getting very tired and very worn out. We had a guard on me twenty-four hours a day, and that was costin' a lot of money. So I went back to New York then. I realized I was taxing everybody at this point, and I was endangering people. Besides, they'd already closed the theater. So I went on back to New York and did some more show business. Then I got cancer and came home.

Q. *Did you modify your actions because there was a physical threat to some of the people you loved most? Did you really not care much about the social criticism of the people around you?*

A. No, I did not. And I think my family was against me. My grandmother and my mother were not; it was the rest of the family who were not integrationists. They weren't against me slyly or anything. They just didn't want to be involved. They were frightened. But I didn't care. And I didn't quit because of their threats.

Lucille's social ostracism extended beyond her friends, her extended family, and her church and provides a telling glimpse of what it must be like to follow one's conscience against overwhelming social pressure.

Q. *Let me ask you about the reaction of the church and the political authorities or the business community to your integrationist activities. How did you feel they viewed what you were doing? And how did that affect you?*

A. They were fighting me. I lived in a segregationist state. They were all segregationists. I sometimes felt there wasn't another integrationist in the state. The governor, of course, was actually in the Ku Klux Klan. Some of the finest people in this state were in the Ku Klux Klan. In fact, once, when I was hurt, I went to a doctor, a man my mother had known for a long time. This was in the middle of the night. He said, "I'm going to doctor you, but don't ever come to me again, because I have no respect for you." Mother said she was going to turn him into the Medical Society, but the Medical Society didn't have any patience with me either. I was a very hated person in a very hateful situation. People don't know what it was like. People pulled in their ears and their necks. They stayed home and they stayed quiet. They were too afraid. There was no network of people supporting me at all.

Lucille pictures herself as acting alone, without support from a network of like-minded integrationists; although she does mention an occasional contact with a kindred spirit, she appears not to have drawn on these for support. Like Otto, who "just got mad" when he saw what the Nazis did to Jews, like Melissa who went through hard times alone, Lucille's mainstays were her own anger and determination.

People ask me, was it lonely for me? I guess so. Yes, it was; it was. But when something's done wrong, I get awfully mad, and I think this carried me through a lot of it. There were quite a bit of horrible things going on then; some of them were supported by Governor Faubus. Then there's the White Citizens Council and the Ku Klux Klan. They were money-wise, and they brought in these gangs of blacks who they paid to help them. These blacks came out of Chicago. They were just gangsters. They didn't care whether you were white, brown, yellow, or blue; they couldn't care less. They were brought here to beat up and hurt the people standing up for the negroes.

Mrs. D. D. Terry was the wife of the congressman, D. D. Terry. And she put black girls who were talented, in opera or whatever field, she would send 'em to schools and get 'em out of the state. She'd do things like that. So there were some people who helped. But it never appeared in the paper.

Then there were those people who just sat on the fences. People who said, "Well, I know they should deserve some rights, but I don't know quite where I stand." If the people who had been fighting for the blacks were hurt, especially brutally hurt, by black people, then the ones on the fences would say, "Well, here's Lucy B——. She's done nothin' but knock herself out fightin' for 'em, and they beat her half to death."

They never allowed it to get into the papers, but these negroes who beat me up, these were paid people. These weren't our Arkansas negroes doin' anything. They didn't have knives, [any] one of 'em; they didn't have guns. This was all lies that were being said, that they bought every gun that every store had, that they could have killed us all off. That was ridiculous!

What was interesting to me was that Lucille, and so many other altruists, have such a strong sense of what is normal that they cannot really understand why other people do mean things, do not help others in need, or persecute those who do. This was clear as Lucille continued her discussions on race and helping people.

Q. *How does this make you feel, though, about other people, when you were willing to go on the line and be beaten and risk your life, and other people weren't? How do you feel about that?*

A. I couldn't understand it. But I knew it was none of my business. I told people what I was and what I believed in. I really had no right to tell them *they* had to believe my way. I tried to show 'em and tell 'em, and it was very frustrating. I was terribly frustrated, especially when kids in the theater would say, "Miz B——, I can't come to the theater anymore. My mother and daddy said this was a bad place." It would hurt me very much. But they were afraid for their children.

Q. *What was it that made you keep on doing it? Was it because you felt it was the right thing to do, or were there some other emotions that were more important to you?*

A. No. I knew it was the right thing to do, and if enough people stood up, maybe we could gather enough, then we could stop it. And the law did come in, finally.

Lucille here voices a common thought among altruists: if we would only work together, then we could stop the injustice. Like many rescuers and like other heroes and heroines, Lucille does not consider herself extraordinary but rather goes out of her way to mention others whom she felt did more than she.

I've met and known Daisy Bates well for a long time. She was the woman who got these nine children to go to school, to an integrated school. She worked with 'em and trained 'em what to say and what to do. I met those nine. One girl still is not well. She was the one that had the kids come up to her, after they forced 'em to take negroes into the school, they came up to her and they said, "This is acid and we're gonna ruin your face." Then they threw it in her face. It was so traumatic for her psychologically that she went blind and went crazy and had to be treated medically. And it was nothing but water. Now *this* is the kind of torture that we all went through. But those children were children. I think they're to be admired and should be awarded heroes' awards, because they stood up and walked to that school with people callin' 'em everything in the world. They were lined up along the streets, the white people were, as these little kids would walk to school, and these big grown-ups would scream at them. It was a very ugly period, one of the ugliest. I think Arkansas ruined herself.

And you know, another thing that happened. Our chief of police, he fought for the negroes. He really tried. He begged me, he said, "Lucille, get out of the state. You're just another problem on my back." I said, "No, I'm not goin'." They later found him and his wife shot to death in their kitchen. All we got publicly was that they committed suicide. But that never happened. Everybody *knew* that was not suicide. I've talked to policemen since then, policemen that I was close to, who didn't wanna stir up any trouble, but who told me there's no way they committed suicide. The whole thing has never been cleared up. Somebody wanted him out of the way because he was arresting people. He was helping black people, and he was just wiped out, that's all.

At this point, our discussion turned from the specifics of Lucille's life to her own thought process while she was engaged in her civil rights activities. Lucille did not describe herself as a particularly brave person or as someone who tried to change the world. Indeed, her self-image seemed somewhat at odds with her fights against injustice and efforts to protect the underdog.

I'm very strong-willed and stubborn and hard-headed. My family would be glad to call me any of those names! But I'm not a mover and a shaker; I'm not one of those people who makes things happen. I accept what they give me. I don't like it, but I accept a lot of it. I think that's all we can do; we try our best to do everything we can.

I wouldn't say I was a brave person. I wouldn't go and say, "I'm a brave person" or "I'm a hero." I'm *not*. There are too many people that do far, far greater things than I have ever done. *They* are the real heroes. I hate the word hero. You know, I got that award—what's it called? oh, the Andrew Carnegie Award—I got the medal for heroism. I didn't feel I deserved it. I was not ashamed that I got it, but I'm self-conscious about it, because I don't think about myself that way. And it just bothers me when people say, "Boy, you were sure brave!" Then I get to stammering and can't say anything because [I'm so embarrassed]. I don't know. We didn't call it brave or heroic in the old days when they went out and did things they had to do, so why make such a big deal about it now?

This idea of normalcy, of doing what one has to do, played an important part in Lucille's perspective. It was evident as she spoke of her army experiences: she described herself as patriotic but was careful to note that she was not a John Wayne patriot, or even a heroic person. Like many other altruists I interviewed, Lucille did not want to "make such a big deal" about doing things that had to be done. Like other altruists, Lucille characterized herself as someone rather ordinary, even as she told me of performing extraordinary deeds: "I don't think I'm so unusual in this. I know I'm someone who's willing to take a lot of responsibility on in the world. But I don't think I'm anything special."

I found Lucille's participation in the civil rights movement particularly interesting in light of her professed insecurity and her strong need for people to like her.

Q. *You say that you want people to like you. But you obviously had a lot of people who did not like you because of some of the things you were doing in the integration period. Yet you still continued. So obviously you were able to live with that in some way.*

A. Well, I had to. That was more important.

Q. *Do you think of yourself as a rugged individualist?*

A. I'm rugged, and I'm an individual. I'm rugged in that I'll dive into anything that I think it's necessary to dive into. I don't go around in fights all the time. But I'm not some horrible person, you know.

Q. *Are you somebody who marches very much to your own drummer?*

A. Yes, definitely. But I don't think I'm a loner. I'm just so self-conscious all the time—this sounds funny—that people won't like me, or don't like me, or I've insulted them. Because my folks used to say, "Oh, well, that's Lucy. She's always into something."

Now, I'm not an aristocrat. It's not that I want to be an aristocrat, but all my kinfolks are. They all belong to lovely country clubs. . . . I don't know how to say this. I don't mean that I'm crying in my own puddle. I feel very self-conscious. [If you] know me, you won't think so. You'll think I'm the most outspoken moron you ever saw. But I want people to like me, and I don't know that they do. That's honest. That really is.

Lucille related several stories that characterized her as a loyal friend.

I was nominated for a sorority and didn't get in, because of two things. I was goin' with a fireman's daughter—she was my best friend—and in those days, firemen and policemen weren't the upper class; they were the lowest of all class. And they asked me if I was accepted for the sorority, would I drop my friend? I said, "Well, no! Can't you invite her to come in too?" They told me no. Then they asked me again, "You won't drop her?" "No, I won't. I don't think you're right if you're asking me to do this."

So I didn't [get in]. I found out later that I was blackballed for two reasons. One, I wouldn't drop a "common" friend, and the other was that we had an outdoor toilet and didn't have electricity. So I ran away. I was so hurt, I ran away. It wasn't that I really wanted that, to be accepted to the sorority. What I wanted was to be liked.

See, when I was growing up, we lived way out in the country. I had no contacts, no social contacts at all, no people to go to little parties or do little things with. Now I think, what an ass I was. So what? Why did I worry all that time about wanting to go to things?

But I'm the black sheep of the family. They loved me, but I was the black sheep in the sense that they'd say, "Lucy, you do the craziest things. I just wish you wouldn't get messed up in this." All I can say is that I took on the idea that I gotta do what I do. But I know I'm hurtin' my family. They want me to be nice and in a little pink dress with little bows, and I want to wear jeans and old tennis shoes and run through the woods and play with the animals and the squirrels and things.

So I hurt a lot of my life. I hurt an awful lot. I have a lot of fears that I've been trying to figure out why they are.

This does not fit the preconceived image many of us carry of a strong, gutsy heroine, fighting against all odds to achieve justice. But it resembled the self-image of many of the other altruists I interviewed, who tend to see themselves as normal people, complete with all the hurts, insecurities, and neuroses that plague the rest of us. Despite this insecurity, altruists like Lucille seem to have a trust in life that is critical in their dealings with other people.

Now, I do something that *everybody* says not to do, and that's pick people up on the highway. I figure God knows me enough that he's not gonna let them hitchhikers hurt me. I haven't picked up one yet that didn't have a tragic need. Usually, I'll take 'em into the city, either give them a few bucks or help them get going on to Memphis. Get them started, that kind of thing.

Sometimes something funny happens. Either God or whatever you wanna call it directs me. I can be going down a street that I never went down before in my life. I make a turn into a street and I say, "What did I make that turn for? I'm supposed to be going down Third Street." I make that turn, and a couple of blocks down I'll find a little animal lying in the street in pain. It's been hit by a car, and nobody pays any attention to him. I end up bringing him home and loving him. If I can't find his owner, I'll fix him up, have him in the hospital and so forth.

I think there's a meaning for this. I don't know, and I probably won't know until I'm dead, why this is constantly happening. I don't mean once a year. I mean the whole year. Some people even tell me, "I don't wanna be around you. You're always into somethin'." That's the best I can explain it.

I credit my grandmother with this. See, she would stop and she'd ask, "Did you hear that?" I'd say, "No." Then she'd tell me, "That's a bird calling for help." I didn't see anything, but she saw. One time she saw a snake going up a tree. "Lucy," she said, "you get up that tree and pull that snake down. He's goin' after that bird nest." So she made me conscious that all things alive are worth saving, no matter what or what situation they were in. If you had the power to do so, to help them, then do it. If you didn't, well, that's another matter. But I guess sometimes God just thought that I could.

The idea that we are surrounded by living things that have value and who need help, if we can but see this need and our common bonds, ran like a leitmotif throughout Lucille's narrative and was typical of all altruists, from philanthropists to rescuers.

Lucille's world view suggests that a concern for the good of others constitutes an important part of her basic identity. While Lucille recognizes that others do not feel such a concern, she does not blame them for this. Lucille was not alone in this: a similar generosity toward others existed among most of the altruists I interviewed.

Q. *How do you view basic human nature?*

A. I don't know how to answer that question. It's hard to say, since it's changed over the years. I think people are becoming more thoughtless, more thinking of themselves only. Man wants to do good, but he's become less a fighter. He doesn't like to get involved. I don't hold it against him if a man doesn't get involved. If a man doesn't get involved, I don't think we ought to say, "Well, here you are, a man, and you didn't do anything." Maybe the man [who doesn't get involved] is built on a different thing. I don't know what his background was. But I do not call anybody a coward, 'cause I just don't believe that all humanity can respond. We've grown up a whole generation of "protect yourself and your own priorities." The younger ones, younger than I am now, well, I just think this is their whole thing, to follow their own personal priorities and not do anything else. But I don't blame anybody that won't rush into something like that. We're all made different.

I don't hold it against anybody that no one came [during the rape]. Our neighbors were all gone to work that day, except one little old lady across the street. That night, my friends called her and said, "Do you know what happened here this morning?" She tells them, "Yes. I heard it. I looked out my window, and this little gray-haired woman was running and beatin' the hell out of a nigger and just cursing him." Then she said, "I went and got in my bed and pulled the covers up over my head."

Mostly, I think that's the typical attitude, for both women and men. It's "Mind your own business." But not me. I can't do it; I just can't do it. I don't meddle in people's business, but I can't stand to see anybody hurt.

Q. *What do you think accounts for the fact that some people go to bed and pull the covers over their head, and another woman, like you, who has just as many excuses for not going and helping someone, will still go ahead and help?*

A. I don't know. I think individuality has to do with what a man is. I don't put people as essentially bad or good. I think some of them are afraid, and I can understand this. They know that nobody'll help 'em if they run out there. This was a knowledge that was in the back of my mind [during the rape]: "Nobody's gonna help me and I'm gonna get killed." In fact, two women drove by in a car, and [when] they saw what was going on, they hit the gas and took off. I was sorry they acted that way, 'cause they could have gone in and called the police. Knowing they did nothing, that's hard for me. But I can't categorize men or any other woman as being a coward because they didn't do it. Somewhere in their backgrounds, somewhere along the way—And I think everything we do now is determined by what our background is, whether we consciously know this or not. It's how we were raised, how we were talked to, how we were treated; and, not education as far as school, but more general education—that's what determines our natures all the way along our lives.

Lucille then talked about the boundaries she draws between her own needs and her own identity and those of other people, relating this in particular to occasions when she put herself in danger to aid others.

Q. *Let me ask you a little bit about the process that goes on when you risk your life [as when you broke up the rape] and take part in something like the civil rights movement. What is it that motivates you? Do you just feel sorry for the person you rescue or help? Or is there actually some further connection you feel with the person you help, to the point where you almost feel their pain or their need as your own? Do you understand what I'm asking?*

A. Yes, I understand. I think it's their need, and that I get people around me not doin' anything or not caring. Like with the girl, the one the guy was raping. She was a beautiful thing, and it was her need. I had to use what courage I had or whatever I could have. It's the need. It's like somebody kicking a little dog around. I'd stomp their head in. That's another thing I can't stand, the misuse of animals. But it's the need. Not pity, but realizing what this person is going through, knowing that I've been through a lot and I can take it, but they don't know and they can't take it.

I asked Lucille to delineate her concerns about her own safety when she approached the rapist. Was she worried about her life, especially since she had a daughter (albeit one fully grown) who could have been affected had Lucille been hurt? I later rephrased this question, asking it in the context of Lucille's civil rights activities and focusing on the potential threat they posed to her mother's safety and the anxiety she must have felt about Lucille's. Both times I found that Lucille had never thought about how her actions might be affecting those close to her. It seemed as though this was the first time it had ever occurred to her that her daring stance might have been a source of pain to her loved ones.

Q. *Were you worried at all during the rape about the possibility that something would happen to you and that your daughter would be left alone? In other words, was the welfare of your family or loved ones relevant? Did that go through your mind while you were attempting to save someone you didn't know?*

A. You mean, was I afraid I would be killed and then he would hurt her?

Q. *No. I'm asking two questions. One is a very specific question. I have young children, and I know I'm much more careful with myself now that I have children, because I know if anything happened to me that they would be left without a mother. Did any of that go through your mind, that your daughter would be left alone?*

A. Oh, it kept going through my mind that I was dying. I knew that my heart was beating way over what it should be. I thought, if I can just hold out long enough. But I thought that it would hold out.

Q. *But you weren't afraid to die yourself?*

A. No, I'm not afraid to die. I don't *want* to die, but I'm not afraid of it.

Q. *It wouldn't affect your decision to risk your life in some way for someone else, even if there was the possibility that you may be making a decision that would jeopardize your own safety as well as the safety of others close to you?*

A. I think I know what you're asking. Sometimes you have to jeopardize the most precious thing you have. Sometimes people have to take those chances, even knowing their children, their sisters, their brothers, their mothers might be hurt. Down deep you know that in the end, you'll win, but not unless you are willing to push. I was jeopardizing my mother when I stood up for integration, because they did all kinds of ugly things. But I knew that.

I then asked Lucille if she could distinguish between a sense of duty or responsibility to others and empathy. Which factor was more important in her treatment of others? For Lucille, as for most other altruists, duty was less central than empathy and empathy—as we shall soon discover—less important than a certain perspective on life.

Q. *So you actually believe you felt this girl's pain [the girl who was being raped] and her need as your own?*

A. Yes.

Q. *It wasn't so much a moral obligation that you felt but more that you genuinely felt her need yourself?*

A. Oh, I don't think anybody now considers you a bad person if you overlook something or somebody being beaten up and you stay inside your house. People don't think of it. They don't blame anybody for any moral problem. The moral was that it was wrong. I feel like that person is crying out for help and is helpless.

Q. *Am I hearing you say that a sense of duty isn't enough to make people risk the kind of things that you risked? It's more empathy with the other person?*

A. It's empathy with the person. Duty, in that kind of case, not so necessarily. Duty in the army, yes. But even in the army, for example, I saw a man throw a poor native, a Sudanese, into the Nile River. In those days they said if you go into the Nile River, you could call yourself dead, it was so filthy. And here this man thought he was a big American, and he just threw this poor little Sudanese into the river. I just jumped in there and got the Sudanese and pulled him out. I overranked the guy, and I ordered him back to camp. The [Sudanese] guy, I straightened him up and asked him if he was alright.

I don't know exactly why I did this. It was my pity, and my shame that my own troops would do a thing like that 'cause they were "better"—or so they thought—than the Sudanese. The Sudanese worked for us to earn money, and they were treated worse than the blacks in the South. So it was the need of the person and the shame the person was getting, the humility and the shame and the hurt the person was getting that I feel.

This clarified Lucille's prior discussions of duty and empathy and suggested that her actions were motivated by something even more basic than duty, morality, or empathy: the need of the other person to be helped. Given Lucille's perspective on life, it was very simple: if someone is in need, you help them.

Like the philanthropist described in chapter 3, Lucille seems to have taken her own hurts and turned them into a deeper understanding of how others might feel when they are vulnerable or wronged. This entails empathy but differs subtly, as the following illustrates.

Q. *When you were taking part in these activities—the rescue of the young girl and your activities for civil rights—did you ever think maybe a loved one of yours might be in a similar situation? Did you ever think that this could be someone you knew over there being attacked? Did any thoughts like that go through your head?*

A. No. No. I just thought of it as a person over there in need.

Q. *Do you think your [childhood] hurts made it easier for you to understand how black people would feel in the civil rights period or perhaps how the young girl was feeling during the rape?*

A. I think so. It certainly helped me realize that hurting, social hurting, especially when you're little, really burns you. And I think it did help because I didn't want to see people be hurt.

Q. *Do you think you empathized with them because you'd been there yourself?*

A. Oh, definitely, yes.

Q. *Let me just ask you one last question. If we wanted to get more people in the world like you, what would you tell us that would be useful in doing so? Do you have any suggestions?*

A. The fact that we grew up poor and didn't have all those material goods affected us. I thought about that last night. The fact that I, and many people, were poor meant we were more conscious of another person not having something. We were more conscious of what we had. If we had a nickel, we should give three cents of it away to someone we thought was in need. Going through that, knowing what it was to not have enough—oh, I tell you, I ate beans sometimes till I thought I would die. We would boil beans and eat 'em, and that was it. There were just lots of things that we didn't have. We walked everywhere.

It wasn't that we sacrificed but that we knew what it was to need things. We knew what it was to be able to help another. I'm grateful. Not for the depression—but I said the other day, "Do you know what we need for these young kids today? We need another depression." I mean a hell of a depression, where they have to get out and work, and they have to realize that people are people and they aren't just somebody you'd con out of something.

I think we're stronger people, the people that lived in the thirties. We're stronger physically; we're stronger mentally. And when we did have a chance, when we had better things, we knew how to appreciate them, and we knew how to give and divide. I'm speaking of me. I never had enough money to give anybody much. But I still figure out of my pension how much I can give to somebody if I have a friend who needs something.

It's nice that people nowadays have nice things. I don't regret that people have nice things. But we don't have any values anymore. Everybody's trying to figure out what they can get into to make 'em another million. Do you know what's funny is the millionaires that I know—I'll tell you their names, but you have to not use them 'cause of what I'm going to tell you now—my mother one time asked one for a loan. He told her he didn't loan money; people had to earn money. But he didn't give her a job. And he didn't give her any money!

This suggested that Lucille feels people with money have obligations to help others. I pursued this in our next exchange.

Q. *What do you think about wealthy people who don't give money to charity? Do you think they're failing to discharge their obligations to society?*

A. Definitely. People say, "Well, they earned their money. They have a right to do what they want to with it." That may be true. You earn the money and do what you want to [with it]. You can go stomping it in the ground and throw it down the toilet. But if we quit realizing humanity's needs, well, I'd like to see the world start all over again, frankly, and see if it couldn't keep on a level.

In this regard, Lucille differs slightly from philanthropists like Melissa and even more dramatically from entrepreneurs like Billy. But Lucille shares a belief in the work ethic with both the entrepreneur and the philanthropist. She also resembles Melissa in feeling that although people sometimes do need help, they also have to make an effort to help themselves.

Q. *You mentioned several things in your life that have perhaps been emotionally difficult for you: your father leaving, your mother losing the house, going through the depression. Was there any one particular critical moment or emotional period in your life when you felt that you desperately needed help from somebody else?*

A. No. Because I wouldn't accept it. Does that make any sense? I have had some real hard times. After her second husband died, my brother convinced Mother that since I was a Catholic, that if Mother left her money to me, then the Catholics would get all her money too. So he convinced Mother that she'd better let him have it. He said he'd handle it and then give her the interest off of it. He got it all, every single dime; everything she had. Then he never came around her again. He never gave her any money. I could not take it to court, because I would've had to declare Mother incompetent. I could've done that, since she was very sick. But I wouldn't have declared her incompetent, even if it meant we could get all the money back. I would never do that to her. So we were very hard up. The only thing I did was to beg hospitals, when it came time that she had to go in one for an operation. They let me pay it off on time payments. So I only ask for what I can pay back. But I asked for time.

Her funeral, when it came, I had no money. My brother quit paying on her funeral policy, and it expired. So I went down and I said, "I'll pay you. I just can't pay you all of it now, and I'm gonna buy the cheapest little coffin here. I'm not gonna put a lot of money into her funeral, 'cause she asked me not to. But I will eventually pay you." They did that; they let me pay over time. It cost two thousand dollars for the funeral, and I didn't ask for anybody's money toward the funeral. But I would send them a little bit each month. It took me a long time to pay it all off, and by the time I'd paid that off, I had a lot of hospital bills that I was paying off on the same principle. Only one doctor sued, and I got confused and thought the funeral company was suing me. This collection agency kept calling. They'd ask me, "What are we gonna do with you? We only give people ninety-day loans to pay off a funeral." They were just giving me an example, but I didn't know who they were calling for. So when they kept asking me, "What are we gonna do?" I finally said, "Well, I don't know what to do. I don't have it, and if you wanna go dig her up, you go right ahead."

I never heard another word from 'em! I'd send 'em about twenty dollars a month, but they never called me back. I have had friends who lent me money, though I never wanted to borrow it from them. And in the tough emotional times, when I was a kid, my grandmother was there for me, assuring me that those things were not important. There were far greater things in life to think about, and I shouldn't get upset over some kid snubbing me or saying I was trash.

Finally, I asked how Lucille's world related to her heroism in breaking up the rape. Like Billy, Lucille sees the world as a good place. But Lucille is much more sensitive to the needs of others. In this, she typifies the altruists as a group.

Q. *Do you think man can control his fate?*

A. Yes, I do. I think that 99.1 percent comes from the beginning, from birth, from the seed taking hold. What is done in those years is what some way or another—maybe in a way you wouldn't expect—provides lessons that tell you how to love, how you learn about society, how you get along with society, and what felicity you have. Because I think we're all basically good.

Q. *Can you tell whether you have any personal ethical credo that guides your life?*

A. As trite as it is, everything I do every day must always be aware of what's around me and be able to help or not help, depending on whether they need help or not. But always be aware of the humanity around me and what is their cause and what is their need. Not that I can always fill their need, but that's part of it. Do unto others as you would have them do unto you.

I believe that I'm dedicated to humanity in my heart. I give my grandmother the credit for this. She taught me that. If I was to feel obligated to anybody, it would be her.

This strong love for all humanity, and a feeling that all living things have value and should be protected, succinctly captures Lucille's view of herself in relation to others. In this regard, Lucille epitomizes the altruistic perspective.

CHAPTER 5

Rescuers of Jews in Nazi Europe

HOWEVER we define altruism, most of us would readily agree that people who rescued Jews in Nazi Europe are altruists, approaching pure altruism on our conceptual continuum. Because the rescuers I encountered were such diverse and fascinating people, this chapter excerpts narratives from two interviews rather than only one. Both the respondents were Dutch rescuers, but there the apparent similarities end. Tony described himself as a spoiled little rich kid when the war began, only nineteen and serving in an elite military unit. Bert was a thirty-year-old worker from a small town called Wobrugge, where he lived above a pharmacy and dry goods store he operated with his wife, Annie. In part, I chose these two men precisely because they are so very different: they illustrate the tremendous range of personality, situation, and background found among rescuers, even those from the same country. But I had other reasons as well. I chose Bert because he was one of many rescuers who had a wife and children whose lives were endangered by his rescue activities. This intrigued me at a personal level. I can imagine making a joint decision with my husband to risk our lives together, but as a mother of small children, I cannot even imagine risking the lives of my children, for anyone. I chose Tony because he was so unusually articulate about his actions, able to verbalize and thus draw my attention to distinctions I might otherwise have missed. In particular, Tony made me aware of the subtle considerations affecting life and death decisions. Tony also articulated the essence of what I call the altruistic perspective, the sense altruists have that they are linked to others through a common humanity. What was even more remarkable was that he articulated this view immediately, almost in the first sentence of our telephone interview. This reassured me, since I knew Tony could not possibly have picked up any subtle cues from me that might have led him to express such a view. Let me thus begin this chapter with what is almost a verbatim transcription of my first interview with Tony. When the interview began, all he had been told was that I was a professor writing a book on altruism and that I wanted to interview him because of his wartime experiences and his efforts to rescue Jews, actions that later resulted in his being awarded the Yad Vashem medal.[1]

Q. *Why don't we begin by your telling me a little bit about yourself.*

A. Well, you told me you were studying altruism, and I have very strong thoughts about altruism. I'm not talking about the suicidal type of thing. That's totally different. Just risking your life, that's not a form of altruism.

Personally, I'm not particularly Christian, insofar as men believing in the resurrection of the Lord and stuff like that. But I do believe that one of the most important teachings in Christianity is to learn to love your neighbor as yourself. I was to learn to understand that you're part of a whole, and that just like cells in your own body altogether make up your body, that in our society and in our community, that we all are like cells of a community that is very important. Not America; I mean the human race. And you should always be aware that every other person is basically you. You should always treat people as though it is you, and that goes for evil Nazis as well as for Jewish friends who are in trouble. You should always have a very open mind in dealing with other people and always see yourself in those people, for good or for evil both.

This captures the essence of altruism. Through the use of extensive excerpts from narratives with Tony and Bert, I concentrate in the rest of the chapter on filling in this portrait of people who closely approach pure altruism. Both men briefly describe themselves and their lives before and after the war, and then turn to more detailed descriptions of their particular way of seeing things.

Tony

Tony's family was bourgeois in its attitudes, economic situation, and education.

I was born June 28, 1919. I'll be seventy in a week. My mother was Belgian-born, and her mother was French. My father was Dutch, and we have a very long family history. They started off as fairly simple country doctors, all the way back to 1650. For instance, my paternal grandfather was a psychiatrist. I'm mentioning him because he's rather different. He started off as a navy doctor. He sailed around the Cape in navy sailing ships and was in the Indian wars. He became one of the very first hypnotist doctors. Then, later on, he became a psychiatrist and was a close friend of Freud and Jung.

My mother's father was a military man who worked his way up from a farm boy to a general. He became the first military commander in the Belgian Congo, when the king was forced to turn over that colony from a private possession to the Belgian government. My Belgian granddad was a friend of Stanley, of the Livingston and Stanley. I have other relatives going all the way down to the Battle of Waterloo. It's a bourgeois family. The one side had military and the other had medical people, all the way back to 1650.

Tony's childhood was spent in comfortable affluence, his family traveling between their home in Amsterdam and various country houses.

I'm the only child. I grew up in Amsterdam. We traveled a fair amount in Europe, mostly going to Brussels and Paris, sometimes to Switzerland, but not much beyond that. In some ways it was a very happy childhood, in others not. I was very spoiled in material things. My mother was a social climber. She would have liked very much to have been part of the aristocracy or the very upper-upper classes, but she was not. My father was a very wealthy dentist, so she played the upper-class game whenever she could. She had lots of antiques and lots of money and status symbols around. I was never very much into that.

Despite his family's economic wealth, Tony did not enjoy an idyllic childhood. Although they treated Tony quite well, his parents frequently fought with each other.

My father and mother were always fighting, ever since I was a little tiny kid. My mother was very Latin and quite possessive. My father made the mistake once. So many men do it. It's really not in their minds; it's not that important. Just a little fling with some cutie somewhere, which didn't mean he didn't love my mother. But there's the difference between male and female feeling about it. One has to build the nest, after all, and the other is supposed to go and fertilize the world. Male and female minds, they're two radically different approaches.

But my mother found out about it, and for the next thirty years she talked about it constantly. "I should have left you, but. . . ." She was always going on about it to the point that now, in retrospect, it's funny. But at the time, as a kid, it wasn't.

Once the war started, they were very political. But before the war they were a good Dutch conservative, loyalist family. And it was interesting what happened to them after the war.

I left in 1947. My parents stayed, but they lost all their money during the war. They had invested in real estate, and the four properties they owned, three of them were destroyed. Our big home in Amsterdam was very badly damaged. It was taken over by the Germans. The investments my father had in Indonesian stock all lost money. Then, too, my mother lived rather high on the hog. It took a long time for her to let go of her lifestyle. They used to have three maids and a butler, just for the two of them.

After the war, there was a housing shortage in Holland. The socialist government told everybody with a large house that they would be forced to take in boarders. They could keep three rooms to themselves, and if they had more rooms, they had to take another family into the house. So my mother was forced to take two other families into the house. There was no more help, and the whole lifestyle collapsed. Basically, she used up too much of the family money. They kept sending me money as though it was in the good old days, till one day I suddenly realized they were totally broke. So I suggested they come to America, which they did. They arrived with five hundred dollars. My father hoped he could be a dentist here, but that was impossible. He ended up in the kitchen of the Santa Monica Hospital, and my mother ended up as a nurse's aide. They both lied about their age so they could work. My mother worked till she was seventy-five. My father worked till he was seventy. They managed to get their social security and a little pension from the hospital. It was the first time in my life I remember them not quarreling and really loving each other.

In addition to the uncertainty and unpleasantness he felt from his parents' quarrelsome marriage, Tony's childhood was lonely.

I was a lonely child. Because I was an only child, my mother was very protective, and I was a mama's boy for quite a while. To give you an example, when I finally went to high school, which was my first moment of liberation, she insisted I wear my sailor suit. This was as bad as [it would be to] wear a sailor suit to high school nowadays! But it had an odd effect. It did teach me to live through situations that are painful, to not give a damn about what people think of you, and just do what you think is right.

Tony did not want to go to law school and avoided a scene with his parents by deciding to first fulfill his military draft requirements. His father's family connections got Tony assigned to an elite cavalry corps, composed primarily of aristocrats who shared Tony's then conservative, establishment outlook. This military assignment, however, was to change Tony's life once the war began.[2]

When the war broke out, I was in the First Regiment of Motorized Hussars. We happened to be transferred just north of The Hague a few days before the war started, causing us to be the only regiment situated between the royal family and the government in The Hague and where some five thousand German paratroopers landed. Thanks to our good training, we beat off the Germans, with both sides suffering heavy casualties. After four days the German airborne forces capitulated, and they never did get through to The Hague or the royal family. But then, the next day, after the terror bombing of Rotterdam, the Dutch government and the Dutch army as a whole decided they had to capitulate to the Germans. We went to our [German] POWs that evening and told them that *they* now were in charge of *us*. We mutually decided to leave things to the next day and get some sleep.

Our regiment was a copy of a German motorcycle regiment, so the Germans were very anxious to get our equipment. Our commander did not want them to get it. He went counter to the [capitulation] orders and made a huge bonfire and destroyed everything we had. Because of that, he later died in a concentration camp, and we were held as prisoners of war, while the rest of the Dutch army was released right away to go home.

The Germans held us for about a month or so. Then they decided it would be better policy to let us go. They thought since the Dutch were Germanic, if we were recognized as such, we would eventually join the German effort. [By the time we were released], I had already hidden some weapons and a motorcycle. And that's when we—some eighty army officers—started a very primitive, nonviolent little resistance movement. Mostly we just were talking about it, not knowing what to do exactly. But a girlfriend of one of our guys was rooming with another girl who was dating a German soldier, and things leaked out. The Germans managed to get an address list for all of us. They came to everybody's home during curfew. I was one of the lucky three who was not at home that night; I was spending the night with a girlfriend. I got a quick call from somebody saying, "Don't ever go home again, because they want to pick you up."

The other seventy-seven officers were all executed. That changed the situation! Up until then, it was almost a game, this little resistance movement. We were so klutzy about all this. We were terribly naive. Nobody is more naive than army officers. We were young, too, just kids. But the executions suddenly showed us the total realities of what the German occupation was going to be like.

After I was condemned to death, I hid with various friends whom I knew. It took a while to get false papers. Then after a while, I had good false identity papers and I could get back on the street. And, oh, of key importance, I had a friend who worked in the National Archives where they keep all the I.D. cards. In Holland, every person has something like a driver's license, but without being a driver. You have to have an I.D. card. And my friend in the National Archives lifted my master card out of the files. So I didn't exist. We did that with several people in the Resistance. On paper, I no longer existed.

So that's how I got involved with the Resistance. Living underground, I have a false identity. I formed my own little resistance movement of twelve guys, which was fairly well equipped. Our principles were not to go out and kill Germans but rather to do espionage. We wanted to keep a low profile, because anything you did, the Germans would go and shoot hostages and unrelated innocent people. So what we did mainly was invisible: sabotage, espionage. I then got involved with a larger remnant of the Resistance, and we contacted a variety of other resistance groups.

Not surprisingly, his brief combat experience and his being condemned to death by the Nazis had a great impact on Tony, making him more aware of commonalities among people.

A great part of my education came from World War II, when I was condemned to death in 1941 for having hidden weapons and being part of Underground activities and hiding Jews and American pilots and things like that. They didn't catch me, but I suddenly had to leave the wealthy, upper-middle-class family and go into hiding. That was an eye-opener. I was told right away by a friend of mine, "Look, if you're ever in trouble in town and there's a raid on the street and you have to go into a house somewhere, if you're anywhere near the red-light district, go to any of the houses of the prostitutes. They'll hide you. They don't like the system. They'll hide you." And they would. They were risking a death penalty for that. But those women would always hide you. They were the people whom I had looked down upon socially before that. And I ended up working with a variety of much lower-class people than I would ever have associated with in my previous existence. That was a great eye-opener, to find that these people were in no way different. It's like the old saying by George Bernard Shaw: How do the poor differ from the rich? The difference is that they have no money.

Tony's story suggests the haphazard way in which rescue activities often began and the extent to which operations that strike us as carefully planned arose by chance. The origins of such undertakings intrigued me. How did people come to rescue Jews? Were they approached by Jewish friends? Or did the rescuer usually initiate the contact? Did rescuers tend to work within a network? I consider these questions more systematically in later chapters, but it is useful to consider Tony's experience in this regard, for it is not atypical.

Like most other rescuers, Tony felt that his desire to help Jews arose naturally and spontaneously, a normal response to what he saw as a deteriorating situation. Tony carried out his first rescue *before* he was condemned to death, during the brief period after he and his army buddies had been released but before their resistance activities had been discovered by the Germans and the other members of his unit shot. (The rescue, in fact, was not related to his work in the political resistance, which Tony kept totally separate in his own mind.) His narrative suggests that Tony was more aware of the pending danger than were his many Jewish friends, who quite understandably found it difficult to imagine in advance anything as horrific as the Holocaust.[3] He, then, not they, initiated the first rescue efforts.

Sometimes when I saved people I'd do it myself, alone; sometimes with my parents; sometimes with other friends. That's what I'm trying to say: it's all very loosely knit. Sometimes you are nothing more than a go-between, trying to find a place where someone could hide.

The trouble with the Jews did not start right away. They knew they had to play it safe. I'm trying to remember the exact dates it really started with the Jews. I don't remember, but it started out very calm. First of all, nothing was going to be done against the Jews. A lot of Jews expected that it might continue that way. And then the Germans brought up a form. They said, "Just for identity purposes, we want to know everybody who is of the Jewish faith. We want to know what your background is, because we know that the Jewish people don't like the Germans, and we want to be sure to know who you are and where you are." And the Jews signed voluntarily. Well, they were effectively told [to do it], so it was not really voluntarily. Everyone was given the form that marked how many Jewish ancestors you had, whether you were religious, if you were going to a synagogue, and all that.

I had a lot of Jewish friends, because my high school had a lot of Jews and Amsterdam had a population of close to between ten and fifteen thousand Jews, which is something like 8–10 percent of the population. Right then and there, I told all my Jewish friends, "You don't look Jewish. Why would you turn yourself in this way?" It's one thing if you're very Semitic-looking, because there was a penalty if you didn't fill it in. You go to a concentration camp. So I suggested, particularly to friends who really didn't look that Jewish, I said, "Don't fill the stupid thing in. Let them do the work. Why turn yourself in that way?" And some of them did, and some of them didn't.

The first person Tony helped was the Jewish father of one of Tony's friends from high school.

I thought it might be wise for him to get out of [his house] before the Germans came for him. So I just went by his house. We got on our bicycles and we bicycled to my parents' house. It was that simple. It was my idea he needed to be hidden. . . . This was during the period right after the war began but before my colleagues were all arrested. But after the fighting I'd been through, I knew what was going on.

I think I said to this Jewish gentleman, "Hey, why don't you go into hiding?" "Yeah, where will I hide?" he asked me. "Oh, I'm sure we can figure out something. Today you can go stay at my parents' home. I'm sure that'll work out. We have this little country house in the Lake District, this little summer shack there. We're probably all going to go for a few days' vacation anyway. Why don't you come along and you can stay there with us? It's in the Lake District. They're not going to come there and look for Jews."

That's how it started, my hiding Jews. Very casually.

Tony's narrative provides a feel for the insidious subtlety of German policy toward Jews. It suggests how cleverly the Nazis played on Dutch feelings toward both foreigners and refugees during the depression and the war. The Nazis also exploited the Jews' reluctance to believe what was happening to them and their confusion as they finally tried to salvage what they could from the slowly expanding nightmare.

In the beginning, not much happened. Then, inch by inch, it came. The Jews weren't allowed in certain restaurants. They were taken out of certain businesses for "security reasons." Then it changed. They were not allowed to use the movie theaters, not allowed to go to a regular restaurant. They had to go to their own restaurants, their own movie theaters. Gradually they lost all their businesses. First they had a German manager with the business and they could still be involved with it. Then they were kicked out. It was all done gradually.

But the most evil thing that the Nazis did was to form the Jewish Council. They got some very wealthy upper-class Jews in Amsterdam. The last one was Mr. Asher. They put him in charge of the Jewish Council. The idea was that these upper-class Jews would organize the situation of the Jews. They would be the spokesmen for the Jewish community. Mr. Asher had been a friend of Hermann Goering. He'd sold him a lot of diamonds at the time, and they developed a friendship, because Goering was always interested in intelligent Jews, in *rich*, intelligent Jews. And what the Germans made this Jewish Council do was to encourage all the Jews to follow all the German orders and organize their own departure later on, and in an organized manner. First they were going to "country work camps." The idea of the Germans was that the Jews had been too much in the money business and too much into diamonds and jewelry and stock market, all those things that were from a social point of view less desirable. "These [Jewish] people should learn to be real people and work on farms, work on the land like the Dutch farmers." They said things like that.

That type of propaganda was not totally disliked by certain people in Holland. You must remember that, like any highly visible group, any ethnic group, there's always a percentage of people that are less desirable, that can be very obnoxious. You know, 90 percent of the Jews would be very, very well liked, very nice. But then there was a percentage of Jews who were living very high. They had very high-profile lives, throwing around too much money. Too much property. Those are the ones that came out of Germany or out of Russia with quite a bit of money and could be sort of arrogant. There was a percentage of Jews who did that. And, of course, the result was that there was a certain anti-Semitism against those people in the society. Not against Dutch Jews, who had been in Holland forever. Even Dutch Jews were a little anti-Semitic about some of these German and Russian Jews who would come with a lot of money and who had left everybody else behind. It was a very intricate thing.

The above discussion of hostility to foreign Jews interested me, since my conversations with other Europeans (not rescuers) revealed the same attitudes. But these Europeans were not merely describing anti-Semitism as Tony is; they were expressing it.[4]

Tony's narrative also provides a glimpse of what life was often like for rescuers after the war, as the stress of daily tension began to take its toll, both physically and emotionally. Too much of what Tony thought he was fighting against he now sees springing up anew all around him. Other rescuers shared this postwar disillusionment. For some, it focused on the recognition of indigenous Fascist elements or on the uncivilized (and often hypocritical) reaction against collaborators.[5] Many rescuers decided to leave Europe after the war ended. "I put a big 'Do Not Disturb' sign on the past and got on with my life," many rescuers told me. So it was for Tony, who left Holland to begin a new life in the United States.

The stress of those four years during the occupation, always being in hiding, always being looked for, and surviving—but because I was surviving, surviving by being always on my toes and being a good actor the times when I got caught, I had no problem with that at all during the war. But two or three months after the end of the war, it expressed itself in a nervous breakdown. And the girlfriend I was dating, she wanted to get the hell out of Holland, too. I can fully understand now. She ended up marrying an American and took off.

A lot of things happened. We'd had such high hopes for the Dutch government. We thought we were fighting this great cause and that we would have a great country after the war. We'd volunteered to go fight the Japanese, but they [the Dutch government] didn't want us to do this at the time. Then they called us up eight months later to go fight the Indonesians, who were our old best colonies and who had been literally liberated by the Japanese from the Dutch colonial system. The Indonesians didn't want to go back to a colonial system. I was very upset about [the Dutch policy in Indonesia]. I thought we should let them have their freedom and work with them as friends. There was a good possibility of doing that. I was really disappointed in the Dutch government at the time.

I had gotten a medical discharge because of my nervous problems. But I didn't want to stay in Holland, and I came to America. So that's how I came here. I worked in the movie business, which is what I'd wanted to do. And I never went back to Holland, not until 1988. I was technical advisor for the movie *The Diary of Anne Frank* in 1958, but except for that one visit, I never went back until my wife [who is American and had never been to Holland] desperately wanted to go. And I sort of settled the old account.

The summer I completed my interviews with Tony, he and his wife, Susanne, decided to move to Holland. They now live in a small town on the seaside. Tony spends his time writing, translating a family history written by his psychiatrist grandfather, friend to Freud and Jung, and completing an anthropological analysis of the comparative mythologies surrounding Santa Claus and the Christmas tree. He has given most of his memorabilia from the war to the Rijksmuseum in Amsterdam.[6]

Tony's Perspective: Self in Relation to Others

Tony's perspective emerged quite early in our conversations, in both the humorous and the tragic episodes he recounted from the war. But always it resembled the perspective of other rescuers in certain dimensions that I believe are critical for understanding altruism.

Q. *How would you describe yourself? How do you view yourself? What kind of a person are you?*

A. Oh, about thirty pounds overweight. My body is seventy years old and starting to disintegrate in various places. But my mind, well, that's the peculiar thing. If I look in the mirror, I'm always shocked. I see this old man looking back at me. [But the person] in my thinking and my mind, and even in what I would like to do with my body, I am much younger. I'm just experiencing the frustration of stepping on the gas pedal and the thing doesn't move very much.

In terms of personality, I guess I'm fairly gregarious. I can get a little grumpy, mainly out of frustration or under too much stress. Generally I'm trying to do more than I can humanly do. I try to work too hard, and then I see my clock running out. So I'm trying to catch up and finish work that I want to finish.

Tony described himself as realistic and cautious but unafraid of death, a view he attributed in part to his wartime experience but which appears to predate the war.[7]

When the war started, I was a spoiled little rich boy. I was shy. I was a bit of a sissy. But I was a careful person, and I had read a lot, and I was very realistic. I had a vivid imagination. I fully imagined the war to be just exactly what it was going to be, with people being blown to bits and all that. So when the war started, I was not at all surprised, whereas several of the other army officers I was around were totally flabbergasted. They had not expected war to be what war was. They were more the "rah-rah" military. Several of them went to pieces when it started. I was always very phlegmatic about living or dying. I always figured if I got to die, I got to die. I was not terribly afraid of dying. That's maybe a weird thing, and I don't know where I got that. Certainly I was never reckless. If anything, I was a little chicken and a little overly careful. But the idea of death itself was never something that frightened me.

I have always been extremely realistic about life and death. You're born. You live. And it's the game you play, the game of life. You play it as well as you can. And then at the end, you get your reward and you die, and you don't have to struggle any more. This happens to be my own philosophy. It's not what you get out of life; it is not the rewards you get. The reward is peace when you die. Life begins like a very tough tennis tournament. You do it, not for the money, but for the fun of playing that game and playing it as well as you can. That's my life's philosophy, basically. We all know that the game won't last forever. It's like going to see a good movie. You know it's going to end, and after that you go to sleep. And that's sort of a time to relax. It's time to rest, like going to sleep.

I asked about how Tony sees people, curious to learn if he had specific views of human nature that might have influenced his rescue activities. Cognitively, Tony resembled other rescuers in focusing on the extent to which everyone carries the potential for good and evil. This made him unwilling to explain away something like the Nazi era through a simple retreat into the idea of "national character," the belief, for example, that the Germans are, as a group, more authoritarian or vicious than other nations and cultures.[8]

I don't believe in just or unjust causes or just or unjust wars. I believe in good people. It's very difficult to explain. To give you an example about good and bad, it's so hard to define. I differentiate in my own mind between what I consider is righteous and what I consider is bad. Not whether it's done by a German, by an American, by a Jew, by an Arab; that's irrelevant. I've been in those countries. I've spent time in Israel; I've spent some time in Arab countries. The people are the same on both sides. They could all get together if they wanted to, but education works so strongly against it. There's propaganda in education.

Q. *Why do you think some people are able to see this and to reach out across the boundaries of race and nationality and see others as human beings?*

A. Well, two things prevent it from happening. First, some people have very closed minds. They're terrified of letting go of their security blanket, whatever it is: religion, Marine Corps membership, Jewish or Christian faith. Any of these things can separate me. Without them, then I suddenly would have to face my own humanity.

The second reason is the lack of exposure. I hear people talking about homeless people, saying, "Well, they're all a bunch of drunks. They admit they don't want to work." They don't realize that there are many homeless people who are simply mothers without a husband who cannot get transportation, cannot get their wardrobe or their hair done sufficiently to get a job, and who consequently are totally trapped in homelessness. Yet here people lump them all together and say, "None of these people really wants to work, and they're all a bunch of drunks, and that's it."

If they spent one afternoon in downtown L.A. or even in the park in Santa Monica and looked and learned to see through their eyes, they could not give that same answer. But most people look away. They don't want to see because it's disturbing. I see this now, and I fully believe the people who lived next to the concentration camps and say, "We never saw anything." Of course they didn't see anything! They didn't want to see. You don't want to think of your son sitting there getting his jollies out of torturing people or sticking them alive in an oven.

Tony's compassionate understanding of why people ignored the suffering of others was remarkable, given his past. It was not clear, however, whether this generosity extended to political leaders.

I have compassion for the people who are little people, who are hiding and don't want to know. But the higher you get politically, if you are somebody like Kurt Waldheim, aiming for these top positions, no. I do not have compassion for people like that who refuse to see and admit what's happening to others. To me, they are far more evil than even the concentration camp guard, who did as he was told.

The kind of people I sympathize with are people like a German acquaintance of a friend of mine. My friend is a German Jew who lives in Malibu. He was in Germany and he went into a restaurant that was full. He had to sit at somebody else's table. They fell into conversation, and they hit it off and eventually ended up corresponding with each other. One was a German man. And my friend is a German Jew.

Recently my friend got a letter from the gentleman, who told him, "Look, I have so much enjoyed corresponding with you that I can no longer be dishonest. I want to let you know that during World War II, I was a lieutenant in the Gestapo. But I never killed anybody or tortured anybody. Still, I feel terrible about my connections with this. It has been more than forty years ago, but I do not feel that I can honestly keep up a friendship with you without you knowing this. Do you still want to stay friends with me?"

Now, to me, that's a very different attitude than what I see from Kurt Waldheim. I respect that man in the restaurant, the one who wrote my Jewish friend. He's grown. We all can grow. We're not doomed; we are not doomed to forever be a sinner. We can at any moment in our lives decide to change things, and that requires courage too.

Closely related to this optimistic assessment of the individual's potential for growth and change is an even more important feature of Tony's perspective: his belief that good and bad lie in all of us.

I've always been interested, ever since World War II, in understanding what caused this Nazi monster to come to be. And I finally realized, every time you see the monster, you basically are looking in the mirror. All over the world, there's a certain attitude. It's not any one nation. It's not because they are German. It worked well in Germany because of the tradition of discipline. It doesn't work as well in Holland, because Dutch people are very ornery and horrendously independent. They'll say, "Screw you" and go their own way.

The idea that we need only look in the mirror to see both good and evil seemed associated with Tony's belief that we all are one people. This first emerged in our discussions of whether we are essentially alone in the world or have group ties that bind us to others.

I think that we are as much together as the cells in our body are together. They are individual; they each strive for their own little survival. Yet somehow they also will sacrifice themselves at times for the whole—or they are made to sacrifice themselves. Whether that is conscious or not, none of us has any way of knowing.

We cannot today exist as individuals. Oh, maybe one or two of us can go off in the wilderness and exist. But as a modern-day American or modern-day European or Chinese, there is no way to survive in this world unless we see ourselves as part of a whole in some way. The big difficulty is to do that without falling into the trap of totalitarian government.

Q. *How do we do that though, Tony?*

A. Just the same way the body does it. It's almost an instinctive, involuntary sort of sensing. It's a combination of education, of new morality, of learning love, of caring, of setting your goals so your happiness is not necessarily based on collecting the most you can possibly collect. It's knowing that your happiness is based on your sympathetic vibrations with your environment, with nature, with the other mankind around you, and on a certain degree of courage, which I describe as being aware that life does not last forever.

I found it significant that Tony did not fall into either of the two poles of a *Gemeinschaft/Gesellschaft* dichotomy.[9] Tony rarely discussed groups in terms of "us" and "them." But he was not an individual actor. Instead, his world view appeared to encompass more than his own community, with all people viewed simply as human beings rather than as members of any particular group.

I don't feel that the Nazis are monsters. I never felt that way. The Nazis were normal German people who, through education, training, cultural thinking, and greed, ended up where they were. And tomorrow it's our people. And the day after tomorrow, it's somebody else. History teaches you that the minute you destroy an enemy, you look behind you and he's standing there in your own ranks. You have to many times look in the mirror to make very sure that he hasn't crept into your head.

We have to watch for the "old yellow gooks" mentality. It is much easier to shoot at or burn the "yellow gooks" than to shoot at and burn some other farm boy just like yourself. But the evil and the good can be in all of us; good and bad is in all of us. You have to look in the mirror. We're always looking in the mirror.

Nazi persecutors and Jewish victims are not two different kinds of human beings but have, at bottom, the same moral potential for Tony. The sense that we all are part of one whole permeated his narrative. Other rescuers shared this world view, this particular way of seeing things, a way that differs significantly from the perspective of entrepreneurs and which appears to become increasingly evident as we move from philanthropists to heroes and on to rescuers. For Tony as for other rescuers, because we are all one, we are all part of the same life force. All forms of life have equal value, have equal capacity for good and for evil. This conviction kept Tony from needlessly risking martyrdom, since his life had value too, and contributed to his remarkable forgiveness for the Nazis.

Feeling a part of a whole also colored any discussions of his accomplishments, reducing them in Tony's mind to the matter-of-fact, a phenomenon that I had noticed in Lucille's narrative and that emerged frequently in the narratives of other rescuers.

Q. You don't consider yourself a hero?

A. No. I always have trouble with that definition. What exactly is a hero? It can be a total lunatic who does something and happens to succeed in doing something that basically was an absolute madcap thing. To me, the closest thing to a true hero is the guy who is terribly scared and does it anyway. To me, that is a real hero.

Q. And you were not a hero, because you weren't scared?

A. Well, there were moments that I was scared. . . . This is confusing. When you think of a hero, you think of some Greek god standing there, defending the pass against five thousand Persians and knowing full well he'll be beaten. That is the true hero in the classic sense of the word.

Q. You don't see yourself as a hero?

A. No. I'm a cautious hero.

Q. Well, most people would say that what you did was an extraordinarily good deed and that you should be rewarded for it. Do you think you did anything unusual?

A. I don't think that I did anything that special. I think what I did is what everybody normally should be doing. We all should help each other. It's common sense and common caring for people.

Q. Let me ask you one last question. If we would like to have more people like you in the world, what can you tell us that would be useful in doing this?

A. Oh, I don't know if I'm really the world's most desirable citizen. Let's not get too focused on me. We live on one world. We are one people. Working together, basically we are all the same. We can behave or we cannot behave. To me, behaving means working in harmony with the world and around you, harmony in the same sense that a big symphony orchestra is in harmony with each other. By being in harmony it creates something very, very beautiful. If you get one man who plays the wrong note, then you lose it. And yet, a good conductor is not a dictator. He is a friend and a guide, and it's a pleasure to work with him. And tomorrow, maybe you take over and conduct. You share it all.

This particular way of seeing things, as unusual as it may be in the world at large, was common among rescuers. It is clearly evident in Bert, another Dutch rescuer, who differs from Tony in most other respects.

BERT

In outward appearances, Bert's life could scarcely differ more from Tony's. Raised in a large family in a small town, Bert seemed to have led the simple, idyllic country life of the Dutch workers depicted in Van Gogh's portraits. Indeed, I was struck most by his simplicity, by the gentle strength of the man. Bert was a man of few words, of few passions. But he was unswerving in his faithfulness to what he felt instinctively to be right, even when this meant taking unpleasant action. Consider how Bert describes his family background, what he was doing when the war broke out, and how he came to save Jews.

I am a Dutchman. I love that little town I am born in. When I dream, in my sleep I am in Holland. We grew up in a small town, in a tight community. The population was no more than three or four thousand. We knew everybody, especially through the family store [we owned]. You have a kind of love for people because you know so many of them.

I had wanted to break out of Holland. We had a family store, and I had two older brothers in the store and I worked with them. We never fight. We are tremendously good to each other. But I don't want to be forever involved in the store. So I went for two years to Finland. Then the trouble started with Russia, around 1938 or 1939, and I came back. Just before the war, I came back out of Finland.

When the world war broke out, I was still working with my brothers. But I had met Annie. She was a pharmacist, and we saw something in that way. So with the help of friends we got money enough to buy a drugstore. That was in 1941. We married in 1941, and we started a drugstore.

Like many other rescuers, Bert did not help only Jews. He also took in a Dutch couple who were in the Underground and had lost their home in the brief Dutch war with Germany. Bert's actions toward this couple, however, show that rescuers were not saints; they were human beings, fully capable of getting angry, and they could and did take unpleasant measures when necessary.

> Now, this one friend who helped us, he had a paint factory. But he was arrested and sent by the Germans to a concentration camp. The morning that he was picked up, I was over at his place. His wife was miserable, of course, and she said, "I have two people here in this house. I have to send them away now, since they are in the Underground and we have so much trouble with the Germans."
>
> So I took them to my house. They were the first ones to come to my house. It was a couple. They were not Jewish themselves. They were supposed to bring Jews from Holland to Spain. Now, they were from a well-educated family, but the man's behavior was the way that I came to the conclusion that running the Jews to Spain was not number one priority; getting money from them was number one. Of course, there has to be money to get Jews to Spain. But this was a case of taking the money and not bringing Jews over the border. *That* I found out slowly, and then I dismissed them. I put them out of my house.

Bert's description of how he first took in someone Jewish demonstrates the extent to which rescuers wasted no time agonizing over what, to others, might appear a difficult moral choice.[10]

> Annie had a girlfriend from before the war. I met her, I think, in 1935, at Annie's house, before we were married. Hennie Juilliard was her name. She was a very nice person. Very smart. She was from a poor Jewish family, but she spoke modern languages and was very well educated, because she went to night school endlessly.
>
> The day she came, I was for the time in Amsterdam. I had often to be going to Amsterdam, since to buy goods, finding actual goods to buy, was harder than to sell the goods in the store at this time. So I had often to be going to Amsterdam. This time, when I came back, Hennie was sitting there. She asked if she could talk with me. I knew immediately what she want. My go ahead was emphatically, "Of course." She didn't even have to ask. We arranged that of course she stay. So that was the first person I saved.

Like all rescuers, Bert knew there were great risks involved in what he was doing. He took precautions to protect the people he was hiding, although he was "too much of a lazy loafer" to do it early on and without prodding from his wife, who Bert says was much smarter than he.

We had a large building for the pharmacy, and we built a secret room in it. The fire wall was located just between the wall to the next house, which connects with ours. The wall between two houses is automatically a fire wall, to close you off from your neighbor. The funny thing is that the fire wall takes a lot of the roof from the neighbors'. Between the houses is all this room. There is no use for it, and it was big enough for ten people to stand there. So what I did was to cover part of the attic with the same material as was in the rest of the attic. Then we stain it a certain color, using tea, to look like the color of paper as it gets older. I make a shelf over the top, over the seam of the door, so you couldn't see the door that swings open and close to seal off the room.

Even with these precautions, Bert was still betrayed. It is important to remember that during the war people were turned in to the Gestapo for many reasons. Some informants felt it their patriotic duty and were committed to the Nazi cause; others were seeking monetary rewards (often no greater than five dollars) or extra ration coupons; still others were avenging an old grudge or saving their own skins or bailing out one of their family members from jail.

One time we were betrayed. It was a busy morning in the store, and I was with my back to the entrance. One of my helpers was a man named Joost. I could see from his face that there was trouble. In the same second, there was a hand on my shoulder. "Are you the boss?" this voice says. By turning my face, I could see a German colonel, or some kind of officer. Then I see there was a soldier outside. I see another one by the house door, another by the front door, and one by the back. There were all over German soldiers. The house was surrounded. We couldn't get out.

Joost opened the back door in the hallway. There on the landing, halfway up this very wide staircase, was one of the women we were hiding. She got the idea something was going on. So she ran back into the living room and told the Jews what was happening. The Jews quickly went through the staircase to the third floor. They disappeared into the hiding place about five minutes later.

The German officer saw Joost and said to me, "What's he doing?" I said, "He's cleaning bottles." In those days it was a big deal to clean bottles. There was not enough bottles to go around, so people had to bring bottles in. So that's what I told this German Joost was doing. And Joost was, indeed, cleaning. He didn't come back in. He just was cleaning bottles in the little kitchen there.

Then the German ordered me upstairs. We came in the living room. There was sitting my wife and little Eric, my son, born in 1943. He was a year and ten months old. And then there was the sister of Hennie, a girl who had blue eyes and blond hair, so she was okay. But there was an old woman by the name of Sarah. She looked so Jewish, she was straight out of the

Bible. I feel very bad about it when I see her sitting there. I think it can be the end of everything. Another soldier was already talking to her. And just when I came in, he said, "You are Jewish. I see it before my eyes." Sarah was quick enough to jump up and say, "That's an insult! I don't take that!" And she started hitting him. So the colonel, he said, "Let her go. She is not Jewish. She just looks the Jewish type."

While this is happening, I look down. I saw lying on the floor, there was a handbag with thirty cards, food and ration cards, for my own family and for all the people in the house. Now, all these distribution cards should not have been there, of course. My mother-in-law was also sitting there. She had lost her house in the war, so she was with us. She saw these cards, too, and quick said to the German, "I was just ready to go shopping. Can I go?" And the German said, "Go." She scooped them all up, quick, so he won't see them. She took the cards and went off.

Then the Germans ordered me to the attic. The attic was very big. By that time I had already built two bedrooms in the attic, we had so much people. When the Germans come in the attic, they started immediately knocking all around, knocking on the walls to see if there was a false wall. I was so sure that they would never find it. But I was worried. My only hope was that everything could go all right and that they please leave the house without the others. I was thinking about the little kids and the older people.

Bert escaped detection this time although he was arrested twice during the war. Both times he was released unharmed and the Gestapo never discovered his hidden Jews.

Although both Bert and Tony were rescuers—Bert hid thirty-seven Jews in his home, and Tony took part in numerous shorter-term rescues—Bert's family background differed starkly from Tony's. Bert was one of eight children in a family that was far from affluent. Despite their modest economic situation, Bert never thought of his family as poor. The idea of helping neighbors—an idea Bert says comes from a time that "is gone now"—was very much a part of Bert's outlook. Despite a rather modest income after he moved to the United States, Bert had raised, in addition to his own five children, a friend of his twin daughters. The first day I visited Bert I also met a woman he and his wife had taken into their home because her alcoholic husband beat her. His treatment of me was both typical of the generosity I found in rescuers and indicative of his general treatment of others: he gave me lunch, urged me to stay for dinner, and sent me off with presents for my two sons. Giving to and caring for others was a normal part of life for Bert, long before and after the war.

I was the fifth child. There are three born after me. I get along very well with my brothers and sisters, still. When we was kids, I was the storyteller. When they went to bed, say at eight o'clock, the younger kids would lie awake until I came to bed at nine.

It was an old-fashioned house. There was a big sleeping room and a big room between, where you hang your clothes on both sides. My sister slept in the other room, and when I told stories to the little boys, I sometimes heard my sister's voice saying, "What did you say? Say it again." She would listen to the stories I told to the two younger brothers. In a way, in a big family, your friends are your brothers. We were friends. But nevertheless we have our duties. I remember that we always had a rowboat, and if we behaved good, then we can always go in the rowboat.

We were not what you would call rich, but I remember growing up much better off than most of the laborers' kids. Eighteen guilders a week was the income from my father.[11] We weren't poor. The clothes were always from the older kids, and the younger kids wore the hand-me-downs. In our house, when something was still good from an older brother, then it was normal to pass it down. We were by far not spoiled. There was always meat on the table. We had a good life.

Around you, you see people who are poor. I remember a widow. She had three kids and could not work much. They stayed in the house all the time. They were the poor devils, these kids, not only poor but a little bit dirty, too. And on Monday, this widow or one of the kids always came and they got homemade bread and a pound of butter, maybe a few other things. That went on for years. Some of the people, they got help in the same way.

That time is gone now. There is no way that kind of thing happens here. Every once in a while there comes a fellow at the door with a story that he needs some gasoline and he can't start his car. I never worry when I go to the door. I am somebody who is not light, and why should I be afraid?

Bert was very close to his family, especially his father, who died when Bert was twelve. His father's death was catastrophic for Bert, an incomprehensible event for which he was completely unprepared. How he dealt with this tragedy, however, reveals much about Bert and how he developed his remarkable sense of inner peace about life and death.

My father's death was devastating. My father was so optimistic; maybe that was why his death was such a surprise to me. The day before my father died, I was walking with my brother Nick, who is a year older than I am, and with a neighbor. We were all three walking together. Nick said something, half-crying. He said, "I think father is dying."

I could not believe it! There was a minister visiting father that day. My mother sent him home with the town horse and buggy driver, so his bicycle was still at our place; and the next morning she asked me to bring the bicycle back to the minister, who lived at least ten miles away. It seems far now, but I was used to these things. I drove the extra bicycle with my one hand. And when I came back, I had not forgotten that my father was so sick, but I still did not believe that he was ending his life. And on the way back, I stopped at a friend's house, a friend who had tuberculosis and was in a little tent. I spent an hour or more there before I came home.

When I came home, they said, "You're too late. Where have you been?" I got a terrible feeling. I came in the house, and my oldest brother came down and said, very calmly, "It is all over." I got choked up, terribly. I was lying on the couch in the living room, and nobody could stop me crying. I was hysterical.

Then that night, I got a dream. I never forget it. It saved me a lot of trouble, I think, a lot of grief. I dreamed that my father was standing in front of me, just in front of the bed I was sleeping in. That was my dream. And my father said to me, "Nobody really dies." He said, "I am not dead. I am always there." And the next day, I was calm. When the funeral came, two or three days later, I had no fear. I was so calm, I could handle anything. Because you never forget that.

Do you understand this that I am telling you? It was not a sign. It *was* from him. Not his body but his soul. It *really was* his soul that was there. Oh, yes. You know, when you are very young. You are more open with things like that. So I remember very strong that time of my life.

Bert's Perspective: Self in Relation to Others

Tony was so articulate and verbal that understanding his perspective was an easy intellectual exercise; understanding Bert's required a somewhat different skill.

Bert was the first rescuer I interviewed. I had been studying altruism for several years, reading in the vast literature on the subject and thinking about how I would go about constructing my own empirical examination. I had some vague ideas about what I might find and was excited at the possibility of doing my first interview with an altruist. What I was not prepared for, what nothing in my reading or conversations with other scholars could possibly have prepared me for, was the actual impact of meeting such a person, who views the world so differently from the way most of us do.

That summer happened to be particularly hot in Los Angeles. Bert lived in a small house in a blue-collar section of Lomita. I parked my car and knocked on the door. A large man, evidencing the frailty of age on his big-boned body, Bert answered the door and invited me into a living room that seemed to overflow with dogs and people. He led me through the kitchen to a small study and introduced me to his wife, Betty, who was sitting at a desk painting watercolors, despite the fact that her hands were swollen and crippled with arthritis. The room was close, not air-conditioned, and filled with the aroma of the elderly and the infirm. The dogs curled up around my feet as we began the interview by my asking Bert to tell me about himself and, in particular, how he came to rescue Jews during World War II. His English was heavily accented, and I experienced a momentary panic as I realized that, on top of the heat and the dogs, I was having difficulty understanding what he was saying.[12]

As Bert continued to speak, however, all these difficulties dropped away, and I found myself—I don't know how to express it any other way—in another world, one that was kinder and more humane than the one I ordinarily knew. This difference centered directly on the way Bert saw himself and on his particular perspective on life.

> I am a brusque man. That's the way I am, from the old country. My nature is that I forget very easy bad things, about my own troubles. I remember the good fellows. Oh, I do remember two fellows from the wartime, just after the war. I didn't like them, because they misused me, and I never forget it. But I put them out of my life. I never go back to them anymore, and it is over.
>
> I am a pretty straightforward person. I am not too patient. I am now more tolerant. That comes by aging: I got more and more tolerant the last thirty years. I think I am optimistic. I am also a little bit passive. You know, the hiding place, that was one example. When I finally made it in the attic, I did it as good as possible. But it was high time it was done. My wife Annie had hoped it would be done a couple of months earlier. That time I was a little too much of a lazy loafer. But I don't know about how passive or active I am when I see things in life that come along, and I think maybe I can change it.

I asked Bert specifically about ethical credos and found that this simple man did not subscribe to any particular rules that guided his life.

> I don't have any kind of ethical credo, a personal ethical credo that I use to guide my life. No, I don't think I live by special rules. I know during the war that I was doing things which were against the law, but that didn't bother me as long as it was on behalf of everybody: of my family, of the people hidden in the house. So I guess, though I never thought about it, that maybe I do think there's some kind of higher law than man-made law.

Nor did Bert view his actions as political. Unlike Tony, who was in the Resistance (as were a few other rescuers I interviewed), Bert did not contact the Underground. He did not want to know what was going on. "You never know how you respond when they get those irons on you," he said. "The less I know, the better." Bert considered his rescue activities humanitarian, not political.

> I don't think what I did was political. The Germans came as robbers in the night. The only law we had was German laws. And don't forget, Hitler made

the law. You could see that in what he did with the hostages. When one German soldier was shot, they would go, in the name of the German soldier who was shot, and take every man out of the house and shoot them on sight. We saw that happen. They were not normal. When there were Dutchmen who said things like that were all right, then you felt your nationality very strongly. I am a Dutchman. In the wartime, you really are a countryman. But I am an individual too. An individual, that comes always to the top, I think. Being an individual is first.

Q. *But did you do what you did, risking your life, saving other people, primarily because you were relating to them as another human, or is it because you felt it was your patriotic duty as a Dutchman?*

A. I don't think I gave it too much thought. It was easy to find the money to keep these people all alive. I knew I was on the right track, and nobody could blame me. I had the confidence.

I know people like you always want to know about religion. I am not religious, but I guess maybe I do believe in an afterlife. I don't know much about it. I know my wife, Betty, is sure that after you die, you go still through all the shortcomings you have in life, that you have to redo that before you are clean. She doesn't believe in reincarnation, but it would be nice. There is a story, *The Store of Wisdom.* It tells how when you have killed a man, for a long time you will have to keep on killing that man, until you are sick of it. When you have fornicated, you will fornicate until you never will fornicate again. I guess that makes some sense to me, too. But this is really Betty's idea. I don't think much about this myself.

I believe in the heaven, and heaven is something you have to pay for in order to get in. When you die, you go through everything you did on earth until you really are more aware of what you did that is not right. It's not that they tally up the good acts and the bad acts and if the good acts are more than the bad ones, you go to heaven, but if the bad ones are more, you go to hell. No. That is a little bit easy way of religion. That's not how I believe. No. And you can't go and be a good man on Sunday and then on Monday till Saturday go your way again; then on Sunday become good again. I don't think that.

I know what I did during the war, I did not do for religious reasons. No, it was not religious. I just never thought about it.

Like Tony, Bert's attitude toward religion is not unusual among rescuers. Many of them had some religious affiliation, but they either judged it irrelevant to their rescue efforts or held that a feeling of closeness to others was more important. Indeed, Bert's first response to my inquiries about religion was to smile and laugh. "Oh, I don't believe all that stuff about snakes talking." But he later elaborated, setting his religious beliefs in the context of his family background.

My town was built around two dikes, on the canal. It was a small community but very divided religious-wise. Not between Catholics and Protestants, since there were only three Catholic families. It was the orthodox Protestant ministers who divided it.

My parents were, I would say, normal Protestants and really believing people. But religion-wise, my grandfather already was more or less liberal. We are brought up with the idea that whatever we want to believe, that is alright too. Nobody knows what's better. In our case, they never told me that Christ was the savior of the world. That has nothing to do with believing in God. That is very hard to hear in this country [in the United States]. But there are lots of religions, thousands of years longer in the world than we are. Why are they wrong and we right?

My father was a very wise man, and he never was religious. On Sunday, most of the people in our town went to church, of course. But we [in my family] think that Sundays are almost the same days as the weekdays, especially when you don't go to church. On Sunday, in the summer, we want to sail the boat from the water in front of the house. The boat was there. We just had to go into the yard to get it. But the people going to church were there too. My mother always said, "Don't go the moment that older people are walking around to church. Go a little bit earlier or later. They still know that you go sailing, but you don't irritate them that way. Just let everybody live in his own rights." That's the way we were brought up.

I am religious inside. Very deep. I am a very strong believer. But I don't need a minister. I went for a couple of years to the Christian church, and I see the breaking off of people into different groups, destroying the little churches by silly things, and that was enough for me.

Bert's help for Jews was not an isolated event in his life. Bert did not suddenly become an altruist only at the outset of World War II. He recounted an incident from his childhood in which he saved someone's life.

When I was twelve years old, there was a boy my age who fell out of the rowboat in the canal, in the middle of the canal. I don't think he could swim. He was a kid from the Christian school and swimming was against their orthodox idea of life. My family were liberals in that field.

Now, I had polio as a baby. I worked hard to get over it. I was the fastest swimmer. I want to be that. I had setbacks, of course. When playing at school, I could not ever run the mile run against my friends. But in the water, I could beat them. That made me a bit of a braggart. So [when I see that boy drowning] I dived in the canal, and I swam to him and picked him up. I got a medal from the queen for this. I got in the local newspapers. It was quite a joke.

I don't know why I did this. It was just spontaneous. You don't think; you just do it. When you start thinking, then maybe you figure, "Well, the boy is strong. He cannot swim. Maybe he is in panic. When he gets you the wrong way on the boat, then you both drown." But I just swam to him, and I have to hit him strong on the head when he did try something to pull us both under.

This incident is important for understanding Bert's wartime rescue activities: it shows that he had a certain inclination toward acts of rescue and that these acts were spontaneous, not the product of reflection. I found that this pattern was common among rescuers. (Tony, for example, told me he had saved seventeen people from drowning off the coast of Malibu, where he lived for many years after World War II.) Although this same pattern appeared in a few heroes and heroines (such as Lucille), it was more widespread and pronounced among the rescuers.[13]

Bert insisted that he did not really understand why he had rescued people, that he simply never thought much about it, and that he had no other choice. If he knew then exactly what was involved in rescuing these people, would he still do it over again?

Yes. You asked me earlier if I would have been able to live with myself if I had not rescued these people. No. The possibility was that they should have a very hard situation, and you have the feeling that if you send them back, you don't forget it for your life. So I don't think I could have lived with myself.

Nor did Bert think that what he did was extraordinary or particularly praiseworthy.

Am I brave? Well, now, I should be very mad when you call me a coward. But brave, I don't know. When I look at the fellows who climb mountains straight up, and I see the chance that they lose their life . . . [Shrugs his shoulders]

Q. But dealing with the Gestapo, these were not pussycats you were dealing with.

A. No, but that is something you have to do, and mountain climbing is not.

This simple phrase—"something you have to do"—implied that Bert's actions, at least from his perspective, were inevitable.

I next asked if Bert thought people have a social responsibility to help others who are in need. His answer, particularly the illustration he gives of how some people helped while others did not, demonstrates the extent to which it was difficult to rely on traditional predictors of behavior to foresee who would be a rescuer and who would not.

Having [the responsibility], yes. But using it and knowing it is a different thing. I found that out. You know, I was not so young when the war started. I was thirty years old. I knew many people, old and young, in the small community that I grew up in. You think they are nice people and good to go with. Then the war comes, and you find out they cannot do without a thing. They are so afraid that they will get hungry. After a month or so, they cannot give nothing away. But other people gave lots.

I remember three brothers on one farm. Their father was the farmer to start with, but all the brothers live on houses on the farm. I came there during the war, asking one brother for potatoes. We got from him forty-four pounds of grain, beans, peas. These things could have been sold for a fortune, and he didn't want a dime. I'd ask for one bag, and he'd give two. Many years later, 1980 it was, I was over at the house of friends, and there I met this farmer again. It was his birthday. I said to him, "Remember what you did for me?" He said, "I remember that you drove by. But I don't know what I gave you."

Now this farmer, he had a brother nearby. Annie drove her bicycle there to see if we could get some food. And he gave nothing. Brothers. He was from the other house, on the same farm, from the same family. One is very giving and the other isn't. How do you explain that? I don't know why it is. You know the families. You know each other by birth. You grow up with them. The middle one will help, and the oldest one does nothing. They had the same bringing up, but they turned out so differently.

So I do think people have a social responsibility to help people in need. I do blame people like that couple that took money from Jews but had no intention of getting them to Spain. I cannot stand them.

Q. *If we wanted to have more people like you in the world, what could you tell us that would be useful in doing that?*

A. Well, let me say it different than you ask. When there was a bigger amount of normal people, the world was already much better, don't you think? What the world needs is more idealists. I am not one. I know that sometimes, for the Jewish case, they want to advertise people like me. But I don't know that the world itself is so much better for some old geezer like me. I am not that unusual a person.

Although Bert did not view himself as unusual, most of us would. The fact that he considers himself "normal" reveals much about his canonical expectations of life. These expectations about what constitutes ordinary or normal behavior set and delineated the range of options Bert found available, as is evident in the following excerpt, which hints at the terrible costs of his rescue activities and how he felt about the people he saved.

Q. *How did rescuing these people make you feel about yourself? Did it make you feel good? Did it have any impact on your view of yourself?*

A. Well, don't forget that you live for four years in this [war] situation. Then you cannot feel good before that everything is over. The day it was over, I got a very strange feeling, that it was off me. That the responsibility, the danger was over. Many long years ago, after the war, when I think back on these times, then I found out that the worst time for me was really after the war. After the war, I missed all those people in the house. When things with Annie didn't go well, that was the worst.

Annie collapsed the day the war ended. She died later, from the tuberculosis. And then I had the two kids to raise alone. And financial setbacks came. When you have to hire people just to take care of the kids, your life is not easy. So that was the worst time for me, just after the war.

During the last days of the war, when Annie was more and more sick feeling, the Jewish women in the house were crying and saying how they thought their being there was causing Annie strain and making her tuberculosis worse. I feel terrible. But what could you do? Annie didn't want to throw the people out of the house for her well-being, and that could be the only way. We both had a heavy feeling about this thing, of course. But we couldn't do anything else. We had to go on.

But this was the hardest time. I could not talk to Annie about how I feel about her dying. That would have just made it more difficult for her, to see how upset I am. I had to give her the power to go on, and not to show my fear. I was basically on my own. I have to be strong for her. I did tell her that I could take her to relatives in the south, and I could carry on in Huizen. I already hated to suggest that, since I knew she wanted to be around me. She did not go. She stayed with me and the child.

Also, I could not talk to the others in our house about it, since it would make them feel bad. I could not really tell them how bad it was for Annie. When you tell that to your people in the house, who feel already that it is very hard on her, and when you say you cannot bear seeing your wife like this, well. . . I could not go to somebody else. I had to carry it alone. I had to hide my own fears from them. I handled it by myself, and that was the hardest.

Now, thinking back, I have always a happy feeling that these Jewish people are still alive.

Annie's health problems were exacerbated by the strain of the rescue activity, and Bert told me, one afternoon when the tape recorder was turned off and we were fixing sandwiches in his kitchen, that this had been the hardest thing for him to handle. Bert also spoke a little on tape about his difficulties in raising two children by himself. I found it interesting, however, that Bert expressed not pride in what he had done so much as sorrow at saying goodbye to the people with whom he had shared such a difficult time. This passage reveals much about Bert and the sensitivity he brought to his concerned treatment of others, even when the emotional costs to himself were extremely high. It suggests a man of quiet strength who carried his pain and his loss alone, both during the harrowing days while his wife was dying and for long years after the war.

> After the war, I was much more preoccupied with my personal problems at that point. Then later it was important that Betty [my second wife] not feel jealous of things like this. Maybe that was the main reason that there are already many years before I can think and talk of this time. My kids never hear the stories. Only lately. Or maybe I give them papers that they can carry later and look at later.
>
> The same was true for the Jews, too. After the war, the younger Jews, they start fighting to build up a living. They didn't want to think back on the parents they lose, of the children they lose. That took almost thirty or forty years before they came back to that.
>
> And for me, I have to say that when I married Betty there came a better time. We went to America and the kids do fine.

Things were, indeed, better for Bert after he met and married Betty. They had a happy marriage, raised three children in addition to the two Bert had with Annie, and moved to southern California, where Bert found work as an upholsterer.

Betty, an extremely articulate woman, sat in the corner painting watercolors during most of our interviews. When Bert expressed his puzzlement at all the attention he was receiving because of his wartime activities, she smiled and asked if she could add her own comments.

> Bert does not think about what he does. He's not going to say, "I'm going to go do a good deed." He's impulsive. He lives by a certain moral code, and you cannot get him away from that. He will not go beyond that. I know. I look at our kids, who have Bert as a father, and they will stop on the freeway and help anybody who's standing still. It's not smart. But they do it, all over, when there's a need. I just think it is planted in them. And I also have found that most of the time there is no thought behind it. It's like the woman in New York who lifts the heavy car off a body. You know you can do it. And she did. People will do unbelievable deeds that you don't understand why they are not completely dead. And they just say, "Well, I never thought about it." That's Bert.

Bert expanded on Betty's remarks, picking up on an earlier question of mine and articulating the sense that altruistic behavior is not chosen but inevitable, almost involuntary.

> You asked me, if I knew then exactly what was involved in rescuing these people, would I still do it over again? Yes. Now I am a bit older, of course, I'd have to do it a little bit less. But I never think about not doing it. I never thought about that.

I think it was always fair, what I did. I feel sometimes not so good about the health of Annie. But yet there are very hard things, and you have to go on. It has to be done. There are things in this life and you have to do them, that is all. You do things because you are human, and because there is need.

In 1990, Bert found out he had cancer. In May of 1991, he and his wife traveled to Holland for one last visit. They returned to California in July and Bert died on August 13, in his home, with his children and family around him. He was buried in a simple wooden coffin, marked—at his request—only by a Star of David.

His wife, Betty, died shortly thereafter.

PART III

Traditional Explanations
for Altruism

CHAPTER 6

Sociocultural Attributes of Altruism

> What I did during the war, I did not do for religious reasons. No.
> It was not religious.
>
> —Bert, Dutch rescuer

I SUGGESTED in part I that existing explanations of altruism satisfy only partially and that the missing piece in the puzzle can be supplied by considering cognitive phenomena such as perspective. In part II, I presented impressionistic evidence of how the individual's perspective differs as we move from the self-interested actor to the altruist. I would like now to begin a more systematic examination by considering explanations that stress the importance of sociocultural attributes for altruism.

Do sociocultural characteristics explain altruism? No. Indeed, none of the sociocultural attributes to which altruism is so frequently attributed—such as religious affiliation or residence in a small town—remained consistent predictors once I controlled adequately for a baseline effect by asking nonaltruists the same questions I asked altruists. Furthermore, none of the general sociocultural factors social scientists automatically examine even appeared consistently in the altruists in my sample. The rescuers of Jews, for example, ranged from a very poor woman whose father used to beat her to a Silesian countess, raised in a ninety-three–room castle. Their educational levels were as elementary as the fifth or sixth grade and as advanced as the Ph.D. Gender did not predict altruism: women may be more nurturing but are no more likely than men to be altruistic.[1] Nor is family size a factor; altruists can be lonely only children or can come from large and close families. Neither birth order in a particular family nor that family's position in the community appears to be related to altruism.

Let us look at each of these findings in detail.

RELIGION

Religion is frequently believed to influence altruism.[2] Various explanations of this relationship are put forward, but most reflect the general premise that religions teach people to be kind and to help others.[3] While I found that religion was, indeed, relevant for some altruists, this was far from consistently the case, and I concluded that the overall influence of religion was much more complex and subtle than has been thought. Certainly, religion does not act as the straightforward predictor one might have expected.

For the most part, the altruists I interviewed considered religion irrelevant to their altruistic acts.[4] Such a view is articulated, for example, by both the Dutch rescuers discussed in chapter 5. As Bert put it, "My feeling when doing it [saving Jews] was that it had nothing to do with religion. If I was not a Christian, I would still do it. You have it in you."[5] In discussing his general attitude toward religion, Bert described himself as religious but in a private way. He then recounted how his friends told him that going to church would improve his business, but he found this idea repulsive and refused to engage in a self-serving charade, since he didn't believe "that stuff about snakes talking and all that."

This same attitude was evident in Tony's narrative. Tony appeared to have spent more time than other rescuers thinking about many of the complex religious issues raised during our discussions; he was, therefore, perhaps better able to articulate finer distinctions concerning these issues than were other less verbal altruists.[6] Tony's subtle observations capture what I would characterize as the implicit position of all the altruists I interviewed: (1) Religion alone was not a dispositive influence. (2) What was more important than religion itself was the underlying value for human life that religion often—but not always—fosters.[7]

Tony began by distinguishing between religion as worship and religion as social morality. He then argued that all good religions teach the same social morality, which stresses the importance of working together.

> To me, there are two aspects to religion. One is worship, getting down on your knees and, in fear or in hope, praying to some superior being there that will rule your life. The other is social morality. This is by far the more important part of religion. Unfortunately, the two have been mixed together at times. They're confusing for people.
>
> There's so much superstition involved with the first type of thinking. To me, it is utterly unimportant whether Jesus ever walked on water or whether he walked on the rocks. It is what he had to *say* that is important. Jesus said, "Look, I am the Son of God. We are *all* sons of God. We all have it in us to lead a good, a kind, a moral life. I'm no different. I am you. You can do it."
>
> *That* to me was the teaching of Jesus. Anybody can do it if they want to. Sure, you may endanger your life. Sure, you may get crucified. But if enough of us do it, nobody will get crucified anymore. That is the initial teaching of early Christians and of all religions. There is no difference. All good religions are saying that if we work together and love, fewer of us will have to be crucified.

Q. *So yours is more religion as a morality? Was that relevant in your rescue activities?*

A. At that time, no, because I hadn't studied religion that much at the time.

I tried to touch on another aspect of religion's possible influence on altruism, addressing the more cynical and quasi-economic idea articulated in Pascal's wager. This idea suggests that people who believe in an afterlife of rewards and punishments will be more likely to do good in this world, in order to buy themselves a better position in the next.[8] I asked other altruists about this and received roughly the same two-part reply. First, virtually all of them laughed at the very idea that people would live their lives in such a calculating way. Second, most denied they believed in such a traditional afterlife.

This was articulated in practically the same words by two Dutch women of vastly different backgrounds. The first was a working-class woman who had borne eight children and was now the archetypical grandmother, with incredible sweetness in her round, cherubic face, despite the fact that she had been raised by an alcoholic father who beat her. When I asked her about an afterlife, she leaned over, tapped my knee, and whispered confidentially, "Nobody ever comes back, do they?" The second woman was a psychiatrist, who recalled how she and her artist father had discussed this question. She told me with some bemusement that her father had promised her that, if there was anything there, he would come back and tell her after he died. "I'm still waiting," she said smiling. Since all but a few of my altruists—from the philanthropists to the rescuers—expressed similar views, I conclude that a belief in the afterlife is not a critical determinant of altruism.

What I did find instead among altruists was a world view—closely akin to spirituality—in which all life constitutes an indissoluble whole. This seemed less a religious belief and more a way of conceptualizing the world.[9] Altruists see the world as one in which connections exist and extend, through nature, beyond the death of any one particular individual.[10] Tony articulated this commonly held view.

Q. *Tony, do you believe in an afterlife?*

A. I don't know. I'm an agnostic, in that I do not believe we have any way of knowing until it happens. It is obvious there is a plan in the universe, some plan, some master plan. As an agnostic, I do not believe that we are in a position to be able to judge and to evaluate that plan and how it works. I never have had the feeling that the finger of God points at you or knocks you over or helps you up. No, I never believed that. And for very good reasons!

Tony discounts the idea of a deity who rewards the good and punishes the evil. He explicitly rejected the notion of a connection between religion and altruism, arguing that religious people are just like others and therefore can be weak and petty on occasion.

> **Q.** *Some people have said that religious people will tend to be more altruistic—* *(Tony interrupted at this point.)*

> **A.** Anybody who says that, I would send them immediately to the Middle East, to Beirut, and see how religious people behave towards each other there. The most horrible things in history have been done in the name of religion. So I think religious people are just like everybody else. They can be very moral, very kind. But they're human.

Tony's own religious views were complex; his idea of an afterlife seemed more akin to Hinduism than Christianity.

> I guess I believe in an afterlife, though not in the standard Judaic-Christian idea of men of today. It's more like the one I just described, that you just go to sleep. I don't believe in an afterlife of a heaven or hell, where you sit around on a cloud and play the harp. No, I think the world is a world of energy that is like a cell in the body of creation. I see the whole world as one living body basically. But not our world only: the whole universe. And I'm like one of the cells. So I'm as much a part of that as others. Without me, the universe doesn't exist, anymore than my body exists without its cells. So I'm a part of a whole, and I will go back into that part, in the Indian philosophy sense. Whether any consciousness remains, we'll find out.

Tony then articulated a major theme among altruists: the idea that we are all one, are all equal, and that all life has value. He also typified other altruists in suggesting that any religious influence in his life came more in the form of general morality than it did as a specific church or theology. When I asked him explicitly if religious belief was a factor in his rescue activities, his negative answer echoed those of other altruists.

This same world view is evident throughout the narratives presented in part II. Bert did not attend church and felt religions divide people from each other, thus discouraging the kinds of personal social interactions altruists cherish.[11] While Lucille does touch on religion in her narrative, she does not judge it particularly relevant for either her civil rights activities or her heroic rescue of her neighbor. For Lucille, the value of religion lies in the drama of its ritual, and no particular church has a monopoly on that.

What about altruists' views on an afterlife? The overall pattern for altruists was one of suspended disbelief. Lucille's comments are typical.[12]

> I believe in an afterlife, but I don't believe in hell and heaven. Now, I get popes who'll not like that, and maybe I'll get excommunicated. But I don't believe in heaven or hell. God doesn't punish us; we punish ourselves. Anything we do, we somehow get involved. God's not goin' in and say, "Ah

ha! There's Lucy. I'm gonna jump on her and trample her and send her down to hell."

No, I don't believe in hell and heaven. I believe dying is an evolving into another series of life. What you haven't accomplished here, you do there. Like if you didn't get out of grade school, then you've gotta start in grade school again. I'm not saying I believe in reincarnation. What I believe, it's hard to say. We don't become stagnant and wait for our bodies to float up to meet our spirits. I think the body is a materialistic thing that rots and is done. The spirit, as we call it, the *me*, the *we*, evolved into whatever we've gained. If we've been mean son-of-a-guns and bastards, then we're gonna go into that kind of place until we learn to do decent. We're gonna have to just go through the same classes, over and over again, until we learn 'em.

Lucille's idea that we all repeat our past mistakes until we learn from them was articulated again by Bert and almost in the same words. To my surprise, this same attitude—one which seemed somewhat unusual to me—was expressed by several other altruists.

Like other altruists, Melissa noted that religious people were very human, often no better than nonreligious people. After her first husband died, for example, some of the people at her church hurt her deeply by choosing that moment to approach her for contributions for the new minister's home and never even mentioning her bereavement. Melissa concluded from this that you should "not give expecting anything in return. Give because you want to, because if you expect it, you're going to be very hurt." This idea was typical of altruists, and it was not related to the next life or to their possible position in it. Their altruism does not emanate from the desire to get to heaven, and for most of them the afterlife consists of the spirit of the person living on in the hearts of others.

I also found another reason for discounting religion's influence on altruism: there was no standard breakdown along religious lines between altruists and the individuals interviewed as part of the baseline sample. Isabelle, an Italian Catholic philanthropist married to a Jewish man, whose family initially had disapproved of their marriage because of the religious difference, offered an instructive comment about the role of religion in her philanthropy.

Forget being Catholic or Jewish. I don't care what you are. That is very secondary to me. Take the word "God" and stretch it and it's "good." If you have an aura of goodness, then goodness begets goodness. I don't give be-cause I am Catholic. It has nothing to do with that.

I can relate this to the camp we started for needy children. I had no idea what was going on there till my husband said, "Izzi, do you realize what is happening here?" He showed me that through children who need help many of the Jewish people were hanging out together with the Catholics and they all were working together with a common bonding. I didn't even realize that. They all said they'd help, without asking whether this was a Catholic charity or a Jewish charity or whatever. It was just that a child needed help, and so they all came and contributed.

Doing good for another human transcends religious differences for altruists, as is illustrated in Isabelle's discussion of her personal life and her own interfaith marriage. Her comments resonated with ideas expressed by other altruists about the importance of believing in each other and in a shared humanity.

Sam and I did some of this in our own marriage. I know that when my oldest daughter was in school, it was very unusual for people from different religious backgrounds to marry. The teacher asked if my daughter would stand in front of the classroom and answer questions. One question was, "What do you believe in?" And that little girl, a seven-year-old girl, said, "Well, we believe in each other."

Beyond statements such as these, which suggest religion's irrelevance for altruism, several altruists I interviewed identified themselves as agnostics or even atheists. I should add, however, that these were equally balanced with a small group of altruists who *did* belong to organized churches and were deeply and conventionally religious. A rescuer named John was typical of this latter group. His father had been a minister, and John, on the Gestapo's Most Wanted List because he organized and operated an escape route to take Jews to Switzerland and Spain, was a devout Seventh Day Adventist whose life was permeated by religion. Yet even John said, "I don't think you had to be religious. You had to have love in your heart."

Perhaps more significantly, even for the devout, human life was something of greater value than church membership or religious doctrine. This was starkly illustrated in a story told by a Polish woman who was a deeply religious Catholic girl of eighteen when the war began. Irene's experience, especially her actions when she felt a conflict between her church and the call to help the afflicted, is most revealing and worth relating in some detail.

Irene was away from home for the first time, at nursing school, when the Germans and Russians partitioned Poland. While trying to minister to some of the Polish soldiers, Irene became caught in the midst of the fighting. Raped and beaten by Russian soldiers, she was left to die in the snow. She woke to find herself in a Russian hospital, her eyes so swollen shut that she could not see. A Russian doctor cared for her and then let Irene work in the hospital until she was repatriated.

Returning to a dismembered Poland, Irene discovered that her family had disappeared into the portion of Poland annexed to Germany. Since she was not able to contact her family, Irene stayed with a friend from nursing school. One Sunday, as the two girls left church, Irene was seized by the Germans and pressed into slave labor in a munitions factory. On the day a German major visited the factory for inspection, Irene fainted while standing on line. Although the usual punishment for this was death, the major spared Irene, because she told him she wanted to work and had fainted only because she was malnourished and allergic to the fumes from the ammunition produced in the factory.

The major took pity on Irene and put her to work in a German diner, where she worked as a waitress, serving the German soldiers under the major's supervision. One of her duties included waiting on the major, who was occasionally joined for meals by the local Gestapo commander. As she served the men, Irene gradually realized that she could overhear the local Gestapo commander informing the major about planned raids on the Jewish ghetto, including the dates when these raids would occur. She began telling the Jewish kitchen staff not to go home on those nights. Eventually, she constructed a false back in a linen closet in the diner, where twelve of the kitchen staff could hide during the night of a raid.

This continued for some weeks. Then one day Irene heard the Gestapo chief telling the major the final liquidation of the ghetto had been ordered. Irene was heartsick and panicky. She wanted to help but had no idea what to do. Then the German major asked her to supervise the cleaning of a villa he planned to occupy. Seizing on this opportunity, Irene told the Jewish staff to meet her that night at the villa, where she hid them in the coal cellar. Twelve Jews lived in the villa of the German major until early in 1944, when the Russians liberated the area.

Let Irene continue the story in her own words:

One day in September, I was in town. Suddenly, out of nowhere, the Gestapo was pushing everyone from the streets to the marketplace. They forced us to witness a Polish couple with two little children and a Jewish couple with a child being hung in the middle of the marketplace. They forced us to watch, to see what happens when someone befriended a Jew. I closed my eyes. I could not watch. But you can hear the breathing, the cries of the children. And I was like a zombie, numb. There were signs on every street corner saying, "This town is Jew-free. Whoever will help Jew descendants is dead."

So I knew what could happen. But that doesn't matter. I mean, they were human beings. I knew I didn't have to help. I took the responsibility. And I believed so strong that for reasons God put me there, so everything will be fine. I did have such a strong belief in that. But I was shaken that day, seeing those children hung.

Coming to the villa, I opened the door. I closed the door; I even locked it; but I pulled the key out. Usually, I pulled the key and put it in the inside lock and turned it in the lock, so when the major would come in he could not walk in; he would have to ring the bell. But that day I was so shook up that I took the key and walked straight into the kitchen. I put the things down. I came back with something, put it in the sink, and I was looking white like the snow. I was trembling.

Four of the girls came out, as they usually did when I was alone in the kitchen. The door was locked, and we had a warning system. They knew I was not normal, and they asked me what happened. I said, "I'm catching cold." I could not tell them what I had witnessed, because it would put a guilt in them. I could not do it.

I was standing with the door open, and the major walked in on us. He saw me. And he saw the four girls. He was just standing. His eyes was unbelieving. His skin was shaking. He looked like he'd seen a ghost. Without saying one word, he turned around and went to his library.

Well, I did have to go and face him. There was not any other way. He knew [some of] them from the laundry room. When I went in, he began to scream and yell at me. "How did you dare to do so? Behind my back! I trusted you! I give you home! I give you protection! Why?"

To secure the major's silence, Irene had to agree to be his mistress. The devout young girl went to the church to confess this sin and to ask for forgiveness. The priest, who quickly figured out what Irene was doing, told her to turn in the Jews and stop endangering her mortal soul. "I turned around and walked out of the church, and I have never gone back," Irene told me.

Obviously, Irene's story is remarkable for several reasons.[13] But what was most touching to me and what seems directly relevant in assessing the importance of religion for altruism was the fact that Irene related most of her story with no difficulty. She demonstrated surprisingly little awkwardness in recounting the most brutal and inhumane aspects of the war: the clearing of the ghetto; life in slave labor conditions; being raped, beaten, and left to die in the snow. Several times during our conversations I offered to stop the interview or at least to turn off the tape recorder, fearing that recounting the story was too difficult for Irene or that recording it was a violation of her privacy. Yet throughout all our interviews, the only part of her story that Irene found too horrible to tell on tape was the exchange with the priest. And so the first time she told me of it, in tears, it was not recorded. Only in a later interview did she give me permission to include this incident, saying, as she leaned over to pat my hand, "It's okay, honey. You can use it if you like."

Others may interpret Irene's behavior differently, of course, but what this signified to me was that the break with her church was the most difficult thing Irene went through during the war. And yet, when there was a tension between the needs of human beings and what the church told her to do, a tension that was particularly wrenching for Irene because of what it said to her about the church she had so loved, the choice was clear: "I turned around and walked out of the church, and I have never gone back."

This emphasis on the sanctity of life itself, rather than on religious teachings or membership, was articulated for me by many altruists. Like Wilhelmina, the Berlin rescuer who described herself as "pious from the inside," most altruists seemed less traditionally religious and more like people who had established a personal credo, a faith in or relationship with a higher power they had themselves discerned or intuited. This was clearly captured in Irene's narrative, when she told me about leaving the Catholic Church because of the priest's anti-Semitism and in our subsequent conversations, when she remarked that she did not need a building to find God. Even less traditional is Otto, an articulate German-Czech rescuer who described himself as a Kantian pantheist and noted, "I have no formal religion. . . . I can get along without any revelation." When asked if he believed in an afterlife, he replied, "Absolutely not. Not an individual one."

While most of the altruists I interviewed had strong ethical codes, this was also true for the nonaltruists. Certainly there was no correlation between religious affiliation and altruism, no behavioral difference between Catholics and Protestants, for example, or between conservative churchgoers and their more liberal brethren. And the personal religious views of altruists did not diverge significantly from those of the traditional rational actors I interviewed. Not one person interviewed felt that their actions here on earth would affect their situation in an afterlife.[14] Being good was not a strategy to buy themselves a better place in paradise. Most people just laughed at the idea, as Tony did. Some (like Melissa) added, "I don't believe that."

What I concluded from all these interviews was that altruists share something that may bear superficial resemblance to but differs critically from what we would commonly think of as organized religion or even religious belief. I would identify it, instead, as a spiritual feeling of closeness to others or a belief that we are all part of a human family. This belief is a key commonality among altruists and will be more fully addressed later. This way of looking at the world and at themselves in relation to others differs significantly and consistently from the view I found among entrepreneurs, who find nothing wrong or unnatural about acting as self-interested individual actors.

It is therefore particularly useful to make a distinction between religion as church membership and religion as the source of a particular world view in which all life is valued. It is this particular perspective and not religion as a sociocultural phenomenon that can explain both why so many religious people are not altruists and why so many nonreligious people *are*.[15] What generates altruism is seeing oneself and others as human beings of value, not being religiously faithful or adhering to any particular theology. This helps to explain the situation in the Middle East, cited by Tony, and the hostilities of religious wars, in which both sides pray to God as they go out to slaughter other human beings.[16]

For all of the following reasons, then, I discount the importance of religion on altruism. (1) Most altruists themselves draw no connection between their religious views and their altruism. (2) Even those altruists who do believe in an afterlife—and these are by no means the norm—do not do good in this life in order to do well in the next. (3) Typical rational actors are just as likely to be members of religious groups as are altruists. (4) There is no traditional institutional religious breakdown among altruists, no difference between Protestants or Catholics, between liberal and conservative churchgoers. (5) For all altruists, the sanctity of human life transcended religion. To the extent that this view is associated with religion, religion may seem related to altruism, but the relationship is misleading. The direction of the influence comes from the altruist's perspective, not from religion itself.

Family Background, Wealth, and Occupation

What about other sociocultural characteristics, such as the individual's or his or her parents' wealth, occupation, socioeconomic status, or education? These are logical factors to explore, given their general importance for other significant forms of social and political behavior.[17] Let us first examine the wealth and occupations of altruists and their families.

The rescuers alone reveal the tremendous diversity of altruists' family backgrounds and socioeconomic situations. Bert was from a Dutch family of modest means and worked in a dry goods store during the war. His education stopped in high school. Peter was a Slovakian peasant. Alida was born into a poor, working-class family and was raised by a physically abusive, alcoholic father. Neither she nor her husband, a shipbuilder who also hid Jews, was well-educated. They had eight children, some of whom went hungry during the war because their parents gave their food to strangers.

In contrast, Wilhelmina was a wealthy Berliner and extremely proud of her famous family. Margot, a rescuer born in Heidelberg, had a French governess, who taught Margot French before she learned German. Margot's father was head of General Motors for Europe, and she grew up amidst family friends like former U.S. secretary of state Charles Wilson. An only child, Margot was sent to boarding school in Geneva and lived in Spain, Italy, and England to become fluent in the languages she would need for service in the German diplomatic corps. After completing her university studies, she was sent on a grand tour of Russia and Central Europe to learn more about these regions. She left Germany for Holland, along with her parents, husband, and children, before the war began and in opposition to Hitler. Another German rescuer, Maruska, was a countess from a wealthy, and anti-Semitic, Silesian family; her brothers and sisters married into the German nobility. Maruska rebelled against her family, ran away from home, earned a Ph.D. in veterinary science, and ended up traveling as a veterinarian with a circus.

Other rescuers were from the middle class. Leonie was the daughter of an artist in Maastricht; Irene's father was a Polish architect; Knud's family were Danish coopers (makers of barrels); and John's Dutch father was a minister, who raised his children in his parish in Switzerland.

Consider the family occupations and family wealth of the philanthropists as another example. Melissa's parents were not professional people and left the Midwest during the depression to avoid economic ruin. The person Melissa most admired was her grandfather, who was a farmer. Isabelle's parents were Italian immigrants who worked in a small business in New York. In contrast, Mac's parents were quite wealthy, and Harry's family had been both wealthy and nationally prominent since the eighteenth century. (Harry counted at least one cabinet member in his family. His brother was a congressman, and his grandmother's art forms one of the best private collections at the New York Metropolitan Museum of Art.) Jimmy's father made his money while Jimmy was growing up and was described by his son as a skinflint. The same diversity of economic levels was evident among all the groups analyzed.

In terms of their own education and occupational positions, altruists are equally wide-ranging. When the war began, Otto had completed university and was an engineer. Knud was serving in the Danish police force. Leonie was in the Dutch equivalent of high school, and Irene was a nursing student; Leonie later became a psychiatrist and Irene an interior decorator. While many of the rescuers I interviewed were too young during the war to already have established professional occupations, the range of postwar occupations was great, including an inventor and an engineer, a psychiatrist, several housewives, a veterinarian, and the owner of a health food store in Pasadena. Nor was there any one educational pattern. All in all, the rescuers were a varied group.

The same diversity existed for other altruists. In addition to Melissa, for example, I found among the philanthropists one former fashion model, one retailer of children's clothes, one engineer, and a State Department employee on the Far Eastern Desk. Philanthropists' educations also ranged widely: some had only a high school degree, while at the other end of the scale there was a graduate of Yale Law and one Ph.D. in physics who was educated at both Princeton and Cambridge Universities.

Other than their common trait of financial acumen, the entrepreneurs also formed a diverse group, differing widely in training and occupation.[18] The only billionaire in the sample made his money developing and marketing public storage rentals. Roger is an urban planner with an advanced degree from Berkeley. The lone female entrepreneur, who preferred to be identified only as "Mom," was trained as a nurse. She made her money in holistic health products and in pop art memorabilia from the 1950s and 1960s. Justin was trained as an accountant and ran his own electrical company. Billy made casting parts for cars. And Warren is a jack-of-all-trades, a layman who mastered a difficult medical field in order to develop the first successfully marketed heart valve for humans.

This same diversity of family background, socioeconomic situation, occupation, and education was evident in all the groups I interviewed, from the entrepreneurs and the philanthropists to the heroes and the rescuers. Given this variety, I concluded that these factors are not significant correlates of altruism.

FAMILY POSITION

Family position is frequently cited as an influence on altruism, one often related to education, family wealth, and socioeconomic status. The basic logic here is that the position of the person's family in the community might influence altruism, since people raised in more prominent families are both accustomed and expected to take charge of local affairs and have the ego strength and leadership qualities necessary for altruistic endeavors.[19] I did not find such a correlation in the altruists I interviewed, however, and will argue later that what is germane in the family position argument is its *potential* intermediate effect on a person's view of her or himself and not the actual position of the family per se.

If we recall the chapters about Billy and Melissa, for example, we are reminded how similar their backgrounds are in this regard. Both were uprooted while in high school and came to California with families that were trying to build a better life. Their families were respectable but, as newcomers of modest means, hardly prominent in the community. Yet despite these similarities in family position, Melissa became a philanthropist and Billy did not.

Furthermore, family position can have a mixed effect on an individual. Lucille's kinfolk were accepted into Little Rock society, and her grandmother enjoyed national stature as a writer, but Lucille did not characterize the position of her own immediate family as exalted, noting instead how poor they were and how little social status they had. How would we then classify her on a "family position" variable? Lucille also felt inferior to her other relations because of the poverty of her immediate family and her father's desertion. As Lucille's example illustrates, how one feels about one's family position may be both highly subjective and more significant than external assessments of family social position; the influence flow could then be more personalistic than it is a straightforward relationship between family social status and altruism.

Nor is it clear that family position works to develop feelings of increased responsibility for others. Bert's family, for example, was solid Dutch working-class, respectable but not prominent in the community. Yet Bert felt very comfortable with that, talking at one point about how his family, though hardly rich, always found some little thing to give others in greater need. Tony's family was affluent and bourgeois, with several members receiving public acclaim. But this did not engender social security in Tony, whose mother constantly fixed her eye on the next rung in the social ladder and was not content with the prominence already enjoyed by the family. The personal effect of this on Tony was quite negative. (He spoke at one point of its causing him to be placed in a prestigious military unit filled with aristocrats who used social position to put others down.) Insofar as Tony did develop the view that a certain social position means taking on more responsibility for others, this view appears to have emanated more from his commanding officer in the cavalry corps than from his family's status. And Tony seems to believe that greater privilege brings greater responsibility, a concept somewhat different from the idea that family position itself requires one to act in a certain way.

> The other man who influenced me was my military commander in the school for cavalry officers. He taught us if you want to be an officer and a gentleman, [if] you want those privileges, that means that if there is a war, if the country is attacked, [then] you cannot look down on a soldier for being scared or for wanting to desert out of fear. But since *you* wanted to be an officer, you have to be the first one to get killed when that happens. You cannot expect it from others. You want that privilege, you pay for it when the time comes. That's the type of responsibility he taught me.

Furthermore, when I did ask rescuers who came from prominent families about the effect of this on their altruism, they seemed baffled by the question. Margot asked quizzically why this should be related to her activities on behalf of Jews.

Q. *Your family was rather prominent, wasn't it?*

A. Yes.

Q. *Did that have anything to do with your actions toward the Jews?*

A. No, no. Not at all. Not a damn thing to do with it. I never even thought of that. Why should it matter?

Even more significantly, there were many other rescuers (Bert) and heroes (Gerald) whose families were not prominent in the community. A wide range of family positions was evident for all the other groups I considered as well: heroes and heroines, philanthropists and entrepreneurs.

I have already suggested that social position may have a mixed effect on a family member, as it did for Tony. But occasionally the prominence of an altruist's family served to make altruistic activities less, rather than more, likely. Lucille's case, while complicated, offers an example of how this process might work. Lucille talked at great length about how she felt inferior when she was growing up, because her immediate family was poor and her extended family was more proper and socially acceptable. Even now, she said, she cannot fit into what they want her to do and be, "wearing pearls and being all ladylike." The relatively prestigious social position of her extended family did not serve as a source of emotional strength for Lucille. Indeed, the disapproval of her socially prominent relations served as an additional psychological burden Lucille had to carry during her integration activities, when she had to accept the shame of knowing she was embarrassing her kin by her actions on behalf of blacks. Nonetheless, she persevered in her aid of others.

I would guess (and I shall analyze and document this hypothesis in detail in chapter 10) that the significant factor is the altruist's perspective on self and that family position enters into the equation only insofar as it shapes the altruist's sense of self in relation to others. The countess Maruska, for example, seemed a rather imperious grande dame, with some of the arrogance commonly associated with the German aristocracy. At one point the Gestapo was searching her apartment looking for hidden Jews. The Gestapo thought there might be someone hidden in the countess's sofa and threatened to shoot into it. Knowing full well that there was, indeed, a Jewish man hidden in the sofa, the countess nonetheless haughtily told them to go right ahead and shoot if they wanted but that she would make sure their office reimbursed her for the loss of an excellent sofa. This illustrates an instance when family position might have given the altruist the nerve and hauteur necessary to carry off the altruistic act successfully, but it seems only tangentially related to the altruistic impulse in the first place.

In general, therefore, I discounted the influence of family position on altruism for three reasons. (1) There was a wide diversity of family background and position among the altruists I interviewed, both in childhood and in the later circumstances in which their altruistic behavior occurred. (2) When asked directly about the relevance of family position to their altruism, most judged it irrelevant. (3) I found extreme diversity of family position among all the people I interviewed, altruists and rational actors alike. This diversity suggests that there is no significant difference between the social position of altruists' families and that of rational actors.

Birth Order and Size of Family

Whiting's important cross-cultural study of children and sharing (1983) found birth order an important determinant of prosocial behavior.[20] Indeed, many studies find birth order a critical factor in much later behavior, with older children generally held to be more nurturing and more driven to achieve. I did not find birth order a significant influence on altruism, however. For the most part, birth order and size of family seemed unrelated to the altruism of the people I interviewed. Some altruists were the firstborn in their families; some were middle children; some were the youngest. Some altruists had close ties to siblings, while others did not. (Melissa was very close to her brother, for example, while Lucille was estranged from hers.) Altruism seems independent of the size of the birth family. Isabelle was a philanthropist from a large family, as was the rescuer Bert. But Margot and Tony were only children. Such variation was the norm.

Surprisingly, even the kinds of caring relations that children had with younger siblings seem unrelated to altruism, a finding at distinct odds with Whiting's work, which holds that children who are given responsibility for younger children tend to be more nurturing adults, regardless of cultures and family ties. Bert talks about caring for his brothers and sisters and how close he was to them. A German rescuer named Bethe told of how she cared for her younger brother after her mother died. Other altruists mentioned similar situations. Yet others (like Tony or Margot) were only children and did not mention other children at all in their discussions of their early lives. Nor did the kind of family situation affect the altruist's happiness as a child: some only children, like Tony, felt quite lonely as a child, while others, like Margot, delighted in having all their parents' attention.

This same variety in birth order was evident among the entrepreneurs, some of whom spoke with great feeling about the importance of their families in their lives, while others scarcely mentioned family. Given this, I concluded that birth order and size of family are not critical predictors of altruism.

CLOSENESS OF COMMUNITY

What about the effect of the community in which one is raised? Does that influence altruism? Some have argued that people who grow up in small towns will develop close ties to others. These ties, reinforced by participation in the same groups and frequency of interaction, mean that community members know each other personally and cannot escape into anonymity. Knowledge of everyone else's behavior is easier in small geographic units, and social interactions act as subtle pressures to reinforce good treatment of members belonging to the same group. Because of all this, people may act more kindly to neighbors in order to avoid social censure or to gain praise and reciprocal kindness from others in the community. Thus small and close communities are said to encourage altruism. This basic argument has been expanded and modified somewhat to apply to small, homogeneous national populations as well. Such an explanation has been offered, for example, to explain Denmark's protection of its Jews.[21]

This basic idea appears, in slightly different variations, in the writing of evolutionary biologists and economists. It will be discussed later and more fully when we consider the importance of groups and networks for altruism. At this point, let us simply take the idea at its face value and ask whether altruists originate more frequently from geographically small and cohesive communities than do rational actors. Do we frequently find a small or close-knit community in the background of the altruists in this study?

A close-knit community was critical for some but certainly not for all. Bert, for example, grew up in a small town near the Zeider Zee, where everyone knew everyone else and where ties were close. This was important to Bert, who told me that when he dreams, he "still dreams of that little town." But other altruists, such as Tony or Wilhelmina, were raised in the large cosmopolitan cities of Amsterdam and Berlin. They led sophisticated, international lifestyles similar to Margot's.[22] Furthermore, close community ties were also evident in the baseline data sample. One wealthy entrepreneur, for example, was raised in Oakland, where his grandmother ran a boardinghouse. He spoke at length about the sense of community he experienced around his grandmother's dinner table. But this did not encourage him to become a philanthropist. And there was no systematic variation in this regard as we moved along the conceptual continuum from self-interested to altruistic individuals. Rational actors do not seem to have been raised in communities that differ much from those in which altruists were raised. I therefore conclude that being raised in a close-knit community is not a critical determinant of altruism.[23]

CONCLUSION

What does the evidence presented above suggest about the general influence on altruism from socioeconomic characteristics such as religion, wealth, education, birth order, closeness of community, and family's social position in the community? None of these attributes, as significant as they may be for other important forms of social and political behavior, can be judged critical determinants of altruism.

In responding to a question about the impact of such sociocultural characteristics on altruism, both Margot and Tony laughingly referred to George Bernard Shaw's response to the aphorism that the rich are different from the rest of us: "Yes," Shaw said, "they have more money." We might equally quip that altruists are different from the rest of us: they are more altruistic. In terms of the social and cultural contexts from which they emerge, however, altruists are just like the rest of humanity: remarkably diverse.

CHAPTER 7

Economic Approaches to Altruism

> **Q.** *I present a lot of papers on altruism at conferences attended by economists. When I tell them about a woman who says giving is such a wonderful thrill, they'll say, "Sure. That's why she does it. She's buying something for herself."*
>
> **A.** Oh, no. Those people are very cynical. It comes back; what goes around comes around, yes. But that's not why you do it.
>
> —Isabelle, philanthropist

IF SOCIOCULTURAL attributes do not determine altruism, we must consider more subtle and sophisticated theoretical explanations. To assess the usefulness of these other approaches, I begin with economics, since economists frequently utilize concepts from other fields, such as evolutionary biology and psychology, and because economists have offered particularly rich and creative analyses of altruism.[1]

No matter how infrequently it occurs, the mere existence of altruism presents an important theoretical challenge for economic theory. Economists recognize this, and we find Adam Smith considering a phenomenon that resembles altruism long before Comte coined the actual term in the 1850s.[2] Recent economic work on altruism arose in response to Titmuss's 1971 work on why people donate blood. This publication attracted widespread attention and stimulated some economists to recognize the importance of altruism as a substantive phenomenon that did not fit easily into the "beloved model of utility maximization subject to constraints."[3] These economists, however, believed that existing economic concepts might elucidate this phenomenon; they did not see altruism as an anomaly that cast doubt on basic economic theory.[4]

In other words, contemporary economists follow their predecessors in treating altruism as a subtle variant of self-interest, and I consider a broad range of these economic explanations in this chapter to assess how well they explain the altruistic activity of the people I interviewed.[5] I begin with explanations suggesting that altruism is pursued for the rewards such behavior brings, rewards that range from honors and praise to more tangible material benefits. Altruism of this kind is often referred to as goods altruism. I then consider what economists call psychic benefits from altruism. Under this category, I review several different explanations for altruism: participation altruism, a taste for altruism, and altruism to alleviate guilt or to win approval. Although these explanations vary slightly, each essentially views altruism as behavior aimed not so much at benefitting the recipient as at making the altruist feel good about him or herself. Within the general economic framework of goal-directed behavior, such individuals are considered by economists to have unusual utility functions, but their behavior can still be fitted into the basic economic paradigm. Only their goals differ from those of more "normal," self-interested rational actors. I next consider the concept of reciprocal altruism, which treats altruism as behavior designed to engender similarly benevolent behavior. It is thus a short-term strategy designed to further long-term self-interest and has been offered by both economists and evolutionary biologists to explain both altruism and closely related behaviors, especially cooperation.[6]

All of these explanations come straight from economic theory and rely on the tools of economics for their intellectual power. But economists have also imaginatively and creatively borrowed concepts from other disciplines in order to explain altruism, and I consider these explanations as well.[7] Early economists, attempting to explain the existence of both self-interest and human benevolence, posited a dual utility function within each individual. This notion has been coupled in recent years with ideas from evolutionary biology concerning group versus individual selection and has led economists to ask whether people construct a kind of equilibrium model to balance their need to pursue self-interest with their need to pursue the interests of the group. This approach follows the early economic anthropologists who suggested that altruism is a luxury item, to be indulged in once more basic needs are obtained. Underlying all of these economic explanations is the idea that altruism results from a basic cost/benefit calculus.

My own empirical findings are, overall, quite striking. They suggest that economic models do have some explanatory value for quasi-altruistic activities by rational actors (such as giving, helping, or sharing) but much less for the purer forms of altruism.

GOODS ALTRUISM: HONORS, PRAISE, AND MATERIAL REWARDS

Let us consider first any obvious potential benefits that might accrue to the altruist from his or her behavior, focusing on the rescuers of Jews as the individuals whose acts best represent pure altruism. None of the rescuers were motivated by money. Indeed, it is a requirement for receiving the Yad Vashem medal that the recipient did not save Jews for monetary or material reward.[8] Most rescuers, in fact, lost money because of their efforts on behalf of Jews.

For example, many rescuers who were affluent before the war lost most of their wealth because of their activities on behalf of others.[9] At the other extreme, many poor rescuers lacked food for themselves and their families, yet they willingly shared the little they had with others. Two conversations illustrate the human costs of rescue efforts in terms of sheer hunger and deprivation. The first was a conversation with Alida's daughter, a Dutch woman who was a teenager during the war and who sat in during my interviews with her mother. After the last interview was over, the daughter drove me back to my hotel. On the way, she told me that it was only when she herself became a mother that she realized how difficult it must have been for Alida to constantly have to tell her children that there was no food for them because Alida was giving it to strangers. Alida had not mentioned this.

The second conversation occurred with Bethe, a German woman who during the war had lived in Berlin in a two-room apartment with her husband and three children, plus several rotating "guests" being hidden from the Nazis. Bethe tells a touching story about how she explained to her young son that it was important to share what little they had.

> One day our oldest—he was about eight—said to me, "Tell me, Mom, we haven't enough for ourselves to eat, but we have always guests. They eat here and live here, and we haven't enough for ourselves."

> *Q. And what did you answer?*

> **A.** I knew at this moment that I must now answer so he would understand that it was necessary. So I told him, "Listen, these are people, just like you and me. The possibility to live in an apartment has been taken away from them. They will be sent to the concentration camp." (I explained what a concentration camp is.) "And they don't get coupons [food ration coupons] anymore, and they don't know how to live. They would have to die or go to the concentration camp, and there they'll also die if we don't help them."

> Then he said, "This is quite different." And from then on he shared every apple, everything he received as a present.

This is not a woman who helps others for money or material gain; this is a woman who sees others as "people, just like you and me."

What is even more significant, perhaps, is the fact that the rescuers turned down offers of payment from rich Jews, only occasionally accepting enough money to buy food for their Jewish guests when the rescuers literally had no funds themselves. Bethe spoke directly of this and of her unwillingness to take money from the people staying with them, even though her family's own need was acute.

> *Q. You've mentioned before that the two [Jewish] girls had money. Did they ever offer you any?*

> **A.** No, they never offered us any; but on the other hand, we never asked for any. What we could offer them for food was so little that it would not have been right to ask. But even if we'd had more, I wouldn't have accepted.

A Dutchman also touched on this question of money.

Bert. The Underground had plenty money, and they promised to pay back everything that was lost. I paid one time on five tons of potatoes that I picked up, and I never got that money back, but I didn't care.[10]

Bert went on to voice particularly strong abhorrence of taking money from desperate people in their time of need.

Beyond this, rescuers were often entrusted with money by particular Jews; they deposited it in special bank accounts and returned it to the rightful owners or their heirs once the war was over. Tony, for example, tells how his family had what was called a "rag and bone man," a peddler who sold odds and ends and did various jobs for families in the neighborhood. The man was Jewish and asked Tony's parents to keep some of the valuable items he had accumulated over the years. They did so, and after the war, tried to find the man to return these items, mostly collectibles such as antique silver table pieces. Even after Tony and his parents discovered that the man and his family had been killed in the gas chambers, they continued to search for his relatives until they finally found someone to whom they could return the items. This occurred at a time when Tony's parents were experiencing economic hardship themselves, having lost most of their wealth during the war.

After the war, some governments offered rescuers sorely needed financial compensation for their activities on behalf of Jews. The Dutch government, for example, made such offers to the Dutch rescuers. But the people I spoke with refused such aid. None of this seems consistent with explanations suggesting that altruists are people interested in the possible tangible or material rewards for their altruism.

Nor were the altruists I interviewed interested in more psychological forms of reward, such as honors or praise. It must be remembered that many rescuers, particularly those from central Europe, suffered harsh social ostracism for their acts, even after the war.[11] None of the rescuers I spoke with experienced this postwar ostracism, except for Irene, who was called a "Jew lover" by some members of the Polish Catholic community in the United States because of her actions during the war. But several were the targets of subtle ridicule after the war and heard such sarcastic or disparaging comments as "There goes the big hero."[12]

Still, all the rescuers—and philanthropists and heroes—were very clear that they never expected praise for their actions. Indeed, they were frequently more embarrassed than appreciative of such acclaim. An extreme example of this is provided by one of the heroes I initially contacted. This hero was a man in his forties who liked to hike in the southern California hill country. On one of his hikes, he heard a mother screaming that a mountain lion had carried off her small child. The man ran to where the mother told him the lion had disappeared with the child and tracked the animal until he found it. The child, still alive, was held tightly in the lion's jaws. The man picked up a stick and attacked the animal, distracting the lion so that it dropped the little girl and attacked him instead. He managed to beat off the attack and returned the child, badly mauled but still alive, to the mother. As soon as he got the mother and child safely en route to the hospital, he disappeared.

The incident was reported by the grateful mother, and the man found himself the unwanted recipient of public notoriety and the Carnegie Hero Commission Award. He avoided as much attention as possible, refusing all interviews, including mine. His polite but firm refusal letter informed me that the local honors were unwanted, the national press and television attention unpleasant, and the public acclaim abhorrent.

For similar reasons, several of the rescuers I interviewed refused the Yad Vashem medal, because they felt that they had not done enough to help the Jewish victims of the Nazis.[13] Some philanthropists said they had occasionally allowed their names and financial gifts to be the focus of public attention, but always with reluctance and only because they were told that standing in the public spotlight might encourage other people to make similar contributions to the good cause.

Melissa speaks extensively of this in her narrative. Melissa's discussion is interesting for several reasons, all of which suggest that she cares more about the welfare of others than about her own self-interest. She notes, for example, that philanthropists have another self-interested motive, in addition to their natural modesty, that might make them averse to the publicity surrounding their gifts. Being publicly identified as having given large amounts of money advertises your wealth and may attract burglars or further solicitations. But neither this fear nor her desire for anonymity was enough to overcome Melissa's concern to help others. (Surprisingly, Melissa refers to the desire to avoid attention, rather than the desire for praise, as "that old vanity.")

Melissa noted several instances when she had not wanted publicity but had reluctantly agreed to have her gift publicized, only because the recipient (always an institution, such as a hospital or an arts center) argued that publicity might inspire others to give with similar generosity. This was, in fact, precisely what happened. Melissa recalled one newspaper story in which she had commented that she decided to give money to the Performing Arts Center because she was impressed with the facilities they had installed for the physically disabled. She was delighted to learn later that a disabled gentleman, having read the article, visited the center and then sent in *his* check for $1 million.

The altruist's usual reaction to public attention and praise, then, is one of aversion. One striking example of this comes from the postwar reaction of the people involved in the massive rescue of the Danish Jews. The following story is told by Knud, one of the organizers of the rescue.[14]

On the 29th of September, actually just before Rosh Hashana, we found out from a German shipping expert named Duckwitz that there were three or four hundred police troops from Germany coming into the port of Copenhagen. They were sent to arrest all the Jews in Denmark. Duckwitz informed the Danish prime minister about it.

All the Underground newspapers found out about it at the same time, so we knew everything that was going on. There were roughly seventy-five hundred [Jews] in Copenhagen, and people got all of them out of their own apartments. It was a lot of trouble, because in 1943 Jews didn't believe the Germans would do such a thing. They didn't believe it was serious, because they had heard so many rumors before. But at this time, [the Underground papers said], "This time we know it's going to happen."

Even with all the police troops coming in from Germany and the Gestapo working and everything else, the Germans caught only about four hundred Jews. Most of the seventy-five hundred were moved into apartments of friends, into churches, into schoolhouses, into anything as long as it was out of their own homes. Almost all the Danish population worked in order to protect them [the Jews]. During the next ten or fourteen days, we managed to send most of them over to Sweden. That was where I as a person started my export service of Jews. I became a rescuer.

Knud then told how the Danish war veterans as a group decided that they would not accept individual Yad Vashem medals, asking instead that any Danish awards be made to the country as a whole. I asked Knud why he felt they did not need any more honors, despite this most extraordinary and historically singular accomplishment. Knud said simply, "We had honor enough."

For all the altruists I interviewed, whatever honors they later received—and it is important to remember that, at least for the rescuers, these honors were usually awarded more than thirty years after the altruistic act—were peripheral. For most, they were unexpected; for a surprising number, unwanted. While the majority were pleased by them, they had nothing to do with the intent of, the motive for, the original act of altruism. For no rescuer was the honor ever central.

For altruists, the act is the end. "Seeing the joy that a gift could give" was how one philanthropist described it. Saving someone's life was reward enough for rescuers and heroes. The Polish rescuer Irene captured this succinctly, articulating the difference between the pleasure felt now in looking back on the act and the emotion felt at the time.

> I did not realize then, because I didn't do it for money or glory or anything. But the older I get, the more I feel I am very rich. I would not change anything. It's a wonderful feeling to know that today many people are alive and some of them married and have their children, and that their children will have children because I did have the courage and the strength.

Margot expressed even more forcefully and colorfully her lack of interest in a reward for her rescue activities.

Q. *Many people would say that what you did was an extraordinarily good deed and that you should be rewarded.*

A. That's what they say now. The hell with it. I don't want any reward. You do things because you want to, because you got no choice, and not to have people praise you or make some celebration.

This was the typical attitude of altruists toward rewards or praise for their behavior. As Isabelle so succinctly expressed it, "That's not why you do it. It comes from the heart."

ALTRUISM AS A PSYCHIC GOOD

There is a story told about Thomas Hobbes passing a beggar and giving the man money. Hobbes's companion comments on this with some surprise: Hobbes had argued so convincingly that people pursue their individual self-interest, and yet he himself had just demonstrated such charity to another. Hobbes hastens to correct his companion's misimpression, explaining that he gave to the poor beggar not to alleviate the beggar's suffering but rather because it made Hobbes too uncomfortable to see the poor wretch in such a miserable condition.[15] Many economists, following Hobbes's lead, have developed various explanations for altruism centering on the idea that altruistic behavior occurs not so much to benefit the recipient as to produce certain psychological effects in the altruist. This explanation essentially treats altruism as a mechanism to produce feelings of psychic good: it is the altruist's feelings that are critical, not the recipient's improved situation, which in effect has been reduced to a means to the altruist's self-centered end.

Altruism as psychic good constitutes one of the most intellectually powerful, and at the same time frustratingly tautological, explanations for altruism. It is extremely difficult to operationalize the concept in a way that allows us to design a test by which it can be reliably accepted or rejected. At the general level of psychic utility, about all we can ask is whether the altruistic act did lessen the personal discomfort at viewing another's suffering or make the altruist feel good about him or herself.

Were altruistic activities pursued because they made altruists feel better about themselves? Did they affect the way altruists felt about themselves? The short answer to these questions is no. Altruism is not pursued for the psychic benefit it brings the altruist. While I found psychic benefit may enter into a calculus affecting charitable action by entrepreneurs, the farther we moved toward pure altruism on the conceptual continuum, the less important such a calculus became.

When asked how their rescue activities affected them, most heroes and rescuers noted no effect, insisting that they really had not done anything extraordinary enough to influence how they felt about themselves. A German rescuer living in Holland during the war, Margot was arrested six times by the Gestapo. Yet she insisted she had done nothing praiseworthy. Her terse words distill the general attitude among rescuers.

Q. *How did your rescue activities make you feel about yourself?* (Margot shakes her head.) *It didn't affect you?*

A. Nothing special, no.

To the extent that there was any psychic income attached to rescue activity, it appeared to have occurred well after the fact and took the form of simply being pleased that the people had been saved. It was not a motivating factor in the rescue action itself.

In contrast, I found clear evidence of psychic gratification connected with the charitable giving done by entrepreneurs. As a very general rule, both philanthropists and entrepreneurs tend to give primarily (or exclusively) to people they know, to local causes, or to groups with which they have some connection and where they can see the payoff, rather than to unknown people far away. Billy says explicitly that he gives mostly to kids he knows from the local high school. He mentioned seeing ads on television about famine in Africa or "some other faraway place" but says that even though he is moved by such ads, he never picks up the phone to send in money and is much more likely to give to a local charity instead. I will argue in chapter 10 that this preference for local giving stems partly from a feeling of connectedness with the person helped. In addition, rational actors may enjoy giving more when they can see the pleasant effect their gifts bring. This interpretation would be consistent with the psychic utility argument.

Beyond generalized feelings of pleasure, how does altruism make the altruist feel about him or herself?[16] Unlike heroes and rescuers (people farther toward pure altruism on our conceptual continuum), philanthropists and entrepreneurs noted feeling good about themselves when they gave money. Warren, an entrepreneur who also had given a good deal of money to a local college (and who therefore fell somewhere between the entrepreneurs and the philanthropists on the conceptual continuum), said that he got a "warm, fuzzy" feeling from his giving. But philanthropists always insisted this is not the main reason they give.

Both Isabelle and Herbert, for example, declared quite explicitly that any good feelings they might derive from their philanthropy are an unexpected consequence and not a cause of it. Isabelle's answer lent particular insight on the limitations of the economist's approach to altruism. She is married to a man who owns a well-known fur company, and her social life in consequence brings her into frequent contact with glamorous movie stars and celebrities. But instead of luxuriating in this social whirl, Isabelle spends most of her time raising funds for and working with children who are emotionally and physically abused. I asked Isabelle to explain why she gives away so much money and time, when most of the people she knows do not. Her answer did give clear voice to the economist's explanation of giving, the idea that it makes the altruist feel good. "It's a thrill," she said. But her answer went beyond this and corrects the economist's misleading interpretation of such expressions of joy.

> **Q.** *Let me ask you something. I present a lot of papers on altruism at conferences which economists attend. I'll tell them that I talked to a woman who says that giving is such a wonderful thrill. Then they will say, "Sure. That's why she does it. She's buying something for herself."*
>
> **A.** No, I don't. I wasn't looking to buy anything. I did it because I wanted to. I never realized that I would get that thrill. But when you look at a child, a little girl who was raped by her father and her uncle and who came to our camp, and she sits on a swing, sucking her thumb, a baby and frightened. Then you approach, just to put your arms around her. You hug her and you kiss her and you laugh. And all of a sudden, maybe not all of a sudden, maybe four weeks or four months later, a smile appears and she will play, even though she's frightened. You lighted a candle. This child can see that there is good in the world. You don't do it for yourself.
>
> Oh, no. Those people are very cynical. It comes back; what goes around comes around, yes. But that's not why you do it. It comes from the soul.

Isabelle's response was not uncommon among altruists; and, at least for me, it was not one that could easily be categorized as supporting the economic interpretation of altruism as a veiled form of buying something—even good feelings—for oneself. There is a subtle but critical distinction in Isabelle's answer that removes her altruism from psychic utility and instead suggests that she simply sees the world quite differently from the way most rational actors, and probably most economists, see it.

Although fine distinctions are difficult to draw, on this dimension philanthropists appear to fall somewhere between the typical rational actor and the rescuer or hero. In contrast to most entrepreneurs, the heroes and rescuers helped total strangers, not local people or acquaintances, as Billy did. Most rescuers shrugged off their rescue actions as rather ordinary. Only one rescuer articulated anything even resembling psychic utility: "I was only proud inside," Wilhelmina, a Berlin rescuer, told us, "just for me." Most of the rescuers responded as Margot did when asked how her actions made her feel about herself: "Nothing special. No big deal."

Let us now consider the most frequently discussed variations of the psychic utility explanation: (1) participation altruism, (2) altruism as a taste or preference, (3) altruism as a way to alleviate guilt, and (4) altruism to win approval of critical others.

Participation Altruism

Both economists and evolutionary biologists utilize a concept called "participation altruism." What is important in participation altruism is the altruist's part in causing another's good fortune and not the increased welfare of the recipient. Let me clarify this through an example. Fred is drowning in a lake. Both Ginger and I notice this and try to help him, but Ginger is the actual person who saves Fred's life. According to the logic of participation altruism, I would not rejoice as much in the outcome as I would have if I had been the one who saved him. My participation in Fred's rescue is key, not Fred's rescue itself.

This is only one illustration of participation altruism. Do altruists feel this way? Is it important for an altruist to be the one who helps? Or do altruists just care that the person in need receives help? My findings here are very clear. Altruists do not help others because they crave the joy of being the agent of relief. They care about the other's welfare. A typical response follows.

Q. *Was it important to you that you were the one who saved the people?*

Margot (rescuer). Not at all. They just had to be saved.

This point of view was echoed by other rescuers, some of whom looked at me incredulously when I asked if it mattered more that they were the ones who helped people or that the people be helped.

Q. *Was it of importance to you that the two young girls and the mother with her son were being helped, or was it important to you that it was you who did it?*

Bethe (Berlin rescuer). That they were being helped. It was not important that we did it. But because they came to us and had nobody else, we helped them.

In general, what matters most to altruists is that needy people receive help, not that the motives of the helper be pure. I asked rescuers how they felt about people (including Gestapo agents) who helped Jews late in the war only as protective insurance against the coming Nazi defeat. All the rescuers I quizzed said it was sad that such acts were undertaken only to avoid retribution but that the more important thing was that people were saved, not that they were saved for the right reasons. This same attitude was also evident among the heroes and philanthropists.

A Taste for Altruism

Is there in some people an underlying taste or preference for altruistic behavior? Do altruists simply have unusual utility functions, in which the welfare of others is substituted for their own individual welfare as the goal of their behavior? To examine this variant of the economic explanation of altruism, I began by determining whether any of the particular altruists I interviewed engaged in altruistic behavior frequently enough to reveal an underlying preference for altruism. I asked whether they had performed altruistic acts other than the ones that had brought them to my attention. When I did so, I found surprisingly consistent patterns: people who were altruists at age fifty were also altruists at age twenty. Although the mode of altruism might vary over time, the tendency itself was evidenced at an early age and appeared to remain constant throughout life. "I've always been a person who liked to give, and I've kept that till today." said one of the Berlin rescuers. "All the money I've had, I gave to these social places. I send a lot of money [to good causes]."

Another clear example of lifelong altruism, as we saw in chapter 4, is the heroine Lucille. Lucille was only six or eight years old when she helped a little black girl who wanted to ride a segregated bus in Arkansas. During World War II, Lucille went to the rescue of a Sudanese who was pushed into the river by a bigoted American soldier. Later she took extensive part in the civil rights movement in Arkansas, even though she was snubbed by family and friends, menaced by governmental officials such as Governor Faubus, received death threats from the Ku Klux Klan, and was physically attacked by numerous people on several occasions. In short, a considerable career of altruism lay behind the particular act, late in life, that brought her to the attention of the Carnegie Hero Commission.

Indeed, the people I interviewed had engaged in many noteworthy acts of altruism besides those that drew my attention to these particular individuals in the first place. A surprising number, like the Dutch rescuers Bert and Tony, had saved people from drowning. Mac, a philanthropist, has twice plucked distressed swimmers from the water. His behavior afterward is not atypical. Each time, when asked for his name by the grateful person he had just saved, Mac gave them a phony one, once identifying himself as the colorful "Captain Crunch."

Drowning episodes are not the only occasion for altruism, of course. One philanthropist cares for an elder brother and a sister who has emotional and drinking problems; he has cared for the sister since he was in his early twenties. Even before she had any money, Isabelle was so moved by the plight of emotionally damaged children that she found the time "to do the only thing I could do, make a terrific spaghetti sauce," for 75¢ and then sell it for $1.50. This small effort blossomed into an international food festival to benefit children. Although Isabelle's pet project (a children's camp funded by this money) recently had to close down because of extensive government regulations, Isabelle continues to raise money for emotionally and physically abused children and to act as mentor for several ghetto children who need attention and love.

This pattern of care and nurturance was also evident among rescuers.[17] After he moved to this country, Bert raised several children in informal adoptive arrangements, with no monetary compensation. Knowing the modest economic circumstances of Bert's family, I appreciated the hardship and sacrifice this entailed on everyone's part. Bert continued this pattern until the end of his life. Other rescuers demonstrated the same consistency. The Berlin rescuer Bethe told of caring for her baby brother after their mother had died; she was only a young girl herself at the time. Maruska continues to fight for the rights of Turks and other foreign workers in contemporary Germany. Many similar examples could be cited.

Finally, many rescuers—Margot, Tony, Otto, and Ursula to name but a few—helped hide political prisoners as well as Jews during the war. Both Irene and Maruska specifically identified their actions in saving Jews as part of a lifetime struggle against persecution. This idea was expressed most forcefully by Maruska, the imperious Silesian countess we met earlier. Maruska swam across a large lake one night to take an old woman to safety and then swam back the next night to fetch the old lady her belongings. In refusing praise for her actions, Maruska pungently articulates her general attitude toward helping others.

I belong to a class of people who have been vigilant from youth on. . . . When somebody by nature has a relatively strong personality, then he also should use it to defend and to protect people who don't have this [kind of personality].

Q. Your help for persecuted Jews— [Maruska interrupts]

A. I'd like to generalize this. I helped persecuted people. Whether they were Jews, politically persecuted people, or otherwise persecuted was not important to me at all. I'd like to emphasize this. Here in Berlin-Kreuzberg [a working-class section of Berlin, populated by foreign workers today], I live in a corner which is explosive too. When policemen act evilly during their operations, which happens quite often, I'm always ready to go down on the street and to defend the people. I've always been doing this.

Q. So you are still on the side of the persecuted?

A. Yes, of course. You cannot just look at all this and do nothing. During my whole life, I've always been intervening in things I found unjust. As a child, I already acted like this.

All of this suggests that altruism develops into a consistent pattern of behavior, that there is indeed such a thing as the "altruistic personality," in which the habit of helping others has become so ingrained over the years that the helping response is virtually automatic.[18] While the existence of such an altruistic personality does not constitute definitive confirmation of a psychic goods argument, it is certainly consistent with such an explanation and fits in with the idea that certain people may have a taste for altruism.

Altruism as a Way to Alleviate Guilt

Perhaps, on the other hand, altruism is undertaken to relieve guilt for past actions—another variant of the psychic goods explanation. If I have behaved badly to someone in the past, I may wish to atone for this by engaging in compensatingly benevolent action toward that same person, toward a similar individual, or even toward a random stranger.

I asked all the altruists whether they felt their actions would, or were intended to, atone for past wrongs. Not one person in the sample said they acted to alleviate past guilt. Only one person, a philanthropist called Herbert, came at all close to explaining his actions in terms of guilt. In response to my inquiry about whether guilt had anything to do with his charitable giving, Herbert responded that he did not think so but that his psychiatrist had once told him he suffered from a ghetto conscience. I asked what this meant. Herbert said he was not sure but that he supposed it meant that he felt guilty about having so much when others had so little. This does not seem like the same thing as being motivated by guilt over past wrongs, although it may be a more ambient form of the same phenomenon. But Herbert was the only altruist who made any place for guilt as a factor, and it seems significant that it was his psychiatrist, and not Herbert himself, who suggested that his behavior was motivated by guilt. This may be an instance of an outsider who is a rational actor himself—a psychiatrist used to encouraging people to take care of themselves, perhaps even to be more self-interested—having difficulty understanding the altruist's genuine desire to help others. A nonaltruist may be trying to place the altruist's actions into a conceptual framework that is comprehensible for the other rational actors with whom he is more familiar and—perhaps—more comfortable. In the rest of Herbert's interview he talked at great length about the tremendous joy he experiences in being able to help people and how giving makes him feel part of the creative life force. This was the main explanation he himself gave for his altruism, and the motif of guilt is nowhere apparent.

Altruism to Win Approval

Finally, do altruists help people in order to win approval from critical others? This may be stretching the psychic goods argument a bit but since this argument is advanced by psychologists and economists and bears some relationship to the psychic goods argument, let us consider it here briefly.

I found no one at all in any of my samples who said they act altruistically in order to win the approval of someone, even an important role model. The response of the Berlin rescuer Wilhelmina on this point is representative and captures the important quiet, hidden quality of much altruism.[19]

Q. *Was the opinion of others important to you? Of people on whose judgment you set great store?*

Wilhelmina. But nobody knew about that. Never. Later, I became an "Unbesungener Held" [Unsung Hero, an award given by the German government], and I thought then, "Great, now you've got this record of honor." I always took much pride in that. But I never made use of it that I had this or so. Never. I was only proud inside, just for me.

I interpret "proud inside" to mean not so much that Wilhelmina gloried in doing a good deed that others would approve of but rather that she knew she had been true to herself, that she had not been found wanting when tested by life. This seems significantly different from action designed to win the approval of others.

If we consider the narratives of Melissa and Lucille, we find the same lack of connection between their altruism and a desire for approval from those they looked to as role models. Melissa had her grandfather as a role model, but most of her philanthropy occurred after his death. The same was true for Lucille and her grandmother. While people often internalize a need for approval from relatives long dead, when I asked about this, neither Melissa nor Lucille—or any other altruist—mentioned a connection between their altruism and wanting approval from a role model.

Q. *Were you at all concerned that you might lose the respect of somebody whose opinion mattered to you if you didn't act? Was that at all a factor in your decision? You mentioned that your grandmother had been so important to you. Was that at all relevant, how she would feel about you if you did not act?*

Lucille. No. It didn't matter to me whether anybody approved or believed something else. I had to do what I believed. But I've never felt, "Well, this is what Grandmother believes too." I just knew that I had to do it.

Any connection between role models and altruism is more the traditional idea of another person providing the altruist with a pattern of behavior that he or she now imitates.[20] This again differs subtly from behaving in a certain way *because* you know the role model will like it and will then like you because you have followed the prescribed course of behavior.

Taken as a whole, then, the above evidence fails to support the idea of altruism as a psychic good. Altruism was not engaged in to alleviate guilt or to make the altruist feel good about him or herself. There was no evidence that altruists were seeking to atone for past wrongs through their meritorious deeds. And all were quite clear that the good feelings they had as a result of their altruism were the unexpected and unnecessary consequences, not the motivating causes of the altruistic acts.

How do we assess this negative evidence concerning altruism as a psychic good, in light of the fact that altruists are consistently altruistic? This consistency constitutes the main evidence in favor of the psychic goods theory. But there are other, more convincing explanations for such consistency. The Oliners argue, for example, that the habits of helping begin so early in life and become so rote for the altruist that we can speak of an altruistic personality. Identity construction and view of self in relation to others offer yet other ways of understanding repeated altruistic conduct. Given these alternative explanations, the evidence in support of the psychic goods theory of altruism can be judged only mixed at best. I suspect that Herbert's story about his psychiatrist provides a clue concerning the popularity of the psychic goods argument for economists. Rational actors—be they economists or psychiatrists—who assume that the rest of the world consists of individuals motivated as they are will explain their own quasi-altruistic acts (such as Billy's loans to friends) in terms which they can comprehend. The idea of doing good for others in order to feel good yourself makes sense for many people, especially those who themselves resemble the rational actors at the heart of economics. But this is not why altruists act as they do.

RECIPROCITY

Both economists and evolutionary biologists explain altruism through desires for reciprocal behavior: I will do something nice for you now in the hope that you will treat me in a similar fashion later. My so-called altruism thus is actually a short-term strategy designed to achieve my own long-term betterment. The welfare of the recipient is secondary.

Does such implicit bartering occur? I touched briefly on this topic earlier and noted then that I found no evidence of altruists engaging in altruistic behavior designed to encourage a return in kind. But I did find such behavior among the entrepreneurs, a fact that may help explain why economists (used to dealing with rational actors) find the concept of reciprocal altruism plausible. For altruists, however, the attitude toward reciprocity is aptly summarized by Melissa: "You give because you want to, not because you want anything in return." Like the entrepreneurs. Melissa expressed some concern that her gifts be used constructively by the recipients. But she added a critical caveat: "To be concerned with their response, to me, that's not philanthropy. That's making a loan."

This attitude contrasts significantly with Billy's. Like Melissa, when Billy gives money, he cares about how his gift is used, but he seems more concerned with equity, with being treated fairly in "the deal," than is Melissa. And his

"gifts" resemble loans more than the unconditional giving in which philanthropists engage. This was well illustrated in the story Billy told in chapter 2
about once loaning a friend money and asking for the friend's car as security.
When the loan remained unpaid, Billy demanded the car, even though he
did not want or need it, because it was a point of honor that the money be
returned.

Billy also said that on the occasions when he funds a local high school
student to go to college, he expects repayment and becomes annoyed if he
does not get at least a small token amount sometime after the person gradu-
ates. In explaining this, Billy couches his answer in terms of identity, something I believe is significant and which I discuss more fully later. Billy's feelings about repayment, wanting gratitude for his aid, and helping only those
who deserve it are not unusual for entrepreneurs.

Billy's attitude toward charity probably makes sense to economists, but it is
not the attitude evident among philanthropists, who would agree with Melissa
in describing Billy's form of aid as loans, not philanthropy. The same is true for
heroes and for rescuers, all of whom insisted that they did not engage in
altruism with the expectation of any delayed reward or reciprocal benefit. It is
also important to remember that both the rescuers and most of the heroes
risked their lives by their deeds. It is difficult to use the idea of reciprocal
altruism to explain acts that might cost the altruist his or her life; receiving
repayment in kind seems largely irrelevant when one is dead.

DUAL UTILITIES

Early political economists used the idea of dual utility functions to explain the
fact that the same individuals would sometimes behave in a self-interested
fashion and at other times as if they wanted to maximize group welfare or the
welfare of others.[21] Many early theorists argued that human beings possess a
dual nature: one egoistical and interested only in the welfare of the self and the
other more public-spirited and able to put the welfare of others on an equal
footing with his or her own. Do altruists divide their world into two different
spheres, one in which they are dictated to by self-interest and another in
which they are guided by other-directed concerns? I found some evidence of
this for entrepreneurs and philanthropists but little for heroes and rescuers.

It is important to remember that almost all people do give some limited
amounts to charity, if only to the kinds of local requests that come from one's
children collecting funds to "save the earth" or a co-worker collecting for the
United Way.[22] Entrepreneurs, for example, do indeed give of their time and
money, but I found that those in my sample uniformly give to drives and
causes with which they have a local connection. Billy's coaching of his son's
football team typifies the volunteer activities in which entrepreneurs typically
engage: there is usually a close connection to the activity or to a person en-

gaged in the activity. Such actions can be explained easily through the traditional self-interested utility function.

The same pattern is evident, although less clearly, in philanthropists. Melissa's charities all have a personal connection, often through her husband (the charities associated with McDonald's) or daughter (those serving disabled children). The same is true of Warren's gift of $1 million to a local college. Herbert considers himself a political liberal and gives to causes liberals would generally support, such as the homeless. In common with rational actors, none of these people gives away so much money that they become poor themselves. It is understandable, then, that economists have fastened on the idea of dual utilities as an explanation for altruism. But it does not in fact adequately account for the behavior of altruists in general.

The rescuers offer the most dramatic refutation of the dual utility argument. All the rescuers knew they were endangering their family members through their rescue efforts. Their parents and children, their spouses or lovers might be killed because of their endeavors. Indeed, several people I interviewed *did* lose loved ones because of their rescue activities. Margot, for example, had met and fallen in love with a German named Albert, and they were engaged to be married. Albert knew nothing of Margot's rescue work and was neither politically involved nor politically astute. One of the times Margot was arrested, Albert went to her father to see what they could do to get Margot out of prison. Her father advised Albert to do nothing, but Albert went to the Gestapo anyway, to find out why his fiancée had been arrested. Figuring that Albert would know about his fiancée's activities, the Gestapo questioned him. The questioning turned into torture, and Albert was eventually beaten to death. This was one of the most difficult things Margot had to bear, but she did not stop her rescue efforts, even when it was made painfully obvious that her succor of others had cut deeply into what an economist might view as her own self-interest. Rescuers were not people who balanced their own needs with those of others.

Resource Hypothesis

Economists, psychologists, and evolutionary biologists have suggested that altruism may be a luxury item, something to be indulged in only after more basic, self-interested needs are satisfied. Another variation on this theme, frequently referred to as the resource hypothesis, suggests that people strike some balance between what they are willing to do for others and what they do to benefit themselves or their families. This relates closely to the dual utility argument just discussed.[23] Does this occur? Do people wait to give to others only after their own basic needs have been met satisfactorily? Or does the fact that they have given a certain amount then encourage them to give less, according to an internal equilibrium model? These are variations on the resource hypothesis. Working against this idea is the logical possibility that having more resources actually encourages people to give more, thus setting up the kinds of habits of giving that the Oliners (1988) identify as an altruistic personality. This kind of phenomenon would *not* be consistent with the resource hypothesis.

What do the narratives suggest? Overall, the resource hypothesis works best for entrepreneurs, who did demonstrate concern that their own needs and those of their families be met before they gave to others. Ray and Bradley gave little money, and Jordan speaks of "always keeping something back" for himself and his family. The hypothesis has a more limited usefulness in explaining the behavior of philanthropists. Many philanthropists (such as Melissa) appear to engage in a vague balancing act in which their own—or their family's—needs are considered, if not first, then at least on a par with the needs of others. This tendency decreased, however, as we approached pure altruism. What this suggests to me is that earlier works that describe such a phenomenon are correct in using it to explain quasi-altruistic or other-directed activities among typical rational actors.

But does this phenomenon occur among altruists themselves? No. The more altruistic an individual is, the less useful is the resource hypothesis. This is clearly evident in the four narratives presented earlier. Consider evidence from the most dramatic refutation of the resource hypothesis: rescuers of Jews. None of the rescuers I interviewed exhibited a pattern of allocating resources between individual needs and the needs of others.[24] Indeed, rescuers appear to make no distinction between their own needs and those of others.

The general context of war meant that everyone experienced at least some shortages and physical hardship. This was especially true during the last year of the war, often referred to as the Hunger Winter because of the harsh weather and scarcity of food all over Europe, but particularly in the occupied countries, where the Nazis increasingly plundered food and sent it back to Germany. The limitations on ration coupons meant that rescue activities drained away the already scarce supplies of food and fuel.

Beyond this shared wartime limitation on resources, however, there was great variation in the individual resources particular rescuers brought to their situation. Otto was upper-middle-class, as were Wilhelmina and Ursula. Margot was wealthy while she lived in Germany; her father had been head of General Motors for Europe, and Margot was raised in great luxury. In contrast, Alida had eight children who often went hungry to feed their Jewish guests. Bethe was quite poor, living with her husband and three small children in one room so that their Jewish guests could have the other room. Perhaps the most extreme conditions were experienced by Tony and Knud (both condemned to death and living underground), by Irene (living the precarious existence of a slave laborer), and by Otto after he was arrested and placed in a concentration camp.

The critical point is threefold: (1) rescuers had widely varied resources; (2) rescuers did not attend first to their own needs and then to the needs of others, as a traditional allocation-of-resources explanation would predict; and (3) rescuers did not appear to engage in the kind of balancing of needs which the resource hypothesis describes, in which altruistic giving on one side of the equation allows (indeed, almost requires) the rescuer to turn attention to the other side and then pursue self-interest. I therefore conclude that the resource hypothesis does not explain altruism when we examine the situation of rescuers in terms of two of the most basic measures of resources: food and finances.

But what about other types of resources? Few rescuers had tremendous resources in any of the other areas we might judge significant. Irene was young, away from home for the first time, and separated from her family after the partition of Poland. (She never did see her parents again and did not see her sisters until the 1980s, when she failed to recognize the "old women" waiting at the airport as her younger sisters.) Raped, beaten, and left for dead in the snow by Russian soldiers, she experienced some of the most traumatic aspects of war. It would be difficult to paint a portrait of anyone less likely to find either the material or the psychological resources necessary to risk her life to save strangers. Moreover, even when Irene began her rescue activities, she had no physical resources of her own, since she was in a slave labor camp, surrounded by German soldiers and living in one tiny room behind a kitchen in a diner where the soldiers were fed. Yet she managed to hide twelve Jews in the laundry closet and smuggle food to others who were hidden in the woods.

The same was true for other rescuers. Leonie was only seventeen, staying with her sister in Rotterdam and cut off from her home in Maastricht, which had been liberated by the Allies. To begin her rescue activities, she had to argue with her older sister, in whose home she was a guest and on whom she was dependent. Knud and Tony were in hiding, sleeping wherever they could. Otto continued his rescue activities even after he was sent to the concentration camp, bribing guards and Gestapo officials alike. When I asked him about the riskiness of this, he responded that you had to learn to be a good psychologist to know which guard or official might be susceptible to a little flattery, which to bribes, and which to intimidation.

I could continue, but the point should be clear. All of the rescuers endeavored to help others even though they lacked what the traditional hierarchies of needs suggest are the apparent prerequisites for selfless action: food, fuel, physical safety, and emotional support from families or friends.

Costs and Benefits

Finally, let us consider what may be the central concept underpinning all economic analysis: the idea that people think in terms of costs and benefits. Indeed, this idea lies close to the heart of all disciplines and social theories that assume people are self-interested.[25] In its extreme form, it proposes that most human social behavior can be explained by assuming people pursue their goals, subject to what economists call information and opportunity costs.[26] People are further said to assess these various components in terms of a rational calculus, which exists and is critical regardless of whether or not the actor is conscious that he or she is pursuing it.[27]

Is this theory accurate? Can it explain altruism? Are altruists aware of both the costs and benefits of their actions before they act? Do they engage in this kind of rational calculus? I spent a great deal of time during all my interviews trying to answer these questions, and the answer is unequivocal: no. Rational actors may engage in cost/benefit analysis when they assess whether or not to help others or give money to charity. Altruists do not.

Begin with the two purest cases of altruism in this study. Both the heroes and the rescuers knew the dangers and the potential costs of their actions; yet uniformly these costs were considered irrelevant. Both the heroes and the rescuers seemed surprisingly oblivious to risks to their own safety. Their attitude was uniformly very matter-of-fact: "Yes, you knew there were costs, but so what? One does these things." I heard over and over responses like the following.

Q. *So you were quite aware of the big risk you took?*

Wilhelmina (Berlin rescuer). Yes, yes. Of course.

Q. *Have you always been conscious of the possible risks and consequences of your actions?*

Maruska (Berlin rescuer). Of course. It would have been a bit naive not to know the consequences all this implied.

No one expressed this more eloquently or with more gentleness and compassion than Bethe, the Berlin rescuer who hid Jewish people in her home even though she had three small children who were endangered by her actions.

We knew what could happen. If they had caught us, we would have been taken away. The children would have been taken away. We absolutely knew this. But when they're standing at the door, and their life is threatened, what should you do in this situation? You could never do that [turn them away].

Yes, rescuers knew the costs of their actions; there were far too many public executions and disappearances not to know the punishment for hiding Jews. The costs were simply never relevant to the rescuers' efforts to save lives. This was so even in the most extreme cases, where the costs were most painfully evident. Irene's behavior the day she was caught hiding Jews is both telling and typical. On this particular day, Irene had just been forced to witness an execution of a Polish family caught and punished because they were hiding Jews. To this day, when she describes the scene, Irene recalls and relives the anguish she felt as she listened to the cries of the children suffering the slow death of strangulation by wire. She noted the signs at the execution that said, "This is what happens to people who help Jews." She was so affected by this that she returned home "shook up, white like a sheet." Yet when she herself was caught that same afternoon hiding Jews in the villa of a German major, her main plea to the major was to let the Jews go. She begs that they not be blamed for something she has done. Such behavior is so extraordinary that even to comment on it seems to risk demeaning it somehow. To explain it away by saying that Irene was merely willing to pay the cost, or that the benefit to her outweighed the potential costs, seems to miss the essential quality of Irene's behavior.

I did address this question of costs and benefits directly, however, and when I did so, Tony articulated what I believe is the subtle but critical distinction here, one that explains how rescuers could be aware of the costs at some level and yet remain totally unaffected by them at a deeper one. Tony explained that the potential costs—the danger, the tension, the inconvenience—all these things were viewed tactically. They affected *how*, but not *whether*, a rescuer might proceed with the rescue activity. Such considerations were irrelevant to the undertaking. In the following excerpt our conversation seems to wander a bit and takes on an unusual quality as Tony compares the dangers of rescuing someone during World War II to the dangers of driving in Los Angeles in the 1990s. But I include the entire conversation because it is important in documenting the rescuers' awareness of their perilous position and in assuring the reader that I am not quoting selectively.

Q. *Let me ask you a little bit about the costs of your actions. Were you conscious of the potential costs for you and for your family?*

A. Yes. As I said, those are decisions everybody makes every single day of their lives. Anytime you drive to downtown Los Angeles, you totally accept random challenges. You don't give it a second thought. [*Shrugs*] Sometimes you think about it a little bit.

Q. *But what you did was a little more dangerous than going to downtown Los Angeles.*

A. Yes; it is more dangerous. Though actually you don't realize how dangerous driving is.

Q. *You didn't think about the risks when you tried to save someone?*

A. We were cautious. It's just like you are in driving. You say, "I'm taking a risk driving there. It's dangerous driving at rush hour. Maybe I won't take the freeway." You take certain precautions.

Q. *The idea that you could be losing your life for this, it never really affected you?*

A. Oh, it sunk in at times. But it's just like flying. I'm going to fly [next week]. I know we've had three major air crashes, and I really don't like flying. But what am I going to do about it? Not go on the trip?

Q. *So does a calculus of the risks have any relevance to your decision to undertake the action?*

A. Not too terribly much.

Q. *Let me be sure I understand you. Is what I'm hearing you say is that there is a conscious calculus that goes on, but that it's a tactical kind? This calculus does not really have any impact on the decision to help other people, to rescue people. Is that what you are saying?*

A. Yes. It is.

After my conversation with Tony helped focus my attention on this distinction between tactical concerns and the basic decision to save another's life, I was able to pose this question more pointedly and articulately to other rescuers. All of them agreed with Tony's assessment that this distinction was critical. I asked Margot about it, drawing her attention to the fact that she had lost her children for a while because of her first imprisonment and that she had carried on an extended affair with the Gestapo commander for Amsterdam in order to get information of value to both the Jews and the Resistance. These "costs" for me would be unbearable; they were the most difficult for me to understand, because they were extended over a long period and thus could not be explained away as impulsive and spontaneous. Yet Margot insisted that she never thought of them.

Q. *Do you mean to tell me that the entire time you were in prison, the entire time you're sleeping with this guy, you never ever stopped to think about the costs of what you were doing?*

A. I never even thought of it.

Q. *You never asked yourself, "Why me? Why do I have to do this?"*

A. I only wondered what had happened to my kids. But after that, I never gave it a thought. It was war, honey, and everybody killed everybody. You didn't have time to think: yes, no, count your buttons, and all that crap. No way!

When I asked the heroes about costs calculations, I heard similar responses. Lucille's is typical. Such considerations were so irrelevant to her that she seemed surprised when I asked her about this and at first did not know what I meant.

Q. *How conscious a decision do you make when you do something like this? You're particularly interesting for me to talk with, because you not only rescued someone, like the Sudanese man or the girl who was being raped, but you also took part in a more ongoing kind of commitment to other people through your civil rights activities. How conscious are you of potential costs for you and your family when you decide to do this kind of thing? And is there a difference between the kind of on-the-spot rescuing that you did for the young girl as opposed to a more ongoing kind of commitment in the civil rights movement?*

A. I guess now that you put it that way—and I've never thought of that, and I may have been wrong—I never thought what it would cost my family or that it would hurt anybody around me. Now you bring that up, I think, I wonder how many people I hurt by doing what I thought was right but not caring whether they got hurt or not. It never dawned on me that it would cost any money or hurt my family money-wise. I never thought of my family. Now, all of a sudden, I realize that sounds selfish. You ask it that way, and I think, "My God, I never did." I see now what I put on my people's backs. But I never thought of that before.

Given the above evidence concerning cost/benefit calculus, my conclusion has to be largely negative. The notion of a calculus of costs and benefits appears to have a limited usefulness in explaining acts by traditional rational actors, such as Billy, who seems aware of every penny he gives to others and whose limited charity takes the form of loans for which he expects gratitude and repayment. Billy's behavior seems entirely consistent with the kinds of cost/benefit calculus economists insist we all follow. This same process also seems to have a very slight explanatory power for those philanthropists who, unlike Melissa, are affected by praise. But they have virtually none at all for heroes or rescuers. Altruists simply do not function in such terms and are surprised and mystified when asked how such a cost/benefit calculus affected their altruism.

Conclusion

How useful are economic explanations of altruism? They have some pertinence to the limited charitable giving or volunteer activities engaged in by rational actors, like the entrepreneurs I interviewed. They have a limited utility in explaining actions by philanthropists, many—but not all—of whom do seem to tend first to their own needs and to those of their families before they give to strangers. But economic explanations fail abysmally to explain actions by heroes or the rescuers of Jews, people who come closest to pure altruism on our conceptual continuum.

Economists are unable to explain such extreme forms of altruism in part because they define altruism as action which either benefits others with no gain to the actor or which benefits others more than it benefits the actor. This somewhat relativistic definition excludes or ignores the possibility of self-sacrifice. It directs discussion into "mine and thine" terms[28] and assumes that actors think in terms of individual benefits and costs. Consequently, economists predict that altruism will not occur when the costs are too high.

But altruism does exist. People do help others even when the costs to themselves *are* higher than the rewards they receive from their action. They do sacrifice for others. Their behavior simply cannot be explained through the traditional rational actor paradigm that assumes all actors are isolated self-interested individuals. This individualistic paradigm in turn blinds economists to the shifting identities and group ties that constitute a strong part of human nature.[29] While such close reliance on an individualistic conceptual paradigm may work well to explain the behavior of some persons, particularly those who are willing to incur only small costs to their own welfare in order to help others, it is vastly less successful for those whose altruism—to adopt the economist's vocabulary—costs them their own individual welfare, perhaps even their lives.

I thus conclude that these economic explanations can continue to help us understand only the behavior of rational actors. It is time to admit the limitations of the economic conceptual paradigm and concede that its intellectual tools are better suited for certain individuals and particular situations than for others. Altruism is one area in which the limitations of the economic approach are abundantly evident.

CHAPTER 8

Explanations from Evolutionary Biology

> **Q.** How conscious are you of potential costs for you and your family when you risk your life to help someone else?
>
> **A.** I never thought of my family. I see now what I put on my people's backs. But I never thought of that before.
>
> —Lucille, heroine

ALTRUISM presents a major theoretical challenge for evolutionary biology, a discipline that relies heavily on the Darwinian concepts of individual selection and survival of the fittest.[1] Behavior in which one organism acts to promote the survival of another organism, rather than his or her own survival, violates this individual selection principle. The empirical rarity of altruism offers the possibility of explaining it away as an aberration; but its persistence makes this more difficult and presents a serious theoretical challenge for evolutionary biologists.[2]

In general, evolutionary biologists explain altruism in one of two ways: kin or group selection.[3] Both the kin selection and the group selection hypotheses attempt to explain altruism within the biologist's paradigm of individual selection. Essentially, the group selection hypothesis retains the Darwinian principle of natural selection while arguing that the process works not on individuals directly but rather via groups.[4] The basic argument runs as follows. As individuals, altruists do not fare as well as egoists in the normal Darwinian sense, but groups that possess altruists may have a competitive advantage over groups that do not. Groups therefore will develop some mechanism to protect their own altruists in order for the group *as a whole* to compete more effectively in the biological process of natural selection.

In contrast, the kin selection hypothesis sees the process of natural selection as working through the gene rather than through the group or the individual organism.[5] Consider two brothers, Harry and Dave. Both brothers share gene Q and can pass this gene along to their offspring. But that gene might best be passed on to future generations through Harry's dedicating his life to protecting his brother's children (who also carry gene Q) rather than by producing children of his own, since his children might further drain scarce resources and jeopardize the survival of all children who carry gene Q. Harry's decision to forego having children thus might appear self-sacrificial to many;[6] but from the perspective of a kin selectionist, Harry's behavior is rational, since it is the gene, rather than the individual organism or group, which is the relevant unit for natural selection. Harry's selfish genes, therefore, may pursue their interests most effectively through sacrificing one or more organisms (Harry's children) to protect offspring of related organisms (Dave's children) which carry the same gene.

Neither kin nor group selectionists discuss how the original altruists get there in the first place or how their altruistically sacrificed genes are transmitted. They focus not on individual choices but rather on statistical explanations for choice in long-term genetic reproduction. Moreover, evolutionary biologists concerned with altruism allocate relatively few of their discussions to human altruism.[7] Even the few works that discuss human biological predispositions toward aggression or altruism fail to isolate specific structures that can be linked to altruism.[8] For our purposes, this creates a gap in their theory. Because evolutionary biologists offer explanations that closely resemble economic explanations, which do concern human altruism and individual action, I include in my discussion of biological explanations of altruism those economic analyses that have adopted biological concepts. These concepts include the concept of reciprocity (I help you so you'll help me later), the clustering phenomenon (groups of altruists encourage each other), and the extension of self-interest to kin or critical group members (helping you protects me, my group, and my genes, too).

The most important recent analysis that forges explicit links between the two disciplines is by the economist Gary Becker, a Nobel laureate whose work has had considerable influence on contemporary theories of altruism. Becker casts the biological arguments in economists' terms, maintaining that biologists have stopped short of developing models with rational actors who maximize utility functions subject to limited resources. Biologists rely on what Becker calls the "rationality" of genetic selection; that is, the environment encourages behavior more suited for survival and discourages behavior less suited. In contrast, economists "have relied solely on individual rationality, and have not incorporated the effects of genetic selection" into their models.[9] Becker wants to create a more powerful analysis by joining "the individual rationality of the economist to the group rationality of the sociobiologist" (1976b:284). To do this, while still retaining actors who pursue individual self-interest, Becker follows the earlier economic tradition of treating altruism as a problem in interdependent utility functions, arguing that in certain circumstances "altruism pays."

Becker supports this claim through a three-step argument. (1) He equates consumption with fitness in biological terms. (2) He argues that altruism initially implies reducing one's own consumption to increase the consumption of another. But (3) the altruist's selfish beneficiaries (the egoists) will not want to hurt the altruist. Why not? Because hurting the altruist will limit the altruist's future ability to contribute to the egoist's own consumption. If the damages the egoists would otherwise have inflicted on the altruist exceed the cost of the altruist's contributions to them, then the altruism actually "pays," because the altruist is better off and thus more likely to survive than is a comparable self-centered individual.

Becker claims that this social interaction framework is superior to the socio-biologist's genetic fitness framework. Why? Because, Becker argues, his frame-work allows for the primacy of egoism and explains how altruism can survive within a world of egoists. This means, for Becker, that "[models] of group selection are [thus] unnecessary since altruistic behavior can be selected as a consequence of individual rationality" (1976:284).[10]

Becker's logic here is masterful in explaining altruism while not disturbing the cornerstone of economic thought: the idea that human nature is essentially self-interested. His argument made two important contributions.[11] It demon-strated that there were circumstances in which self-interested individuals might be induced to maximize joint income, thus permitting both parties to reach higher levels of individual consumption than would otherwise be possi-ble. This conclusion opened the door for important later work on the evolu-tion of cooperation in a world of egoists.[12] Becker also introduced to econom-ics and rational choice theory the distinction between true altruism and a category of behavior that evolutionary biologists[13] call reciprocal altruism and that sociologists[14] call social exchange.

Unfortunately, Becker's analysis also makes several critical errors. (1) His concept of altruism is extraordinarily restrictive. The scenario in which altru-ism pays is logically possible, but only under rather limited conditions. Even someone as sympathetic to Becker's approach as Gordon Tullock commented: "It seems very dubious that any real-world situation would fit the model" (1975:503). (2) Becker's analysis requires the altruist to correctly anticipate the preference orderings of his recipients; this is notoriously difficult to do.[15] (3) Becker ignores the extent to which the biological process of group selec-tion is a nonconscious, outcome-oriented process, and not the result of con-scious choice.[16] Finally, (4) what Becker describes simply as altruism is more accurately characterized as strategic altruism or enlightened self-interest. Here, Becker misapplies the biologists' concept of reciprocal altruism. In Becker's reciprocal altruism, an actor helps others in the "expectation or hope that he will then be helped by them in the future" (1976:821). This can be called altruism only in the most immediate sense: a donation is made, and no *immediate* return is expected or received. It is not altruism in the long run, however, for there is the clear expectation of *future* return. And, more impor-tantly, where this future reciprocity is not expected, Becker argues that the initial "altruistic" act should not occur. Why it does occur under these condi-tions remains unexplained by his model of altruism.

Becker's model thus remains unconvincing because he has defined altruism too narrowly and idiosyncratically. In particular, his concept of altruism does not allow for self-sacrifice; for Becker, altruism always results in eventual individual gain for the altruist. This is certainly not the standard usage of the term; nor is it the usage of evolutionary biologists, most of whom define altruism as increasing the fitness of another at the expense of one's own.[17] On this point, Becker appears to have misread the biologists he claims to follow.[18] He fails to pursue the biologists' emphasis on groups, remaining instead entrenched in the world of the individual actor, who pursues individual self-interest, albeit in a strategic fashion.[19]

Becker's analysis aside, then, how are biological theories applied and tested empirically when it comes to human altruism?[20] When we examine this literature, we find six main concepts developed by evolutionary biologists to explain human altruism. Four of these focus on the social benefits of altruism and speak directly to the group and the kin selectionist arguments. These explanations focus on the community size, on clusters and networks of altruists, and on sanctions to punish defectors from the desired behavior. Two other theories, heavily utilized by economists, were discussed in the preceding chapter—group selection, as it has been utilized in conjunction with the concept of dual utility functions, and reciprocal altruism—and will therefore not be reviewed here.

Favoring of Kin

According to kin selectionists, altruists would tend first to their own needs and those of their families and only then consider and care for the needs of others. Does this happen? Do people wait to give to others only after their own basic needs have been cared for satisfactorily? I discussed a related version of this idea in chapter 7, when I asked whether people strike some balance between what they are willing to do for strangers and what they do to benefit themselves or their kin, thus treating altruism as a luxury item, to be indulged in only after more basic, self-interested needs are satisfied.[21] Let us here consider the biological version of this argument: that individuals attend first to the needs of those in their kin group, widening the circle of concern only after these needs have been met.

We can find clear evidence of this phenomenon among the entrepreneurs, who did demonstrate concern that their own needs and those of their families be cared for before they give to others. Ray and Bradley gave little money to anyone. But Ray, in particular, talks a great deal about what being a family man means to him, and his treatment of his family members seemed generous. Jordan was also a family man, who frequently cared for his grandchildren and spoke lovingly about being raised in a close "ethnic" family, in his case, of New York Jewish immigrants. He related many "crazy family feuds" but held that they really do not mean anything, since "family is family, and you don't turn your back on them." In discussing charitable giving, Jordan speaks of "always keeping something back" for himself and his family and indicates that this is only appropriate.

This same attitude was evident to a lesser degree among philanthropists. Most philanthropists (such as Melissa) engage in balancing acts in which their individual or family needs are considered before those of strangers. Perhaps even more directly relevant for a consideration of the kin selection hypothesis is the fact that none of the philanthropists gave away so much money that they or their families became poor themselves. In this regard, entrepreneurs and, to a lesser degree, philanthropists fit in perfectly with the kin selection hypothesis: they are all wealthy but choose to keep much of their money for themselves or to pass it on to their children.

In contrast, rescuers offer the most dramatic refutation of the kin selection hypothesis. Every single rescuer knew they were endangering their family members through their attempts to help Jews. Under the Nazi policy of kith and kin, the rescuers' relatives, including even their youngest children, could be killed because of their actions. This meant that children far too young to be directly involved in helping their parents would be punished for the parents' deeds. In biological terms, the effects of this policy were clear: those who shared the rescuer's genes could be killed because of the rescuer's actions.[22] The Nazis thus attempted to use biology to deter rescuers but did not succeed.

Since biologists place great emphasis on nonconscious actions, since they stress that it is not necessary that an altruist consciously know that his or her behavior favors kin so long as the behavior itself reflects this favoring, the rescuers' actions acquire particular significance. In behavioral terms it was very clear that rescuers were not favoring kin over strangers. When I did explicitly ask rescuers about this idea, posing my questions in biological terms, the reactions clearly indicated that they did not (at least consciously) think in such terms. The specific answers themselves were often quite amusing, as indicated by Margot's emphatic response to a question concerning her possible fears of endangering her family, and therefore her gene pool, through her actions. "What? Are you nuts?!" Margot responded. "You don't think like that. That's crazy." Margot may be more outspoken than other altruists, but her answer illustrates my point: rescuers make no distinctions between kin and strangers.

There is even more powerful empirical evidence that rescuers simply cannot be fitted into the framework of the kin selection theory. Margot, we recall, was a German living in Holland as a stateless person when Hitler invaded. In addition to her work on behalf of Jews, Margot was contacted by the Dutch Resistance and asked to work for them, with the chilling caveat, "If you are arrested, we don't know you." Margot agreed despite this, and she was, indeed, very much on her own. The first of the six times she was arrested, her two children were left alone in the house, terrified after the Gestapo's midnight arrest of their mother. During her first incarceration, she had no idea what was happening to them.[23] Both of her daughters made it through the war safely, but not, it appears, without emotional scars. One of Margot's grandsons told me his mother remains bitter that Margot, "her own mother," would put strangers ahead of her. Margot never expressed this thought, but she did tell of an estrangement from her older daughter.

Other rescuers also had children who are or were angry with them for neglecting them during the war in favor of strangers. Bert told me that his oldest daughter was for a long time very angry with her mother for wearing herself down so for strangers that she died shortly after the war. Eventually, the daughter went back to Holland and visited her mother's grave in a symbolic—and successful—attempt to lay her resentment to rest.

These are but two illustrations of how rescuers refute the kin selection hypothesis. Rescuers frequently took the little food they had quite literally out of their children's mouths and gave it to strangers. It is perhaps significant that I learned this from family members; rescuers themselves seldom told me such stories. The fact that rescuers did not mention these sacrifices might, of course, mean that they feel guilty about depriving their children; I think it more likely, however, given the general tenor of my conversations with them, that they simply did not see life in such terms. Whatever the cause, the contrast between rescuers and rational actors is clear: treating family better than strangers was not something rescuers did.

An overall appraisal of the kin selection hypothesis thus suggests that it explains entrepreneurial giving reasonably well and, to a certain degree the behavior of some, but by no means all, of the philanthropists. But it fails abysmally to explain the acts of heroes or rescuers.

GROUP SELECTION: IN-GROUP/OUT-GROUP DISTINCTIONS

The group selection hypothesis claims that genetic selection works not through individuals or close kin but through broader groups. In particular, group selectionists argue that in competition among different breeding groups, groups which have some members who act to further group interest will have an advantage over groups which contain only self-interested individuals.[24] *Within* a group, self-interest may be favored, but *among* groups, group interest is the more successful strategy. Thus, the biologically smart groups will encourage a certain number of altruists and will develop mechanisms to both protect and encourage them. According to the theory, altruism is valued by the group not for intrinsic or moral reasons but rather because it serves as a tool enabling the group as a whole to compete more effectively in the biological process of natural selection.

I examine this general idea in several different ways. (1) I ask whether altruists do treat members of one group better than they do members of other groups. Such a distinction between members of different groups, particularly an in-group/out-group distinction, constitutes a central point in the group selection hypothesis. If group membership does not result in differential behavior toward nongroup and group members, then the whole idea of group selection breaks down. (2) I ask if there are group mechanisms that encourage altruism; or, conversely, are there sanctions developed to punish defectors from the established group policy toward altruists? For example, are group members who are designated as altruists punished if they act instead as self-interested rational actors? Or does the group punish members who take undue advantage of altruists, thereby threatening to discourage altruism or even to wipe out the desired group altruists?

Consider rescuers first. War is the closest contemporary instance of the Darwinian battle for survival, and group alliances may surface as people struggle against constant shortages and physical hardship. Certainly, life was especially harsh during the last year of World War II, and photos of this time are filled with scenes of haggard, starving people. Despite this, rescuers did not attend first to their own needs and then to the needs of others, as both the kin *and* the group selection theorists would suggest.

But did rescuers distinguish between members of different groups? Not the rescuers I interviewed.[25] Rescuers did not choose to save one particular Jew over another on the basis of group ties. For the most part, rescuers were not more likely to save a native Jew than a foreign one.[26] They saved Jews whose socioeconomic status differed greatly from their own and Jews with personalities they found difficult.[27] They helped Jews of different nationalities and varied ethnic backgrounds. While group similarities might be important to nonaltruists, what was important to the rescuers was simply that there was need.[28]

The heroine Lucille also illustrates the extent to which altruists fail to make in-group and out-group distinctions. Like other altruists, Lucille treats all people as equal. She risked her life on behalf of blacks during the civil rights period—but she went after the black rapist with a vengeance. Race is irrelevant to her. In a similar fashion, she describes herself as a strong feminist, but she does not favor women over men because of this.

Q. *You sound like you're a strong believer in equal rights for women.*

A. I'm for equal rights of all living creatures, including all humanity.

This was the attitude among all the altruists I interviewed. Altruists do not see the world in terms of in-groups and out-groups, but rather in terms of a shared humanity.

This attitude became less evident as we moved toward the self-interested pole on our conceptual continuum. I noted earlier that entrepreneurs uniformly give to drives and causes with which they had a local connection, and this phenomenon can be explained easily through a biological model stressing ties to kin or group membership. The same behavior is evident to a lesser extent among philanthropists, as illustrated by Melissa's charities, which frequently have a personal connection. Such patterns, while not explained through kin selection, do suggest that ties to groups of some kind are important for entrepreneurial and philanthropic giving.

Among the people I interviewed, I found that differential treatment of in-group versus out-group members exists among entrepreneurs and occasionally surfaces among philanthropists. But it rarely occurs among heroes and never among rescuers. The in-group versus out-group distinction of the group selection hypothesis thus cannot be said to explain altruism itself; such group distinctions are helpful only in explaining giving and other quasi-altruistic activities by self-interested rational actors.

GROUP SELECTION: INCENTIVES AND SANCTIONS

Biologists often suggest that group selection works through sanctions designed to punish defectors from the group-assigned policy of protecting a certain number of altruists. Conversely, incentives may be utilized to encourage these same altruistic policies. Do incentives affect altruism? One obvious incentive, frequently discussed by economists, is the policy of providing tax deductions for philanthropic gifts. Does this affect philanthropy? Here I found the effect less than what previous analysts have noted.

Entrepreneurs showed some susceptibility to tax incentives and were more concerned to receive tax deductions for charitable gifts. For philanthropists, the influence of tax incentives was more complex. Herbert, for example, born into a wealthy family, receives a comfortable, but not excessive, income from a trust. He gives away part of this money, in addition to the family money he donates through a family foundation. In describing his charitable giving, Herbert offered a two-part explanation for the effect of tax breaks on such gifts. (1) Tax breaks and duty can encourage charitable giving among people who might otherwise not give. Herbert said he knew many wealthy people, none of whom he considered philanthropists, whose limited charitable giving is affected by such considerations. But Herbert felt that the critical factor in long-term philanthropic activity, what turns rich people who are only occasional donors into true philanthropists, is discovering the joy of seeing what your gift can do for someone else. And this, Herbert said, has nothing to do with tax incentives. (2) Herbert noted that tax incentives may have had more appeal in "the old days," before tax reform reduced the tax credit one received.

Melissa also dismissed rather curtly the notion that tax incentives lie behind her giving. "You have to have it in the first place in order to give," she told me, adding that you do not receive tax credits that even approach the amount you have given away. Several other philanthropists also noted an obvious fact that minimizes, if it does not refute, the influence of tax incentives on giving: many wealthy people give nothing, despite the fact that they are eligible for the same deductions. (Several philanthropists mentioned particular friends—often much wealthier than the interviewee—who give away no money at all.)

For rescuers and heroes, I found few if any incentives behind their altruism. None of the heroes had ever heard of the Carnegie Hero Commission Awards, for example, before they received one. None had expected praise or reward of any kind for their efforts. As for the rescuers, there were absolutely no incentives to save Jews. All incentives worked in the opposite direction, with rewards and special favors being given to those who informed on both Jews and their rescuers.[29]

This brings us to the other side of the equation: sanctions. The sanctions phenomenon is one noted in general terms by evolutionary biologists interested in explaining altruism. Sanctions, they argue, are applied (or threatened) (1) to prevent members of the group from defecting from the pattern of altruistic behavior to which they have been assigned on behalf of the group or (2) to prevent group members designated as self-interested from taking undue advantage of the altruists in the group. Such sanctions are important tools in the process by which groups with altruists compete more effectively and do better as a whole than do groups without any altruists.

Did sanctions affect the altruists in this study? No one threatened rescuers (or heroes) with any penalty for defecting from their altruistic role. Often, no one even knew about rescuers' altruism. Nor, needless to say, did Nazi society threaten those who harmed rescuers. Rescuers were hardly viewed or treated as "group altruists" in the same way drinking buddies choose and protect a designated driver. Far from it. The idea is almost ludicrous. In fact, the exact opposite occurred. Rescuers were treated as defectors from the Nazi regime and risked severe punishment for saving Jews. Furthermore, there is no evidence that clusters of altruists (rescuers) could defend themselves against defectors from this altruistic policy by cooperating with one another and doing better as a group than did defectors.[30] The biographical and historical evidence from this period suggests precisely the contrary: at least until the very last days of the war, rescuers were mercilessly turned in to the Nazi regime, and their betrayers were rewarded.[31]

Nor do sanctions appear to operate for heroes, none of whom would have been criticized, let alone sanctioned or punished, for not performing the heroic act. Lucille, in particular, speaks of this, noting that the way things are today nobody really worries much about morality. She states explicitly that nobody blames people for not helping someone else. Fear of group disapproval, then, is not what motivates her altruism. She also noted that most people find it acceptable for rich people to hoard their money. "Nobody criticizes rich people for failing to discharge their obligations to society," she said.

GROUP SELECTION: COMMUNITY SIZE, NETWORKS, AND CLUSTERS

Community Size

What about community size? This idea, which relates closely to that of sanctions, assumes a psychological predisposition toward either self-interest or altruism is created through the mechanism of group approval (or the threat of group opprobrium) and that such group mechanisms operate more effectively in small communities.[32] Do both sanctions and social approval work more effectively in small groups? I noted in chapter 6 that the size of the community in which altruists were raised had no relation to their proclivity for altruism. Altruists come from every imaginable kind of community background, from small towns to large urban centers, as was illustrated in the four stories presented in part II. The rather eclectic pattern of community background was typical among the rest of the interviewees. It suggests no pattern, no relationship between community size and altruism. Altruists are not found more often in small towns than in larger cities.

Networks and Clusters

In addition to sanctions and specific incentives, such as tax deductions, there are other, more subtle ways in which groups, according to biologists, foster that degree of altruistic behavior that will give the group an advantage in the process of natural selection. Some biologists focus on the kinds of material benefits and rewards whose importance we considered, and discounted, in earlier chapters. Others note the less tangible rewards, the social benefits, that accrue to altruists because of their good deeds. Evolutionary biologists are joined by anthropologists and economists in proposing elaborate variants on a common theme in social science: the importance of social benefits in encouraging altruism.

One important social benefit is group approval, and evolutionary biologists often point to this as an effective mechanism for fostering altruism. Even though community size seems to be irrelevant to the emergence of altruism, group approval may still exert a powerful influence. The fact that the Carnegie Hero Commission gives out awards for remarkable valor or that newspapers print stories about philanthropists' gifts suggests that group approval may indeed be an indirect benefit of altruism, irrespective of the size of the community. Both the cluster hypothesis and the network hypothesis argue that this is precisely what occurs.

The cluster hypothesis claims that the mere existence and visibility of a group of altruists may influence a person to engage in similarly altruistic behavior, even one who was not originally part of the group. The key here is the imitative aspect of altruistic behavior. An actor sees an example of altruism and finds it preferable, either because of personal values or because key groups or society at large values the action.[33]

In this, the cluster hypothesis differs subtly from the closely related network hypothesis. The network hypothesis refers to a group which resembles a cluster but differs in having a somewhat more clearly delineated membership. This group already may include the actor, or it may be a network which the actor wishes to join. It may be a social club, for example, or an officially designated and publicly displayed list of donors who give money to a college or hospital. If the actor does not already belong to the network, it is the membership in this group, or the desire to become a part of this group, that impels the actor to behave altruistically. If the actor already belongs to the network (e.g., the social club), it is his desire to avoid an awkward or uncomfortable position within it that triggers his action. What distinguishes the cluster hypothesis from the network hypothesis is a more specifically defined network that carries some particular benefit and not simply the imitative aspect of behavior that lies at the heart of the cluster hypothesis.[34]

According to the network scenario, the behavior that appears altruistic is actually nothing more than the desire to obtain the social benefits associated with altruistic behavior. This is less clear with the cluster hypothesis, in which the imitative aspect of behavior may theoretically, at least in part, be genuine, insofar as the imitator internalizes the altruistic standard of the cluster. (Unfortunately, works analyzing the cluster hypothesis do not clearly specify *why* the actor wishes to imitate the behavior.) The critical distinction we must focus on here is the difference between cluster or network altruists on the one hand and true altruists on the other. The cluster or network altruist mimics altruistic behavior to gain something for him or herself, if only the feeling of belonging. For the true altruist, no ulterior motive or intent drives behavior; the altruist responds simply to the needs of another.

To illustrate the cluster hypothesis, let us consider Betty. Betty is a realtor who moves to a new community shortly before the nearby hospital begins a building fund. She notices that all the other realtors are giving money to the fund. Although she herself does not really care much about the hospital, she gives to the fund because all her other business associates give liberally, and it seems like "the thing to do." What Betty wants from her so-called altruism may be only vaguely defined, even for Betty, but it has more to do with the desire to be like others in the group than with helping the needy party or cause.

For an example of the network hypothesis, imagine another realtor named Janice. Janice is also new to the same community, but she is a social climber who gives to the local hospital because she consciously desires acceptance into the town's social set and believes that a generous (and publicized) gift will enhance her chances. So far, Janice's actions could still be explained by the cluster hypothesis. But Janice may want a more tangible form of reward, such as being elected to the hospital board, where she will make contacts advantageous to her business. Or she may hope to impress people by having her name listed on a prominently displayed donors' plaque in the hospital entrance. Janice may even already have achieved a certain prominence in the community and be an elected member of the hospital board, a largely honorific position that she has accepted for her own mixture of social and business motives. Everyone else on the board gives generously to the hospital building fund (for *their* own reasons, from the altruistic desire to help others to the more self-centered desire to have expanded hospital services), and Janice joins in only (or at least primarily) because she fears she will look penurious if she refuses.

In neither of these examples is the altruistic impulse genuinely motivated by the desire to help the hospital. For the cluster philanthropist, the key is a modeling effect; Betty goes along with the group behavior without thinking about it for herself. For the network philanthropist, the key is a more conscious desire to belong to a particular social network.

What do we find when we examine these hypotheses? The lack of concern for social acclaim among altruists has already been noted in earlier chapters. The insignificance of group approval as a motive for altruism is most readily obvious among the rescuers. There was no group approval of their deeds. The immediate society, the official political system, and, in many cases, the rescuer's dearest friends and family members, all were ignorant of or opposed to the rescuers' acts.[35] Alida, a Dutch working-class mother of eight who hid Jews and took in several Jewish children, was severely chastised by her father for risking her own children's lives and denying them food in order to feed strangers. She continued her rescue activities nonetheless. Alida's experience is just one example of the extent to which rescuers not only lacked group approval for rescue activities but also encountered active resistance, even from their nearest and dearest. The families of a few of the rescuers were both anti-Semitic and in political agreement with Hitler's policies. Irene spoke with great pain about living in a psychological no-man's-land that continued to haunt her after the war, even in the United States; she was viewed with distrust by the American Jewish community because she was Polish (and therefore was suspected of being anti-Semitic) even as she was rebuffed by the Polish Catholic community in this country because she *had* helped Jews. Since group approval is the basic assumption underlying both the network and the cluster hypotheses, rescuers would seem to constitute rather clear refutation of these explanations for altruism. But let us consider these ideas in more detail before discarding them. What about the importance of clusters of altruists? Does the existence of small groups or clusters of similarly motivated actors encourage altruism? Here, the evidence is mixed for entrepreneurs but negative for altruists.

At one extreme is Roger, a multimillionaire in the baseline sample of entrepreneurs. Roger earns over $1 million a year as president of a company owned by a billionaire, a philanthropist who made significant cash gifts (totaling many millions of dollars) while Roger worked for him. In addition to this immediate example of altruism, Roger frequently has to attend charity events as part of his job. All of this puts him into constant contact with other rich people who give money to various causes. Yet Roger himself engages in only limited personal giving. (He did not want to discuss the extent of these gifts, saying only that they were "minuscule" and that he certainly is not a philanthropist.) Roger noted that he finds no difficulty at all in resisting the tremendous social and business pressure to make more significant personal contributions. He was cynical about the kind of social benefits from charitable giving that both the cluster and network hypotheses promise. He described the charity ball phenomenon, in which people spend $50,000 to raise $1 million, as perfectly sound business practice. But he himself dislikes this kind of event. He told of being invited to charity balls by fund-raisers who try to flatter him into giving by saying how much people would like him to attend. "I tell them they can either have me or have the money: which would they prefer?" Roger grinned. "Guess which they choose."

Roger is not susceptible to social pressures, but such independence is not the norm for the other entrepreneurs I interviewed. Most of them did at least occasionally donate small amounts to charity or attend charity balls, for both social and business reasons. Some of these entrepreneurs thus seemed susceptible to influence from the behavior of those around them, at least insofar as their charitable giving was concerned.

The same was true with philanthropists, most of whom gave at least some money simply because it was expected. This was usually to local charities, however, such as a nearby hospital or small gifts in response to neighborhood solicitations. Philanthropists' large gifts, however, were unaffected by the behavior of others. Herbert, for example, gives to some causes, such as the Boy Scouts or the local hospital, because he sees himself as having an obligation to his community. (This is the sense of community discussed earlier and refers to a particular geographic locale and/or social circle.) But Herbert was clear that this kind of philanthropy was in the "good citizenship" category and constituted neither the bulk of his philanthropy nor the part of it that mattered most to him. Other philanthropists made the same distinction.

In sharp contrast, the heroes were unaffected by what others did or did not do. Gerald, for example, was visiting a ski resort in Massachusetts when he heard an angry crowd yelling and screaming as they attacked a policeman. Gerald plunged into the mob of nearly one hundred people, most of whom were young and in good physical shape, to save the policeman from being beaten. As the others stood by cheering, some of the youths then turned on Gerald, beating him and later trying to run over him in their cars. This hardly constitutes group approval.

In a similar fashion, it seemed significant that Lucille, who talked at length about her civil rights work, never mentioned working with other civil rights activists. Though we know historically that there were existing networks throughout the South, Lucille seems not to have been recruited into such a network. Nor does she appear to have sought comfort, solace, and support from any existing group of like-minded individuals.

Determining the effects of clustering and networks on rescuers is both easier and more difficult, in part because of the need for extreme secrecy that surrounded their wartime activities. On the whole, I found no evidence of an effect from clusters, while the networks that arose were more the product of altruistic activities than the cause of them. Let me elaborate, discussing the importance of clusters and networks simultaneously, since the two concepts are so closely related.

While I found none of the rescuers helped Jews because of influence from others, the logistics of rescuing Jews usually necessitated contact with others in what then amounted to a kind of informal network. With varying degrees of closeness, seven of the rescuers worked with organized resistance groups. A typical case is that of Leonie. a young Dutch rescuer. While staying with her sister in Amsterdam, Leonie hid two Jewish girls in the apartment. Her sister was terrified. After three days of tense discussions, Leonie realized that her sister was about to crack under the emotional strain. Leonie decided that she needed a safer hiding place for the girls. She approached a woman who she suspected was hiding Jews and asked for her help. The woman was, indeed, hiding Jews herself, and she put Leonie in touch with others who could provide a haven for the girls.[36] Leonie thus became part of a network of rescuers. But this network arose *after* she had become a rescuer, not before, and it developed in order to facilitate her altruism. This, of course, is the exact reverse of the process described by evolutionary biologists who argue that altruism develops to facilitate network membership. Instances such as this (and there were many) led me to conclude that networks are not necessary for altruism to appear, however crucial they may be to its efficacy.

Like Leonie, most of the other rescuers had to depend on neighbors or friends turning a blind eye to the increased demands for extra rations of food or medical supplies. Does this constitute a network? Perhaps. But since all of these networks arose in order to further rescue activities, they also seem more the result rather than the cause of the altruistic action. While many rescuers *did* need the assistance of others in order to successfully save Jews, they usually got it after the rescue effort had already begun. Bert, for example, said he knew there were people who sold him food cheaply; he assumed they may well have suspected he needed the food for Jews without ration cards. Assessing the evidence on this aspect of the clustering effect is difficult. The danger of rescue action necessitated secrecy and therefore would work against cooperation with others. (Bert said he preferred to work alone, without contact with any Resistance groups. "The less I knew, the better. You never know what you will say when they get those irons on you.") Yet any ongoing rescue effort usually required some tacit support or assistance from others, who might be called upon to give food, misfile papers, or simply look the other way. In addition to this general or tacit support, of course, there were rare instances of entire communities rescuing Jews. (Le Chambon in southern France is one example of this.)[37] In these instances, clusters of already existent altruists may have encouraged or even brought out altruism in other people.

In my sample, however, I found more instances of rescuers who felt group disapproval and, as a result, broke group ties in order to save Jews. Irene's break with the Catholic Church is one instance of this. Countess Maruska's break with her family and aristocratic friends is another, as is Leonie's argument with her sister.[38]

Furthermore, those rescuers (such as Margot, Otto, and Tony) who were active in organized resistance movements undertook their political action simultaneously with or after initiating rescue actions. It seems significant that these people did not view rescuing Jews as another form of political resistance to the Nazi regime.[39] Tony, as we saw in chapter 5, kept Resistance activities and rescue activities separate.

Certainly, no one undertook rescue activities in order to affiliate themselves with a group or to experience social prestige or group fellowship—often cited as motivations for cooperation and altruism.[40] In part, of course, this is because danger necessitated ad hoc arrangements. Tony told me that rescue networks "came up by themselves. As the need arose, people ended up getting involved." Rescue networks certainly did not serve as clubs which one wished to join.

No rescuer I interviewed had been recruited into rescue activities by any official group, although both Margot and Otto were recruited into political activities. Margot was contacted by the Dutch government and asked to help the Resistance because of her extensive language skills. But this was *after* she had already begun helping Jews. Overall, the experience of Bert, the Dutchman who rescued people with his first wife, Annie, is typical.

> Annie had a girlfriend from before the war. The day she came [to stay with us], I was for the time in Amsterdam. This time, when I came back, Hettie was sitting there.

Hettie asked if she could talk to Bert.

> All at once I had the feeling why she came. I never thought it over. "She stays," I said. "I hope Annie has already told you that it's all right." We arranged that of course she stay. My go-ahead was emphatically "Of course." So that was the first person I save. And her husband, Pom, whom I had never seen, of course he had to stay too. He didn't come right away, because he was still trying to save a little Jewish kid, a nephew, but that did not work out. On both sides their parents were gone already; there was plenty of misery around them. So Pom came sometime later.

Bert's rescuing was automatic and spontaneous, emanating from the need of Annie and her husband to be saved. It was as simple as Bert's "of course he had to stay too."

I conclude that networks and clusters or the desire for social approval are largely irrelevant for altruism. Nowhere is this more dramatically demonstrated than with the rescuers, most of whom operated on their own, without encouragement from others and without formal group support. Rescuers were not usually recruited into tight groups, as were some Resistance workers. Nor did the loose support networks that did exist provide the kind of tight group membership for which people might risk their lives. Finally, because of the danger and the extremity of the Nazi methods of torture, many rescuers (such as Margot) isolated themselves from loved ones who might otherwise have given them emotional support in their activities. They did not want their loved ones to know anything that might be extracted from them or involve them in danger. Given all of this, I cannot interpret the existence of informal or formal contact with other rescuers, or even participation in Resistance activity, as corroborating the cluster or network hypothesis. Networks and clusters of altruists may have occasional influence on quasi-altruistic behavior by rational actors; they have no significant influence on altruists themselves.

KIN SELECTION AND CHILDREN WHO CARE FOR OTHER CHILDREN

Cultural differences in the care of young children are not usually analyzed by evolutionary biologists, but because such factors relate directly to the ideas of kin and group selection, I include them in this chapter.

In general, explanations from evolutionary biology (and the economic explanations based on biological concepts) allude to culture's role in answering the question of how, when, and why particular groups determine their peculiar ratio of altruism and self-interest. These works sometimes note that the mixture varies greatly among different cultures. But for the most part, evolutionary biologists (only a small percentage of whom study altruism among human beings anyway) leave the consideration of cultural influences to anthropologists. Economists follow the same tack, making culture and cultural values exogenous variables, outside the range of an economist's purview.

One of the best cross-cultural studies on altruism is Whiting's anthropological research (1983) on children in six cultures, work which did address the comparative importance of kinship ties on altruism in human beings and across cultures. Whiting examined different patterns of child-rearing. She considered children who were raised not just in the traditional Western nuclear family but also in more extended families where grandparents, aunts, uncles, and cousins interacted closely. Whiting also examined societies in which children are raised in common, living in what are called women's houses until a certain age, at which point boys undergo an initiation ceremony and join the men. In constructing her analysis in this fashion, Whiting tries to isolate both the role of culture (which relates to the general theory of group selection) and the kinds of biological ties the kin selection argument emphasizes. Whiting concludes that children who are put in charge of other youngsters become more socially responsible and caring adults than those children who are not given such responsibilities. This finding, Whiting argues, holds true whether or not the young care-givers are related to their charges through ties of blood or kin.

Whiting's work provides valuable evidence about altruism, particularly for biologists concerned with human acts of altruism. Whiting's is one of the rare studies in this area, however, and is seldom even cited by economists or evolutionary biologists. In general, questions concerning culture's role in setting a mix between altruism and self-interest—either for the individual or the group—are left unanswered by the biologists and by the economists who have borrowed these biological concepts and successfully applied them to human altruism.

Unfortunately, I can provide only a cursory examination of Whitings's interesting work, since my sample consists only of people raised in Western nuclear or extended families. But questions about early experiences of caring for other children, including children not related to the altruist, revealed little evidence of this in my sample. Only some of the rescuers had engaged in such child care relationships. (Bert and Bethe had cared for their siblings. Others had no such experience and later blithely handed over their own children to governesses.) Indeed, not all rescuers had nurturing personalities, a factor that appears implicitly to underpin Whiting's work. Tony in particular speaks quite honestly about his own failings as a father. His honesty in assessing his family ties is remarkable, even though what he recounts is extremely sad at a personal level.

> Unfortunately, my children were a major disaster. They grew up not only in divorce but also right in the middle of the worst end of California hippiedom, in the drug culture. They burned out on acid and on drugs. They got into crime. My son—I haven't seen him for years—he's sort of got it together. He became a Jesus freak originally. Then he joined a slightly less extreme religious group, which helped him. They got him back to where he could at least do some work. His brain is pretty well fried, but he can still do good carpentry work. He's about thirty-five now, and finally, after years, at least he can survive on his own. But he was gone so long that in many ways, he sort of died. The relationship no longer exists.
>
> The same thing happened with my daughter, who is about thirty-three. She went through the exact same thing and hit the road. She tried just about everything. Recently she sent a note for the first time in almost six or eight years. Most of the time, whenever they did that in the past, they wanted

money. And we decided it was best to leave things the way they were. We both had learned to survive without each other. There wasn't really very much left. It's sad, but that's the way it was. So in many ways . . . [*Pauses*]

I hate playing games and pretending. There is nothing worse than being a family and pretending you love each other and pretending you're being polite with each other when really there's nothing there. There is none of that normal warmth that exists between family and children. That's the negative page in the story.

Tony was not alone in combining detachment from family with caring for strangers. The same trait appeared among other rescuers and heroes. The pattern of caring for younger children varied as greatly for the philanthropists and entrepreneurs as it did for the heroes and rescuers. (Some entrepreneurs, such as Ray or Billy, were extremely close to and nurturing of their own children; others were not.) Perhaps a larger sample would lend greater insight on this question. But my interviews do not indicate that altruism is linked to an early experience of being given the responsibility of caring for younger children.

CONCLUSION

Altruism presents a particularly thorny theoretical problem for evolutionary biologists, who base their discipline on Darwin's notions of individual selection and survival of the fittest. Their general response to altruism has been to argue that individual selection works through either kin selection or group selection. There are few biological works on human altruism, and these do not specify the origin of altruism. Nor do biologists tend to focus on individual choices but rather on statistical trends in long-range genetic selection.

My overall conclusion concerning biological explanations of altruism is that they work reasonably well for behavioral patterns of rational actors in general and for some philanthropists but have nothing to contribute to our understanding of the more extreme forms of altruistic behavior. The individualistic paradigm and implicit assumption of self-interest on which Darwinian biology is based appears unable to account for situations of genuine self-sacrifice for people not of one's kin or social group. What evolutionary biologists are explaining, then, is not altruism but rather the limited and isolated acts of charity or volunteer work in which even the most self-interested rational actor engages intermittently. To understand altruism and altruists themselves, we need another theoretical framework.

CHAPTER 9

Psychological Discussions of Altruism

> Psychology and psychiatry . . . not only describe man as selfishly
> motivated, but implicitly or explicitly teach that he ought to be so.
> —Donald Campbell, 1975 Presidential Address to
> the American Psychological Association[1]

THE FIELD of psychology is dominated by the assumption of universal egoism.[2] Most psychological explanations of altruism reduce it to veiled forms of self-interest, utilizing concepts similar to those found in economics and evolutionary biology.[3] Is altruism actually just a way to feel good about oneself? To alleviate guilt for earlier wrongs? To obtain praise for being a good person? This dominant view began to shift subtly, however, during the mid-1970s, as some psychologists became more willing to accept the existence of altruism.[4] Two factors may account for this greater intellectual receptivity toward altruism among psychologists.

(1) Psychology is widely practiced as a helping profession. Psychologists who themselves are interested in helping others therefore may prove more receptive and willing to believe that other-directed behavior actually does exist without any ulterior motive. (2) Psychology has a general concern with identity. This may encourage psychologists to consider variations in identity formation and to be less ideologically committed to the model of self-interested identity and personality structure.[5]

Whatever the causes, some of the richest explanations of altruism come from psychology. The contributions of psychologists fall into two general categories: (1) behavioral works that ignore motive, arguing that we can observe only the consequence of inner processes, not those processes themselves, and (2) works which contend that an agent's motives and intentions are critical determinants of whether an act is altruistic or self-interested. The current thinking among most psychologists concerned with altruism falls primarily into the latter category, and the best recent empirical analyses discuss motive and intention extensively, despite methodological difficulties in doing so.[6]

The easiest way to summarize recent psychological studies of altruism is to divide them into two main approaches: the developmental and the social psychological. Developmental psychologists stress learning and learning stages as predictors of altruism. They begin with Freud's assumption that all behavior is ultimately rooted in an attempt to satisfy the self. This egocentricity is modified as the child grows and identifies with critical others, thereby developing a superego. This superego then suppresses the basic selfish desires, and altruism emerges, either as a result of guilt (imposed by the superego for moral transgressions) or as a result of the internalization of values and standards learned in early childhood.[7] Much of the developmental work on child psychology that addresses altruism directly focuses both on the stages at which children start to give to others and on tracing the process by which this natural proclivity to share grows and develops into a more full-fledged ethical system.[8] This developmental approach frequently explains altruism as a result of the child's learning to value other human beings.[9] Some scholars further hold that altruism, along with other forms of moral action, occurs only at the highest stages of ethical growth[10] or after other psychological needs have been satisfied.[11] Others reject such a stage theoretic approach,[12] arguing that people can change and that motivation, in particular, may evolve or regress.[13]

In contrast, social psychologists who analyze altruism move beyond the individual actor and examine the interaction between the individual actor and the external world. Like developmental psychologists, social psychologists also examine social learning, self-reinforcement, and critical role models; but they broaden the inquiry to include factors such as the altruist's familiarity with the person helped or the surroundings in which the altruistic act takes place.[14] Like developmentalists, social psychologists frequently ask about individual values, occupational interests, psychological well-being; whether the altruist is an extrovert or an introvert, a leader or a follower; how open the actor is to new experiences; and other personality traits.[15] But they also consider situational predictors, such as the physical environment in which the altruistic act occurs,[16] and the particular characteristics of the individual in need of help.[17]

If we can characterize developmental psychologists as generally explaining altruism through a focus on the individual, then social psychologists can be described as explaining altruism more as the outcome of an interactive decision-making process in which the internal characteristics of the actor join with the external environment in a pattern of mutual influence. To illustrate how the best works in psychology move across the expositional categories and intradisciplinary boundaries presented above, consider the Oliners' recent work (1988) on people who rescued Jews in Nazi Europe. Although the Oliners themselves categorize their approach as social psychological, their work actually seems somewhat broader, considering a wide variety of predictors, from role models, empathy, and family ties and bonds to acceptance of responsibility and patterns of disciplining children.[18] In this regard, their work reflects the state of the art in psychology in general.[19]

Many of the predictors of altruism explored by psychologists are also discussed by scholars in other disciplines using different terminology.[20] Since the basic explanations and concepts are so similar, with only specific terminology differing, depending on the discipline in which the concepts are discussed, and since these concepts already have been discussed adequately in earlier chapters, when the basic explanations and concepts of a psychological approach match those we have already covered in other disciplines, I will not review them here.[21]

These explanations include developmental factors[22] such as (1) socialization and learned ethical values, (2) stage theoretic forms of cognition and affect,[23] and (3) altruists' social learning processes, such as relations with parents. Social psychological approaches treat altruism as an interaction between the altruist and the environment and explore factors such as the characteristics of the person being helped or the altruist's familiarity with that person. Situational factors, such as the physical environment in which altruism occurs, tap the "interactive" aspect of altruism and, by providing insight into the contextual dependence of altruism, deliver us into the tricky realm of cultural influences.[24]

DEVELOPMENTAL INFLUENCES ON ALTRUISM

Relations with Parents and Role Models

Perhaps the simplest developmental explanations concern socialization patterns, especially role modeling by parents and critical others and the transmission of particular ethical values.[25] Do altruists exhibit consistent patterns of relations with parents and/or critical role models or reflect at least subtle differences from more traditional rational actors in their parent-child relations? How similar are the ethical messages transmitted by critical role models to altruists and to rational actors?

To my surprise, I found no systematic evidence supporting any of these explanations of altruism. I found no consistent pattern of parental relationships among altruists, nor did I find any consistent expression of the importance of such ties. Instead, certain kinds of relations with parents seemed to appear almost at random, in one hero but not another, for one rescuer or one philanthropist but also for some entrepreneurs. This occurred in all dimensions, such as closeness to versus distance from parents, "good" versus "bad" relations, severity versus leniency in patterns of child-rearing, and so on. Some altruists, like John, received clear exhortations from their role models to be altruistic; others, like Jimmy, claimed to have had no critical role modeling for their altruism. Some, like Wilhelmina, even denied having critical role models at all.

The complexity of role modeling is readily apparent as we reconsider the stories told in detail in part II. Billy described close ties to his father, who had no business sense, a skill that Billy prizes highly and one that constitutes a critical part of his entrepreneurial personality. His father "worked seven days

a week because he loved it, and he never had the thought of making money."
His father's lack of interest in money seems hard to reconcile with Billy's expressed "greed [for]. . . the good things that you could have in life, that money could buy for you." Instead, Billy's interest in money and his entrepreneurial spirit seem to have come directly from his mother, whom he described as "mostly Irish and a hard-charger," a woman who ran her own hair salon. Billy remains close to both his parents and credits them with being the central personalities in his life, although he makes it clear that his father was his main role model.

> I think I've tried to pattern myself a lot like him. My dad's the kind of guy that can accept life. He's a very positive thinker. I'm a very positive thinker. . . . My dad's a very mild person. He has no temper. He doesn't get mad. I never get mad.
>
> My mom is a very fiery, outspoken, dominant person. My mom has always been the aggressive one, and I think I'm kind of in between the two. Maybe, if you wanted to put it this way, you could say I got my basic personality from my dad but my business sense from my mom. I think that's about the way it worked out.

Billy is illustrative of other entrepreneurs in taking his sense of family and his entrepreneurial spirit directly from his parents. This corresponds to developmental psychology's emphasis on social learning and role models.

What about Melissa? Melissa did have a strong role model for her philanthropy, her grandfather. When we hear Melissa discuss her role models, we are struck by how many key psychological factors she mentions and are reminded that role models need not be parents. (Indeed, Melissa describes her parents as being rather immature, as people whom *she*, effectively, had to parent.) The dominant force in Melissa's life was her grandfather, who taught Melissa the value of hard work, pride, caring for oneself and one's family, personal independence, and philanthropy.

> **Q.** *Did you have anybody you were particularly close to as a child or an adolescent?*
>
> **A.** My grandfather. Definitely. My mother's father. Both my brother and I were real close to him. He was a strong father figure to us. He taught us our values, and I think he was where we got our pride, because he was a very proud man. He was a very disciplined, hard worker and very successful. He was a farmer, and in those years farming was difficult. There weren't many successful farmers, but he happened to be one and we looked up to him.

In addition to learning her values of hard work and family ties from her grandfather, Melissa also clearly identifies her grandfather as a model for her own philanthropy.

Q. *Was your grandfather a philanthropist? Did he help people in any particular way?*

A. Yes. At that time the farming communities were very neighborly. Neighbors helped neighbors. And that was the way that he would help. And, gosh, he also helped us. He helped his family. It was more the church, neighbors, and family, because it was more of a closed community thing, the way they lived.

Melissa had related earlier how weak her parents were, describing how she and her first husband effectively had to parent them and watch over them, much as her grandfather had done when Melissa was a child. This idea of watching out for family members who may need protection was also a pattern she seems to have acquired from her grandfather. Melissa traces her strength, philanthropy, and love of children directly to her grandfather; she likewise explains her methods of child-rearing, which stress reasoning and explaining rather than physically punishing children for childish offenses, as being directly modeled after her grandfather's.[26]

Melissa's narrative underscores the tremendous importance of a critical role model for her later life. This fits in perfectly with the importance psychologists attribute to role models and social learning for general development. But what strikes me when we compare Melissa's narrative with Billy's is the extent to which Billy and Melissa resemble each other, not just in their close attachment to particular role models but also in the messages they took from these role models. Work hard; take care of family; be honest—the messages are virtually identical in both cases. And yet Billy is not a philanthropist and Melissa is. When we assess the importance of role models and parental ties for altruism, then, we have to note both the differences in the parental relations exhibited by Billy and Melissa *and* the similarity in the messages they received from critical others. If everyone has role models, and particularly if the messages taken from these role models are so similar in content, then role models cannot be critical determinants of altruism. Thus the traditionally described importance of role models for altruism may be less than has been suspected.

As we review the narratives presented in part II to assess more fully the importance of parental role models and their ethical messages for altruists, we again encounter similar variance in role models for heroines and heroes and for rescuers. Lucille emphatically stated that she hated her father, telling me flatly that she wouldn't discuss him or even tell me his name. She admired her mother but spoke more about her grandmother as a role model. Although Tony bore his parents no ill will, he expressed little affection or deep emotional ties toward either of his parents. When asked who was instrumental in his formation, he does mention his parents but he places them at the same level of importance with seven other people, from his nurse to a teacher and a film director friend. In contrast, consider the other rescuer discussed in chapter 5. Bert was extremely attached to his parents, especially his father. This evidence suggests that for every altruist who "fits" the parental role model theory, there is another who does not.

Nor is this inconsistent pattern of parental ties limited to altruists; it occurs for the individuals in each of the groups I interviewed. Consider the entrepreneurs other than Billy. Both Roger and Jordan were close to their grandmothers; but Bradley and Warren mention no one from their pasts, and "Mom" speaks only in passing of her parents.

Among the philanthropists, Jimmy describes his father as a skinflint and his mother as being dominated by Jimmy's father. Jimmy was fond of a particular uncle because he was a guy who always knew how to have a good time; but when I asked if this uncle was a role model or even someone to whom Jimmy had formed especially close bonds, Jimmy said no. "He was just someone who was fun. He had no influence on my philanthropy." Mac disliked both his parents, whom he described as cold and distant, but Isabelle worshiped both of hers. And Herbert described a beloved mother who would have done anything for her children.

Despite superficial evidence suggesting the importance of parental ties and role models, therefore, I concluded that the existence of role models was not critical in determining altruism. For the most part, altruists had, in fact, been instilled with high ethical standards by a critical role model. But this was not uniformly so. Furthermore, the role models mentioned specifically by all the altruists varied greatly, from Lucille's stridently feminist grandmother, fighting with policemen on picket lines in the early 1900s, to rescuers who had anti-Semitic parents. Perhaps more importantly, I found that all the rational actors I spoke with also had role models, and so far as I could ascertain, the moral messages transmitted by role models appeared to be remarkably similar for both altruists and rational actors: honesty, fairness, justice, equality, respect for others. There appeared to be no one standard pattern of parental tie or relationship that influences altruism. Even the kinder and gentler pattern of child-rearing that Melissa mentions, in which children are reasoned with rather than punished through spanking, did not appear dispositive among the people I interviewed. (One rescuer, in fact, had suffered abuse as a child at the hands of an alcoholic father.)

At first, this may challenge, or even offend, a basic hope most of us share as parents: a belief that if we can just give our children a loving and secure emotional environment, they will turn out to be fine young men and women. On closer examination, however, it actually serves to underline two points I have noted before but which are perhaps worth repeating. (1) Altruism is not the same thing as becoming a fine, loving person. Altruism may intersect with certain kinds of ethical behavior, but it is not the same thing as general probity or good character. I need to make it abundantly clear that I am not assessing, or even commenting on, whether particular kinds of parental ties affect a child's emotional or moral development. I am asserting only that these ties do not seem to predict altruism. (2) Altruists look much like other human beings in many dimensions. Relations with parents are clearly one of these. Some altruists loved their fathers and hated their mothers; some felt the opposite. Some loved and respected both parents; others had atrocious relations with their parents. Some altruists had lost one or both parents at early ages and were raised by loving relatives; others experienced similar losses without this comfort. But the critical point remains: exactly the same variety was evident among the nonaltruists. I therefore conclude that in terms of both childhood relations with critical role models and the ethical messages transmitted through the socialization process by critical others, the altruists' experiences mirror those of the rest of humanity: they are complex and varied and cannot be reduced to a single explanatory pattern.

Stage Theoretic Approaches to Altruism and Deviation from Ethical Values

According to the dominant view, ethical development proceeds in certain stages.[27] In the earliest stages, moral principles are said to be rooted in self-interest, fear of punishment, and desire for reward. Some individuals then go on to acquire an emerging concept of self-identity within the confines of their institutionalized moral community and are motivated by the idea of being a good member or citizen conforming to community norms. Those individuals whose development stops at this level exhibit conventional morality. At the highest stages of ethical development, analysts expect to find individuals with postconventional morality, rooted in universal moral principles that transcend community norms.

My own data were difficult to interpret on this point. I did find some support for a stage theoretic argument, with altruists voicing clear expressions of universal morality. But there were also important deviations from such existing principles, deviations that can be interpreted as regression to an earlier stage and which, therefore, would work against a stage theoretic explanation for altruism. More importantly, I found to my surprise that it was the rescuers, the individuals who came closest to pure altruism on my conceptual continuum, who deviated most from the universal moral principles of ethics and morality. Furthermore, this deviance was necessary in order to act altruistically, and the guilt felt at such deviations varied greatly from rescuer to rescuer.

To illustrate this, consider an excerpt from a rescuer called John. This passage captures some of the guilt, confusion, and emotional turmoil John felt when he realized that his wartime lying, deceit, and cheating meant he was deviating wildly from all the ethical principles instilled by his minister father. This and similar excerpts from the accounts of other rescuers record the experience of guilt at failing to live up to the ethical messages transmitted through the social learning process. Such comments also point out the extent to which altruists often need to break with role models and the ethical systems these role models impart *in order to* perform their altruistic acts.

John was a Dutchman but was raised in the border country between Switzerland and France, where his father was a minister in a parish near Geneva. John was interesting for many reasons, not the least because his background so resembled that of Klaus Barbie that a film was made discussing the similarities between the two men and asking why one became the notorious Nazi "butcher of Lyon" while John found himself on the Gestapo's Most Wanted List.[28] The following conversation came after a discussion of John's ethical development and the extent to which his rescue activities flowed naturally from the lessons he had learned from his father. Unprompted by any further probing on my part, John launched into the following remarks, clearly airing a concern that had been on his mind independent of my investigation.

> And even very strangely, I always learned to be truthful, to say the truth, never to lie. But when we came before the German Gestapo, who wanted to raid, and they ask, "Were these people [Jews] in your house?" it was for me very natural to lie, to say, "I don't know." Only after the war, I say, "Was I right or not?" I don't know.
>
> In Holland, my story is the story of many people. You may know the story of that lady, Corrie ten Boom, who was a Dutch lady who helps the Jewish people. She say the same thing: "When it happen, I say 'No. I not have Jews here in my room.'" Very naturally, she lies. Only later, after the war does she wonder, "Am I right or wrong?"
>
> See, thousands of people in Holland have the same question: Was their conscience right or wrong? And see, even now, I say, "Was I right or wrong?" I don't know.
>
> **Q.** *But at the time—?*
>
> **A.** [*Interrupting*] No question. No problem if it's right or wrong. *It was right!*

Several other rescuers raised this same issue, volunteering unsolicited information about how they had not only lied but even killed during the war. "How did you feel about this?" I would ask. The answers varied greatly. Some rescuers expressed deep regret and anguish over murdering someone, even a Nazi.[29] Others did not.[30] Margot provides one interesting example as she describes an interaction with the Gestapo commander for Amsterdam.

We [the Resistance] had a man planted in the Gestapo. It was a policeman, a Dutch policeman. One day I had to contact him. So I call him up at Gestapo headquarters [for Amsterdam]. A man answers, and I said, "Is Mr. —— in?" This was referring to my friend, you know, the one who is the spy. "No, he's not in. You got a message?" this voice asks. I said, "Yes. Would you tell him, please, dinner is at eight." You know, that was code. That was the end of the conversation.

So later when my friend comes to me that evening, he said, "You dolt!"

I said, "What happened?"

"You know who you talked to?" he asks.

"No. What do I care who I talked to? What happened?"

Now, there was an expression in Dutch. When you want something, you say, "Riks for that." For your sweater, for example. Riks was money. It was worth about two dollars and fifty cents, or two guilders. It's like saying, "A penny for your thoughts," or "I'd give anything to have that."

So my friend says, "The person you spoke with is the Gestapo commander for all of Amsterdam. And he tells me, 'You got a message. "Dinner is at eight." Riks for that woman, for that voice.' He wants to meet you."

I said, "Wonderful!"

He said, "No way."

"Oh, yes," I said. "You have a nice lunch tomorrow, and you introduce me."

And that's what happened. That guy [the Gestapo commander] became my friend. You wouldn't believe what I went through with a friend like that!

Q. *So you became friendly with the Gestapo commander for Amsterdam, while you were hiding Jews and helping the Resistance?*

A. [*Nods*] Friendly! Honey, you don't know what I went through with such a friend. You know, a person who has not been there cannot really understand. It's impossible.

Margot then told me she had conducted an affair with the man in order to get information for the Resistance.

One time this man [the Gestapo commander], when he comes into my house, I was standing there, staring, just looking in the street. The Germans took young people away from the street. It doesn't matter whether they were Jewish or not. That had nothing to do with it. They had to work in the German factories in the east. And he comes, and I look at him and I said, "Isn't that awful?"

Now, I tell you something that is true, darling. Honest to goodness. This is something that I never forget. I said, "Isn't that awful, taking away these young people?"

He just shrugged his shoulders and said, "So what does one more or less matter?"

I turned around and I said to him, "I want to tell you something. The Germans will never win the war. Never! There will be a time that you will ask me to help you. And I will say to you what you say to me now: 'So what does one more or less matter?'"

I said those very words to that man, to this Gestapo commander. He got up and came over to me. And he said, "You are a little kid, and I love you." And he kissed me on the forehead.

I told him, "I got to go. But you're going to learn a lot." He just laughed.

Now, here the war's over. I got to tell you this. My people—like the FBI, but in Holland, it's more like the police—they came to me when the war is over and say, "Have you got time tonight?" I said, "Yes, sure. I always have time. Why?" The war was just over. I said, "Why? What happened?" "We have to go to the camp, to the German camp," they tell me. "Okay," I said. "Fine."

So they picked me up at ten o'clock at night. We got up there. It was up north, west of ———. I didn't know what my people wanted. And we got in there, and they asked for Mr. Such-and-Such. I don't even remember the name.

Now, this German Gestapo commander was a general. He was always dressed immaculate. His boots were shined. His nails were done. His hair was beautiful. Now, in comes a man. No shoes on. Dirty feet. Dirty nails. Disheveled hair. Horrible-looking. It was him. And he sees me and gasps. One of the men says, "Do you know that lady? Tell me about it." I hadn't told anybody about this event, you know [the story I just told you], when I said, "The war will be over, and you won't win." And he falls on his knees and he says, "You know I only did what I was told to do." And I despised him like you wouldn't believe! He just clung on to my legs, and he says, "You have to help me."

And when he was through begging, I said, "So, you're through?"

He said, "Yes, please."

I looked at him and I said, "I know, not too long ago, somebody was standing at my window and said, 'What does it matter, a few of these more or less?' when those poor Dutch youngsters were taken away. Now, I said at that time, the tides would be reversed. And since you are ready, I want to ask you people to kill this gentleman, because we don't need one of these 'more or less.' Good night."

I opened the door and I walked out. And the next day the Dutch hanged him. They got the whole story. When or where, I don't know, because I didn't tell them. Isn't that something?

Margot later commented more directly on her ethical beliefs.

Q. *Do you have any particular ethical credo that has guided your life? Any system of ethical beliefs?*

A. You don't steal. You don't hurt anybody. You don't lie. Well, I lie sometimes. When I was in the Resistance, I lied a lot. When I was in Prague [when the Nazis invaded], you should have heard what I told them! I didn't believe it myself.

Did it bother Margot to lie and deceive people, particularly since she had just told me honesty was a critical part of her ethical system? "Honey, are you nuts? These were the Nazis!" As usual, Margot's reply was concise, colorful, and to the point. But she articulated what several other also alluded to: a kind of social contract that had been broken by the Germans, who came—as Bert said—"like thieves in the night" and imposed their law on others.[31]

Examples like Margot provide some support for the idea that the rescuers were developmentally sophisticated enough to recognize that the moral order had been violated by the Nazis and then acted (as did Margot) to restore the equilibrium.[32] But this does not completely explain what remains an anomaly of rescue behavior. Rescuers habitually lied, frequently stole, often neglected and endangered their families, even occasionally conducted illicit sexual affairs and murdered people in order to save Jews.

Comparing Margot's account with John's, we see the tremendous variance in guilt and emotional turmoil felt when rescuers deviated from the ethical standards they had been taught as children. This added to my difficulty in finding a clear pattern to any influence on altruism from the development of moral reasoning. Given the similarity of ethical belief systems transmitted to altruists and to rational actors, I feel confident concluding that ethical systems themselves do not critically determine altruism. (This is not to suggest that ethics do not influence behavior—presumably, the ethics of a serial killer differ significantly from most other people's—merely that the specific contents of ethical belief systems do not account for behavioral differences between rational actors and altruists.)[33] But beyond this, it seems clear only that while altruism may have some relation to development in moral reasoning, altruism is not the same phenomenon, and the influence on altruism from moral reasoning is unclear.[34]

INTERACTION WITH EXTERNAL ENVIRONMENT

Let us now assess some of the interactionist variables noted as important by social psychologists. Such explanations emphasize the interactive decision-making process between the individual altruist and the external or social conditions that might encourage altruism. Certain of these factors were discussed in earlier chapters, when we discounted the impact of community size, group approval, and group sanctions on altruism. Let us now ask whether familiarity with the person helped, his or her particular characteristics, and the immediate circumstances of the encounter have any bearing on the probability of altruistic behavior.

Familiarity with the Person Helped

There are many stories from World War II in which Jews were saved because they happened to see someone they knew before the war, and this person was moved to compassion by their plight.[35] Such anecdotal evidence has been supplemented with more systematic studies which find that altruists are more likely to help people they know than they are to help total strangers.[36] We noted earlier (chapter 8) the frequent link between entrepreneurs and the organizations to which they gave money or the groups for whom they volunteered their time. This pattern was also evident in some of the philanthropists. These findings suggest that altruism may be encouraged by familiarity with the needy person. Is this the case?

In general, no. Altruists may, indeed, help those they know, but their altruism is not limited to such individuals. The mixed evidence on philanthropists probably reflects their mid-position on the conceptual continuum between self-interest and pure altruism. If we consider the rescuers or heroes, however, a different picture emerges. None of the heroes except Lucille had experienced any prior contact with the people he or she saved, and Lucille's contact was peripheral, being limited to knowing that the young girl was a neighbor and to having said hello to her on one previous occasion. A few rescuers did know some of the Jews they saved. The first person Tony rescued, for example, was the father of a school friend. But in no case did rescuers make a distinction between Jewish people they knew and those they did not know. Tony saved many other people in addition to his friend's father, and he clearly indicated that this familiarity was not the reason he saved the man. Beyond this, most of the rescuers I interviewed had no previous acquaintance with the Jews they helped. This was true for Margot, Knud, Maruska, Alida, John, Irene, and Peter, for example. For all rescuers what was important was that people needed help, not whether or not they knew the person in any kind of ongoing relationship.

In general, then, I conclude that familiarity with the person being helped is a factor of some importance for entrepreneurs; its importance exists to a lesser degree for philanthropists. Overall, however, its significance so decreases as we move closer to pure altruism on our continuum that we would have to discount it as a factor significantly influencing altruism itself. As with some of the economic explanations discussed in chapter 7, familiarity with the recipient appears to explain the limited quasi-altruistic activities of rational actors but not the actions of altruists themselves.

Characteristics of the Person Helped

Are altruists more likely to aid someone they find attractive in some way? Someone with whom they have a common bond, such as nationality, gender, or old school ties? Are people more likely to assist a small and innocent child than they are to aid a querulous older person? What about a person who is simply a more difficult individual to deal with on a daily basis? Do factors such as these enter into the calculus of altruists, especially those who risk their lives to help others?

Nonaltruists clearly make such distinctions in their charitable giving, as Billy's narrative illustrates, and there is a glimmer of such considerations among philanthropists also. But altruists in general appear unaffected by the characteristics of the needy person. Rescuers readily acknowledged the variation in the personalities of the people they saved. When asked, they openly acknowledged that some people were more difficult to deal with; some grumbled all the time, demanded special treatment, refused to take precautions necessary to avoid endangering others in the group, insisted on leaving hiding places to walk in the open air.[37] These people were as difficult to love as to save. But not one rescuer refused to aid anyone because of these reasons.[38]

> **Margot.** I like people. Listen, to me it's like this: either you like a person or you don't. If you like him, you do what you can. If you don't, you don't. The hell with them. You don't have to kill them. You can still say you don't like them.
>
> **Q.** *Are you saying that the fact that you don't like somebody doesn't mean you can't help them?*
>
> **A.** That's right.
>
> **Q.** *Would you help people you don't like?*
>
> **A.** Absolutely.
>
> **Q.** *Would you help a person that you thought was terrible?*
>
> **A.** If something happened to that person, certainly. If I can help somebody, I will be happy to do it.

Margot articulates the general pattern among altruists. It is not necessary to like the person being helped in order to help them, nor are the characteristics of the needy person determinative. Rescuers did not seem to gravitate more to Jews they found sympathetic.[39] Women were not more likely to help other women. Children and babies were not particularly cherished because they were more innocent. (Babies were also noisier, of course, as were children in general.) My readings about the other side of the moral equation, about those who perpetrate genocides such as the Holocaust, suggest the killers are far more affected by the characteristics of the victim than are altruists.[40] Neither familiarity with nor the characteristics of the person in need of help explained the actions of the altruists I interviewed.[41]

What about Margot's refusal to help the Gestapo commander after the war was over? Does her turning him over to the Dutch with the suggestion that they kill him indicate a judgment about him as a person, and therefore support the theory that personal characteristics determine whether help is given or denied? Possibly. It is equally possible, however, that Margot is responding emotionally to years of anger and personal sacrifice. I should perhaps have probed more deeply into this incident, asking Margot to interpret it for me. I did not do so because I felt it was too sensitive for Margot to discuss easily.

This returns us to the other rescuers who killed people in order to protect Jews. If we interpret such actions as reflections of rescuers' judgments about the moral innocence or guilt of the people they killed, such acts might provide insight into rescuers' assessment of the characteristics of the person to whom aid was denied. Certainly they could reflect an implicit judgment made about the relative worth of the individuals whose lives are threatened. In this sense, some of the rescuers must have judged guilt and innocence contextually; that is, violence, including the taking of a human life, is not always wrong. My impression given the general context of the narratives, however, is that these deaths were less a moral judgment than the necessary, albeit distasteful and morally reprehensible, part of helping the Jewish victims of the Nazis.

My general conclusion, then, based on data that are admittedly difficult to evaluate, is that there is only ambiguous support for the view that the characteristics of the person being aided influence altruism. The only characteristic that seems consistently and directly relevant for altruists is the need of the recipient.

Situational Influences on Altruism

Security in Surroundings

Finally, let us consider situational factors that might influence altruism.[42] Social psychologists often stress the interaction between the individual altruist and the environment, especially the altruist's sense of security in these particular surroundings. They argue that it is far easier to help someone whose car breaks down outside your home in the middle of the afternoon and with all your family around you than it is to stop on a deserted street late at night in the middle of a rainstorm. Did the surroundings make a difference for the altruists I interviewed?

Again, the rescuers prove highly informative. John told me that he organized an escape route for Jews to Switzerland because he knew the border country and could therefore easily take people across, acting as a guide. In minimizing the danger of what he did, John ignores the fact that hundreds of other people knew the border country well but did nothing to help Jews. Nor does he mention that he also organized a similar escape route across the Pyrenees, a geographic area with which John was *not* previously familiar.[43]

Of course, many rescuers did save people on their home turf. (Bert is one example; Alida and Knud would be others.) But just as many did not, performing their acts of altruistic heroism in unfamiliar surroundings. Otto and Irene, for example, saved people after they themselves were in German camps (a concentration camp and a slave labor camp, respectively). Peter, while stationed in a post away from home and caught in the uncertainty of war and the shifting alliances of the Czech and Slovakian governments, forged masses of documents for Jews, saying the Jews were critical to the war effort and should be spared.

The heroes provide an equally diverse group in this regard, with some of their rescues taking place in familiar surroundings but others on unknown terrain. Lucille illustrates both situations. The rape she broke up occurred just down the block. This was familiar territory, even though there was no one else home during the day and she says she was frightened. Her youthful kindness to the little black girl trying to get onto the bus with a chicken also occurred in Lucille's hometown and with her grandmother present. But her civil rights activities led her into situations that would intimidate many of us. She frequently stopped to pick up hitchhikers while she was alone in the car. Jumping into the Nile River to save a Sudanese is another example of Lucille's altruism in unfamiliar territory.[44]

Overall, then, since acts of altruistic heroism seem to occur just about as often in unfamiliar terrain as in familiar, I do not judge this explanation of altruism to be convincing.

Bystander Behavior

One final situational variable concerns the presence of friends or other potential altruists, a factor often referred to as the bystander effect. This theory suggests that altruism (or its absence) can be predicted by what other people do during the crisis. It is a view inspired in part by the infamous Kitty Genovese incident, where a young woman was brutally murdered outside an apartment building filled with people listening to her cries.[45]

While the presence or behavior of bystanders may encourage or discourage helping behavior by nonaltruists, I found little to support the idea that this factor affected altruists. As Lucille was capturing the rapist, two women passed by in a car but accelerated and drove to safety once they realized what was transpiring. Lucille noticed this but was undeterred. Nor did the hostility of her neighbors during the southern civil rights period discourage her. Gerald charged into a crowd of onlookers who were cheering as several youths beat up a policeman. Certainly the rescuers were not deterred by the fact that others around them did nothing.

The bystander effect, therefore, like other situational factors, must be discounted as a critical determinant of altruism.

CONCLUSION

The kinds of influences emphasized by developmental and social psychologists may encourage quasi-altruistic acts among entrepreneurs, but they produce neither consistent nor definitive explanations for the behavior of the altruists I interviewed.

The socialization patterns, the nature of altruists' relations with parents and role models, patterns of social learning, and the specific content of the ethical messages transmitted by altruists' parents and other role models—none of these differed significantly from those of nonaltruists. When we consider stage theoretic explanations for altruism, we find some evidence that altruists subscribe to universal moral principles, marking them as individuals who have reached a high level of development in their moral reasoning. But it was the rescuers, precisely those individuals who come closest to approaching pure altruism in my sample and who most frequently express the universal moral principles of the highest stage in moral development, who deviated most wildly from their learned ethical beliefs, and they did so precisely in order to save victims of Nazi persecution. Their altruism necessitated this deviation from their learned ethical systems. Finally, a consideration of interactionist and situational influences likewise discloses little effect from such factors. Neither acquaintance with the person being helped nor the security of being in a familiar physical environment affects altruism. Altruists seem unaffected by bystander behavior and even by whether or not they like or dislike the needy person. The only characteristic of the person that seems relevant for altruism is, in fact, their neediness.

PART IV

The Altruistic Perspective

CHAPTER 10

The Altruistic Perspective: Perceptions of a Shared Humanity

> You help people because you are human and you see that there is
> a need. There are things in this life you have to do, and you do it.
>
> —Bert, Dutch rescuer

> We all belong to one human family.
>
> —Irene, Polish rescuer

I HOPE the preceding chapters have substantiated my claim that remaining within the paradigmatic confines of self-interest can produce only limited explanations for altruism. Let us now ascertain whether perspective does, as I have asserted, supply the missing piece in the puzzle of altruism and detect critical differences between altruists and rational actors.

My findings concerning perspective differ from more traditional analyses of cognitive influences on altruism, which tend to stress the development of moral reasoning or suggest that helping behavior stems from attempts to replicate democratic norms or beliefs in a just world.[1] Indeed, we saw in chapters 6 and 9 that moral development, as usually conceived, had little impact on altruism. "Good" people are not necessarily more altruistic than ordinary mortals, and the specific substance of altruists' ethical belief systems differs little from that of the rational actors I interviewed. While there are clear cognitive influences on altruism, the influence does not take the form traditionally suggested in the literature. Instead, the relevant cognitive component centered more on altruists' world views and canonical expectations about what constitutes normal behavior and on their perceptions of a shared humanity. This is reflected in altruists' insistence that they have not done anything extraordinary or praiseworthy. It also made their altruism a logical outgrowth of their sense of self in relation to others, giving altruistic acts a reflexive or instinctual appearance and removing them from the conscious process of moral reasoning that is often stressed. Let me document these surprising findings below, suggesting both how my findings differ from the more traditional cognitive explanations and then presenting the evidence supporting the importance of perspective for understanding altruism.

World Views

In assessing the relevance of cognitive development to altruism, I took the conventional knowledge about the importance of moral development as a point of departure. In chapters 6 and 9, I discussed the effect of the content of ethical beliefs on altruism and asked if people with highly developed ethical systems are more likely to be altruists. Although this constitutes one of the simplest, most intuitive and longest-standing explanations for altruism, it did not appear to be a strong predictor of altruism. A comparison of entrepreneurs (the baseline sample) with other groups suggested no difference in the specific content of ethical systems: virtually all the individuals I interviewed, from entrepreneurs to rescuers, described ethical systems in which truthfulness, honesty, family, and clean business practices figured prominently.[2] Equally astonishing, the ethical systems of traditional rational actors appeared just as highly developed as those of the altruists I interviewed. In their daily lives, rational actors demonstrate what most of us would judge equally high standards of morality and honesty. They have analogous experiences with critical role models, and the specific ethical messages transmitted by their role models reveal remarkable correspondence to the messages received by altruists. Chapter 9 thus presented ambiguous but essentially negative evidence on the importance for altruism of moral development as traditionally conceived.

What did seem to strongly influence altruism was world views and canonical expectations about normal behavior. World views constitute extremely powerful influences on altruism, with the critical factor being the altruist's perception of self in relation to others. But contrary to earlier findings, this perception was not framed in terms of group ties. Indeed, altruism is not a product of the altruist's perceptions of others, in terms of the others' particular group or their individual characteristics or likability;[3] nor was it a reflection of the altruist's views on human nature or beliefs in a just world. Rather, it is a reflection of the perceived relationship between the altruist and *all* other human beings. Altruists share a view of the world in which all people are one. This world view appears to bond them to all humanity in an affective manner that encourages altruistic treatment.

This was not what I had expected to find. I originally thought world views might affect altruism in one of two different ways: (1) People who saw the world in terms of communities and groups—frequently described as having a *Gemeinschaft* mentality—would be more altruistic, especially toward those in their own community, than would individuals who see the world as a place in which ties between people are volitional.[4] (2) As a variant of this, I thought altruists and nonaltruists would be distributed in some pattern along a continuum between these two world views.

To my surprise, I found only limited and superficial evidence for either of these phenomena. In terms of world views, clear cognitive differences existed. There were indeed subtle shifts along the conceptual continuum, from self-interested rational actors to altruists, with philanthropists falling somewhere between the entrepreneurs and the rescuers and heroes.[5] But the crucial dimension was not the expected *Gemeinschaft/Gesellschaft* distinction at all. To my surprise, most analysts since Hume appear to be wrong: group ties and group membership do *not* appear to be critical predictors of altruism.[6] Rescuers and heroes are just as likely to be loners as they are to belong to a group. Some come from tight-knit, cohesive communities, and others do not. The same was true for philanthropists and for rational actors.

In terms of world view, the groups closest to the self-interest pole of the continuum were more likely to think in terms of group ties, particularly ties to their families.[7] All of the entrepreneurs and—to a slightly lesser degree—the philanthropists seemed to care for the needs of their families first or to give to causes with which they felt some association or tie.[8] This evidence suggests there is some support for the idea of the importance of perceived group ties on philanthropy and the quasi-altruistic activities in which rational actors engage. But this was not true for altruists farther to the right on my continuum. Rescuers did not distinguish between in-group and out-group members when they risked their lives to help strangers. They neither asked nor appeared even to consider whether they had something in common with the people they saved.[9]

Q. *Was there anything in common about the people you helped?*

Margot. No. They were just people.

Q. *You didn't know most of the people that you helped, then.*

Margot. No. I know a lot of them now, of course, the ones that stayed in my house.

Consider in this regard the extraordinary rescue of 85 percent of the Jews of Denmark.[10] Some have attempted to explain this phenomenon by suggesting that Denmark considered indigenous Jews more Danish than Jewish. In contrast, a Danish rescuer (Knud) suggests simply that the Jews were people who needed help, and so he and the other Danes helped them. Knud further underscores this by relating how many of the Danes were anti-German, and yet helped Germans opposed to the war to escape to Sweden, even though, as the war was ending, the tide of refugees pouring into Denmark became a flood. Knud's attitude here, as before, was not to ask whether these refugees were "good guys" who had been persecuted by the Nazis or Germans fleeing the destruction of war. The relevant fact was that they were people who needed help.[11] "We helped them with food, schools, hospitals. There were some non-Jewish refugees who came up too. We couldn't distinguish between the Danes and Norwegians and the German and Jewish refugees from other countries, but we certainly took care of all of them."

Altruists exhibited a world view that can best be described as universalistic. This was more important than societal or group ties, more important than liking a particular person. This universalism was evident in the extent to which altruists commented on the value of nonhuman life and—as we shall soon see—lay at the core of altruism.[12]

The Just World Phenomenon

I wanted to know whether altruism could be explained through the idea that those who feel people are good and the world is just[13] will act in a manner that confirms this view.[14] I knew of the desolation felt by Jewish and political refugees after the fall of France. One Jewish survivor described this desolation but said he had continued to be optimistic because he "couldn't have lived" if he had not been an optimist. This is the motif I would have expected to find if someone acts in a way to validate particular beliefs about the world. It is the kind of finding that would substantiate the "just world" phenomenon. But I found it among none of my altruists. Not one rescuer, for example, mentioned being motivated to save Jews because of a need to confirm a belief in a just world. There was far too much evidence to the contrary to maintain this myth. Yes, rescuers felt Jews were treated unjustly. But they did not save Jews in order to assert or confirm their own beliefs in a just world.

Nor did altruists act to validate beliefs that people were good. I asked specifically about views on human nature. Most people I interviewed felt human nature was mixed, sometimes good, sometimes bad. Their remarks reflect both the complex nature of altruists' views on human nature and the degree to which these views are unrelated to their altruism. Here is Melissa's evaluation.

Q. How would you describe man's basic human nature? Do you think people are essentially good, or bad? Or are people more self-interested or other-regarding?

A. That's an interesting question. I'm kind of ambivalent about it, because I think they're both good and bad, but basically I think people are pretty much self-interested. But you know, there are so many exceptions.

There was, if anything, a slight tendency among both altruists and rational actors to find self-interested behavior the norm. There was, moreover, no indication that a higher opinion of one's fellow human beings would encourage better treatment of them. The following exchange with Margot represents the general tenor of the responses on this point.

Q. *How do you view human nature? Do you think people are basically good or basically bad?*

A. Well, you cannot say. I don't know if they're good or bad. That has nothing to do with it.

Q. *Do you think people tend to think about other people very often? Or do they tend to be more self-centered?*

A. I don't think they think much about people.

Q. *Let me ask you about how you view other people in relationship to yourself. How do you see other people?*

A. Some are boring, some are interesting.

Q. *In terms of relating to them, though, do you feel a strong sense of community? Do you believe there are some people you meet and you decide whether you want to be friendly with them or you don't? Or do you believe that there are ties that we are born with?*

A. No, I don't think we have ties. I think you meet somebody—like I met you—and I think, "There's a fabulous person. I like her." And that's it. It's one person I like. And then again, I'll meet someone else and say, "Oh, that guy is terrible."

Q. *Would you help the person that you thought was terrible?*

A. If something happened to that person, certainly. If I can help somebody, I will be happy to do it.

Q. *Do you feel you have a choice here? [Margot shakes her head no.] It just happens? That's just the way you are?*

A. Yeah. You don't just stand and think. You have no time to think. Suppose somebody drowns. If you stop to think, "Shall I? Shall I not? Eeny, meeny, miney, mo." You can't do that. You either help or you don't. You don't walk away. You don't walk away from somebody who needs real help.

My overall impression is that altruists do not feel obligations toward others because of any felt communal ties. Margot likes people or doesn't like people on an individual basis, almost as her fancy dictates; in this, her feelings toward people appear to be volitional. But liking them does not determine whether or not she will help them. On this point, Margot was clear. You don't have a choice over whether or not to help someone. "You don't walk away. You don't walk away from somebody who needs real help"—even if this is someone who "is terrible." My original ideas about how world views would affect altruism were dead wrong. Margot fits the associational model, in which ties toward others are a matter of choice, up to the individual. Yet for Margot, while liking people is optional, helping them is not.

Self-Image

What about self-image? Does this affect altruism? In trying to discern that part of a world view most closely associated with altruism, I found the altruist's self-image to be far less salient than the altruist's view of self in relation to others. The relational aspect of this world view appears critical, for I found no evidence supporting earlier claims that it is *only* the altruist's sense of self that is relevant.[15] Altruists do not necessarily see themselves as leaders, or even as people who must "do the right thing."[16] When I asked people to describe themselves in some detail and to answer particular questions about themselves, things began to come into an intricate focus. Altruists' views of themselves, like the self-images of entrepreneurs, were quite mixed. Some altruists felt insecure (Lucille), while others felt they could tackle the world (Otto). Many rescuers described themselves as family people (Bert), but so did many entrepreneurs (Billy, Justin, Ray). Furthermore, not all altruists considered themselves family people (Lucille and Tony did not). Some altruists described themselves as brave and fearless. (A perfect example is Maruska, the Silesian countess who stared down the Gestapo over a sofa.) Other altruists appeared extremely timid and shy. (Alida was a Dutch rescuer, whose sweetly tentative, smiling face peered shyly out from behind the curtain as she waved good-bye after our first interview.) Some altruists described themselves as people with many friends, always caught up in a whirl of social activities (Margot). Others saw themselves as alone (Irene).

These are but a few of the dimensions explored during discussions of altruists' self-images. What was most striking was the great variation in how altruists saw themselves. In addition, the view of self often fluctuated wildly within one person over time. This should not be surprising: people have different moods, ups and downs. Altruists are just like the rest of us in this regard.

There was, however, one notable characteristic shared by all the altruists I interviewed. All saw themselves as people strongly bound to others through a common humanity. Let me describe this perception more fully, and then suggest how it is manifested in particular canonical expectations about what constitutes normal behavior, with heroes and rescuers in particular insisting that they had not done anything extraordinary and moreover had no choice but to do what they had done.

NOT SIMPLE EMPATHY BUT PERCEPTIONS OF A SHARED HUMANITY

The sense of being tied to others differs subtly but significantly from empathy, a concept whose importance for morality has long been noted.[17] The term "empathy" itself comes from the German *Einfuhlung*, meaning "feeling into," and was introduced into the vocabulary of American intellectuals early in the twentieth century by psychologist Edward Titchener. Interestingly enough, however, the term empathy was first widely used to characterize not morality or psychological states but rather a mode of aesthetic perception, as in the way an observer entered into the artist's mind when regarding a painting, a fact I found intriguing as I developed my own concept of perspective.[18] As a term, empathy moved from this more limited conceptualization to its present use after psychotherapists adopted it. Kohut referred to empathy in discussing the bond between parent and child, using the term to indicate any aspect of a positive affective bond.[19] Rogers used the term empathy to denote how the therapist enters into and achieves understanding of the patient's state of mind during psychotherapy.[20]

As currently used in psychology, empathy denotes more than simply feeling my way into another's perspective; it suggests that this newly acquired understanding of another's feelings is joined with my concern, regard, or pity for those feelings to form a bond that then results in altruistic behavior.[21] Many scholars feel that it is this kind of empathy that engenders altruism, helping, and prosocial behavior.[22] The dominant view is that the "capacity to put oneself in another person's shoes is behind most altruistic behavior."[23] Counterarguments suggest that the perspective-taking aspect of empathy in itself is not sufficient to cause altruism, since this increased understanding need not necessarily be utilized for the other person's welfare.[24] Since the psychological literature rests heavily on laboratory experiments or simulations in which empathy is operationalized in many different ways, an analysis of empathy and altruism in real life situations—so-called naturalistic settings—seems particularly useful.[25]

I found empathy does appear to explain the other-directed behavior of traditional rational actors. It is reflected, for example, in the pattern of entrepreneurs' gifts, which are made primarily to recipients with whom the donors feel a personal connection or bond.[26] Empathy's influence abates somewhat, however, as we move toward altruism. Melissa does resemble entrepreneurs in giving mostly to people and causes with which she has some empathetic tie or identification, but other philanthropists appeared not to need this tie to inspire their generosity.[27] Nor was a personal link necessary for heroes or rescuers. Below is a telling exchange with Margot.

Q. *Was empathy a part of your rescue activities?*

A. Meaning what?

Q. *Feeling that this could be me.*

A. No. Never even thought of it.

Q. *You didn't think of that at the time?*

A. [Shakes her head no]

Q. *Did you feel sorry for the people? Pity?*

A. I don't know. I didn't feel anything, to be honest.

Margot's insistence that she did not think at all, indeed, that she had no empathic feelings that went through her head before she rescued people, was characteristic of both heroes and other rescuers. Empathy seemed less important for those people who come closest to approaching pure altruism on my conceptual continuum. Altruists like Tony, Bert, and Lucille require no particularistic empathic link to others to want to help them. They need not experience any complex perspective taking or role playing in order to help others.[28] Nor do they talk about feeling another's pain as their own. What is more significant than putting themselves in another's place, and what *was* common to all the altruists I interviewed, was a bond with the person in need of help that arose out of a particular perception of themselves in relation to others. Altruists seem to conceive of themselves as part of all mankind rather than as members of any particular group or subgroup. This perception of themselves as part of a common humanity, and not personalistic or empathic ties to family, gender, and religious, national, or ethnic groups, most aptly captures the systematic and consistent differences between paradigmatic rational actors and altruists. I believe it is this particular perspective that creates the bond that encourages altruism.[29] Because of this, I have characterized the heroes and rescuers, and to a lesser degree the philanthropists, as John Donne's people, embodiments of the world view Donne expresses in the seventeenth Meditation of the *Devotions upon Emergent Occasions*.

> No man is an island, entire of itself; every man is a piece of the continent, a part of the main. If a clod be washed away by the sea, Europe is the less, as well as if a promontory were, as well as if a manor of thy friend's or of thine own were. Any man's death diminishes me because I am involved in mankind, and therefore never send to know for whom the bell tolls; it tolls for thee.

Unlike many of the rest of us, people like Bert and Lucille and Tony need not send to know for whom the bell tolls. They know. This perception of themselves as one with all humankind is such an intrinsic part of their perspective, of the way they define themselves, that they need not stop to make a conscious decision when someone is drowning in a lake or knocking at the door asking for help. This spontaneous aspect of altruism was clearly illustrated in virtually every interview I conducted, as articulated by Ursula, a Berlin rescuer who—significantly—voiced it not in response to questions about how she saw the world or herself in it but rather on her own initiative, in an attempt to explain that she had not acted out of duty.[30]

Q. *Do you consider it to be your duty to help someone in difficulties, even if that exposes you or people who are close to you to danger?*

A. This is a strange question. At that time, one had quite another attitude than at the present prosperous time. We were simply much more welded together, we and our Jewish friends. We knew they needed us.

The idea of being welded together, of belonging to one human family, surfaced over and over again in my interviews; indeed, I was struck by the similarity of expressions used, particularly since I myself was careful to avoid terms such as "one family of man" and never suggested such a view in my questioning. Tony, in fact, articulated this viewpoint in the first few moments of our first telephone interview, at a time when he knew only that I wanted to speak with him about his wartime experiences in connection with research on altruism.

> I was to learn to understand that you're part of a whole, and that just like cells in your own body altogether make up your body, that in our society and in our community that we all are like cells of a community that is very important. Not America; I mean the human race. And you should always be aware that every other person is basically you. You should always treat people as though it is you, and that goes for evil Nazis as well as for Jewish friends who are in trouble. You should always have a very open mind in dealing with other people and always see yourself in those people, for good or for evil both.

This idea was voiced by all the rescuers and the heroes I interviewed. "Everything is dependent on everything else, and if we wipe out any one of the other, we're going to lose that much more in the nature of things," Lucille told me. Otto extended this explanation even further by drawing a connection between the mass murder of the Jews and one's perceptions of a shared humanity.

> This is also one thing which I wanted to tell you. . . . I was always intrigued by the question: How could seemingly normal people become killers? Once, I got an interesting answer. In a camp in Upper Silesia, I asked one of our guards, pointing at the big gun in his holster, "Did you ever use that to kill?" He replied, "Once I had to shoot six Jews. I did not like it, but when you get such an order, you have to be hard." And then after a while he added, "You know, they were not human anymore."
>
> *That* was the key: dehumanization. You first call your victim names and take away his dignity. You restrict his nourishment, and he loses his physical ability and sometimes some of his moral values. You take away soap and water and then say the Jew stinks. And then you take their human dignity further away by putting them in situations where they even will do such things which are criminal. And then you take food away. And when they lose their beauty and health and so on, they are *not* human anymore. When he's reduced to a skin-covered skeleton, you have taken away his humanity. It is much easier to kill nonhumans than humans.

Otto paused:

On my medal, the Yad Vashem medal, there is an inscription. It says, "Whosoever saves one life, he has saved the entire humanity." And I think the inversion of that is also true. Whoever kills one innocent human being, it is as if he has killed the entire world.

My explanation of altruism, then, centers on this sense of a shared humanity, a perception of self at one with all mankind. It is a much vaguer and subtler concept than the traditional ones—such as religion or role models—that social scientists like to identify. It lacks the comfort of explanatory concepts such as psychic utility or group or kin selection, which are equally intricate but which do not challenge existing orthodoxies based on the norm of self-interest. It differs in nonobvious but significant ways from psychological explanations emphasizing empathy or perspective taking or extensivity. Yet it was the common factor among all the altruists I interviewed, the only one that refused to go away under the most careful scrutiny.[31]

I would characterize it as a different way of seeing things; it certainly represents a different way of seeing the world and oneself in relation to others. Altruists have a particular perspective in which all mankind is connected through a common humanity, in which each individual is linked to all others and to a world in which all living beings are entitled to a certain humane treatment merely by virtue of being alive. It is not any mystical blending of the self with another; rather, it is a very simple but deeply felt recognition that we all share certain characteristics and are entitled to certain rights, merely by virtue of our common humanity. It constitutes a powerful statement about what it means to be a human being.

This was articulated in various ways by all the altruists I interviewed. It is illustrated by Bert's quote at the beginning of this chapter: "You help people because you are human and you see that there is a need. There are things in this life you have to do, and you do it." It is evident in Leonie's matter-of-fact statement about how we must treat each other: "A human being who is lying on the floor and is bleeding, you go and do something." It is Tony's recognition that in some sense we all are part of one life force and thus are all related: "I see the whole world as one living body, basically. But not our world only: the whole universe. And I'm like one of the cells. I'm as much a part of that as others. Without me, the universe doesn't exist anymore than my body exists without its cells. I think that we are as much together as the cells in our body are together." Bert's statement focuses on the humanity of the actor, Leonie's on the humanity of the person in need, and Tony's on the extent to which these two intertwine.

Many altruists extended this beyond the world of human beings to include all living things. Margot talked about the humanity of dogs. Lucille spoke of not harming any living thing, even spiders. Others spoke of "the good earth" itself (Knud) or the animal and the vegetable kingdoms (Tony). Life itself was something to be valued for these altruists.

This perspective entails several important consequences for altruists. (1) It means all people have value; this includes the altruist. It means that when altruists sacrifice themselves for others, it is not because they feel they do not have worth of their own. (2) No groups are better than others, since we are all one, are all part of a common and cherished whole. (3) There are no "bad guys" and no "good guys," only people. (4) This, in turn, appeared to give many (but not all) altruists a tremendous understanding for weakness and human frailty and a remarkable forgiveness of even the vilest of deeds.[32]

All these things are evident in Tony's narrative.

> I was impressed with the individual of Jesus as a man, just like you or me, ahead of his time, starting to face these new concepts. Whenever they said, "You're the Christ," he refused [to take the title]. When they said, "You're the Son of God," he'd tell them, "We are all sons of God." Now, if you think of God as creation, then we *are* all part of creation. We *are* all sons of God. And I realized, simply and without getting too deep into these philosophies, that Christ, Buddha, Gandhi, they're all the same person. They are all the hero with a thousand faces. That's what I learned. It's helped me.
>
> I've always been interested, ever since World War II, in understanding what caused this Nazi monster to come to be. And I finally realized, every time you see the monster, you basically are looking in the mirror. I don't feel that the Nazis are monsters. I never felt that way. The Nazis were normal German people who, through education, training, cultural thinking, and greed, ended up where they were. And tomorrow, it's our people. And the day after tomorrow, it's somebody else. History teaches you that the minute you destroy an enemy, you look behind you and he's standing there in your own ranks. You have to many times look in the mirror to make very sure that he hasn't crept into your head.
>
> We have to watch for the "old yellow gooks" mentality. It is much easier to shoot at or burn the "yellow gooks" than to shoot at and burn some other farm boy just like yourself. But the evil and the good can be in all of us; good and bad is in all of us. You have to look in the mirror. We're always looking in the mirror.

This sense of being a part of a whole, but a whole that includes everyone, that includes all living things, from evil Nazis to their innocent victims, and a whole in which we ourselves share the good and the evil, this constituted the world view shared by all the altruists I interviewed. It was striking and, I believe, significant that this world view, in turn, provided a particular anchor for what constituted normal behavior.

Canonical Expectations about Normal Behavior

The self-descriptions of the altruists I interviewed reveal little common thread except the view of themselves as ordinary people, "nothing special."[33] Altruists' descriptions of what they did suggest over and over again that they considered their altruism only "normal" behavior. This implied quite different canonical expectations from those of rational actors. It revealed an entirely different world view, a different way of defining what was "normal" and then naturally and without reflection acting in this "normal" fashion. I believe these canonical expectations about normal behavior account for the anomalous fact that altruists, including rescuers of Jews, insisted they were not special because of their actions toward others. The quotes from Bert, Leonie, and Margot (below) are but three of many virtually identical responses that indicate altruists do not see themselves as extraordinary people.

> **Q.** *Let me ask you one last question. If we wanted to have more people like you in the world, what could you tell us that would be useful in doing that?*
>
> **Bert.** Well, let me say it different than you ask. When there was a bigger amount of normal people, the world was already much better, don't you think? What the world needs is more idealists. I am not one. I know that sometimes, for the Jewish case, they want to advertise people like me. But I don't know that the world itself is so much better because of some old geezer like me. I am not that unusual a person.

I asked Leonie a similar question.

> **Q.** *I was told that you refused to take the Yad Vashem medal of honor. Is that right?*
>
> **Leonie.** Yes.
>
> **Q.** *Why is that?*
>
> **A.** Oh, I don't know. There were people who had done so much more. What I did, that was just very little. I hadn't really done much, and so I don't feel. . . [*Pauses*] What I did was such a normal thing to do that I don't want to be put on a pedestal. It's not that kind of thing.

This reluctance to view themselves as special was evident in other rescuers, as is demonstrated by Margot's response to the question posed in a slightly different way.

> **Q.** *How would you view yourself? How would you describe yourself? You said you were an extrovert. How else would you describe yourself?*
>
> **A.** I never would describe myself. I have my good sides and my disagreeable sides. I can be a bitch, and I can be nice.

Q. *Well, when I go home tonight, my husband will say, "What was this woman like?" What should I tell him?*

A. Well, what would you say? Nothing, nothing special. Just a person. Just an ordinary person.

Q. *You don't see yourself as anything special?*

A. No, I'm nothing special.

Q. *You don't think you did anything extraordinary?*

A. No, definitely not.

Q. *How can you say that?*

A. Because I didn't do anything extraordinary. Lots of people help others. No, I certainly didn't do anything special. No, absolutely not. I didn't do that much.

This from a woman who risked her life, lost contact with her young children, was imprisoned six times, and conducted an affair with the Gestapo commander for Amsterdam to get information for the Resistance, and whose fiancé was beaten to death by the Gestapo because of her actions. If we can take her at her word, and after knowing Margot well for many years now I believe we can, then her canonical expectations about how the world operates, of how people behave toward each other, of what is "normal," all these certainly differ from the view held by most rational actors. But this appears to be the world as altruists see it. More particularly, it is how they see themselves in relation to others. Tony articulates this better than I.

I don't think that I did anything that special. I don't know if I'm really the world's most desirable citizen. Let's not get too focused on me. What I did is what everybody normally should be doing. We all should help each other. It's common sense and common caring for people. We live in one world. We are one people. Working together, basically we are all the same.

Q. *You don't consider yourself a hero?*

A. No. I always have trouble with that definition. What exactly is a hero? It can be a total lunatic who does something and happens to succeed in doing something that was basically an absolute madcap thing. To me, the closest thing to a true hero is the guy who is terribly scared and does it anyway. To me, that is a real hero.

Q. *And you were not a hero, because you weren't scared?*

A. Well, there were moments that I was scared, but I mean. . . [*Pauses*] This is sort of confusing. When you think of a hero, you think of some Greek god standing there defending the pass against five thousand Persians, knowing full well he'll be beaten. That is the true hero in the classic sense.

Q. *You don't see yourself as a hero?*

A. No. I'm a cautious hero.

Q. *Well, most people would say that what you did was an extraordinarily good deed and that you should be rewarded for it. Do you think you did anything unusual?*

A. I don't think that I did anything that special. I think what I did is what everybody normally should be doing.

All the altruists I spoke with responded in similar ways. They disagreed with my assessment that their deeds were extraordinary in any way. They saw themselves as acting "normally, just doing what anyone would do," even though the rescuers, at least, *must* have known that everyone else was *not* behaving so "normally" or the Jews would not have needed help in the first place.[34]

Altruism as Reflex, Not as Choice

I believe these particular expectations and world view explain why altruism so frequently appeared reflexive, not the result of a conscious process in which reason subjugated the passions. "One thing is important," Otto told me. "I never made a moral decision to rescue Jews. I just got mad. I felt I had to do it. I came across many things that demanded my compassion."

This spontaneous response seems more comprehensible for the heroes, who are presented with an immediate life-or-death situation that is soon resolved. But what about the rescuers, who had ample time to rethink the costs of their actions? Here, the evidence is all the more striking because of the ongoing nature of rescue activity. Surely, during the long nights spent by Otto in the concentration camps or by Irene in the major's bed, one would become all too conscious of what one had done. Yet all the rescuers insisted, over and over again, that there was no choice to make. "It's pretty near impossible not to help," Margot told me in our first interview. Later, after I knew Margot better and felt I could ask her more directly about her experience with the Gestapo commander, I probed more deeply on this point, particularly about the extent to which she had made a choice to do what she did and how she weighed the costs of her actions. My own background as a political economist, trained to think in terms of costs and benefits and conscious calculus, may have made it more difficult for me to accept that anyone could do such extraordinarily difficult things without thinking about them. But Margot's case was particularly enigmatic for me: as a mother, I would find it impossible to endanger my children, and as a woman, I cannot imagine what it must take to conduct an affair with someone you so despise, even in order to save lives.

Q. *You started out, almost before we even began the interview, talking about making conscious choices, and you said you didn't really think you did that. Was there a conscious choice that you made?*

A. I don't make a choice. It comes, and it's there.

Q. *It just comes. Where does it come from?*

A. I don't know. I don't think so much, because I'm not so smart. I got nothing much to think with.

Q. *. . . I'm asking—I don't want to put words in your mouth here—but what I've heard other people say when I've asked them this is that they didn't think they could live with themselves if they'd not helped Jews. Is that true for you?*

A. It has nothing to do with it.[35]

Q. *It was just totally unconscious?*

A. Yes. You don't think about these things. You can't think about these things. It happened so quickly.

Q. *But it isn't really totally quickly. There's a tremendous amount of strategic planning that has to be done.*

A. Well, I was young. I could do it. Today, I don't know. I'd have to try it. But I was thirty-two years old. That was pretty young.

Q. *You didn't sit down and weigh the alternatives?*

A. God, no! There was not time for these things. It's impossible.

Q. *So it's totally spontaneous? It comes from your emotions?*

A. It's pretty near impossible. You couldn't do that [turn someone away]. That's no way [to be]. . .

Q. *How about the repercussions of your actions? Did you think about what might happen because you were doing this?*

A. You don't think about it. No way.

Q. *You didn't worry about possible consequences for you, for your family?*

A. No. No way.

I quizzed Margot on this several times later, only to receive virtually the same answer on each occasion.

Q. *You never thought about what you were doing?*

A. Never gave it a thought.

Q. *But all this time, when you're sleeping with this guy [the Gestapo commander], when you're in prison and you don't know where your children are, surely—*

A. I never gave it a thought.

Q. *You never asked yourself, "Why me? Why do I have to be the one?"*

A. No. I only wondered about my kids. Listen, it was war, honey, and everybody died. You didn't have time to think, to count your buttons, "yes," "no." No way! You acted. You had to act.

Many other altruists articulated this same spontaneous and reflexive aspect of altruism, supplying valuable information concerning the extent to which ethical behavior emanates from reason[36] or feelings.[37] The altruists I interviewed rejected this traditional juxtaposition for discussing the importance of moral reasoning. They suggested not that the conscience wins out over the baser passions but rather that altruists' views of themselves in relation to others is so central a factor in their altruism that such a debate never even arises. Instead, altruists see the world differently. Their behavior results from the recognition that the actor is human and therefore required to act in a certain way, and that the needy person is human and therefore entitled to certain treatment. Humanity plus need: This is the only moral reasoning, the only calculus for altruism. This is a far cry from the cost/benefit calculus which I had been trained to apply to human behavior.

The spontaneous aspect of altruism was closely related to the extent to which altruists said they had no choice in their actions. This again was most striking when we consider the rescuers and the risks they incurred, not just for themselves, but also for their families. Despite these risks, the idea that there was no choice in their actions constituted a kind of leitmotif that ran throughout my conversations with the rescuers. This was tied into the kind of differentiation Tony made between feeling an unquestioning commitment to save Jews and making a conscious choice about *how* best to go about doing this. Tony was extremely articulate in describing what I would call a tactical concept of conscious choice: he consciously considered *how* best to help others but not *whether* to help.

Q. *What about your rescue activities during the war? You knew that the risk was very high that you would be caught. You'd already been sentenced to death and were living underground. Weren't you in rather a risky situation as far as that went?*

A. Yes, but it was a controlled risk. I might be taking a high risk, but I was not taking an uncontrolled risk. To me, that is an important difference. You have to constantly take risks. Your whole life is based on that sort of decision, and those decisions cannot be totally selfish. You have to think of your fellow man, not just yourself, for when you save your fellow man, you save yourself, too. It is the principle of life you are trying to help.

Tony was not the only rescuer to describe this lack of choice. For all rescuers, even those who were not articulate enough to express it as clearly as Tony, the determination to help was never in question; it presented itself instead as a given, and it emanated from their sense of themselves in relation to others.[38] Indeed, at some time or another during our interviews, virtually all the rescuers looked at me, almost with bewilderment, and in effect asked, "But what else could I do? They were human beings, like you and me."

> **Q.** *How did you decide to rescue Jews? What was the decision-making process that went through your head when you began all this?*
>
> **Margot.** Honey, I never even thought about it.
>
> **Q.** *You never thought about what you were doing? About what it might mean for you or for your children?*
>
> **Margot.** I swear to God, I never even gave it one moment's thought.

Other rescuers reported similar experiences.

> **Bethe** (Berlin rescuer). We knew what could happen. If they had caught us, we would have been taken away. The children would have been taken away. We absolutely knew this. But when they're standing at the door, and their life is threatened, what should you do in this situation? You could never do that [turn them away].

This remarkable feeling that they had no choice concerning whether or not to risk their lives for strangers was firmly entrenched in the altruists' perspective on themselves in relation to others. It is this shared perception of themselves as part of an all-embracing humanity that was the one common characteristic that consistently and systematically distinguishes altruists from other individuals. It gives rise to an instinctive response that guides their actions in saving others and makes even life and death decisions nonconscious. Their perspective, their view of themselves as part of all humanity, constitutes such a central core to their identity that it leaves them the sense that they have no choice but to aid others in need.[39]

CONCLUSION

How can we best explain the differences between altruists and the paradigmatic self-interested individuals who exist at the heart of disciplines as wide-ranging as psychology, evolutionary biology, economics, and rational actor theory? The most important and consistent difference centers on systematic similarities in perspective. All altruists have a particular way of seeing the world, and especially themselves in relation to others. All the altruists I interviewed saw themselves as individuals strongly linked to others through a shared humanity. Their perspectives differed consistently and significantly from those of traditional rational actors in this one regard.

Two important behaviors flowed naturally from this. The first suggests that altruism does not correspond to the accepted wisdom in Western ethics, in which moral actions are believed to arise from the dominance of reason over the baser passions. For both the heroes and the rescuers I interviewed, decisions to risk their lives to help another person appeared spontaneous and simple. There was no night of anguish spent searching one's soul to find the strength to do the right thing. "You do things because you are human and because there is a need," one Dutch rescuer said simply.

Closely related to this was a second interesting phenomenon: in describing their activities, altruists claimed to have had no choice in their actions toward others. In explaining this, John—the rescuer on the Gestapo's Most Wanted List—said, "I think that it came as a natural reaction from the inside. Like a mother. Normally, you don't teach a mother how to love her baby. She has that naturally. Maybe not the father, but the mother. And so your instinct that you develop in yourself is to react that way. And so it was a quite natural development, not 'Should I do it or not?'" This lack of a cost/benefit calculus, indeed of *any* conscious calculus, was especially remarkable in individuals who had to decide whether to risk not just their own lives but also those of their families. Yet, uniformly, rescuers insisted that they never thought about it, never saw a choice there to make. "The hand of compassion was faster than the calculus of reason," Otto told me, articulating both the spontaneous and the nonreasoning aspect of altruistic behavior.

When I focused on the constancy of this perspective and asked how susceptible it is to external appeals to group identities and empathy, the results were also surprising. This particular perspective seems constant, being evidenced at an early age in all the altruists I interviewed. It is not strongly related to group ties, however. While both familiarity and empathy occasionally explain some of the philanthropist's altruism and much of the entrepreneur's quasi-altruistic behavior, neither of these explains acts by rescuers or heroes.

At first I had difficulty reconciling this consistent and striking phenomenon with findings by other scholars, findings ranging from philosophical discussions based on inference and logic to empirical works utilizing experimental or large-sample statistical studies, and suggesting that a multitude of factors explain altruism. But then I realized one important fact: the particular perspective that constitutes the heart of altruism might easily be activated by many different factors, from genetic coding and religious teachings to group or kinship ties and psychic utility.[40] Metaphorically, I compare it to different people traveling to the same destination, such as a family reunion or a party. Depending on where each individual starts the journey, each person will take a different road, but all the roads eventually have to enter the same town or there can be no arrival at the common destination. So it is with altruism.[41]

In focusing on so many different trigger mechanisms of altruism, and engaging in the inevitable scholarly debates about which is in fact the determinative one, perhaps we scholars have mimicked the fabled blind men who went to see the elephant. Each touched and described a different part of the elephant's body. In describing the elephant as ropelike (because we felt the tail) or like a pillar (because we felt the leg) or pointed (because we felt the tusk), we have each been partly in the right and all been partly in the wrong. If the particular perspective I have just described occurs consistently among *all* altruists, if it becomes more evident—and it does—as we move from the philanthropist to the hero and on to the rescuer, then it seems reasonable to describe it as the critical influence accounting for altruism. But it may be prompted by many different factors. This explains why earlier studies which emphasize such different explanations for altruism are, at least to a certain extent, correct. But it also suggests why so many of these earlier studies have disagreed with each other and why so much scholarly debate continues to exist. Analysts simply focused on different trigger mechanisms and missed the critical underlying attribute.

In stressing the critical role of perspective, I am not suggesting that other factors never encourage altruism or that we should expect any single factor to explain behavior as complex as altruism. What I am asserting is that the role of perspective is so constant and significant that it appears to be critical.

I asked altruists, particularly rescuers of Jews, why they felt they had been able to rescue Jews when others had not, why they had this ability to see the common humanity when others did not. Here is Tony's response.

Q. *Why do you think some people are able to reach out across the boundaries of race and nationality and see others as human beings, while the rest of us don't?*

A. Two things prevent it from happening. First, some people have very closed minds. They're terrified of letting go of their security blanket, whatever it is: religion, Marine Corps membership, Jewish or Christian faith. Any of these things can separate me. Without them, then I suddenly would have to face my own humanity.

The second reason is the lack of exposure. I hear people talking about homeless people, saying, "Well, they're all a bunch of drunks who don't want to work." People don't realize there are many homeless people who are simply mothers without a husband who cannot get transportation, cannot get their wardrobe together to get a job, and who consequently are trapped in homelessness. Yet here people lump them all together and say, "None of these people really wants to work, and they're all a bunch of drunks, and that's it."

If they spent one afternoon in downtown L.A. and looked and learned to see through their eyes, they could not give that same answer. Most people look away. They don't want to see because it's disturbing. I see this now, and I fully believe the people who lived next to the concentration camps and say, "We never saw anything." Of course they didn't see anything! They didn't *want* to see! You don't want to think of your son sitting there getting his jollies out of torturing people or sticking them alive in an oven.

Tony highlights the importance of giving a human face to misery, of not abstracting it away from you and thereby minimizing its importance.[42] In this regard, it is significant that the altruists I interviewed kept referring to the importance of "seeing" others. This importance of perceptions, of seeing the common humanity, of looking beyond the unkempt hair of Tony's homeless person or the dirt and filth on Otto's unwashed Jew, constitutes a critical feature of altruism.

My analysis suggests that earlier explanations of altruism may have failed to discern the critical explanatory variable by instead accurately identifying the various factors that may trigger the emergence of this different way of seeing oneself and one's world. While the various trigger mechanisms may precipitate the development or growth of an altruistic perspective, it is the perspective itself that constitutes the heart of altruism. Without this particular perspective, there are no altruists. What causes it in any particular altruist may be many different factors, as innate as a genetic predisposition toward altruism, as explicit as parental exhortations to think about others, as transient as situational factors. But it is the common perspective that any of these external mechanisms trigger, and not the triggers themselves, that remains critical. It alone consistently and systematically predicts altruism among all the individuals I interviewed. It consists of a common perception, held by all altruists, that they are strongly linked to others through a shared humanity. This self-perception constitutes such a central core to altruists' identity that it leaves them with no choice in their behavior toward others. They are John Donne's people. All life concerns them. Any death diminishes them. Because they are part of mankind.

CHAPTER 11

Perspective and Ethical Political Acts:
Initial Thoughts

ARE THERE broader theoretical insights to be gleaned from our analysis of altruism? I believe so. It seems clear that perspective offered a less limited approach conceptually than did explanations that rest on assumptions of self-interest. This suggests the value of moving beyond theories based exclusively on self-interest if—as was the case with altruism—we desire a more complete understanding of important social and political phenomena. In particular, we should consider the importance of the cognitive and the value of utilizing concepts such as perspective when developing theories that concern ethical political behavior. Thinking about the elements of such cognitive theories is my task in this last chapter. I hope these modest first attempts at theory construction will stimulate others to build on my initial work, to incorporate cognitive concepts such as perspective into their own theories, and to move beyond the paradigmatic confines of self-interest when constructing theories about ethics and politics.

I begin the chapter by sketching my theory and contrasting it with rational choice theory.[1] I then discuss some possible advantages offered by my theory and suggest the categories of political action for which it appears relevant. I conclude by suggesting several specific empirical phenomena it might successfully explicate. Throughout this discussion, I limit my remarks to human actions that fall at the intersection of politics and morality and refer to this domain as the realm of ethical political behavior.

THE LINK BETWEEN COGNITION AND BEHAVIOR

Perspective on Self in Relation to Others

The essence of the theory I propose can be stated succinctly: Ethical political action emanates primarily from one's sense of self in relation to others. This perspective effectively delineates and sets the domain of options perceived as available to an actor, both in an empirical and a moral sense. Certain situations[2] present choices[3] that affirm or deny one's basic perception of self in relation to others.[4] As a general rule, ethical political behavior flows naturally from this core perspective. To pursue an action that deviates in any significant regard from this necessitates a personal shift in identity that can occur only at great psychological cost and upheaval for the actor.

Let me mention three caveats and then sketch the rough outlines of the central points covered by this theory.[5] The theory is prelusive; future work will need to elaborate on the conceptualization, origin, and development of identity, defined here only in general terms to refer to one's sense of oneself and one's character.[6] Such elaborations undoubtedly will clarify and modify my initial formulations.[7] Similarly, a more complete specification of the nature of the cognitive process underlying perspective is required, with special focus on the interplay between identity and incoming information and how structural contexts shift and affect both core identity and perspective.[8] Finally, while I believe the theory has broader application, at this time I restrict discussion to ethical political behavior, defined narrowly as acts involving both the political institutions of the state and individual ethics.[9]

Origin of Ethical Acts Not Conscious. The prime force behind ethical acts is not conscious choice but rather deep-seated, intuitions, predispositions, and habitual patterns of behavior related to our central identity.[10] The factors that produce what Hutcheson called our moral sense range from genetic programming to social roles and culturally inculcated norms; they include, but are not restricted to, values we know consciously that we hold.[11] Our actions in situations that tap into ethical concerns are motivated more by our sense of self than by any conscious calculus. Indeed, conscious cost/benefit calculus rarely determines ethical political acts. Such behavior touches our core values and triggers a different calculus, one in which actions are aligned as closely as possible to the actor's sense of self. In such instances, any cost/benefit calculus is restricted to the strategic assessment of *how* such action can best be carried out, not *whether* it will.

This emphasis on central identity should not imply that an actor may not have conflicting identities.[12] If identity excludes some set(s) of actions, it also may leave available another set of actions, that is, an array of possible behaviors. We need to so construct our theories that they allow both for ambivalence and for these shifts in, and conflicts of, identity.[13] Our sense of self "selects" the ethical options perceived as available much as we select from a series of options on a computer menu. My menu, for example, includes WordPerfect, e-mail, and Chess. I choose WordPerfect because I am a writer or e-mail because I am an academic who communicates with other scholars. I never use Chess but include it on my menu because I am a mother whose sons occasionally play chess on my computer. Similarly, I "select" a decision-making mode in accordance with the situation and the particular part of my identity that comes into play.

Ethical Political Decisions and Core Values. Most everyday decisions that involve a conscious calculus entailing choice do not engage our basic sense of self. These decisions involve most economic acts (e.g., where to eat or which car to buy) and many political acts (e.g., whom to vote for or whether to donate money to a particular political campaign). This is only a general rule; it does not mean that some individuals might not treat economic or political decisions as ones that relate to their basic identity. Individual core values, after all, vary drastically from one person to the next. Nor does it mean that any given individual may not vary in the way he or she regards a particular kind of economic or political act.

Consider as examples decisions in areas as disparate as voting, dressing, and marriage. In general, I may use a rational choice calculus to decide how to vote or what dress to buy, but not whom to marry. This is not necessarily the case, however, for voting may become a kind of moral referendum, when, for example, the candidates represent opposing stances on a war or on abortion or when a question concerning increased funding for prisons is understood as a test of toughness on crime. Even something as trivial as choice of clothing may emanate from identity and perspective; I want to feel dignified at a state banquet but alluring at an anniversary dinner with my husband. And, although I, myself, would once have thought it rare, I have learned that some people do apply a rational calculus to marriage.[14] (Shortly before our marriage, a lawyer who worked with my husband commented that by choosing an academic for a wife my husband was diluting his income. Presumably a hard-core rational choice theorist would explain my husband's choice through the nonpecuniary advantages of marrying an academic, or me in particular. To a young man in love, the remark seemed strange and revealed a rather different perspective on life from his own.)

I hope the above examples suggest how important it is to understand when and how an action touches on core values and when it does not. Situations that tap into core values will bring identity and perspective into play; those that do not will be resolved by the more traditional cost/benefit calculus. Whether a particular situation actually taps into this sense of self will vary both from person to person and over time for the same individual. Each individual locates issues on an inner continuum: some have only superficial significance; some strike at the basic sense of self; and there are innumerable positions in between. But generally people have a kind of master identity that determines how they deal with both kinds of issues. Theoretically, the same individual could respond differently to roughly identical issues and situations at different points in his/her life cycle.

Identity Supersedes Consciously Held Moral Values. In this selection process, identity is more basic than conscious adherence to moral values. As a general rule, most people do not sit down and consciously survey alternate sets of moral values, assess them, and choose one to follow as a guide for their lives. Rather, adherence to moral values, whether this adherence is loose or rigid, evolves out of one's core identity.[15] This core identity includes our innermost sense of who we are and what ties and obligations we believe we have to others.[16]

Decisions as Recognition, Not Choice.   Our basic conception of ourselves is fundamental and preset for most adults. If an act touches on our basic sense of self, then the act becomes less a choice than a recognition, akin perhaps to an inner realization, reflecting a statement of who we are at the most fundamental level of self-awareness. This self-recognition involves an acceptance that only certain options are available to us because of who we are or, more precisely, who we perceive ourselves to be. It is the perceived identity that is key, not the actual identity itself, although for most people these should relate fairly closely. Fully understanding the extent to which we discover identities will involve us in a discussion of the relation between the forms of identity we can grasp consciously and the unconscious substance of identity, including the role of cognition and emotions.

Actors Discover, Rather Than Create, Their Identities.   Identity is not created by an actor so much as it is revealed to an actor through his or her own acts and by the realization that the actor cannot do X but feels compelled instead to do Y.[17] It therefore seems more appropriate to speak of a person's recognizing, rather than creating, his or her own identity. This may be because core identity emanates at least in part from genetic factors and early childhood experiences, and develops at such an early age that its basic construction cannot be said to result from an adult's own free choice or will. We may modify our identities later in significant ways but only at great psychological effort.

Perspective More Important Than Identity.   A crucial influence on behavior is perspective on oneself in relation to others, not merely one's sense of self. Furthermore, it is the self-knowledge or recognition of this relationship that is critical, not the actual or objective existence of that character or identity. The key to action is our perspective on ourselves in relation to others and not objective, third-party assessments of this perception. For example, genocidalists frequently see themselves as the victimized parties honestly acting to redress a grievance. What to an objective observer is a barbaric act of murder, genocidalists perceive as a preemptive strike necessary to ward off their own destruction.[18] Thus, a belief about one's identity in relation to others leads to action in accordance with the perspective on the particular identity relationship; the perceived identity (genocidalist as potential victim) becomes more salient than the reality (genocidalist as mass murderer).

CONTRAST WITH RATIONAL CHOICE THEORY

Since rational choice theory is considered both a normative and a positive political theory, it seems particularly appropriate to compare it with an alternative theory focusing on acts that occur at the intersection of ethics and politics.[19] In doing so, I am not arguing that rational choice theory is wrong, merely that it has limited application and that analysts must apply it only when relevant. The following discussion should demonstrate that some acts emanate from a kind of rational choice calculus but that others require a different theory. As a general rule, acts that emanate from core values will be better explained through a cognitive theory emphasizing identity, such as the perspectival theory proposed here, than through rational choice theory.[20] But acts that do not tap into our basic sense of self may be explained quite satisfactorily through rational choice theory.

Example 1: Choice of Restaurant. Most people may not care deeply about where they eat. But if I am a religious Jew and feel I can eat only in a kosher restaurant, then my choice of restaurant reflects my identity; expanding my options to include a meaningful consideration of whether or not to eat nonkosher food would pose a threat to my identity. Thus my identity defines the range of options available to me. Only after I have satisfied the demands of my identity and excluded all nonkosher restaurants may I apply a standard cost/benefit calculus to all kosher restaurants, rationally weighing factors such as the quality of the food, size of portions, cost, ambience, et cetera.

What if I am born a Protestant and convert to Orthodox Judaism at the age of thirty? Before my conversion, a decision to eat nonkosher food did not touch my basic sense of self; after the conversion, it does.[21] This example illustrates how one particular individual might view identical situations differently over time, but will not, at any time, regard as a viable option behavior that violates his or her fundamental sense of self.

Example 2: Response to Sexual Harassment. I may love my job, until I discover that sexual favors are expected as part of my employment. A woman operating in a rational choice mode might subject the situation to a conscious deliberation and calculate whether the sexual demands constitute too high a cost of employment. In contrast, a perspectival mode might lead the woman simply to feel, "I'm not that kind of girl," slap her boss's face, and walk out. (Alternatively, she could view herself as a victim and put up with the demands.) This is the kind of situation, then, that may or may not come into conflict with a person's basic sense of self.[22]

This example is intended to illustrate the importance of identity *in relation to others.* I would hypothesize that a woman who feels her basic sense of self violated by sexual harassment would be less likely to subject her response to a conscious deliberation than one for whom the situation does not touch so closely on her basic identity. Consider, in this regard, the issue of sexual harassment as it surfaced during the confirmation hearings for Clarence Thomas. Might such shifts in perspective concerning one's sense of self be relevant here? If we attempt to analyze Anita Hill's accusations against Clarence Thomas in such a light we might ask the following questions. If we assume

Professor Hill was telling the truth, was her initial silence a result of a conscious deliberation? Of feeling powerless in the situation? Did her feelings about herself change over the years? Was there a shift in her perceived identity in relation to others? Or was it merely that she decided to speak up only after she had tenure and the job security necessary to make doing so less costly, in an economist's terms? To what extent were Professor Hill's actions spontaneous at any stage in the process? To what extent were they the result of conscious deliberation or calculation? How much was her range of choice limited by her view of her identity? Of her perceived relations to Thomas? To others? All of these are interesting questions; few of them would even be asked if we restrict our analysis to a rational choice approach.

This example also underlines the importance of conceiving of core issues and more superficial issues—as with conscious and nonconscious calculations—on a continuum in order to understand how a core issue may become subjected to a rational choice calculus and, in some situations, even take on a degree of negotiability.

Example 3: Response to Theft. Suppose I am visiting New York City for the day. While walking down Fifth Avenue, my purse is stolen, leaving me with no money and no train ticket back to my home in suburban New Jersey. How do I get home? I know no one in New York whom I can call to ask for a loan of money. I have no bank or credit card with which to obtain ready cash. What do I do? What options do I consider?

Most of us who are middle-class would probably go to the police and try to secure a loan. An optimist might approach a stranger on the street, explain the situation, and ask for enough cash to get home. A savvy shopper might ask to charge cash on a department store credit account whose number could be retrieved through the store computer. Few of us would think of stealing someone else's money, even though robbing someone to obtain money would clearly have been forced into our framework of possibilities by what had just occurred. And few people would think of offering to engage in an act of prostitution to secure enough money to buy a train ticket home. Why not? Are the "costs" of theft or prostitution too high for our integrity? Or is it more probable that such actions would simply not even occur to us and that, if they were suggested to us by someone else, we would know without reflection that such acts are not in character, are not the kind of acts in which someone "like us" would engage? I suspect it is the latter. Our behavior is limited by the range of options compatible with our concept of what is acceptable behavior for "people like us."

Example 4: Wartime Behavior. In an earlier work (Monroe 1994), I described an interview with a German soldier who viewed World War II as an inevitable repetition of history, not something subject to rational calculus.

Kurt said he knew that the German invasion of Russia meant that Germany would lose the war. When asked why he did not resist, even returning, against medical orders, to fight with his unit the day after he had received a serious head wound that necessitated complete rest, Kurt replied that he had to be with "his people" or he was "nobody." His acts during the war were heavily filtered through his perspective on himself in relation to others. Certain acts were not acceptable because of this perspective.

The perspectival constraints on Kurt's behavior are readily evident when we consider the contrasting case of another German soldier who treats the war in highly rational terms, staying in his unit only to avoid being shot for desertion and trying to avoid fighting in all possible ways. Axelrod's discussion (1984) of cooperation provides just such an empirical example, one from trench warfare during World War I. Recognizing the futility of the slaughter, soldiers on both sides of the trenches aimed their guns so that the shells fell in "no-man's-land" instead of on their opponents. This satisfied the high command's need for military action, while keeping the fighting men alive. It may be that the soldiers engaged in an elaborate cost/benefit calculation and decided it was not worth it to be killed in a war that was ending. But it is also possible that they turned to cooperation with the enemy because their individual perspectives had shifted. As foot soldiers out in the trenches, they identified more with the other poor souls they were supposed to kill than with their military leaders back in the safety of high command.

I intend the above examples to convey how explaining ethical political situations involves us in questions of perspective and identity. We need to know which situations touch on an actor's perspective and basic identity and which do not. Doing so will allow for the importance of framing decisions, a phenomenon noted by political economists[23] and by psychologists.[24] It also will help us better understand certain political actions that bear looser relations to ethical values (e.g., behavior in a prisoner's dilemma) as well as behavior by groups of individuals whose acts fall directly at the intersection of ethics and politics, as was the case for those who rescued Jews during the war.

But even more ordinary political acts, such as the decision to vote, might be subject to shifts from the rational calculus to the nonrational realm, depending on the particular individual or on how the individual voter's perspective is constituted at the time of a specific election. For example, new citizens, here to avoid political persecution, may view their first votes quite differently from the votes they cast after twenty years of democratic citizenship and participation in meaningful free elections. Alternatively, a lifelong citizen who is often indifferent to politics may be drawn into action by the sudden existence of an identity issue about which the voter feels strongly, such as war or abortion. To understand ethical political action, then, we need a better understanding of when and how situations touch actors' core values and basic identities.

Advantages in Viewing Ethical Political Acts in Terms of Perspective

Even in its prelusive state, the perspectival theory outlined above already offers several potential advantages as an explanation of ethical political action.

(1) Such an approach builds on the long tradition in Western philosophy that posits an autonomous and intentional self residing behind the mind,[25] but it avoids the metaphysical abstraction of a self that operates outside any human context.[26] By focusing on an individual's perspective on self in relation to others, we automatically include in our purview the world in which an individual is already engaged, thus linking the individual to culture and cultural influences. By focusing on the individual's perceptions of this relationship, however, and not on the relationship itself, we allow for possible genetic components of identity, as with born skeptics, cynics, or optimists, for example, whose innate predispositions lead them to put a certain gloss on events. This provides the individual with a kind of master identity that makes the actor more than merely the product of specific relationships.[27]

(2) The perspectival theory broadens the concept of choice, moving away from the heavy emphasis on discrete, specific choices at a particular moment—the model of economists and rational choice theorists—to one in which choices are treated more as summaries of agents' whole personalities and their entire life experiences.[28] It effectively builds a bridge between the kinds of discrete analysis of rational choice theory and the psychological literature on personality types,[29] thus offering the potential for the kind of rich analysis the Oliners (1988) provided in explaining rescue activity through reference to an altruistic personality.

(3) The perspectival approach incorporates critical aspects of Marxist, feminist, and rational actor theory, possibly reducing such theories to particular branches of a broader theory of the self. This is a strong claim, so let me elaborate.

Consider first the concepts of false consciousness and consciousness raising, utilized in both Marxist and feminist theory. Each of these concepts can also be integrated into a theory of self and others, since both Marxist and feminist theories focus on the idea of identity; only the determinants of the identity (economic class for one, gender for the other) differ. An actor's behavior then is said to follow from these gender or class differences that shape the actor's personality. Acting contrary to one's class or sexual group interests is explained through false consciousness, through a lack of awareness of one's basic and inescapable identity, as defined through membership in this class or gender.[30] By making perspective the primary theoretical explanatory variable, we incorporate critical components of both feminist and Marxist theory and avoid recourse to concepts such as false consciousness to explain deviations from the general theory.

What about rational choice theory? If we conceive of ourselves as rational, egoistic individuals, we will treat others on that basis; if we view ourselves and others as rooted in more communitarian memberships that entail certain duties and obligations, we will respond in a mode appropriate to that perception. Consider one example, that of an actor we will call Ted. When Ted goes to buy a new car, he may well conceive of himself as a rational actor; rational choice theory would then be extremely useful in predicting his decision. But when Ted falls in love and decides to marry or have children, he may no longer see himself as a rational actor does. In such instances, another conceptual paradigm will prove more useful.[31]

Consider further the question of when Ted will pursue strategies to further his individual self-interest and when he will act to further the interests of the particular group or collectivity to which he belongs. Rational choice theorists concerned with collective action have long been aware of the importance of group identities and membership. Some have argued that individuals join groups because the group mediates resources for that individual or provides side benefits.[32] But surely other forces also determine group memberships. (Parent-offspring bonds or socialization provide two such determinants.) The logic of social (as well as economic) competition is often mediated by a group, and the group to which Ted gives allegiance at a particular moment may be determined both by the particular problem he confronts and by his key identity perception at the time.

The marital relationship offers an instructive example of both these factors. In general, Ted and his wife relate as a couple, a single unit, in dealing with the problems that jointly confront them. But during an argument, each shifts perspective and conceives of her or himself as an individual with interests that conflict with those of the spouse. While political negotiation may resolve many clashes of this sort, just as many may be resolved by Ted and his wife simply recognizing that they still feel part of the group (in this case, the marital couple) or recognizing that their ties have so shifted that they now feel alienated and detached from the spouse, that they cannot flourish as the people they are within the confines of this particular relationship.[33]

(4) A theory of perspective allows for change by focusing on the evolving pattern of individuals' perceptions of their relations to others and to society. To illustrate how shifts in an individual's perspective on his key identity in relation to others may well affect the group dynamic, consider an actor called Jim. Assume Jim is a faculty member undergoing tenure review. Jim may perceive his relations with others as undergoing changes. Jim may continue to see himself in the same way, but because he perceives important shifts in the way he is viewed by others within his group—for example, if he begins to feel abused, devalued, or taken for granted—then his behavior may alter to correspond to his new perception of others' perceptions of him. As a result of this difference in Jim's perspective, the entire group dynamic may shift dramati-

cally. What is critical is the perception of the change in Jim's relations with others, not the reality of these changed relations.

This emphasis on the evolving pattern of perceptions incorporates the importance of symbols, which anthropologists argue give meaning to action.[34] It also enters the role of emotions as focusing agents, directing our attention toward particular problems and solutions, something psychologists concerned with rational choice have found important.[35]

(5) The perspectival approach allows for the framing of options, especially insofar as the framing of a choice affects an actor's concept of his or her own identity. It allows a place for manipulation (by the media or by an individual) and for ideology to influence behavior. If I view myself as a valued member of a coalition, for example, I may find it easier to go along with an unpopular group decision. But if I feel undervalued, I may respond as an individual thrown back into Hobbes's state of nature. Depending on my perspective on myself in relation to others, then, my behavior may emanate from quite different aspects of my identity: I may respond as a highly individualistic actor or as a group or team player.

Actors will shift between their individual and group identities at different points in time and depending on key stimuli. Every actor (group or individual) probably has an average point on a continuum where they tend to hover between individual self-interest and group or collective interest. But actors may not be fully conscious of the extent to which they move along this continuum; thus, behavior may result from both unconscious and conscious decisions. Parsing out the critical parts of the process by which actors shift back and forth from individual to group or collective identity will not be easy. An attempt must be made, however, since much psychoanalytic work suggests its importance.

(6) The perspectival approach allows directly for cross-cultural variation. Some rational choice theorists are now trying to introduce culture into their models.[36] Elster, for example, proposes two successive filtering devices that influence choice.[37] The first defines the "feasible set" of options "circumscribing the range of possible action," and the second consists of the process by which an actor chooses from these feasible options.[38] I would argue that cultural variations enter at a more basic level, through one's identity perception, which is strongly influenced by one's culture's perceptions of the actual (and the desired) relationship of the individual to society. This is why canonical expectations constitute such important influences on behavior.

Consider how perspective on self and others allows for changes over time, changes that are analogous to variations across cultures. Even the most cursory knowledge of history reveals tremendous shifts in views on the individual's relation to society. Most of us in contemporary Western society have difficulty fully comprehending a belief in the divine right of kings or societies that practice human sacrifice. The gap between "us" now and our ancestors then (a temporal change) is as great as the gap between modern feminists who consider female circumcision barbaric and those who feel it fills legitimate social functions (a cultural variation).

Or consider a more basic illustration of shifts in Western views concerning the self in relation to others. Both the concept of rationality utilized by traditional economists and Simon's concept of bounded rationality reflect a post-Enlightenment framework that separates the individual from the collectivity. Interests are not identified this way in many non-Western societies, however; and even in Western society, men (not to mention women) as individuals have conceptualized their relationships with society quite differently in other historical eras. Consider just three variations.

Post-Enlightenment political thought assumes individual actors pursue self-interest. A less individualistic, more organic view, however, might argue that individual self-fulfillment results from taking part in the life of the *polis* or society. Under this view, individual and group happiness cannot be separated. The good life is the life spent in contemplation, discussion, and performance of civic duties. Such an organic view is found in some of Plato's works and in works by other classical Greek and Roman theorists.

A more organismic view of the individual's relation to the collectivity is found in works by medieval theorists such as Aquinas.[39] According to this organismic view, each individual has his or her function to fulfill within society, while at the same time maintaining a distinct identity within (but not separate from) society. This view approaches those held in many contemporary non-Western cultures and may explain why Western decision models (based on individualistic assumptions) fare so poorly outside the Western market system.[40] A successful theory of human behavior should allow for these complex ties. A cognitive analysis along the lines of perspective seems a potentially productive route to pursue.[41]

(7) By explaining action through perspective on self in relation to others, behavior can be understood as a result of outcomes (both conscious and non-conscious) and strategies, not just choices.[42] For example, consider a political candidate called Wilbur. Wilbur begins his candidacy thinking of other people and genuinely desiring to run a clean campaign in which issues are discussed openly and fairly. But if, during the campaign, Wilbur feels unfairly attacked or believes the opposition violates what Wilbur believed were commonly held norms in an egregious manner, he may shift to a self-interested, or even a combative, mode. This means self-interest and other-directed behaviors need not be inputs to our models (as they primarily are in rational choice theory) but may also be outcomes of the process, affected and perhaps even determined by the dynamics of the interaction itself. This allows for feedback and for structural and institutional factors to determine behavior.[43]

(8) Finally, although perspective emphasizes the cognitive and the perceptual, this approach still allows for the rational and the emotional; these ele-

ments simply enter the process at a more secondary level. All of these factors—rational and emotional—become part of the cognitive, through the actor's original cognitive framework for analyzing the world, through the process by which the actor filters new information and gives it meaning within this existing framework and through the options the actor perceives as available at a particular point in time. The cognitive provides the key to understanding cultural, developmental, and possibly even genetic inputs.

Possible Empirical Tests of the Theory

One of the challenges involved in developing any general theory lies in establishing empirical tests to determine its validity and limitations. Can we construct a series of tests to empirically examine the value of my theory of perspective? I believe so.[44] Let me conclude by suggesting two areas in which this theory might provide further insights of interest to political scientists: cooperation in prisoner's dilemma situations and voting. I choose these two areas precisely because they are so different substantively and because they would, at least as I conceive of them, be tested using quite different methodological techniques. In each of these tests, however, analysis focuses on determining how action is affected by cognitive differences in perspective.[45] I then contrast these explanations with those produced using rational choice theory.

Prisoner's Dilemma

In its simplest form, the prisoner's dilemma refers to the quandary experienced by two prisoners being questioned by police about a crime jointly committed. Police officers isolate the prisoners and tell each that if he cooperates with authorities, his sentence will be reduced. The suspects understand that since the evidence is skimpy, if neither prisoner confesses both will receive a minimal sentence (say, one year in jail). But they also know that if one prisoner confesses and the other does not, the one who confesses will receive no jail time, while his accomplice will receive a heavy sentence (say, ten years). If both prisoners confess, both go to jail for an intermediate time period (say, five years). What does the prisoner do? Trust his fellow prisoner and take a chance on freedom? Or make sure that he is not the person sold out?

In discussing cooperation in the prisoner's dilemma situation, I focus on one of the most important recent works in that area, *The Evolution of Cooperation* (Axelrod 1984), both because this work had such an impact in the field and because it demonstrates so clearly the value of combining a rational choice approach with a theory that focuses on the self in relation to others.

Axelrod sets his work on cooperation into a game theoretic framework, a framework popular in economics and decision theory and one which analyzes interactions of decisions of individual people (or organizations) whose behavior has the potential to affect each other. Game theorists generally ask how self-interest, tempered by the knowledge of the interests of others in the situation—be it a hypothetical game of strategy or a real life situation, such as war—will lead to mutual accommodation and group activity. Axelrod's particular interest is in understanding how cooperation evolves between two players in an iterated or repeated prisoner's dilemma situation, in which during a single play each player gains from cooperation but can potentially gain more by following a strategy of pure self-interest. The critical factor centers around the uncertainty in predicting what the other player will do. One's own welfare depends on correctly anticipating another's action. It is a situation in which individual rationality, defined traditionally as the pursuit of individual self-interest, leads to a worse outcome for both individuals than is possible had they cooperated.

Axelrod set up iterated prisoner's dilemma games in a computer simulation in which game theorists submitted different strategies. Time and again, the reciprocating strategies yielded better results than either noncontingent cooperation or largely uncooperative strategies. The overall winning strategy was tit-for-tat, which begins by assuming cooperation and then does whatever the opponent did on the preceding move.[46]

Why and how does this cooperation emerge? Axelrod points to several critical conditions: (1) the possibility of future interactions; (2) the initial existence of a cluster of reciprocating cooperators, necessary for cooperation to become a viable strategy; and (3) a cooperative strategy that is able to respond quickly and in kind when provoked by the failure of others to reciprocate. Axelrod supplements his technically derived conclusions with evidence from other sources, including the live-and-let-live system that evolved during trench warfare in World War I. Soldiers simply ceased firing or deliberately fired over the heads of the enemy, in what evolved into cooperation between the soldiers to keep each other alive, even though these actions violated their specific military orders. One interesting question, then, concerns how clusters of cooperating individuals first form. Given that certain conditions exist that facilitate cooperation, why does it sometimes emerge under these conditions and at other times does not? Here is where identity and perspective become relevant and would deepen our understanding of the particular empirical example of the soldiers.

Pretend for a moment that you are a soldier in the trenches of World War I. Do you identify yourself primarily as an individual or as a member of a group? What ties do you have to different groups that compete for your loyalty? Is your primary identity as a German or French national?[47] Or do you see yourself as a doughboy stuck in a hellhole filled with dirty water, just trying to stay alive, along with your fellow recruits? How does your perspective on yourself in relation to these various groups shift?

Such questions suggest that trench warfare cooperation may have evolved from the development of a different kind of identity perspective, one in which individual soldiers' primary referent groups shifted. After long weeks in the trenches, soldiers no longer saw themselves as French or German but rather as individuals with more in common with foot soldiers on the other side of the guns than with noncombatants of their own nationality. The critical group, the one most salient for their well-being and existence, if not identity, had now shifted. The enemy was now the commanding officers who gave orders to break the de facto armistice that was protecting the common soldier. Perception of themselves in relation to their own high command *and* in relation to the soldiers across the trenches had undergone a change. With these shifts in perspective came changes in behavior.

The above-described scenario is entirely speculative, of course. But it would be interesting to interview individuals in this kind of situation to understand how they saw the world, and how their perspectives shifted over time and depended on certain changes in external conditions. If once we move away from actual everyday situations, similar to the World War I example, into the experimental world, it should not be difficult to devise a narrative format, or even to devise survey questions to examine the perspective of participants in prisoner's dilemma situations. We could ask detailed questions about individuals' views of themselves in relation to others. Such questions would be posed (1) before participants begin the prisoner's dilemma games, (2) during the game, and (3) before and after varying the behavior of the opponent in the game. Such tests should yield valuable information concerning which individuals would be more likely to cooperate than others in a prisoner's dilemma situation. They could yield information about the constancy of the role played by these cognitive perceptions and indicate whether the players' perspective and their behavior shift at the same time, in ways specified by the theory and in response to specific kinds of action on the part of the other player(s).

Voting and Civic Duty

Analysts have long been confounded by the existence of certain citizens who appear to receive benefits from voting that are less than the costs to them. Still, they vote. Why? To explain this phenomenon, voting analysts have elaborately modified the basic model of rational choice, the most widely accepted modification being one in which a "civic duty" factor has been admitted.[48] Essentially, the civic duty model assumes that certain voters find utility in the feeling that they are performing their civic duty when voting. They vote, therefore, even when the personal costs of voting outweigh the benefits, because of the pleasure they receive from feeling that they are fulfilling their duty.

This civic duty factor taps into some of the basic identity issues that should, according to my theory, affect voting. Why not combine the two theories to construct an interview procedure that allows us to distinguish between two kinds of voters: (1) rational voters, that is, voters who calculate costs and benefits, and (2) voters who act out of a more basic identity construct, in which their perspective on themselves as citizens causes them to deviate from the basic rational choice model? The latter group (identity voters) may register higher on a civic duty score, but they also may have other identity factors that affect not just their decision to vote but the specific vote choice itself. Voters who support third party candidates or candidates like Gene McCarthy or Ross Perot, even after it is clear that their candidate is not electable, may have various motives. Perhaps they wish to send a message of disaffection to the party leaders; this, of course, would be easily explained using a rational choice model. But perhaps such voters also act as they do because they feel it is important to themselves that they stand up and be counted on a matter of principle. If this is the case, their behavior would be explained more easily by reference to identity. Understanding what their third party vote signifies would provide information useful in predicting future electoral behavior.

These are only two examples of how perspective might usefully be applied to the analysis of political phenomena. I have performed a similar analysis of religious fundamentalists.[49] Nozick's analysis (1992) of American reluctance to adopt methadone programs provides yet another illustration.[50]

Conclusion

How can we best understand ethical political behavior? Over the years, many theories have been developed, from rational actor theory to cultural theory to Marxism. In this chapter, I presented an alternative theory, one that emphasizes the cognitive components of human behavior and, in particular, one's fundamental perspective on self in relation to others. I argue that ethical political behavior ultimately emanates not from class membership, cost/benefit calculus, utility maximization, or the conscious adoption of and adherence to certain moral values but rather from our fundamental perception of ourselves in relation to others.[51] This perspective may shift subtly depending on external stimuli, but essentially it flows naturally from one's perception of self in relation to others, a perception that effectively then delineates and defines[52] the domain of options an actor perceives as available, both empirically and morally.[53]

While this theory owes much to early works by social psychologists and sociologists like William James and George Herbert Mead, it moves well beyond the traditional sociological response to economics.[54] It draws on an earlier tradition in psychology and political and normative philosophy that understands action as the outcome of identity, through the individual's self-defined relation to others.[55] Beyond this, the theory focuses on individual action, not the dynamics or the mechanisms of collective choice. Nor do I attempt to suggest the ways in which my theory of political behavior would yield explicit predictions about how specific people in particular circumstances would behave differently than some other theory would propose they should.[56] Finally, my main goal is not to critique existing political theories, such as Marxism, rational choice theory, or cultural theory, although one implication of my remarks is that key elements of these theories can profit by being used in conjunction with a theory emphasizing perspectives on self in relation to others.

Conclusion

AT THE END of a long journey it is instructive to look back over one's travels, to survey the terrain in order to understand where one has come and what one has seen and done. So it is with a book. What has our discussion taught us about altruism as a substantive phenomenon? About the different theories of social and political life? About ourselves? These are the issues I address in these concluding remarks.

I begin with a simple but important methodological caution. The world is not divided into altruists and nonaltruists; the potential for altruism exists in all people. Indeed, many of us perform occasional acts of genuine altruism, and all but the most misanthropic engage in limited and sporadic volunteer activities or charitable giving. We engage in quasi-altruistic behavior, in other words, without being altruists. Scholars concerned with altruism itself, however, must take care to distinguish between altruism and closely related pro-social acts, such as giving, sharing, or cooperating, and should not confuse these diverse phenomena in empirical work. While we need to make appropriate use of controlled or baseline data samples—and indeed must be wary of analyses that omit such comparisons—we must recognize the subtle differences in behavior that emerge as we move along a continuum from pure self-interest to pure altruism. Works that dichotomize behavior, attempting to sort complex acts into only two categories—altruism and egoism—will miss many of the subtle manifestations of altruism.

Once we recognize altruism's relation to, but critical differences from, commonly analyzed forms of other-directed behavior, we begin to find answers to important substantive questions about altruism itself. We understand, first, why there are so many contradictory findings concerning altruism. A study which draws conclusions about altruism based on how two-year-olds share toys speaks only tangentially to a study in which altruism is conceptualized and operationalized as cooperation among ants or as the allocation of family resources among charities and kin. These are critical methodological distinctions and ones that have engendered much conceptual confusion and substantive misunderstanding over the nature and causes of altruism.

Substantively, my analysis suggests that none of the traditionally offered sociocultural correlates of altruism unfailingly and systematically explains altruism or behavior by altruists. It suggests, further, that remaining within the paradigmatic confines of self-interest produces only partial explanations of altruism. Such traditional analyses offer some limited insight concerning quasi-altruistic acts by rational actors but fail to explain altruism itself.

The essential failure of both traditional sociocultural correlates and the more elaborate social science theories to provide adequate explanations for altruism leaves us in a quandary: What is the critical component that *does* account for altruism? How can we best explain behavioral differences between altruists and the self-interested individuals who exist at the heart of disciplines as disparate as evolutionary biology, psychology, and economics and rational choice theory?

Perspective provides the critical component, particularly the altruist's perception of self in relation to others. Earlier studies of altruism have failed to identify this critical explanatory variable, focusing instead on the many different factors that may precipitate or encourage the development and growth of this altruistic perspective. This perspective provides a feeling of being strongly linked to others through a shared humanity and constitutes such a central core to altruists' identity that it leaves them with no choice in their behavior when others are in great need. It is this perspective that best distinguishes altruists from traditional rational actors.

Three important and striking behavior patterns flowed naturally from this altruistic perspective. These concern spontaneity, choice, and the constancy and universality of the altruistic bond.

Altruistic behavior does not arise from the dominance of reason over the baser passions.[1] Many rescuers, for example, endured long periods of danger and suffering; some were tortured; some spent time in prison or concentration camps. Despite this, however, their decisions to risk their lives to help another person appeared spontaneous. This was all the more remarkable because rescuers knew how terrible the possible consequences of their acts could be. Yet they responded simply, as they felt any ordinary human being would respond to another's need.

Closely related to this finding was a second, of equal interest. The altruists I interviewed claimed to have had no choice but to help others. This lack of choice was increasingly evident among the rescuers, the individuals whose acts most closely approximate pure altruism. For these altruists, canonical expectations about what constituted normal behavior appear to limit the range of choice perceived as available, both morally and empirically.

When I focused on the constancy of the altruistic perspective and asked how susceptible it is to external appeals to group identities and empathy, the results were also surprising. While both familiarity and empathy with the person in need explain some of the philanthropists' altruism, neither factor accounts for acts of rescuers or heroes. For heroes and rescuers, there is indeed a bond established between the altruist and the person helped, but the bond is universal, available to everyone merely by virtue of their existence. This is not the more particularistic empathetic connection traditionally said to occur through entering into the other's place, although it does bear a superficial resemblance. Moreover, the particular bond that arises in response to an altruistic perspective seems surprisingly constant, being evidenced at an early age in all the altruists I interviewed.

These are my substantive findings concerning altruism. What do they suggest about broader issues in social theory? Here I find three implications of note. First, the attempt to smuggle self-interest into acts of altruism makes clear how difficult it is for disciplines founded on the assumption of self-interest to comprehend and explain altruism. To remain true to their intellectual foundations, analysts working within these disciplines struggle to explain away altruism as merely a veiled form of self-interest or as a strategy to obtain deferred benefits for the self. This is as true in economics as it is in evolutionary biology. The same tendency exists, although to a slightly lesser degree, in psychology.

Second, many social scientists, perhaps suffering from a kind of physics envy, want to create a general theory of social behavior.[2] But why must one theory explain everything? Perhaps it is preferable to recognize that there exist inevitable limitations in even the best social theory. We need not strain to fit everything into any one particular paradigm, be it self-interested, communitarian, or perspectival.[3] The fact that a theory does not explain all empirical phenomena does not mean that we should discard the paradigm entirely.[4] I have tried to take care while criticizing theories based on self-interest to make it clear that I still find such theories useful; I merely find them more limited than their advocates suggest. Paradigms based on self-interest, for example, work well in explaining the helping, charitable, and volunteer activities undertaken by traditional rational actors. They can and should continue to be utilized to explain such acts. But they do not explain altruism itself or behavior by altruists. Shifting our attention to the appropriateness of different paradigms can free us from the futility of debates over which paradigm is right or better.[5]

Yet even as we recognize that a theory need not explain everything to have worth, we also must grant that the theory should be reevaluated when even one case clearly contradicts its basic tenets. Altruism constitutes such a case; it cannot be explained fully within the confines of theories based on the assumption of self-interest. Accepting this frees us intellectually to treat our understanding of altruism as an analytical tool to glean more general insights into social and political theory.

The dominant theories in economics, evolutionary biology, and psychology assert that people are self-interested. These theories claim to be positive, descriptive of actual empirical reality and not just reflections of the writers' personal value judgments, norms, or preferences. My examination of altruism shows there are clear limits to the applicability of these theories. This in turn suggests that the ends of human action implicitly endorsed as natural by these theories, ends that stress efficiency and survival, also are limited. In particular, they constrict the range of human activity to an individualistic pursuit of self-interest. Yet, as one rescuer so expressively articulated it: "Life is possible because a certain amount of people are not selfish and believe in sharing with others. If there is no love and sacrifice, no concept of others, then maybe life would be possible in some ways, but it would be a terrible tragedy." Insofar as theories based on self-interest claim to originate not in value judgments but rather in scientifically and objectively derived empirical observation, they lend an aura of inevitability to what is not, in fact, predetermined. One particularly disturbing limitation of these theories concerns the ways they conceptualize human identity. A study of altruism reveals just how limiting this conceptualization actually is.[6]

Of course, people do pursue their own individual self-interest. But surely there is more to being human than merely a struggle to survive or the efficient rational calculation of advantage.[7]

When we stress calculation, for example, we tend to reduce things and people to the calculable, to homogeneous units that lose their individuality and distinguishing characteristics.[8] Our study of altruism, if it teaches us anything, reminds us of the importance of seeing the human face, the person needing help, of moving beyond the anonymity of just another nameless victim, one more faceless Jew shipped off to a concentration camp, another child killed in Bosnia or dying from famine in some distant land. When we think in terms of "actors" or "agents" instead of individual people like Otto or Margot or Tony, when we speak of "utilities" and "preferences" instead of human emotions, desires, and passions, we rob our discourse of much of the human aspect of social science.[9] I am not suggesting we should not be as objective and analytically rigorous as possible, but we should always remember that in social science we deal with human beings, living and breathing people, and not just numbers or aggregates.[10]

Beyond this, a study of altruism should remind us that squashing some behaviors into a self-interested paradigm robs them of their meaning. Love cannot be bought and still remain love. Nor can justice.[11] The kind of religious belief that comes only because a clever rational actor deems it prudent to place a Pascal's wager is not really belief at all; it is mere expediency. So it is with altruism. If we subscribe uncritically to intellectual theories that reduce significant social phenomena—such as altruism, marriage, and prejudice—to mere acts of rational calculus, we limit our understanding of human action.

My analysis of altruism has demonstrated that self-interest provides an inadequate basis for an all-embracing theory of human behavior. As unfortunate as it is to misunderstand altruism, it is far worse to allow a theory to so intensely focus our attention on the selfish aspect of human behavior that it distorts and limits our understanding of what it means to be a human being. This is not something I want us to do. It is not necessitated by empirical reality.

In this regard, I conclude with an excerpt from an interview with Madame Trocme, a French rescuer whom I myself did not interview but who resembled many of the rescuers I came to know.[12] Madame Trocme was the wife of the Protestant pastor in Le Chambon, a French town where many Jews were successfully hidden for much of World War II. Her husband openly preached brotherly love, arguing that aiding Jews was not a political act but simply a normal expression of Christian compassion. Pastor Trocme's message was not well received by the Nazis, and he eventually had to hide in the woods to avoid arrest. Worse, the Nazis eventually sent a patrol into Le Chambon and rounded up the Jewish children hidden in the town, including in their arrests Trocme's cousin and the Jewish boys he was supervising in an orphanage.[13] In the excerpt quoted below, from *The Courage to Care*, Madame Trocme describes the day the Jewish boys were taken from the orphanage.

> They thought I was the maid of the house. They let me in. I went in the kitchen. I tried to go into the dining room, where all the students were in a line, and my cousin, Daniel Trocme, was first one in the corner. Then the Gestapo screamed, and they kicked me out. But they didn't kick me out of the house. I could go into the kitchen. So it meant I was the maid. It meant I was somebody belonging to the house.
>
> I saw all those boys, passing, to go into this little room where there was a man with a little booklet with many names, and he was interviewing them one by one. Most of them who went through said or had a piece of paper: "Send this to my mother." "Here is the address of my father." "I have a letter for my fiancé." "I have some money in my room."
>
> And when my young son came with me, at the moment when they left, he didn't want me to go alone. And he was so upset to see those Gestapo beating one of those Jews who were in line coming down, going down to the trucks. Beating them, beating those young boys, saying, "Schweine Juden! Schweine Juden!"
>
> And when I saw all those young people getting in, and my cousin said, "Don't worry. Tell my parents I was very happy here. Tell them I like traveling, that I go with my friends."
>
> And when they left, my son was green, I would say, I don't know, like a sick boy. And he said, "Mother! I am going to avenge later. Such things cannot happen again! I am going to do something when I'm grown up." And I said, "But you know what your father says. If you do such a thing, someone else is going to revenge against you. That is why we are never finished. We are going to go on, on and on. You must forgive. We must forget and do better."
>
> He was silent. And we left. And Daniel never came back.

Others will draw their own meaning from Madame Trocme's story, but what she says to me is twofold. First, she illustrates the importance of altruism in presenting another model of what it means to be a human being, a model that her very existence proves is both possible to achieve and richer than the model presented by the predominant theories in evolutionary biology, psychology, economics, and rational choice theory. Second, she supplies an answer to the age-old question: Why do we live? What do we live *for*? As a teacher concerned with ethics, as a parent raising young children, I am often hard put to answer this question. I know, of course, that I cannot provide an answer for my students any more than I can for my children. But surely, if I have learned anything of value, I should be able to provide some tiny insight on why it is important to treat others well, on why we should do good rather than evil in this world.

For me, answers from religion, from philosophical treatises devising elaborate Pascal's wagers, or the biological emphasis on transmission of genetic matter satisfy only partially. Madame Trocme's life supplies a more complete answer. We do good because that is what makes us human, fully and richly human, and not just greedy and graspingly self-centered. "We come into this world with nothing, and we take nothing out," one of my rescuers told me. All we have in the end is the dignity and integrity of our person. But this is enough.

"Remember," Madame Trocme said in explaining why she did what she did, "that in this life you will come across lots of circumstances that will need a kind of courage of your own. Not about others, but about yourself. I would not say more."

Notes

CHAPTER 1
THE PUZZLE OF ALTRUISM

1. Among the earliest authors subscribing to this view are Machiavelli (1513/1984), Hobbes (1651), La Rochefoucauld (1691), Mandeville (1714/1732), Bentham (1789/1876), and Nietzsche (1888/1967). All these regard self-interest as both the normal and the preferable form of human behavior. In contrast, Bishop Butler (1729/1896), Rousseau (1755/1950), Hume (1740/1896, 1751/1902), Smith (1759/1853), and Kant (1785/1889) argue that altruism (or a similar phenomenon called by a different name) is a basic part of human nature.

2. See Mansbridge 1990 for a discussion of liberal political thought; Etzioni 1988 for a discussion of self-interest and economic theory; Schwartz 1986 for the relation of self-interest to biology, economics, and behavioral psychology; and Kohn 1990 for a review of the literature on self-interest, altruism, and human nature.

3. Since I am trained as a political scientist and political economist, I naturally focus my theoretical attention on economics and rational choice theory, the intellectual godchild of the economic method, which spread throughout the rest of social science (see Monroe 1991). My focus on rational actor theory also arises out of the prominence enjoyed by rational choice theory in social science. The importance of rational choice theory is reflected in the existence of the Public Choice Society and by the awarding of the Nobel Prize to James Buchanan, Herbert Simon, Gary Becker, and Ronald Coase and the presidency of the American Political Science Association to William Riker, all important rational actor theorists.

4. Work on attribution theory (cf. Heider 1958; Jones and Davis 1965) discusses problems of inferring other people's motives from their acts.

5. We might also juxtapose deliberate and impulsive acts, particularly since the latter suggest inborn tendencies toward altruism. Biologists focus much attention on reflexive, nonconscious acts. Economists and psychologists tend to be more divided in their orientation, with some analysts ignoring any consideration of costs to the agent and others excluding acts that are reflexive or nonconscious. See, inter alia, Batson and Shaw 1991; Batson 1991; Campbell 1975, 1978; Hatfield, Walster, and Piliavin 1978; Krebs 1970, 1982; Midlarsky 1968; and Wispe 1978.

6. Oliner et al. (1992) discuss this in biology and psychology.

7. On the whole, evolutionary biologists define altruism to require self-sacrifice or the risk of such sacrifice. Many psychologists do the same (e.g., Campbell 1975, 1978; Hatfield, Walster, and Piliavin 1978; Krebs 1970, 1982; Midlarsky 1968; and Wispe 1978), although some do not (e.g., Batson 1991; Batson and Shaw 1991). Economists do not, as a general rule, define self-sacrifice as an intrinsic part of altruism.

8. I did this for several reasons. Excessive conceptual refinements debase the general concept of altruism and confuse ordinary-language discussions of it. They also engage us in fruitless terminological debates about what kind of altruism is explained through

particular predictors. This becomes especially troublesome if we wish to communicate across disciplines, where terminological differences already intimidate and confuse those not among the cognoscenti.

9. Krebs and Van Hesteren (in Oliner et al. 1992) have recently advocated this approach.

10. Staub (1991:151) effectively argues for this approach.

11. This approach is only one of many ways to think about altruism. For other conceptualizations, see, inter alia, Batson 1991, Losco 1986, or Nagel 1970. While the precise definition adopted is one on which reasonable scholars may honestly differ, my later presentation of findings should suggest how critical it is to structure the definition of altruism so as to allow for its subtle variations while not losing our focus on the basic phenomenon. My intention here, however, is not to engage in extensive discussion of the various conceptual attributes of altruism but rather to arrive at a working definition that both captures its most critical components and allows us to distinguish it from other, closely related behaviors, such as sharing, helping, cooperating, and giving. I believe my definition does this.

12. Becker 1976.

13. Eisenberg 1986: chap. 3; Batson 1991.

14. These are discussed and analyzed in chapter 6.

15. Hunecke 1981–82, 1985; Fogelman 1994.

16. Economic explanations are discussed in chapter 7.

17. Biological explanations are discussed in chapter 8.

18. Kohlberg (1976) and Gilligan (1977, 1982) are perhaps the best-known authors from this school of thought.

19. Psychological factors are discussed in chapter 9.

20. I began my study of altruism as a political economist dissatisfied with what I saw as an overemphasis in my field on the idea of cost/benefit as the reasoning process underlying political behavior. This dissatisfaction led me to consider other ways in which information is processed and organized and to focus on the role of cognition in general as an influence on behavior. My early work in comparative politics made me sensitive to the importance of different world views. These scholarly experiences were reinforced at the more personal level through my daily family interactions. My closest relationships taught me how conflicts and divergent behaviors often emanate not from different values or interests but rather simply from different perceptions of a shared reality and from different ways of processing the same information. All of these factors initially encouraged me to consider the importance of cognition and world views in my own work.

21. Reykowski (1984) suggests that there are actually three paths; he includes humanistic psychology as a separate strand whereas I treat it as part of developmental psychology.

22. For specific early works in general psychology, see William James's *Principles of Psychology* (1890) and Sigmund Freud's *A General Introduction to Psychoanalysis* (1917/ 1920). For early works that focus on altruism, see Herbert Spencer's *The Principles of Psychology* (1870,1872), which argues that we can expect to find altruism within its proper place (the family unit); Kropotkin's *Mutual Aid* (1902), which focuses on the instinct of human solidarity as the primary fact of human evolution; McDougall's work (1908) on parental instincts as the most powerful of all instincts. Contemporary psy-

chological arguments stressing empathy as an explanation for altruism include those by Hoffman (1975, 1976, 1981a, 1981b), Krebs (1975), Sagi and Hoffman (1976), and Simner (1971). Rosenhan (1970, 1978) and Rosenhan, Salovey, Karylowski, and Hargis (1981) focus not so much on empathy as on general affect and emotion as predictors of altruism. Lerner (1982) and Lerner and Meindl (1984) explore the role of identity and identity relations in helping behavior and the desire for justice for others. Piliavin and Piliavin (1973) consider empathy and guilt as they affect bystanders. And Reykowski and his associates (1982, 1992) develop the idea of identity and its impact on altruism. Batson (1991) presents an excellent review of much of this literature. The recent edited volume by Oliner et al. (1992) contains several interesting pieces focusing on identity and empathy.

23. See, inter alia., James March Baldwin's work in *Psychology Review* at the end of the nineteenth century, Jean Piaget's work (1948) on the structures of thought at different stages of development, and L. S. Vygotskii's analysis (1978) of the interplay of cognizing individuals in a structured environment.

24. See Kohlberg (1976, 1984) or Rosenberg (1988), inter alia.

25. Based on an experiment in which he asked subjects to fill in the missing sequences in a series of stories, Bartlett (1932) concluded that we all have characteristic scripts that we carry about in our minds. The early schema work grew out of this kind of analysis.

26. I am grateful to Shawn Rosenberg for his help in leading me through the intricacies of the historical development of work on cognition.

27. Kahnemann, Slovic, and Tversky 1982; Bruner 1988, 1990.

28. Kolm's analysis (1983) is one of the few examples.

29. Jerome Bruner, one of the founding fathers of the cognitive science revolution, now argues that cognitive science has become too technical, losing sight of its original goal to discover and "describe formally the meanings that human beings created out of their encounters with the world, and then to propose hypotheses about what meaning-making processes were implicated" (1990:2). Instead, Bruner argues, computing became the model of the mind, and analysts neglected the concept of meaning in favor of the concept of computability. This reductionism offered advantages but carried high costs.

30. Geertz 1973:49.

31. There is some discussion in the field over the extent to which judgment and awareness constitute two separate activities. I do not address this debate.

32. I speak of cognitive-perceptual frameworks rather than cognitive frameworks, both to avoid offending scholars who may employ the latter term in a sense quite different from mine and to adopt a terminology that has not been already widely utilized by other scholars of altruism who are engaged in more technical linguistic and conceptual debates. In general, however, the idea of cognition as being clearly tied to perceptions is neither radical nor controversial. See, inter alia, Kuhn 1962.

33. Children provide marvelously delightful examples of how cognitive-perceptual frameworks operate. One friend told of her two-year-old son's surprise and joy when he was taken on his first Halloween outing. The boy could hardly believe that he could knock on a door and a perfect stranger, without being asked, would open the door and thrust great mounds of candy into his hands. Equally puzzling was the fact that his mother allowed, even encouraged, him to take candy from strangers. Both his mother

and I wondered what would happen the next night, when life suddenly returned to its normal state and the poor child had to readjust his perceptions of reality in a less satisfying direction.

One of my own sons provided a similar illustration of cognitive-perceptual frameworks in action. Born and raised in southern California, Nicholas was visiting my mother in Illinois during summer holiday. He awoke before dawn one morning and enticed his sleepy mother to the kitchen for a snack. As he sat happily munching cookies and milk, he noticed an unusual sound on the roof. "What's that noise?" he asked. "That's just rain on the roof," I replied. "Oh, right, Mom," he said with the scornful disdain that only a child can muster for a particularly dense parent. "It never rains in the summertime."

Given Nicholas's experience, this was, in fact, true. It did rain only in the wintertime in the world as he knew it. The fact that the rain was occurring was something out of the ordinary, given his particular cognitive-perceptual framework.

34. I ignore the question of the extent to which there is an objective reality that can be perceived apart from cognitive representations. Most cognitive psychologists assume there is not. See Abric in Derlega and Grzelak 1982.

35. The importance of expectations is a frequent theme in social science since de Tocqueville's analysis (1839/1955) of the importance of expectations for the French Revolution.

36. This is discussed in the exchange in *Psychological Inquiry* (1991:2, no. 2: 107–58).

37. Canon originally referred to an ecclesiastical rule or law enacted by a council or other competent authority in the Roman Catholic Church and approved by the pope. The term now refers generally to the body of rules, principles, texts, or standards accepted as axiomatic and universally binding in a culture, society, or field of study.

38. Some cognitive psychologists use the term representations to refer to what I mean by perceptions. See Abric in Derlega and Grzelak 1982 or Batson and Shaw 1991 for alternate usages.

39. See Roger G. Barker's work (1978) on perceptions.

40. For a discussion of the innate and cultural aspects of mothering, see Chodrow (1978).

41. Confucius, Plato, Aristotle, Cicero, and St. Thomas Aquinas discuss different world views in vastly different cultures and historical periods. Sorokin (1955:Foreword) describes these differences in detail in reference to Tonnies's idea of *Gemeinschaft* and *Gesellschaft*.

42. Loomis in Tönnies 1955.

43. See Turner 1987 on self-categorization or Heider 1958 and Hornstein 1982 on the importance of "we-feeling" for behavior.

44. See Taylor 1989 or MacIntyre (1962/1976) for the communitarian view and Rawls 1973, Dworkin 1978, or Nagel 1987 for the contractarian or liberal view.

45. Capitalist society is typically offered as the quintessential *Gesellschaft* world view. See Loomis in Tönnies 1955.

46. The importance of "attachment to other people seems quite important in social relations, yet remains poorly understood" (Baton and Shaw 1991:113).

47. Empathy is a relatively new word, originating as a term in art and used by

Titchener in 1909 to translate the German *Einfuhlung*, the process of intuiting one's way into an object or event to see it from the inside. Clinical psychologists had adopted the word by the 1950s to refer to understanding the client's point view, thus making the term closely synonymous with role taking or perspective (Batson and Shaw 1991:113). Early discussions of what contemporary scholars refer to as empathy utilize the term sympathy, Adam Smith being but one notable example.

48. Eisenberg 1986 and Batson 1991.

49. The term empathy did not exist when Smith wrote, and he appears to mean what contemporary scholars refer to as empathy.

50. Oliner and Oliner 1988:376, n. 11.

51. Eisenberg 1986:154.

52. Langer et al. 1978; Oliner and Oliner 1988; Piliavin et al. 1981.

53. See Hoffman 1976, 1981a and Krebs and Russell 1981 on perspective and Batson and Shaw 1991 or Batson 1991 for a slightly different approach to both empathy and perspective taking.

54. There is too vast a literature on the importance of identity for behavior to discuss it here. The literature on identity and altruism is more limited.

55. See DeJong 1979; Eisenberg and Cialdini 1984; Eisenberg 1986; or Oliner and Oliner 1988.

56. For example, Reykowski (1984) found that people going through conflict about their own self-worth tend to evaluate events in terms of the effects on themselves. Staub (1979) argues that there is a curvilinear relationship between self-esteem and prosocial behavior. He found that people with moderate self-esteem tend to be more prosocial. On either side of the median point, however, prosocial behavior diminishes. Individuals with high self-esteem are self-satisfied, and those with low self-esteem are insensitive to others.

57. There is a useful but uneasy tension here. I assume people have a central core concept of self but they recognize that they also exhibit different aspects of this self and that their central identity has multiple components.

58. The Oliners found rescuers were more empathetic toward others' pain than nonrescuers but also that they were more likely to get involved and to stay involved because of their general sense of responsibility and tendency to make commitments (1988:174). Rescuers' empathy with the weak and helpless did not emerge from feelings of personal vulnerability, however, since, in comparison with nonrescuers, rescuers on the whole felt that they could control events and shape their own destinies.

59. Role taking is usually divided into one of three types. Perceptual perspective taking refers to the ability to understand the literal visual perspective of another. Cognitive perspective taking denotes the ability to predict and understand another's thoughts, motives, intentions, and behavior. Affective perspective taking describes the ability to infer another's feelings and emotional reactions. See Batson 1984, Hoffman 1975, 1976, Krebs and Russell 1981, or Staub 1979 for discussions of this.

60. Kohlberg's famous studies posed hypothetical moral dilemmas and asked the subjects what the person in the story should do. Gilligan inquired about similar situations and asked subjects what they would do. Aside from other differences between these important studies, most analysts now agree that the different results are at least in part a reflection of such subtle differences in wording.

61. In chapter 11 I use my empirical findings on altruism to suggest a more general perspectival approach to understanding political behavior.

62. These groups were selected arbitrarily insofar as other groups could have fulfilled the same function, which was to represent different behavioral points along the continuum. My goal was to select groups that would cluster at different points on the behavioral continuum, and these groups seemed to do this. Other possible groups to consider might be volunteers (as examples of quasi-altruistic activities) or doctors and other medical personnel who refuse to work with AIDS patients (as examples of rational actors). There also was some crossover among groups; for example, one of the people contacted because he was a successful entrepreneur told me he had recently given an anonymous gift of $1 million to a local college. Behaviorally, then, I would locate this man somewhere between the entrepreneurs and the philanthropists.

63. See Mansbridge 1990 or Monroe 1991 on this.

64. While other groups could also be utilized for baseline data, I selected entrepreneurs because of their central role in economic theory and because they corresponded closely to philanthropists in critical ways, especially in their financial resources. Essentially, economists locate the reason for capitalist expansion in the innovation of entrepreneurs. This leads to capitalist construction and the establishment of new firms that seek profit and finance from bank credit. Firms follow the innovator until the initial gains are exhausted. As businesses repay the bank loans, deflation occurs, along with consequent readjustments in the economy, including both booms and busts. See Schumpeter 1942 for the classic discussion of entrepreneurs' importance for capitalism.

65. For an excellent discussion of how individuals integrate individual needs with their desire to help others, see Wuthnow 1991.

66. I tried to match philanthropists and entrepreneurs on background characteristics, such as age, gender, geographic origin, etc.

67. One of these individuals was interviewed by a graduate student, Michael Barton, while I sat in the room and asked occasional questions. Unfortunately, some of my research materials for the heroes was lost during two cross-country moves that occurred during the writing of this book. The material on heroes thus relies heavily on my early notes, on a joint analysis of these interviews, on Barton's thesis, and on the remaining interviews for which I have full documentation.

68. Despite the extremity of the altruism required to fit into this definition, the Carnegie Hero Fund Commission has made more than seven thousand awards since it was established in 1904 to honor heroes.

69. Oliner and Oliner 1988.

70. The political context of rescue behavior makes this an especially rich source of observation for political science, particularly if attention is given to national and cultural differences.

71. I also interviewed one man who had rescued people but who was Jewish and therefore not eligible for a Yad Vashem medal. His interview is treated only as background material and is not counted among the ten rescuers whose narratives are analyzed.

72. Bruner (1990) notes the importance of doing this.

73. Bruner (1990) describes a similar phenomenon in the research he conducted with Susan Weisser. He notes that their interviews with the Goodhertzes also involved

the give-and-take of ordinary conversation, in which the interviewer expresses natural and expected responses (such as visual and verbal expressions of sympathy when told something sad), since not to do so would violate the rules of ordinary dialogue (123–24).

74. See Langer 1991.

75. This makes narrative an important tool in what Garfinkel (1981) refers to as ethnomethodology.

76. I encourage other scholars to reanalyze my narratives using such techniques.

77. In administering mass surveys, for example, interviewers typically are told to interrupt respondents who digress into stories, since the stories do not fit conventional categories. While this is an understandable research methodology when we are trying to construct large-scale statistical surveys, it is less justifiable where our interest lies in subtler influences on behavior. Certainly the concept of the human self that emerges from such interviews risks becoming artificialized by the very interview method, and influences on behavior may appear clear when in fact they are more complex and intricate. (I present several instances of this phenomenon in chapter 10.)

78. See Mandler 1984 or Rummelhart et al. 1986, inter alia.

79. Analysts concerned with the schema and the self focus not just on the person's words about himself or herself but also on the way the person interacts with the interviewer and the stories the speaker tells about daily activities, relationships, etc. I have used the general concept of an organizing cognitive framework rather than the more technically developed concept of a schema precisely because I treat the concept as a heuristic and wish to avoid becoming sidetracked into an epistemological discussion of schema as a concept. For readers interested in more technical definitions, the classic definition of schema utilized by cognitive psychologists, such as Mandler (1984) or Rummelhart (1986), has its origin in Kant and usually entails five properties. Schemas are (1) not images, (2) generative, (3) organized structures, (4) nonconscious, and (5) constructive.

80. See Lakoff 1987 on language; Casson 1983 on anthropology and cultural patterns; or D'Andrade (n.d.) and Quinn and Holland 1987 on the methodological issues in the identification of culturally based schemas. See Tannen 1986 and 1990 on gender and language and world view.

81. See Riker 1995 for a critique of such experimental studies on rationality.

82. See Bruner 1990.

83. These tests are myriad and include the ones utilized by the Oliners (1988), the various measures of social responsibility (Staub et al.), a Machiavellian test of orientation toward other people (Christie and Geiss 1968), the Rokeach values scale, and Kohlberg's measures of moral reasoning (both described in Staub et al. 1984 and Berkowitz and Lutterman 1968).

84. By publishing the transcripts (or the kinds of extensive excerpts from the transcripts that appear in chapters 2 through 5 of this book), however, these data become available to scholars who may wish to analyze or utilize them to construct more technical models of the cognitive process.

85. I am aware that my methodology will be found lacking by those social scientists who prefer large survey samples or controlled experiments, who do not find the presentation of the cases in chapters 2–5 systematic enough, or who find the interpretive

technique insufficiently objective. A full methodological discussion of the value of narrative and the limitations of self-reporting lies beyond the scope of this book.

86. These fell into four categories. (1) Could traditional survey research and large-sample statistical analysis detect the delicate shifts in behavior along my conceptual continuum from self-interested to altruistic acts? (2) Would mass surveys and large samples prove adequate to reveal phenomena as subtle as perspective? (3) Would the sensitivity of the analyst be eroded by the deluge of data typical of the large-sample statistical studies on which traditional survey research relies? (4) Finally, would quantitative techniques effectively squash a complex reality into statistical correlations and tables and charts?

87. I had never met any of these people before I interviewed them, but they were often friends of friends, and therefore I had a personal introduction.

88. The interview with Bert, for example, was only partially transcribed, since the sound was bad and Bert went into and out of Dutch. This partial transcript was sent to Bert, however, for his approval.

89. As the people I interviewed came to understand that we would be speaking for only a short time, with a limited duration agreed upon in advance, I wondered also if the phenomenon that psychiatrists have noted in therapy was occurring: the subject raises the difficult subject only at the end of the interview, precisely because he or she knows it cannot then be discussed at great length and therefore feels safe in broaching the topic. This can only be supposition, of course, but I did notice that more difficult personal issues often were raised toward the end of our telephone conversations.

90. Condensation was necessitated by the sheer size of the transcripts, frequently more than 150 pages. The shortest interview lasted approximately two hours; the longest interview stretched over twenty hours and many months and several hundred pages of transcript.

91. All but a few interviews were analyzed independently by three to six students and colleagues who worked on the project and later met with me to discuss their classifications of the transcript. In particular, the analysts were asked to identify sections of the interview that revealed information on specific hypotheses found in the literature. For example, they would determine whether or not the subject was the oldest child or had been made responsible for the care of young children, a factor Whiting suggested should encourage altruistic behavior.

CHAPTER 2
THE ENTREPRENEUR

1. I have changed the interviewee's name and some minor details to protect his anonymity.

2. This was a characteristic that the Oliners (1988), among others, found to be an important influence on altruism.

3. As we shall find in chapter 7, this is not what is predicted by economic theories of altruism.

4. An alternate explanation might be that he prefers anonymity *only* when he is giving to people he does not know—for what may be quite practical reasons, that is, he does not want the world beating down his door looking for donations.

CHAPTER 3
THE PHILANTHROPIST

1. See chapter 2.

2. See Wuthnow 1991 for an excellent discussion of volunteer activities.

3. Billy used similar phrasing in describing his reasons for his (much more limited) gifts to others.

4. In this, they present a challenge to theories that associate such a self-perception with altruism (Oliner and Oliner 1988).

5. The idea that giving is done because it makes the philanthropist feel good about him or herself has been one of the central economic explanations for altruism. Neither Billy nor Melissa seemed concerned with thanks, although Billy's protestations ring less true than Melissa's when we consider his actions. Melissa seems concerned more that the gift be used constructively than that she be appreciated for her part in the transaction; Billy seems concerned with both.

6. In saying this, I am making a judgment that in the case of the woman who insisted she would pick up the money immediately, Melissa was hurt by the woman's pushiness. Similarly, when the church members asked her for money for a new parsonage, Melissa seemed grieved by their insensitivity to the pain she might be in over her husband's death. Billy's attitude seems more a concern that his generosity is not appreciated.

CHAPTER 5
RESCUERS OF JEWS IN NAZI EUROPE

1. The conversations reproduced in this chapter come from audio tapes of several telephone conversations plus personal visits during the summer of 1989. Additional interviews were filmed.

2. The war alone cannot account for the particular differences in perspective noted between rescuers and nonrescuers, since the war obviously affected everyone, albeit in vastly different ways; that is, some helped Jews, some did nothing, and some assisted in the persecution.

3. This is important to remember as we discuss people who rescued Jews, think about those who did not, and ask why so many people seemed to go too acquiescently to their deaths. Without unambiguous evidence of Nazi policies, it was extremely difficult psychologically to believe that anything so dreadful could be instituted by a civilized people. This has been discussed fully elsewhere (Arendt 1963/1992 and Stern 1989, inter alia).

4. See Monroe 1994.

5. I spoke with one rescuer who was asked by his government to be a Nazi-hunter after the war, locating and bringing to justice indigenous Nazis. He did so until he realized that only poor Nazis were being punished; rich ones usually received only token fines.

6. The Anne Frank Institute and the State Institute for War Documentation also have some of Tony's materials.

7. Tony's narrative also suggests the extent to which he broke with his conservative,

bourgeois Dutch background. It reminds us that fascism was linked to anticommunism and protection of traditional values in the minds of many Europeans with Tony's background.

8. For an excellent discussion of this, see Stern 1989.

9. This surprised me, since I had originally expected people who thought of themselves as native to a community to be more likely to help others. What I had not anticipated was the extent to which group membership entails the existence of an out-group, a distinction between "us and them" that may serve to increase the likelihood of ill-treatment for members of the out-group. See Monroe 1995b for further discussion.

10. I later discuss the extent to which rescuers saw no alternative to their altruistic behavior: for them it was not noble conduct but merely normal, what any human being would feel impelled to do under the circumstances.

11. In contrast, Tony told me the pay for an unmarried major in the Dutch army at this time was approximately fifteen guilders a week. Eighteen guilders for Bert's family of ten was thus hardly excessive.

12. I am grateful to Bert's family for reading through the final transcript and correcting minor errors.

13. This finding supports the Oliners' contention (1988) that there is such consistency to people's behavior that we can reasonably speak of an altruistic personality.

CHAPTER 6
SOCIOCULTURAL ATTRIBUTES OF ALTRUISM

1. Simply by chance, more of the German rescuers interviewed were women. Overall, my sample of rescuers was more balanced between men and women.

2. See Huneke 1981–82 or Fogelman 1994, inter alia. There are many ways to conceptualize and define what it means to be religious, from formal membership in a religious institution to inner spirituality. The debate over the importance of religion has been particularly heated in relation to rescue activity since there were many instances of anti-Semitism by individual priests or clergy and cases of religious authorities who were indifferent to or supportive of Nazi policies toward the Jews. For purposes of my study, I relied heavily on self-categorization by interviewees. I considered them religious if they considered themselves so.

3. Developmental psychologists often argue that everyone has some altruistic tendencies and that the altruists we actually see are simply those who have grown into their full potential. Such developmental psychologists often point to religion as a critical factor in this development. See Batson 1991; Oliner et al. 1992; and chapter 9 of the present study.

4. This finding appears to trouble some scholars from religious schools or departments of religion. I can only remind them that these are simply my findings, which I must report honestly.

5. This quote comes from an interview Bert gave to Ellen Land-Weber (undated manuscript, 17). I am grateful to Professor Land-Weber for sharing it with me.

6. I should note, however, that the gist of Bert's shorter responses correspond with Tony's more elaborate answers.

7. Tony's responses also illustrate the advantage of a free-flowing interview over one

containing only specific survey questions that then are coded into predesigned catego-ries. Had I not let Tony talk freely, without directing the flow of the conversation in any but the most general manner, I would have missed the richness and complexity of his answers.

8. Pascal argued that it was logical to act as if one believed in God. He reasoned that God either exists or he does not. If he does not exist and you do not believe in him, then you have lost nothing. If he does not exist and you do believe in him, you have lost little. Perhaps you have circumscribed your behavior somewhat, but this is not a major cost. On the other hand, if God does exist and you believe in him, you have won a great deal with little cost. But if he exists and you do not believe in him, your loss is infinite, for you are damned eternally. Thus, Pascal argued, the sensible wager is to assume that God does exist and act accordingly.

9. One could, of course, argue that religion simply provides a particular way of cognitively conceptualizing the world, but I do not believe that is the ordinary-language usage, nor is it the way my interviewees utilized the concept.

10. The closest articulation of this idea would probably be a philosophy resembling Emerson's transcendentalism.

11. Ironically, the divisions Bert spoke of originated in different sects of Dutch Protestantism.

12. Lucille had converted to Catholicism even though it caused her to be disinher-ited by her mother, to whom Lucille was very close. I would mark Lucille as one of the more religious altruists I interviewed, but note that she does not fit into any traditional religious categories.

13. Like Bert, Irene showed remarkable reluctance to impose any guilt on the people for whom she was sacrificing her safety and well-being.

14. The idea of reincarnation expressed by Bert and Lucille seems different from the standard idea of a purgatory in which you pay for your sins.

15. This has been a particularly difficult issue for researchers on rescuers of Jews in Nazi Europe. Many professed Christians, and even some official spokesmen for the Church, did little to help the Jews, and far too many religious figures responded, as did Irene's confessor, with anti-Semitism and hate instead of Christian charity.

16. During the Gulf War both George Bush and Saddam Hussein made public state-ments to the effect that "God was on our side." One reporter asked the head of the World Council of Churches whose side he thought God was on. "I think God is on the side of the suffering," he replied.

17. Large-sample studies of such factors include Oliner and Oliner 1988 and Klingemann and Falter 1993, among others.

18. The entrepreneurs, like the philanthropists, all had financial acumen. Only one philanthropist seemed relatively unsophisticated financially; all the others were either naturally clever with money or had been forced to develop their financial expertise in order to handle inherited money.

19. Leadership is discussed in chapter 10. See Goldberger 1987 or Oliner and Oliner 1988 for a consideration of such factors.

20. Prosocial behavior, of course, need not be altruism. I consider findings from such studies, however, since other analysts frequently interchange the two terms.

21. See Goldberger 1987 for fuller details.

22. Tony does speak of the homogeneity of the Dutch population, but he seems to

emphasize the Dutch attachment to liberty, their independent spirit, and their sheer "orneriness" as being more critical factors. Furthermore, this seems only one of many possible explanations he offers for the Dutch treatment of Jews. None of the other Dutch rescuers I interviewed made reference to any Dutch national character as an explanation for their acts of rescue.

23. There are more subtle variants to this communitarian argument which concern the extent to which people's relative security in their surroundings influences whether they are willing to engage in altruistic activity. I return to this issue in later chapters.

CHAPTER 7
ECONOMIC APPROACHES TO ALTRUISM

1. For examples of various economic approaches to altruism, see works by Valavanis (1958), Arrow (1963), Frohlich (1974), Becker (1976), Wintrobe (1981), and Margolis (1982). See Monroe, Barton, and Klingemann 1991 and Monroe 1994 for reviews of this literature.

2. See Wispe 1978:304, Lopreato 1984:296, and Batson 1991:chap. 1. Comte argued that people exhibited both egoism (the impulse to pursue self-gratification and self-interest) and altruism (the unselfish desire to "live for others").

3. Phelps 1975:2.

4. This fitted nicely into the movement closely associated with Gary Becker (1976), in which the economic approach is applied to subjects traditionally outside the purview of economics, such as marriage, suicide or discrimination.

5. See Becker 1976, Margolis 1982, 1991, and Axelrod 1984, inter alia. Economists also stress the size of the social unit in which altruism is manifested, arguing that existing clusters of mutually reinforcing altruists will encourage further altruistic activity (Axelrod and Hamilton 1981). Here again, we discern the intermingling of hypotheses, with clusters of altruists filling the function of social or situational factors. In an analogous fashion, it is argued that mutually supportive altruists act as mechanisms through which learning occurs, since it is frequently assumed that a modeling effect is at work. This, in turn, is linked to the assumption that people behave altruistically to avoid group disapprobation, to win group praise, or to gain the reciprocity discussed above. These concepts are discussed later.

6. Alexrod's work (1984) on cooperation is one of the most important in this area.

7. As I do so, there may be some overlap. When the overlap occurs with evolutionary biology, which often considers nonhuman altruism, and when these same concepts have been modified and utilized by economists to apply directly to human behavior, I discuss them under economic explanations. I do so because my interest is in human behavior. When the overlap is simply a case of interdisciplinary borrowing of concepts, as often occurs with economists and psychologists or anthropologists, I discuss the explanation under the category of the discipline with the most fully developed explanation or the discipline in which the concept was first discussed.

8. There is a rigorous examination process that occurs before anyone can be certified a rescuer by Yad Vashem, and the issue of financial gain from the rescue is thoroughly investigated as part of this inquiry.

9. Tony, Margot, and Otto are but three examples. It is, of course, difficult to distin-

guish the extent to which these individuals lost fortunes because they helped Jews or simply because they opposed Hitler.

10. My interview with Bert extended over ten hours but was difficult to transcribe because of language difficulties. This quote comes from an interview Bert gave to Philip Alexander. I appreciate Dr. Alexander's kindness in permitting me access to his interviews.

11. See Block and Drucker 1992 for documentation.

12. Both Tony and Bert mentioned hearing this kind of remark.

13. Leonie was one such person; she said that others had done much more than she.

14. See Goldberger 1988 for a discussion of the Danish rescue mission.

15. The story has been told in several forms; I am indebted to Joseph Losco (1986) for first bringing it to my attention.

16. I later discuss the fact that both the philanthropists and the entrepreneurs were more likely to take care of the needs of their families before they considered giving to strangers. A similar pattern occurred for psychic utility.

17. Many rescuers had saved lives of people before and after the war; often the rescues involved drowning accidents.

18. See Oliner and Oliner 1988.

19. Some of this is understandable for the rescuers, who needed to exercise extreme discretion in order to avoid arrest; but the same reticence appeared in other altruists, many of whom wanted to remain anonymous and not receive praise.

20. This relationship will be discussed more fully in chapter 9, when we consider psychological explanations of altruism.

21. "The tension within economics begins with Adam Smith, who expressed somewhat contradictory views of man in his two published works. Each of the two books he published about society presents only one of these two models of man while forgetting the other. In *The Wealth of Nations* he affirms that it is 'vain' for man to expect the 'help of his brethren' from 'their benevolence only.' However, the first sentence of his first book on society, *The Theory of Moral Sentiments*, runs: 'How selfish soever man may be supposed, there are evidently some principles in his nature, which interest him in the fortune of others, and render their happiness necessary to him, though he derives nothing from it, except the pleasure of seeing it.' Why then does man with the altruistic 'moral sentiments' of the *Theory* display the egoistic behavior of the *Wealth of Nations*? This contradiction between the two works was even given a label by German scholars: 'Das Adam Smith Problem'" (Kolm 1983:22).

Kolm finds in Pareto the most classic expression of man's dual nature but also cites Edgeworth, Bentham, and J. S. Mill among the utilitarians and Leon Walras and Smith (in *The Theory of Moral Sentiments*) as referring to man's dual nature (Kolm 1983:21–22). Kolm also explains how, as the discipline of economics became more rigorous, and particularly after the marginalist revolution in the late nineteenth century, theories proposing a single utility function began to dominate, and economic man was held to have a "fairly constant preference ordering which synthesizes all the desires, aspirations, and inclinations of the individual" (1983:20).

22. See Wuthnow's *Acts of Compassion* (1991) for an insightful discussion of how people balance their limited volunteer and charitable activities with their more self-oriented needs.

23. See Howard Margolis's work (1982) for the most imaginative and fully developed articulation of this concept.

24. Tony comes closest to this when he expresses what I will identify as a tactical calculus that occurs not when deciding whether to help others but in assessing *how* best to help them.

25. The question of consciousness of these costs and benefits is another issue that is discussed shortly. For an excellent discussion of the importance of self interest in social and political theory, see Mansbridge's edited volume (1990).

26. "Information costs" refers to the time and effort necessary to gather information relevant to a decision. "Opportunity costs" are the options foregone by taking one choice as opposed to another, as when I spend one hundred dollars on a blue dress and no longer have it for shoes.

27. Becker's work (1976) is perhaps the most developed example of this.

28. Further evidence of the individual-actor trap that ensnares most economists is found in the exchange between Frohlich (1974, 1975) and Fitzgerald (1975). Frohlich notes that "an altruist may get vicarious utility rewards from bearing a burden for another, but that the reward may be lower than the cost of the help rendered. Under those circumstances the rational altruist would choose not to assume any of the other's burden" (1975:480). Frohlich then notes that this is "an all too common empirical phenomenon," one he argues the reader has no doubt experienced directly. "It is one in which there is a genuine desire to help a friend, to engage in a charitable act, and so forth, but. . . in which the costs of doing so are viewed as prohibitive. . . . In such situations, the altruism is abortive and there is no reduction of the area of contention between the actors" (1975:480–81). Frohlich's comments beautifully demonstrate the weakness in rational choice analyses of altruism.

29. See Elster 1986 on multiple identities.

CHAPTER 8
EXPLANATIONS FROM EVOLUTIONARY BIOLOGY

1. I employ the more neutral term "evolutionary biology" rather than "sociobiology," since for some social scientists sociobiology has come to be associated with subtle forms of racism.

2. Two of the best-known evolutionary biologists are E. O. Wilson (1975) and Richard Trivers (1971), although Wilson's work is controversial because of his later discussions of racial superiority. Boorman and Levitt (1980) present an excellent glossary of terms useful for the nonbiologist interested in biological discussions of altruism. In general, altruism refers to the sacrifice of fitness by one organism (the donor) to preserve or increase the fitness of one or more conspecifics (the recipients). In genetic models of social behavior, an altruist is referred to as the individual possessing a genetically based propensity for altruism.

3. A technical definition of kin selection for a biologist would be selection for altruistic behavior toward genetic relatives. A technical definition of group selection would be selection occurring as a result of competition between demes rather than individuals. (Demes are randomly mating populations that form a closed genetic unit.) See Boorman and Levitt 1980.

4. See Schwartz 1986 or Wilson 1975, inter alia.

5. See Dawkins 1976 for one of the best examples of this work.

6. Remember that evolutionary biologists look not at the pleasure Harry may find in a life free from the cares and responsibilities of children but only at his failure to perpetuate his genes.

7. See Trivers 1971.

8. Panksepp (1986) suggests that both altruism and aggression may be linked to brain structures through neural pathways but concedes that attempts to find such unitary brain circuits have been unsuccessful. Studies of twins by Rushton et al. (1986, 1991) find altruism designed to ensure the survival of genetic information but fail to explain altruism that involves self-sacrifice. See Sellick 1994 for a review of the psychological research indicating that altruism has a genetic component.

9. Becker 1976:284.

10. Becker concludes with a long passage along these lines.

Although an altruist forgoes some of his own consumption to raise the consumption of others, and forgoes some opportunities to raise his own income to avoid lowering the income of others, his own consumption may exceed that of an equally able egoist because the beneficiaries of his altruism are discouraged from harming him. Reasoning along the same lines, one can reach the same conclusion for altruism with regard to genetic fitness: although an altruist forgoes some of his own fitness to raise the fitness of others, and so forth, his own fitness may exceed that of an equally able egoist because the beneficiaries of his altruism are discouraged from harming him.

Therefore, two apparently equivalent statements about altruism by Wilson are in fact quite different. He says "altruism . . . *by definition* reduces personal fitness" (1975, p. 3, my italics), yet simply defines an act of altruism as "when a person (or animal) increases the fitness of another at the expense of his own fitness" (1975, p. 117). Using the latter definition, I have shown that altruism may actually increase personal fitness because of its effect on the behavior of others. Consequently, altruism does not by (Wilson's or my) definition necessarily reduce personal fitness. (1976:291)

11. The importance of Becker's work is demonstrated not just by his Nobel Prize but also by the comments it evoked from several authors (Hirshleifer 1977, 1981; Tullock 1975; Wintrobe 1981). Hirshleifer (1977) used Shakespeare's story of King Lear to argue the importance of having the last word. Hirshleifer's main point (1977, 1981) is that in Becker's analysis, altruism depends upon the possibility of future contact. If the rotten kid has the last word—as the daughters did in *King Lear*, once Lear had relinquished his fortune—there is no reason why altruism should continue. Hirshleifer does mention the possibility that the parent may, while still in full control, constrain his child by "posthypnotic suggestion . . . , cultural indoctrination or even by physical means" (1977:501). This is the closest any of these rational choice theorists comes to discussing the role of cultural constraints on egoism, and Hirshleifer does not develop the discussion beyond this brief mention.

12. See Axelrod 1984 or Axelrod and Hamilton 1981.

13. Trivers 1971.

14. Blau 1968, Homans 1961.

15. Wintrobe (1981) noted this in a comment on Becker 1976.

16. Outcome-oriented is juxtaposed to procedural or process-oriented; a legal trial in which a guilty man goes free but proper legal procedures were followed would be rational from a procedural but not an outcome-oriented definition of rationality. Biologists focus on outcomes and care little for the conscious choices that lead to these outcomes. Biologists look at evolutionary changes over long time periods in which critical changes can occur; certain organisms adapt successfully to the environment and without consciously choosing the adaptive mechanism. A giraffe with a longer neck may not even be aware that certain behaviors affect survival (e.g., eating leaves at the top of tall trees keeps long-necked giraffes alive long enough to procreate). It is the outcome of the process, not the process itself, that is critical. Although the acts in the process must be able to be replicated, this replication need not be conscious.

17. Wilson 1975:117.

18. It is interesting that Wilson is cited by Becker as defining altruism as occurring "[w]hen a person . . . increases the fitness of another at the expense of his own fitness" (Wilson 1975:117, cited in Becker 1976:290). Yet immediately after Becker cites Wilson, Becker proceeds to argue that altruism can actually "increase personal fitness" (1976:291). How can this be reconciled with Wilson's definition? At the least, some conceptual clarity would be useful here. So despite Becker's claim to be applying socio-biological concepts, his 1976 work actually retreats from the useful start he made in 1974 toward incorporating the biological approach. And most unfortunately, it fails to pursue the biologist's emphasis on groups that Becker appeared to be pursuing in 1974. We remain entrenched in the world of the individual actor who pursues his self-interest, albeit in a clever, strategic fashion.

19. Becker is not the only economist who draws on biological concepts. Another approach is illustrated by Margolis, who addresses group interest most successfully to explain why people contribute to the public interest when the return they expect appears inconsequential and the effect on society minuscule. Margolis uses a Darwinian argument to suggest that individuals have dual sources of motivation: every individual has within him both a self-interested person (S-Smith) and a group-interested person (G-Smith). This argument parallels that of early political economists, who assumed a duality of human nature: "man as private, self-seeking individual; man as citizen and social being" (Margolis 1982). Margolis notes that this "dual utility" approach simply reformulates the problem so that we now must move beyond the earlier and relatively simple question of *how* a self-interested individual can use resources rationally to further group interest. Instead, we must ask *when* the individual will use resources to maximize his or her self-interested preferences and when he or she will use them to maximize group-interested preferences.

20. Since my interest is in human behavior, I focus on human altruism and make only occasional reference to the biological literature on generational studies of minute organisms with vastly different structures and behavioral characteristics, e.g., less intelligence, than is the case for human beings.

21. See Howard Margolis's work (1982) for the most imaginative and fully developed articulation of this concept.

22. Lerner (1992) presents convincing evidence that this biological linkage was important in the Nazi genocide.

23. Her father learned that Margot had been arrested and hid the girls in a convent for the rest of the war.

24. Haldane (1932) and Wilson (1975) are two of the best known.

25. Other scholars have found isolated instances of such behavior.

26. This attitude and behavior did exist for a few rescuers. One sees it too in those political authorities who tried to protect Jews they considered native French but who were less likely to try to protect those they regarded as foreign. I discuss this in chapter 10.

27. Bert spoke of this.

28. Christopher Browning's fascinating study (1992) of Germans who were involved in searching out and executing Jewish civilians suggests that a bond between a particular Jew and the executioner often encouraged more lenient treatment or even being saved. But such ties did not exist for rescuers.

29. Interestingly, most rescuers recognized that both sanctions and incentives might affect people. Rescuers did not blame people whose fear of sanctions discouraged them from helping Jews. But rescuers did blame people who turned in Jews for rewards. Tony told of going into a Gestapo headquarters after a bombing raid, disguised as a member of the fire squad sent to put out the fire from the bombing. While in the building, he found a file cabinet with names and addresses of people who turned in Jews for money. Tony removed these files, which were later used to prosecute such people after the war.

30. In the case of the rescuers, any defectors would have to be most accurately represented by those who turned over rescuers to the Nazis.

31. Rescuers were also turned in by neighbors who needed money or food or who held grudges against a particular rescuer.

32. See Trivers 1971.

33. The extent to which learning enters into this underlines my earlier point that it is difficult to separate the various causal mechanisms and that the divisions I have chosen to pursue here to enhance clarity should not be considered exclusionary.

34. Since these two hypotheses are often used interchangeably in the literature, other analysts may adopt definitions that differ slightly from the ones I have employed here.

35. There were a few groups (e.g., Le Chambon) which encouraged altruism. More often, such encouragement to engage in rescue activities might come from immediate family members. But even this support was neither automatic nor necessarily the norm. One survivor told me her rescuer was turned into the Gestapo by his own mother. Such stories, as heart-wrenching and unbelievable as they now seem, were all too common.

36. Unfortunately, this was not a safe haven and the girls were eventually apprehended.

37. There are many books written on Le Chambon, and a video documentary was produced by Pierre Sauvage, who was hidden in Le Chambon as a baby.

38. Leonie never became estranged from her sister. And Leonie's sister was later persuaded to accompany Leonie on a barge that took starving children, some of whom were Jewish, into safety. In this instance, we might count Leonie's sister as someone recruited into rescue activities.

39. I did conduct one interview with a Jewish man who had worked to get people out of Europe. This man, who was not eligible for the Yad Vashem medal because of his own Jewish background, worked with the Resistance to take political refugees to safety.

This meant that he occasionally also helped politically prominent Jews escape from Europe, but he characterized this as arising from political motivation. He was the only person I spoke with who designated as political any of his activities on behalf of Jews. His interview is not part of this analysis and is used only as background.

40. See Alexrod 1984 or Trivers 1971 for fascinating studies on this.

CHAPTER 9
PSYCHOLOGICAL DISCUSSIONS OF ALTRUISM

1. Quoted in Batson 1991:42. Like Campbell, I will include in my discussion research done by psychoanalysts and psychiatrists.

2. It is ironic that the attachment to self-interest and reward as prime motives guiding human behavior developed largely in Freudian theory (based mainly on observations of emotionally disturbed adults) and learning theory (based on observing rats)! See *Psychological Inquiry* 1991: 2, no. 2:107–58 for an overview of the conflicts and debates over altruism among psychologists. Among the experts in the field writing on this issue, Staub (150–53) and Zahn-Waxler (155–58) focus on the extent to which the psychological academy has shifted over time in its commitment to egoism as the underlying basis of human behavior.

3. Altruism as helping designed to gain internal rather than external rewards has a long history in all three disciplines. For example, Becker's psychic income explanation (1976) corresponds closely to the psychologist's aversive-arousal explanation, which argues that we help others in order to reduce some internal discomfort or tension caused by witnessing someone suffer. Aquinas, Hobbes (1651), Mandeville (1714/1732), and McDougall (1908) all described this general phenomenon but did not classify it as altruistic. Some authors (e.g., Karylowski 1982) do classify this as altruistic, while others who discuss this arousal-reduction model (Piliavin and Piliavin 1973 and Piliavin et al. 1982) suggest that the model works more for bystander behavior than for altruistic behavior.

4. Many of these studies concern prosocial motives and evolved into relatively elaborate theoretical models by the 1980s. These models proposed different mechanisms, such as aversive-arousal reduction or negative-state relief, but the common theme was that behavior that appeared selfless was actually egoistically motivated. For numerous cites and references, see the exchange in *Psychological Inquiry* 1991:2, no. 2:107–58; Eisenberg 1986; Hoffman 1975; Krebs 1970; Latane and Darley 1970; Macaulay and Berkowitz 1970; Batson 1991; Zahn-Waxler 1986; or Wallach and Wallach 1983, 1990.

5. Psychology has been concerned with identity and with helping others since its disciplinary inception. So the causes of the timing of this shift probably rest with broader societal factors.

6. See Oliner et al. 1992 and the exchange in *Psychological Inquiry* 1991:2, no. 2 on methodological difficulties in the work on altruism, such as problems of inferring motive from behavior or the limitations of experimental studies as opposed to findings obtained in naturalistic conditions.

7. To demonstrate how the logic of this approach plays out in empirical work on altruism, let us consider just one example. A religious person and an excellent swimmer, Alex is returning home from church and sees a young child drowning in a lake

near his home. He immediately jumps in and saves the child. A developmental psychologist would explain this action through reference to the values Alex learned from a critical role model, values that effectively then suppressed his own self-interested desires. The developmental psychologist may allow for but does not emphasize specific internal states (such as Alex's values, cognition, and emotions). While such internal states are considered, they enter primarily as the results of reinforcement of sociological patterns. The developmental approach emphasizes the fact that particular forms of learning occurred, not the cognitive process that originally led to or encouraged such learning to take place. And unlike economic analyses of altruism, the apparent external rewards that encourage such learning are not discussed. This omission constitutes one of the criticisms of this approach; in the absence of these rewards, it is not always clear where and how reinforcement occurs. See the Oliners' discussion of this (1988:8–12).

8. Bridgeman's edited volume (1983) provides an excellent example of work in this area.

9. Staub (1975, 1979, 1980, 1990, inter alia) presents the most complete model of prosocial value orientation. Other theories specifying the movement from individual characteristics or dispositions to motivational or emotional states and on to action include Ajzen 1988 and Ajzen and Fishbein 1977. Batson and Shaw (1991) offer a rudimentary theory of action in their discussion of hedonic calculus.

10. Gilligan 1977/1981; Kohlberg 1984.

11. Maslow 1962.

12. Both Piaget (1948) and Kohlberg (1984) base their work on the assumption that individuals progress through stages of moral reasoning as a result of a kind of mental maturational process interacting with experience. While Piaget represents a more general cognitive developmental approach, Kohlberg focuses more on the development of moral reasoning. In essence, Kohlberg argues that individuals pass through six stages of progressive moral reasoning, each one more advanced than the earlier ones by virtue of increased ability to resolve issues relating to justice. Although Kohlberg does not focus specifically on altruism, he does discuss helping behavior, suggesting it is only partly explained by the level of moral reasoning since some children can do it very early in their lives.

13. Staub 1975, 1979, 1990; Oliner and Oliner 1988; Sellick 1994.

14. See Goldberger's interesting collection (1988) on the rescue of the Danish Jews.

15. The Oliners, for example, asked both nonrescuers and rescuers of Jews whether they felt like marginal people in their community or whether they felt themselves involved in the community. In this instance, they found little or no significant difference between the two groups (1988:chap. 7).

16. An analysis that focuses on Denmark's physical proximity to Sweden to explain the Danish rescue of the Jews would illustrate the kind of explanation that stresses situational predictors of altruism.

17. Work emphasizing the sympathetic demeanor of a person who needs to be rescued would illustrate explanations stressing the characteristics of the victim. Consider our earlier example of Alex, religious and an excellent swimmer. We found Alex returning from church when he sees a young child drowning in a lake near his home and immediately jumps into the lake to save the child. While a developmental analyst would stress the fact that Alex learned certain values as a child, analysts following the social-psychological approach might explain Alex's actions through a combination of

his strong sense of religious commitment to others or his sense of himself as someone who feels he has to take charge of a situation (both internal states), plus his being in a relatively risk-free situation (a lake near his home) and called upon to help a deserving person (a young child). The social psychological approach thus explains Alex's altruism through a combination of his internal state, plus the particular characteristics of the person helped and the situational circumstances in which the altruistic act occurred. See Piliavin and Piliavin 1973, Monroe 1989, or Staub 1979 for works summarizing findings on the tendency to help those perceived as similar to oneself, works which focus on self-perceptions, world view, and empathy, respectively.

18. Both the Oliners and Hoffman (1970, 1977) find that harsh discipline inhibits the development of altruism, while reasoning with children encourages later altruistic activity. They suggest that this may work through providing a script or pattern for caring for others (Oliner and Oliner 1988:174–85).

19. The Oliners' most central explanation, however, remains a social psychological one, stressing what the Oliners call extensivity. As developed and defined by the Oliners, extensivity consists of the patterns of ethical values of care and inclusiveness. In later work, the Oliners et al. (1992) suggest eight processes make up extensivity. The first four relate to forming attachments to known others: empathy, bonding, learning norms of caring, and participating in caring behaviors. The last four deal with developing a sense of obligation toward the broader society and include diversifying, networking, reasoning, and forming global connections.

The Oliners find that the patterns of caring so permeate the way certain individuals characteristically relate to and shape their sense of commitment to others that they can be said to constitute an altruistic personality. This raises a critical question, often stated as a general criticism of works in this area: How stable are personalities? We have much evidence that people grow and change as a result of later life experiences. Furthermore, if we assume stable personalities, we may underestimate the extent to which participation in one altruistic act influences a person's later behavior, serving as a feedback mechanism that affects the person's identity perception, encouraging more—or even less—altruism.

This last argument reminds us of Margolis's economic analysis of altruism (1982), which posits a trade-off between self-interested acts and other-directed acts. The logic Margolis pursues suggests that, at least for some individuals, the performance of one altruistic act might actually serve to lessen the probability of such future acts. Margolis's analysis would seem to contradict the kind of ongoing altruistic personality the Oliners (1988) find. See also Tipton and Browning 1972.

Regardless of its effect on altruism, the kind of traumatic experience the Oliners consider—rescuing Jews during World War II—*could* dramatically change an individual's basic personality and influence that individual's later acts. Indeed, one of the criticisms of analyzing rescuers now, and asking them about attitudes during the war, which occurred some fifty years ago, has been the extent to which retrospective memory has been shaped by the very acts the researcher is interested in explaining. See Langer 1991 and the 1981 Annual Report of Psychology for a discussion of the methodological bias in self-reported behavior, especially of traumatic events.

Even given all of this, however, and noting that the issue of the continuity of life-span development remains a lively and ongoing debate among psychologists, the Oliners' overall evidence nonetheless seems strong enough to suggest that the assumption of a stable personality is not unjustified and should not be ruled out as one of our research topics to explore further. See also McRae and Costa's *Emerging Lives, Enduring Dispositions* (1984); Baltes and Reese's work on life spans in Bronstein and Lamb (1984); Kelly's early work (1955) on the consistency of the adult personality; or Oliner and Oliner 1988:chap. 1, nn. 59–64 for fuller citations.

20. Psychologists use the term endocentric altruism, or altruism focused on itself, for example, to refer to doing good to feel good about oneself. Exocentric altruism then refers to behavior focused on the other, action designed to increase the other's welfare. To the best of my knowledge, the latter term was first introduced by Karylowski in 1982 and 1984. Karylowski develops a concept of exocentric altruism that resembles what economists discuss under the distinction between goods altruism and participation altruism. "Exocentric approaches assume that improvement of the partner's condition may possess inherent gratification value for the observer, regardless of whether it has been caused by him or not" (1982:399). "The source of gratification lies only in the improvement of the conditions of another person in need" (1984:141). This distinction closely resembles the distinction economists make in their discussions of participation altruism, in which the altruist's pleasure comes from being the agent causing the increased well-being of another; economists contrast it with altruism in which the agent simply wants the other to be cared for and does not insist on being the care provider. See also Batson 1991 or Oliner et al. 1992.

Psychologists refer to aversive-arousal reduction to describe helping another in order to reduce one's own discomfort at witnessing another's suffering (Kohn 1990 or Batson 1991). When Hobbes gave money to the beggar so he would not be upset by the fellow's wretchedness, for example, his behavior might be characterized either as aversive-arousal reduction or as endocentric altruism.

A similar phenomenon occurs with biological explanations, where we find discussions of phenotypes, in which genetic predispositions are shaped by culture in much the same way that the expression of a gene for blond hair is affected by time spent in the sun. Many psychologists who have been influenced by work in evolutionary biology conceptualize altruism as behavior in a biological sense, i.e., as behavior that is maladaptive at the individual level and incompatible with reproductive success. To explain altruism, they turn to the same kind of phenotypic interaction between biologically based altruistic dispositions and cultural influences: genes provide the range of possible behavior, but culture and learning shape the pattern of behaviors that is actually selected. Instead of the biological term "phenotype," however, psychologists refer to an "evolved subjective self-system" that enables humans to transcend biological constraints and become altruistically oriented. See Vine in Oliner et al. 1992.

These are only a few of the examples illustrating the confusion resulting from terminological differences.

21. Some of the psychological explanations already discussed in slightly different categories include a hierarchy of needs (chapter 7), the closeness of community size (chapters 7–8), group approval and group sanctions (chapters 6–8), an altruistic personality (chapter 7's discussion of a consistent taste for altruism), role models and guilt (chapter 7), and the importance of clusters of altruists and the imitative aspect of altruism (chapter 8).

22. Midlarsky, for example, even suggests that age makes people more altruistic (Midlarsky in Oliner et al. 1992).

23. People develop linguistic skills at widely different rates, for example.

24. Culture's influence has been particularly difficult to ascertain. Recent work in a volume edited by Oliner et al. (1992) appears to forge path-breaking ground by redefining how we look at culture.

25. This dates back to Freud (1917/1920) and can be found in virtually all major schools of psychology. Since role models influence general behavior, it is natural for analysts to ask whether they affect altruism.

26. This particular kind of childrearing is something the Oliners found was important for rescuers of Jews, most of whom had been reasoned with, rather than punished physically, as children.

27. See Kohlberg 1981, 1984 or Gilligan 1977/1981, 1982 for the best-known works and Gross (1994) for a careful recent analysis. See also chapter 7.

28. Both men were deeply religious, for example; John's father was a minister, and Barbie had studied for the priesthood.

29. One woman, not in my sample but whose story I saw on videotape, spoke of her reluctance to even take the little gun a friend pressed on her "just in case." She said she never thought she would have to kill anyone and did not want to have a gun around. But when it became necessary to either kill a Nazi collaborator or allow him to arrest the Jewish family she was hiding, she shot the man. She spoke with great anguish of how much she had disliked doing it and had wished there had been another way. She said that she still feels bad about it to this day but would do it over again if necessary.

30. One rescuer told of following a group of Jewish prisoners whom the Gestapo had apprehended in a raid. As they progressed across the barren countryside, some of the Nazis guarding the prisoners went on to headquarters, leaving the Jews guarded by only a handful of Gestapo men who "were then killed." After a long silence, during which these murders—described in the passive voice—hung in the air between us, the man finally said, "Well, we killed them." He then sat silently for a while, clenching and unclenching his hands, before saying, "I have never told anyone this before." This conversation took place in 1992.

31. The phrase is Bert's, but it echoed the sentiments of other rescuers.

32. This explanation would appeal to both developmentalists and to rational choice theorists who subscribe to rational equilibrium models.

33. The ethics could be the same, but the killer's perspective could be so skewed that he does not see a gap between his code and his actions, a possibility I find intriguing given my later findings on perspective.

34. We might think of ethical and altruistic acts as intersecting sets. This particular insight was brought home to me in a highly personal way. One of the first entrepreneurs I interviewed was an extremely nice man, introduced to me by a mutual friend. This entrepreneur was unusually articulate, literate, and well educated. His was one of the first interviews I conducted, and I was still searching for what always remained a delicate balance between having a conversation with another human being and conducting an interview that would be analyzed objectively and dispassionately. As we discussed financial matters, I found myself appalled at the contrast between how much this man earned (well over $1 million a year) and how little he gave to others (virtually nothing). I tried to be nonjudgmental but left the interview certain that my own internal negative judgment must have been revealed through my questions and that I had, as a result, made the man feel bad about himself.

That evening at dinner, I shared my thoughts with my husband, who has a nasty habit of being brutally honest. "Well, you're a nice person, but you don't give away much money. Why are you surprised to find this in someone else?" was the uncomfortable question he posed.

He was right. I am a nice person, one who would score fairly high on most of the traditional measures of ethical development. But I am far from being an altruist of any kind. This humbling realization helped me understand that while altruism may intersect with ethical behavior, there is far from a uniform overlap. The analytical tools needed to understand altruism may be quite different from those required to understand more traditional forms of ethical or moral development.

35. A friend from graduate school told me his Russian Jewish father was saved when the German soldier arresting him realized that they had played soccer together before the war. The soldier told my friend's father to disappear quietly while the other Jews were taken into headquarters.

36. See Oliner and Oliner 1988, Klingemann and Falter 1993, or Browning 1992 for further consideration of this phenomenon.

37. I heard several stories of Jews who simply refused to stay in hiding and would walk around the neighborhood, endangering the other members of the household through their actions. Sometimes the consequences were disastrous; sometimes not.

38. Tony told of one man who was going stir crazy in hiding and desperately wanted to go for a walk. Tony finally agreed and, taking extra precautions, took the man to tea at Tony's parents' home.

39. There are cases of people who saved Jews for nonaltruistic reasons, from financial gain to a general liking or admiration for the Jewish people. See Oliner et al. 1992.

40. On this topic, see Browning's masterful analysis (1992) of mass murderers in Poland.

41. Only Tony spoke at all in terms of saving people who might be more fit, and this was in the general terms of an evolutionary biologist. Noting that one might tend to save a pretty girl rather than an ugly one, he added, "But what is pretty? Pretty means healthier, better able to reproduce." Moreover, Tony only entertained this notion as an example of how *other* people might view things; it was not how he himself made decisions during the war.

42. Other situational factors were considered in chapters 6 and 8.

43. That John's modesty led him to minimize his altruism was evidenced in other incidents as well. At one point, I learned that John had taken a group of Jews across the mountains when the passes were covered with snow. One of the Jewish women asked why John was not wearing any socks; he told her that he preferred to ski wearing only boots. Only later was she told (and not by John) that he had given away so many of his clothes to Jewish refugees that he had no socks left to wear.

44. Concerns for personal safety and security resulting from being in familiar circumstances seem irrelevant for philanthropists, who do not risk their lives through their gifts to others. I therefore do not try to assess the importance of this factor for philanthropy. I should note Melissa's comment that allowing large donations to be publicized lets people know that you have money and where you live, thereby endangering you somewhat. She nonetheless agreed to such publicity when it was likely to encourage others.

45. See Latane and Darley 1970 for the classic work.

Chapter 10

The Altruistic Perspective

1. See Kohlberg 1981, 1984; Gross 1994; and Rawls 1971, inter alia.

2. I originally considered administering some of the standardized tests developed to measure levels of ethical development, such as those constructed for Kohlberg's (1984) typology of ethical development. Limited testing in a pilot study indicated that the tests were obtrusive, time-consuming, and wearing on the subject, interfered with the human interaction critical to a spoken narrative, and yielded less complete information than was obtained through the narrative approach. See also Riker 1995 on limitations of such tests.

3. See chapter 9.

4. Tönnies (1957) referred to these people as having a *Gesellschaft* mentality, in which ties and obligations to others are more tentative. Analogues of this argument exist in biology (kin and group selection) as well as in economics and psychology.

5. Shifts in outlooks were too subtle to be bifurcated, suggesting once again that a simple dichotomy between altruists and nonaltruists oversimplifies reality. In this regard, the methodological decision to use a continuum was not merely justified; it was critical.

6. I describe below how such a mistake could easily arise.

7. This seems to agree with Lerner's work and with similar ideas dating to Tönnies 1957, inter alia.

8. Much of this evidence was documented in the chapter on biological explanations of altruism and will not be repeated here.

9. This attitude was evident in all the rescuers I interviewed. It also existed among the heroes, as Lucille's narrative (chapter 4) illustrates. The young white girl Lucille saved from being raped, the blacks Lucille wanted to help by working with the southern civil rights movement, the Sudanese worker thrown into the Nile—these are a highly diverse group, united by Lucille's perspective, not by any special bond she forged with these particular people as opposed to others.

10. See Goldberger 1988 for details.

11. See chapter 9 for discussion of how other altruists did occasionally make reference to a person's guilt or innocence, but only in connection with occasions (such as Margot's postwar dealings with the Gestapo commander for Amsterdam) when they refused to help people. Presumably, when the altruistic perspective is not triggered, moral judgment *can* sometimes shut out the impulse to help.

12. Tony mentions the vegetable kingdom and the earth itself; Lucille refers to the animal kingdom and tells how she tries not to kill even a spider. The incredible inclusiveness articulated by altruists like Tony and Lucille seems a far cry from any in-group versus out-group distinctions.

13. One theory holds that the motivation for helping emanates from the actor's desire to believe in a just world. This, in turn, depends on the actor's perceived relationship among the participants in the encounter. Consider two actors, Fred and Ginger. Lerner (1982) argued that a perceived identity relationship in which Fred feels himself "psychologically indistinguishable from the other" makes Fred feel that he can experience what Fred believes Ginger (the other) is experiencing. This, in turn, will encourage a kind of "justice of need" that transcends Fred's concern for justice in a more general

sense and causes him to focus instead on Ginger's welfare (Lerner and Meindl 1981:224). In constructing this complex argument, and especially in maintaining that these identity relationships are learned in early childhood, Lerner echoes Hoffman's (1977) emphasis on a developmental process and anticipates the Oliners' (1988) emphasis on the habits of caring. Such habits are, Lerner asserts, more likely to occur with people (such as family members) with whom the actor is closely associated. I will return later in this chapter to the general question of identity and suggest that Lerner came very close to what I believe is the dynamic of altruism, but that the phenomenon is broader in certain respects. I also should note that Lerner's idea is more complex than the analogue I was able to examine.

14. Kohlberg's work on ethical systems (1984) discusses this.

15. Gilligan (1977/1981) also notes the importance of relations for decision making.

16. Other analysts have found these views of themselves significant influences on altruism. See Oliner and Oliner 1988.

17. See Hume's *An Enquiry Concerning the Principles of Morals* (1751/1902) or Smith's *The Theory of Moral Sentiments* (1759/1853), each of which discusses empathy and a quasi-altruistic phenomenon, despite the fact that neither the word "altruism" nor the word "empathy" had yet been coined.

18. See chapter 1 or Kohn 1990:chap. 4 for fuller discussion of this.

19. Kohut 1984.

20. Rogers 1961.

21. Kohn 1990, Batson 1991, and Hoffman 1981, 1984, 1987, 1989a, and 1989b offer elaborate discussions. See also chapter 1.

22. In addition to the works already cited and those discussed below, see work by Piliavin et al. (1982); Eisenberg, Lennon, and Roth (1983); Eisenberg et al. (1987); and Hoffman (1977, 1981, 1989a, and 1989b).

23. Nagel (1970) and Kohn (1990:163) describe this work.

24. Both Williams (1981:91) and Kohn (1990:128–29) discuss the extent to which putting oneself in another's place may be connected with sadism as well as with altruism.

25. The Oliners' work on rescuers (1988) suggests that empathy's influence is often joined with other factors before it becomes critical for altruism. They found no difference between people who rescued Jews and people who did not rescue Jews as far as generalized emotional empathy (defined as general susceptibility to others' moods), but they did find differences "with respect to emotional empathy for others' pain" (174). Rescuers tended to be more affected by pain, sadness, and helplessness. The Oliners found that this was coupled with another psychological factor of importance, the acceptance of personal responsibility reflected in the rescuers' greater task perseverance, commitment to fulfill promises once made, willingness to be involved in friends' problems, and acceptance of the obligation to give of their time for the good of the larger community. Thus, the Oliners concluded that rescuers were not only more empathic toward others' pain than nonrescuers but also more likely to get involved and to stay involved, because of their general sense of responsibility and tendency to make commitments. Furthermore, they concluded that rescuers' empathy with the weak and the helpless did not emerge from rescuers' feelings of personal vulnerability, since rescuers on the whole felt that they could control events and shape their own destinies.

This last factor suggests that a sense of self-esteem might be critical, a characteristic I considered but found too variable among the rescuers I interviewed to be a reliable and consistent predictor.

26. Billy, for example, gives money mainly to people he knows or to local causes. Justin's gifts to Jewish charities are linked to his Jewish grandmother's making him aware of his Jewish identity. Warren gave money to a local college. "Mom" volunteers for organizations associated with her interests in rock music or the environment.

27. Isabelle, for example, focuses her energies on emotionally and physically abused children, even though she has no ties to such children in her personal life. Isabelle is a close family person, for example, who began her philanthropy with cookies for a school party. "I took a wrong turn, which was really a right turn" and ended up in the room where the handicapped and retarded children were taught. There were no festivities planned for these children, no decorations or little treats on the tables, so Isabelle stayed to make them a party and gave them the cookies meant for her son's class. This began her work with disabled and abused children. I think it would be difficult for most mothers to give to others food intended for their own children, even in this non–life-threatening setting.

28. See Kohn 1990, especially chaps. 4 and 5, for a discussion of the importance of, and difference between, perspective taking and empathy.

29. This corresponds to the kind of bonding that goes on through affective empathy.

30. The fact that this quote comes from an interview conducted by Ute Klingemann further minimizes the extent to which I may have inadvertently cued the subject.

31. I have been criticized by Fogelman (1994:157–58) for utilizing too fine a sieve in my search for an explanation for altruism. Fogelman appears to imply that I "lumped Holocaust rescuers into a single category of people who believed in and acted on the idea that all people were part of a fellowship of mankind" (1994:158). This was not my intent, and I think Fogelman misunderstands my concept of careful science, which is to look with ever-increasing scrutiny at a wide variety of explanations and retain only those that appear to be consistently and systematically predictive. Other factors besides perspective may occasionally influence altruism, but they are not consistently significant predictors. It is also true that people may occasionally help others for selfish reasons; but this is not altruism.

32. This forgiveness was not evident among all rescuers. Leonie speaks with disdain of people who turned in Jews to the Gestapo. "Those are animals. These were worse than animals. They got money if they brought somebody in to the Gestapo. And that is the lowest of the low, I think." Tony also described such people as deserving to "hang by the you know what."

33. Lucille, for example, hardly fits the model of a self-confident leader. She sees herself as just an ordinary person, as nothing special. In this she is typical of heroes and heroines, the first group on our continuum to seem to be unaware that what they are doing is extraordinary.

I don't think I'm so unusual in this. I know I'm someone who's willing to take a lot of responsibility on in the world. But I don't think I'm anything special. I'm very self-conscious with people. I want people to like me, and I don't know that they do.

Q. *You say you want people to like you. But you obviously had a lot of people who did not like you, because of some of the things you were doing in the integration period. Yet you still continued. So obviously you were able to live with that in some way.*

A. Well, I had to. That was more important.

Tony offers a sharp contrast to Lucille. A confident, self-aware, philosophical man, at peace with himself, Tony retains a wry sense of humor about himself. He projected quite a different self-image from Lucille's. Still, neither of these two extraordinary people thought that they had done anything unusual.

34. Other scholars have been struck by the extent to which rescuers insist their actions were not unusual. See Oliner and Oliner 1988 or Hallie 1979.

35. I note this part of the dialogue to demonstrate how freely people felt that they could disagree with me and correct my misimpressions. I originally had worried about "cueing" people during interviews and had to laugh at myself as the interviews progressed and I realized how little these people who had faced down the Gestapo were likely to be intimidated by me.

36. Scholars such as Kant (1785/1889), Rawls (1973), and Nagel (1970) have suggested this.

37. This idea can be traced back to Hume (1751/1902).

38. The Oliners (1988) also found this consistency among the rescuers, causing them to conclude that there was an altruistic personality.

39. I have since explored this phenomenon further by comparing rescuers with matched nonrescuers, Europeans who correspond in critical background characteristics to particular rescuers but who did not themselves participate in rescue activities (Monroe 1994). I also conducted a secondary analysis of Browning's (1992) legal interrogations of members of the Reserve Order Police Battalion 101, a unit responsible for the direct murdering of at least forty-five thousand Jewish people in Poland. In their testimony, the men of Battalion 101 described the Jews as inhuman, suggesting that Otto was right: to kill, one must first dehumanize (Monroe 1995).

40. This may explain why one scholar might find empathy (for example) needed an additional component in order to trigger altruism, while empathy alone was sufficient to trigger altruism in certain other people or in other instances. In one person, sample, or experiment, the critical altruistic perspective may be triggered by one factor (such as empathy) but not in another.

41. Altruism is analogous to the family reunion, and the town in which the reunion is held is represented by the particular perspective I have just described.

42. Scholars have noted a similar phenomenon concerning genocide, behavior about as far away as possible from altruism on any moral spectrum. See Monroe 1995 for a review.

CHAPTER 11
PERSPECTIVE AND ETHICAL POLITICAL ACTS

1. I chose rational choice theory as an example of a popular theory with normative and positive content and one often applied to discussions of ethics and politics.

2. I limit my remarks to situations that clearly involve the intersection of ethics and politics, utilizing the narrowest definition of each.

3. We might refer to these as options or alternative forms of action, since "choice" often entails the concept of freedom of action.

4. Because of its interdisciplinary nature, I try to describe this theory using simple language, intelligible to readers in all disciplines and not just to those who are well-

versed in the intricacies of a particular field and its debates. Within space constraints, I try to define terms and make reference to some of the more technical debates in the various literatures, providing references for the reader. (Identity, schema, the self, culture, choice, cognition, and agent are but a few examples of the complex concepts on which much has been written). See Bruner 1988, 1990, Elster 1979, 1986, Johnson 1991, or Taylor 1989 on agency, intentionality, and the self. See Axelrod 1973, Johnson-Laird 1983, and Rummelhart 1986 on schemas and schema theory.

5. These points are interrelated; the order of presentation is not necessarily indicative of importance.

6. Defining a widely used term such as identity is tricky, as Erikson reminds us in the introduction to his classic work, *Identity: Youth and Crisis* (1968).

7. There are innumerable works on identity, and even one of the seminal works (Erikson 1959/1980) notes the difficulties in defining identity.

8. Gary Thom has suggested that the relation between the cognitive and the affective may play a critical, even defining, role in core identity. I have only begun to explore such considerations.

9. There are many definitions of both politics and ethics. A minimalist definition of the political would concern state action of a legal nature. Broader conceptualization would move toward power and influence and the authoritative allocation of values, and eventually into the normative area of how we treat each other—at which point politics and ethics blend together conceptually. Conceptualization of ethics also touches on conceptualizations of identity. Who are we? Are we what we do? Are we what we think of ourselves? Do moral statements concern being good or doing good? Just these few obvious questions suggest why a full discussion of these issues lies far beyond the present analysis.

10. I assume impulses are nonconscious and nonreflexive behavior with motives that lead to action. Intuitions are primitively articulated types of knowledge in which concepts or rationalizations are not well developed.

11. Hutcheson 1728/1971. The relation between social roles and culturally induced norms will be particularly interesting to explore as we try to distinguish deep-seated psychological factors from subcultural variations.

12. James (1890) called this the one-in-many selves paradox, whereby we maintain self-continuity while still acting out different roles and essentially changing personalities situation by situation.

13. Johnston 1991; Elster 1986; or Monroe 1995a.

14. Presumably such a calculus would apply in societies in which marriages are arranged.

15. This treatment of moral values owes much to the concept of moral sense theory discussed by Darwin (1859/1936) in his theory of evolution. The closest parallel in contemporary moral philosophy would be recent work by Bernard Williams (1981) or Martha Nussbaum (1986).

16. There is a vast literature on how identity perceptions emerge, the extent to which self-images are preset, how changeable they are, who changes and under what conditions, and what role independent agency plays in the creation of self. Indeed, one criticism of the economic and the rational choice approach centers on the extent to which economic theory posits a particular kind of actor, thereby limiting the conceptual potential for human development in other ways.

17. Grafstein (1995) argues that individual agents do not choose to have a certain kind of moral character but can usefully learn about their character through the character of their behavior.

18. Monroe 1995b.

19. The examples discussed here concern the cognitive link between perceptions, decision making, and behavior. There are, of course, other distinctions of equal importance, such as fluidity of identity, the extent to which we have multiple or competing identities, or insecurity about our central identity; these need to be built into a final version of a theory of perspective. Because of space constraints, however, I restrict discussion to only two separate categories of actions: (1) acts subject to a conscious calculus versus those not subject to a conscious calculus and (2) issues that strike at our core sense of self and those that touch us at a more superficial level of identity. In general, the more deeply an issue touches on our basic sense of self, the less likely that issue will be subjected to a conscious calculus and the more likely it is to be decided by the individual's overall perspective on life.

20. Conflicts of values: What happens when different and critical parts of our core identity conflict? Traditional rational choice theory suggests that values can be arranged in a hierarchical fashion and a cost/benefit calculus applied. But when values conflict, people need a way to resolve the conflict. Such conflicts might include tension between career and family, the emotional conflict experienced when a loved one has a terminal illness or a parent descends into poor health and senility, or decisions to undergo abortion or relinquish a child for adoption. Although these are individual conflicts, they also touch on societal choices, as in the public debate over child care facilities, euthanasia, and abortion. Other more obviously societal choices include tensions between justice and compassion in a legal system or between equality and democracy in a polity. The psychological literature suggests that several possible cognitive responses frequently occur when core values conflict, from cognitive growth and integration to compromise, cognitive dissonance, severe personality disintegration, or even destruction of identity. (See Tetlock 1986 for one of the better empirical works on this subject.)

Consider one frequently experienced conflict of core values: the tension between profession and family. Consider a group of similar individuals, all of whom have demanding careers and large families they love. John may deceive himself, failing to see that he is ignoring one for the other. His wife, Susan, may give up one value for the other and be unhappy, while Mary decides to concentrate on one and then the other, staying home while her children are young and then returning to her career when family pressures have lessened. Barbara may develop cognitive mechanisms to integrate family and career in more creative ways, such as taking a new baby to the office, running her business out of her home, or job sharing with her husband. For Margie, the conflict may be too great for cognitive growth or self-deception, and her basic identity may crumble or be destroyed. This is the situation in *Sophie's Choice*, Styron's 1979 novel in which a sadistic Nazi forces Sophie to choose which of her two children would be killed.

21. One could also argue that before my conversion eating nonkosher food was also reflective of my sense of self, albeit to a different effect.

22. Other factors might also enter in, e.g., canonical expectations about office behavior.

23. Simon 1984, inter alia.

24. Kahneman, Tversky, and Slovic 1982, inter alia.

25. Kant probably best exemplifies this. For a somewhat idiosyncratic discussion of the role of the self in the development of political philosophy since 1750, see Solomon 1988.

26. This is part of Heidegger's critique (1962).

27. This distinguishes my conceptualization of identity from the more traditional sociological conceptualization (Bearman 1995; see also Sheldon Stryker on master identities which consolidate all our identities and frame and structure our acts).

28. Camus (1946) approaches this concept of choice.

29. The kinds of typologies developed at a theoretical level by Jung and applied at more behavioral and predictive levels in business through the Myers-Briggs tests are obvious examples here.

30. My theory would allow for workers who do not feel defined by class roles or for women who do not see themselves primarily as women but rather as (for example) professionals of some kind.

31. I disagree with Gary Becker's contention that economic theory can satisfactorily explain marriage.

32. Olson 1971.

33. Empirical work on the dynamics of divorce could provide a test of this.

34. Geertz 1973. See also Johnson 1991.

35. See Simon 1984 or Schelling 1960.

36. See Johnson 1991.

37. 1979:113, 77.

38. See also Johnson 1991.

39. Tony appeared to articulate this view, in which the heart is an organ independent within, but meaningless without, the entire body, just as the individual is a separate yet integral part of society.

40. I am indebted to David Easton for alerting me to these distinctions.

41. See Monroe and Kreidie 1995 for studies of Islamic fundamentalists that seem to provide empirical confirmation of such distinctions.

42. By strategies I refer to a plan of action which may or may not be conscious. This differs from the usage in game theory in not directly making reference to the other players. See Rapoport 1966 for the classic discussion.

43. Jaan Whitehead pointed out this distinction to me.

44. I am less sanguine about advancing precise predictions of behavior that could then be empirically tested to validate or invalidate this theory. I should note, however, that rational choice, cultural theory, and Marxism are open to this same criticism.

45. This is particularly important if there are some areas in which rational choice theory may be used profitably in conjunction with the theory of self in relation to others.

46. See Monroe 1994 for further discussion of this.

47. This dichotomy, of course, was something the Marxists got wrong. They thought the working class would refuse to be enticed into a capitalist war and were surprised when the workers responded as nationals of a particular country and picked up their weapons to shoot fellow workers during World War I.

48. Downs (1957) is the best-known example here, but there are numerous empirical and theoretical works that built on his original ideas.

49. Monroe and Kreidie 1995.

50. Nozick (1992) explores the reluctance of Americans to treat heroin addiction through the government's providing methadone to drug addicts, despite experts who argue that this would be a cheaper solution to the problem, He suggests that dealing with the drug problem per se is not the primary concern here for most Americans; it remains secondary to feeling that we as a nation are "tough on crime." Nozick's analysis corresponds closely to the kind of civic duty addition to the rational choice model for voting; it could be explained easily by a rational actor theorist as an additional goal or preference that had to be added into the equation. But Nozick's argument also illustrates how an identity model might be effectively combined with a rational choice model to explain a specific public policy.

51. This does not imply that behavior never emanates from such sources, merely that there is a more basic source of behavior: one's perception of self in relation to others.

52. This perception delineates options in the sense of outlining them in sharp, even vivid, detail. It defines the options by establishing and limiting the ones perceived with such clarity that it becomes difficult to move outside these limitations.

53. This theory differs from schema theory, which is more technical and more exclusively cognitive. My focus is on behavior, not cognition.

54. I refer to the adage that economics is about the choices that people make and sociology is about how they don't have choices. Instead, I draw on an older tradition in normative philosophy, dating from the Greek philosophers and playwrights who discussed politics in terms of what it meant to be a citizen and a human being.

55. While I do, of course, draw on the extensive contemporary literature on identity (such as Taylor's 1989 work) and on the literature in ethics that explains moral action through identity, I find many of the fine distinctions in this recent work more confusing than helpful and therefore do not couch my arguments in the terms of this debate. I would like to express my argument in language that is accessible to both behaviorally oriented political scientists and more traditionally trained political philosophers. See, inter alia, Cropsey 1977, especially those chapters on the relationship of politics, economics, and philosophy; Nussbaum 1986; or Williams 1981.

56. See Green and Shapiro 1995 for a discussion of rational choice models' performance in this regard.

CONCLUSION

1. This idea, articulated in philosophy by Plato and Kant, inter alia, also is evident in literary analysis.

2. Gary Becker advances one of the strongest recent arguments in favor of such a grand theory, but other social scientists, from Marx to Parsons, have presented similar designs. Becker's argument is quoted in part below:

> The heart of my argument is that human behavior is not compartmentalized, sometimes based on maximizing, sometimes not, sometimes motivated by stable preferences, sometimes by volatile ones, sometimes resulting in an optimal accumulation

of information, sometimes not. Rather, all human behavior can be viewed as involving participants who maximize their utility from a stable set of preferences and accumulate an optimal amount of information and other inputs in a variety of markets.

If this argument is correct, the economic approach provides a unified framework for understanding behavior that has long been sought by and eluded Bentham, Comte, Marx, and others. (1976:14)

3. See Gardener 1995.

4. I am disagreeing with those who advocate discarding a theory simply when we find one instance that clearly contradicts it. I am, however, saying that we should look carefully at such "exceptions" to the rules and use them, as I have with altruism, as tools to reanalyze the theory itself.

5. Kohn (1990), inter alia, falls into this trap.

6. This critique has been discussed in various forms by postmodern thinkers like Heidegger and Foucault, as well as by some critics of rational choice theory who work within the rational choice framework itself. See Zuckert 1995.

7. Nussbaum's analysis (1986) of early Greek writings presents an alternate portrait of what it means to be a human being.

8. This is the gist of Heidegger's argument. I am grateful to Cathy Zuckert for pointing out the relevance of Heidegger's argument to me and for helping give shape to my own inchoate thoughts on this topic.

9. See Hirschman 1977 or Whitehead 1990.

10. Much of this is so obvious as to be trite. But I was reminded at a recent conference (March 1993) that we social scientists tend to forget this obvious truth and in doing so may give pain to others. This particular conference was on people who rescued Jews during the war and was attended by several Jewish survivors as well as by academics. Late in the first day of the conference one of the survivors raised her hand and with great passion bemoaned the fact that we were commenting so coldly on what had been her life, that we were failing to capture "the texture" of what the reality had been like.

11. See Calabresi 1978 or Zuckert 1995.

12. It is perhaps appropriate that this interview came to my attention through one of the women I interviewed, a Polish woman who rescued Jews and who, in typical fashion for altruists, was kind enough to share her copy of the film containing this interview with me. I believe the interview was conducted by a Catholic nun named Carol Rittner, who was attempting to understand what made certain people willing to rescue Jews during the war when so many religious Catholics did not. The interview appears in a beautiful film, *The Courage to Care*.

13. The story of Le Chambon has been told by Hallie (1979) and in a movie by Sauvage, *Weapons of the Spirit*.

Bibliography

Abric, Jean-Claude. 1982. "Cognitive Processes Underlying Cooperation: The Theory of Social Representation." In V. J. Derlaga and J. Grzelak, eds., *Cooperation and Helping Behavior: Theories and Research*, 74–96. New York: Academic Press.

Adorno, T. W., E. Frenkel-Brunswik, D. J. Levinson, and R. N. Sanford. 1950. *The Authoritarian Personality*. New York: W. W. Norton.

Ajzen, Icek. 1988. *Attitudes, Personality and Behavior*. Milton Keynes: Open University Press.

Ajzen, Icek, and Martin Fishbein. 1977. "Attitude-Behavior Relations: A Theoretical Analysis and Review of Empirical Research." *Psychological Bulletin* 84, no. 5:888–918.

Almond, Gabriel. 1991. "Rational Choice Theory and the Social Sciences." In K. R. Monroe, ed., *The Economic Approach to Politics: A Critical Reassessment of the Theory of Rational Action*, 32–52. New York: HarperCollins.

Arendt, Hannah. 1963. *Eichmann in Jerusalem: A Report on the Banality of Evil*. New York: Viking Press.

Arrow, Kenneth J. 1984. *Social Choice and Justice*. Oxford: Basil Blackwell.

————. 1951/1963. *Social Choice and Individual Values*. New Haven: Yale University Press.

Axelrod, Robert. 1984. *The Evolution of Cooperation*. New York: Basic Books.

————. 1973. *Framework for a General Theory of Cognition and Choice*. Berkeley: Institute of International Studies, University of California.

Axelrod, Robert, and William D. Hamilton. 1981. "The Evolution of Cooperation." *Science* 211, no. 4489:1390–96.

Baltes, P. B., and H. W. Reese. 1984. "The Life-Span Perspective in Developmental Psychology." In M. H. Bornstein and M. E. Lamb, eds., *Developmental Psychology: An Advanced Textbook*, 493–532. Hillsdale, N.J.: Lawrence Erlbaum.

Barker, Roger G. 1978. *Habitats, Environments, and Human Behavior*. San Francisco: Jossey-Bass.

Bar-Tal, Daniel. 1976. *Prosocial Behavior: Theory and Research*. Washington, D.C.: Hemisphere.

Bar-Tal, Daniel, Ruth Sharabany, and Amiram Raviv. 1982. "Cognitive Basis for the Development of Altruistic Behavior." In V. J. Derlega and J. Grzelak, eds., *Cooperation and Helping Behavior: Theories and Research*, 377–96. New York: Academic Press.

Bartlett, F. 1932. *A Study in Experimental and Social Psychology*. New York: Cambridge University Press.

Bateson, Mary C. 1990. *Composing a Life*. New York: Plume Books.

Batson, C. Daniel. 1991. *The Altruism Question: Toward a Social Psychological Answer*. Hillsdale, N.J.: Lawrence Erlbaum.

Batson, C. Daniel, and Laura Shaw. 1991. "Evidence for Altruism: Toward a Plurality of Prosocial Motives." *Psychological Inquiry* 2, no. 2:107–22.

Bearman, Peter. 1995. "Becoming a Nazi: Network Models of Single Author Narratives." Sociology and Social Networks Colloquium, University of California, Irvine, May 2, 1995.

Becker, Gary. 1976. *The Economic Approach to Human Behavior*. Chicago: University of Chicago Press.

———. 1975. *Human Capital: A Theoretical and Empirical Analysis, with Special Reference to Education*. New York: Columbia University Press.

Bentham, Jeremy. 1789/1876. *Introduction to the Principles of Morals and Legislation*. Oxford: Clarendon Press.

Berkowitz, Leonard, ed. 1972. *Advances in Experimental Social Psychology*. Vol. 6. New York: Academic Press.

Berkowitz, Leonard, and Kenneth G. Lutterman. 1968. "The Traditionally Socially Responsible Personality." *Public Opinion Quarterly* 32:169–85.

Blau, Peter M. 1968. "Social Exchange." In D. L. Sills, ed., *International Encyclopedia of the Social Sciences*, 371. New York: Macmillan.

———. 1964. *Exchange and Power in Social Life*. New York: J. Wiley.

Block, Gay, and Malka Drucker. 1992. *Rescuers*. New York: Holmes and Meier.

Boorman, Scott A., and Paul R. Levitt. 1980. *The Genetics of Altruism*. New York: Academic Press.

Bridgeman, Diane L. 1983. *The Nature of Prosocial Development*. New York: Academic Press.

Browning, Christopher. 1992. *Ordinary Men*. New York: HarperCollins.

Bruner, Jerome. 1990. *Acts of Meaning*. Cambridge: Harvard University Press.

———. 1988. *Actual Minds, Possible Worlds*. Cambridge: Harvard University Press.

Buchanan, James. 1975. "The Samaritan's Dilemma." In E. Phelps, ed., *Altruism, Morality and Economic Theory*, 71–86. New York: Russell Sage Foundation.

Butler, Joseph. 1729/1897. "Upon the Love of Our Neighbor (Sermon 11)." In W. E. Gladstone, ed., *The Works of Joseph Butler*, vol 2. Oxford: Clarendon Press.

Calabresi, Guido. 1975. "Comment." In E. Phelps, ed., *Altruism, Morality and Economic Theory*, 57–62. New York: Russell Sage Foundation.

Calabresi, Guido, and Phillip Bobbitt. 1978. *Tragic Choices*. New York: W. W. Norton.

Campbell, Donald. 1978. "On the Genetics of Altruism and the Counterhedonic Components in Human Culture." In L. Wispe, ed., *Altruism, Sympathy, and Helping: Psychological and Sociological Principles*, 39–78. New York: Academic Press.

———. 1975. "On the Conflicts between Biological and Social Evolution and between Psychology and Moral Tradition." *American Psychologist* 30:1103–26.

Camus, Albert. 1946. *The Stranger*. Translated by Stuart Gilbert. New York: A. A. Knopf.

Casson, R. W. 1983. "Schemata in Cognitive Anthropology." *Annual Review of Anthropology* 12:429–62.

Chodrow, Nancy. 1978. *The Reproduction of Mothering*. Berkeley: University of California Press.

Christie, R., and F. Geiss, eds. 1968. *Studies in Machiavellianism*. New York: Academic Press.

Cohen, E. A. 1973. *The Abyss*. New York: W. W. Norton.

Comte, A. 1851/1875. *System of Positive Polity*. Vol. 1. London: Longmans, Green and Co.

————. 1830–42/1939. *Cours de philosophie positive*. Paris: Bachelier.

Cronin, Helena. 1991. *The Ant and the Peacock: Altruism and Sexual Selection from Darwin to Today*. Cambridge and New York: Press Syndicate of the University of Cambridge.

Cropsey, Joseph. 1977. *Political Philosophy and the Issues of Politics*. Chicago: University of Chicago Press.

D'Andrade, Roy. In press. "The Identification of Schemas in Naturalistic Data." In M. Horowitz, ed., *Personal Schemas and Maladaptive Interpersonal Behavior Patterns*. Chicago: University of Chicago Press.

Darwin, Charles. 1859/1936. *The Origin of Species by Means of Natural Selection*. New York: Modern Library.

Dawkins, Richard. 1976. *The Selfish Gene*. New York: Oxford University Press.

DeJong, P. 1981. "Responses of the Churches in the Netherlands to the Nazi Occupation." In M. D. Ryan, ed., *Human Responses to the Holocaust: Perpetrators and Victims—Bystanders and Resisters*, 121–43. New York and Toronto: Edwin Mellen Press.

Derlega, Valerian J., and Janusz Grzelak. 1982. *Cooperation and Helping Behavior: Theories and Research*. New York: Academic Press.

Dovidio, John F. 1984. "Helping Behavior and Altruism: An Empirical and Conceptual Overview." In L. Berkowitz, ed., *Advances in Experimental Social Psychology*, 2:361–427. New York: Academic Press.

Dovidio, John F., Judith L. Allen, and David A. Schroeder. 1990. "The Specificity of Empathy-Induced Helping: Evidence for Altruistic Motivation." *Journal of Personality and Social Psychology* 59, no. 2:249–60.

Downs, Anthony. 1957. *An Economic Theory of Democracy*. New York: Harper Press.

Dworkin, Ronald M. 1978. "Liberalism." In S. Hampshire, ed., *Public and Private Morality*, 23–46. New York: Cambridge University Press.

Eckstein, Harry. 1992. *Regarding Politics: Essays on Political Theory, Stability, and Change*. Berkeley and Los Angeles: University of California Press.

————. 1991. "Rationality and Frustration in Political Behavior." In K. R. Monroe, ed., *The Economic Approach to Politics: A Critical Reassessment of the Theory of Rational Action*, 74–93. New York: HarperCollins.

Eisenberg, Nancy. 1986. *Altruistic Emotion, Cognition, and Behavior*. Hillside, N.J.: Lawrence Erlbaum.

Eisenberg, Nancy, and Robert Cialdini. 1984. "The Role of Consistency Pressures in Behavior: A Developmental Perspective." *Academic Psychology Bulletin* 6, no. 2: 115–26.

Eisenberg, Nancy, Richard A. Fabes, Denise Bustamante, and Robin M. Mathy. 1987. "Psychological Indices of Altruism." In N. Eisenberg and J. Strayer, eds., *Empathy and Its Development*, Cambridge Studies in Social and Emotional Development, 380–85. New York: Cambridge Press.

Eisenberg, Nancy, Randy Lennon, and Karlsson Roth. 1983. "Prosocial Development: A Longitudinal Study." *Developmental Psychology* 19, no. 6:846–55.

Eisenberg, Nancy, and Janet Strayer. 1987. "Critical Issues in the Study of Empathy." In N. Eisenberg and J. Strayer, eds., *Empathy and Its Development*, 3–13. New York: Cambridge University Press.

Elster, Jon. 1986. *The Multiple Self*. Cambridge and New York: Cambridge University Press.

Elster, Jon. 1979. *Ulysses and the Sirens: Studies in Rationality and Irrationality*. New York: Cambridge University Press.

Erikson, Erik. 1968. *Identity: Youth and Crisis*. New York: W. W. Norton.

———. 1959/1980. *Identity and the Life Cycle*. New York: W. W. Norton.

Etzioni, Amitai. 1993. *The Spirit of Community: Rights, Responsibilities, and the Communitarian Agenda*. New York: Crown Publishers.

———. 1988. *The Moral Dimension: Toward A New Economics*. New York: Free Press.

Festinger, Leon. 1957. *A Theory of Cognitive Dissonance*. Stanford: Stanford University Press.

———. 1954. "A Theory of Social Comparison Processes." *Human Relations* 7: 117–40.

Fiske, Susan T., and Shelly E. Taylor. 1984. *Social Cognition*. Reading, Mass.: Addison-Wesley.

Fitzgerald, Bruce D. 1975. "Self-Interest or Altruism: Corrections and Extensions." *Journal of Conflict Resolution* 19, no. 3:462–78.

Fitzgerald, Thomas. 1993. *Metaphors of Identity: A Culture Communication Dialogue*. New York: State University of New York Press.

Fogelman, Eva. 1994. *Conscience and Courage*. New York: Anchor Books.

Frank, Robert H. 1988. *Passions within Reason*. New York: W. W. Norton.

Freud, Sigmund. 1917/1920. *A General Introduction to Psychoanalysis*. New York: Boni and Liveright.

Frohlich, Norman. 1975. "Comments in Reply." *Journal of Conflict Resolution* 19, no. 3:480–83.

———. 1974. "Self-Interest or Altruism: What Difference?" *Journal of Conflict Resolution* 18:55–73.

Gardner, Howard. 1995. "Green Ideas Sleeping Furiously." *New York Review of Books* 42, no. 5:2–38.

Gardner, Robert. 1986. *The Courage to Care*. Documentary film. New York: Anti-Defamation League of B'nai B'rith.

Garfinkel, Alan. 1981. *Forms of Explanation: Rethinking the Questions in Social Theory*. New Haven: Yale University Press.

Geertz, Clifford. 1973. *The Interpretation of Cultures*. New York: Basic Books.

Giddens, Anthony. 1984. *The Constitution of Society*. Berkeley: University of California Press.

Gilligan, Carol. 1982. *The Contribution of Women's Thought to Developmental Theory, the Elimination of Sex Bias in Moral Development Research and Education: Final Report*. Cambridge: Harvard University Press.

———. 1977/1981. *In a Different Voice: Psychological Theory and Women's Development*. Cambridge: Harvard University Press.

Goldberger, Leo. 1987. *The Rescue of the Danish Jews*. New York: New York University Press.

Grafstein, Robert. 1995. "Rationality as Conditional Expected Utility Maximization." *Political Psychology* 16, no. 1:63–80.

Haldane, J.B.S. 1932/1966. *The Causes of Evolution*. Ithaca, N.Y.: Cornell University Press.

———. 1924. "A Mathematical Theory of Natural and Artificial Selections." *Transactions of the Cambridge Philosophical Society* 23:235–43.

Hallie, Phillip P. 1979. *Lest Innocent Blood Be Shed: The Story of the Village of Le Chambon, and How Goodness Happened There*. New York: Harper and Row.

Hardin, G. 1977. *The Limits of Altruism: An Ecologist's View of Survival*. Bloomington: Indiana University Press.

Harris, Mary B. 1972. "The Effects of Performing One Altruistic Act on the Likelihood of Performing Another." *Journal of Social Psychology* 88, no. 1:65–73.

Harsanyi, John C. 1976. *Essays on Ethics, Social Behavior, and Scientific Explanation*. Dordrecht, Holland and Boston: D. Reidel.

Hatfield, Elaine, William G. Walster, and Jane A. Piliavin. 1978. "Equity Theory and Helping Relationships." In L. Wispe, ed., *Altruism, Sympathy, and Helping: Psychological and Sociological Principles*, 115–39. New York: Academic Press.

Heidegger, Martin. 1962. *Being and Time*. Translated by J. Macquarrie and E. Robinson. New York: Harper and Row.

Heider, Fritz. 1958. *The Psychology of Interpersonal Relations*. New York: J. Wiley.

Hirschman, Albert O. 1977. *The Passions and the Interests: Political Arguments for Capitalism before Its Triumph*. Princeton: Princeton University Press.

Hirshleifer, Jack. 1981. *Scarcity, Self-Interest, Spontaneous Order*. Los Angeles: Department of Economics, University of California at Los Angeles.

———. 1977. "Shakespeare vs. Becker on Altruism: The Importance of Having the Last Word." *Journal of Economic Literature* 15, no. 2:500–502.

Hobbes, Thomas. 1651. *Leviathan; or, The Matter, Form, and Power of a Commonwealth, Ecclesiastical and Civil*. London: A. Crooke.

Hoffman, Martin L. 1989. "Empathy and Prosocial Activism." In N. Eisenberg, J. Reykowski, and E. Staub, eds., *Social and Moral Values: Individual and Societal Perspectives*, 65–85. Hillsdale, N.J.: Lawrence Erlbaum.

———. 1987. "The Contribution of Empathy to Justice and Moral Judgement." In N. Eisenberg and J. Strayer, eds., *Empathy: A Developmental Perspective*, 47–80. New York: Cambridge University Press.

———. 1984. "Interaction of Affect and Cognition in Empathy." In C. Izard, J. Kagan, and R. Zajonc, eds., *Emotions, Cognition, and Behavior*, 103–31. New York: Cambridge University Press.

———. 1981a. "The Development of Empathy." In J. P. Rushton and R. M. Sorrentino, eds., *Altruism and Helping Behavior: Social, Personality, and Developmental Perspectives*, 41–63. Hillsdale, N.J.: Lawrence Erlbaum.

———. 1981b. "Is Altruism Part of Human Nature?" *Journal of Personality and Social Psychology* 40, no. 1:121–37.

———. 1977. "Personality and Social Development." *Annual Review of Psychology* 28, no. 29:5–321.

———. 1976. "Empathy, Role-Taking, Guilt, and Development of Altruistic Motives." In T. Lickona, ed., *Moral Development and Behavior: Theory, Research and Social Issues*, 124–43. New York: Holt, Rinehart and Winston.

———. 1975. "Altruistic Behavior and the Parent-Child Relationship." *Journal of Personality and Social Psychology* 31, no. 5:937–43.

———. 1970. "Conscience, Personality and Socialization Technique." *Human Development* 13, no. 2:90–126.

Homans, George C. 1961. *Social Behavior: Its Elementary Forms*. New York: Harcourt, Brace and World.

Hume, David. 1751/1902. *An Enquiry concerning the Principles of Morals*. Oxford: Oxford University Press.

———. 1740/1896. *A Treatise of Human Nature*. London: Oxford University Press.

Huneke, D. K. 1981–82. "A Study of Christians Who Rescued Jews during the Nazi Era." *Humboldt Journal of Social Relations* 9, no. 1:144–49.

Hutcheson, Francis. 1728/1971. *An Essay on the Nature and Conduct of the Passions and Affections*. New York: Garland.

James, William. 1890. *Principles of Psychology*. Vol. 1. New York: Henry Holt.

Johnson, James. 1991. "Rational Actor Theory as Reconstructive Theory." In K. R. Monroe, ed., *The Economic Approach to Politics: A Critical Reassessment of the Theory of Rational Action*, 113–42. New York: HarperCollins.

Johnson-Laird, Phillip N. 1983. *Mental Models: Toward a Cognitive Science of Language, Inference, and Consciousness*. Cambridge: Harvard University Press.

Johnston, David. 1991. "Human Agency and Rational Action." In K. R. Monroe, ed., *The Economic Approach to Politics: A Critical Reassessment of the Theory of Rational Action*, 94–112. New York: HarperCollins.

Jones, E. E., and K. E. Davis. 1965. "From Acts to Dispositions: The Attribution Process in Person Perception." In L. Berkowitz, ed., *Advances in Experimental Social Psychology*, 2:219–66. New York: Academic Press.

Jung, C. G. 1959. *Basic Writings*. Edited by Violet Staub. Cambridge: Harvard University Press.

Kahneman, Daniel, Paul Slovic, and Amos Tversky. 1982. *Judgment under Uncertainty: Heuristics and Biases*. New York: Cambridge University Press.

Kant, Immanuel. 1785/1889. *Critique of Practical Reason and Other Works on the Theory of Ethics*. 4th ed. New York: Longmans, Green and Co.

Karylowski, Jerzy. 1984. "Focus of Attention and Altruism: Endocentric and Exocentric Sources of Altruistic Behavior." In E. Staub, D. Bar-Tal, J. Karylowski, and J. Reykowski, eds., *Development and Maintenence of Prosocial Behavior*, 139–54. New York: Plenum Press.

———. 1982. "Two Types of Altruistic Behavior: Doing Good to Feel Good or to Make the Other Feel Good." In V. J. Derlega and J. Grzelak, eds., *Cooperation and Helping Behavior: Theories and Research*, 397–413. New York: Academic Press.

Kelly, George Alexander. 1955. *The Psychology of Personal Constructs*. New York: W. W. Norton.

Kihlstrom, John F., and Nancy Cantor. 1984. "Mental Representations of the Self." In L. Berkowitz, ed., *Advances in Experimental Social Psychology*, 2:2–48. New York: Academic Press.

Klingemann, Ute, and Jürgen Falter. 1993. "Hilfe für Juden während des Holocaust. Sozialpsychologische Merkmale der nichtjüdischen Helfer und Charakteristika der Situation." In Günther B. Ginzel, ed., *Mut zur Menschlichkeit. Hilfe für Verfolgte während der NS-Zeit*, 115–56. Cologne: Rheinland Verlag.

Koffka, K. 1935. *Principles of Gestalt Psychology*. New York: Harcourt, Brace and World.

Kohlberg, Lawrence. 1984. *Essays on Moral Development*. Vol. 2. New York: Harper and Row.

———. 1981. *The Philosophy of Moral Development*. San Francisco: Harper and Row.

———. 1976. "Moral Stages and Moralization: The Cognitive-Developmental Approach." In T. Lickona, ed., *Moral Development and Behavior*, 31–53. New York: Holt, Rinehart and Winston.

Kohn, Alfie. 1990. *The Brighter Side of Human Nature: Altruism and Empathy in Everyday Life*. New York: Basic Books.

Kohut, Heinz. 1984. *The Curve of Life: Correspondence of Heinz Kohut, 1923–1981*. Edited by Geoffrey Cocks. Chicago: University of Chicago Press.

Kolm, Serge-Christophe. 1983. "Altruism and Efficiency." *Ethics* 94, no. 1:18–65.

Krebs, Dennis. 1982. "Psychological Approaches to Altruism: An Evaluation." *Ethics* 92, no. 36:447–58.

———. 1978. "A Cognitive Developmental Approach to Altruism." In L. Wispe, ed., *Altruism, Sympathy, and Helping: Psychological and Sociological Principles*, 141–64. New York: Academic Press.

———. 1970. "Altruism: An Examination of the Concept and a Review of the Literature." *Psychological Bulletin* 73, no. 4:258–302.

Krebs, Dennis, and C. Russell. 1981. "Role-Taking and Altruism: When You Put Yourself in the Shoes of Another, Will They Take You to Their Owner's Aid?" In J. P. Rushton and R. M. Sorrentino, eds., *Altruism and Helping Behavior: Social, Personality, and Developmental Perspectives*, 137–65. Hillsdale, N.J.: Lawrence Erlbaum.

Krebs, Dennis, and Frank Van Hesteren. 1992. "The Development of Altruistic Personality." In P. M. Oliner, S. P. Oliner, L. Baron, L. A. Blum, D. L. Krebs, and M. Z. Smolenska, eds., *Embracing the Other: Philosophical, Psychological, and Historical Perspectives on Altruism*, 142–69. New York: New York University Press.

Kropotkin, Petr A. 1902. *Mutual Aid: A Factor of Evolution*. New York: McClure, Phillips.

Kuhn, Thomas. 1962. *The Structure of Scientific Revolutions*. Chicago: University of Chicago Press.

La Rochefoucauld, François, duc de. 1691. *Moral Maxims and Reflections: In Four Parts*. London: Gillyflower, Sare, and Everingham.

Lakoff, George. 1987. *Women, Fire and Dangerous Things*. Chicago: University of Chicago Press.

Langer, Lawrence L. 1991. *Holocaust Testimonies*. New Haven: Yale University Press.

———. 1982. *Versions of Survival: The Holocaust and the Human Spirit*. Albany: State University of New York Press.

Latane, Bibb, and John M. Darley. 1970. *The Unresponsive Bystander: Why Doesn't Anybody Help?* New York: Appleton-Century-Crofts.

Lerner, Melvin J. 1982. "The Justice Motive in Human Relations and the Economic Model of Man: A Radical Analysis of Facts and Fictions." In V. J. Derlega and J. Grzelak, eds., *Cooperation and Helping Behavior: Theories and Research*, 250–80. New York: Academic Press.

———. 1980. *The Belief in a Just World: A Fundamental Delusion*. New York: Plenum Press.

Lerner, Melvin J., and J. R. Meindl. 1984. "Justice and Altruism." In J. P. Rushton and R. M. Sorrentino, eds., *Altruism and Helping Behavior: Social, Personality, and Developmental Perspectives*, 213–32. Hillsdale, N.J.: Lawrence Erlbaum.

Lerner, Richard M. 1992. *Genocide?* University Park: The Pennsylvania State University Press.

London, Perry. 1970. "The Rescuers: Motivational Hypotheses about Christians Who

Saved Jews from the Nazis." In J. Macaulay and L. Berkowitz, eds., *Altruism and Helping Behavior*, 241–50. New York: Academic Press.

Lopreato, Joseph. 1984. *Human Nature and Biocultural Evolution*. Boston and London: Allen and Unwin.

Losco, Joseph. 1986. "Understanding Altruism: A Comparison of Various Models." *Political Psychology* 7, no. 2:323–48.

Lowe, Roland, and Gary Richter. 1973. "Relation of Altruism to Age, Social Class and Ethnic Identity." *Psychological Reports* 33, no. 2:567–72.

Lumsden, Charles J., and Edward O. Wilson. 1983. *Promethean Fire: Reflections on the Origins of Mind*. Cambridge: Harvard University Press.

Macaulay, J., and L. Berkowitz, eds. 1970. *Altruism and Helping Behavior: Social Psychological Studies of Some Antecedents and Consequences*. New York: Academic Press.

Macdonald, A. P. 1971. "Birth Order and Personality." *Journal of Consulting and Clinical Psychology* 36, no. 2:171–76.

McDougall, William. 1908. *Introduction to Social Psychology*. London: Methuen.

Machiavelli, Niccolo. 1513/1984. *The Prince*. Translated by Mark Musa. New York: St. Martin's Press.

MacIntyre, Alasdair C. 1962/1976. *The Unconscious: A Conceptual Analysis*. London: Routledge and Kegan Paul.

McRae, Robert R., and Paul T. Costa, Jr. 1984. *Emerging Lives, Enduring Dispositions*. Boston: Little, Brown and Co.

Mandeville, Bernard. 1714/1732. *The Fable of the Bees; or, Private Vices, Publick Benefits*. London: J. Tonson.

Mandler, G. 1984. *Stories, Scripts, and Scenes: Aspects of Schema Theory*. Hillsdale, N.J.: Lawrence Erlbaum.

Mansbridge, Jane, ed. 1990. *Beyond Self-Interest*. Chicago: University of Chicago Press.

Margolis, Howard. 1991. "Incomplete Coercion: How Social Preferences Mix with Private Preferences." In K. R. Monroe, ed., *The Economic Approach to Politics: A Critical Reassessment of the Theory of Rational Action*, 353–70. New York: Harper-Collins.

———. 1987. *Patterns, Thinking, and Cognition: A Theory of Judgment*. Chicago: University of Chicago Press.

———. 1982. *Selfishness, Altruism and Rationality*. Cambridge: Cambridge University Press.

Maslow, Abraham H. 1962. *Toward a Psychology of Being*. Princeton: Van Nostrand.

Mead, George H. 1934. *Mind, Self, and Society*. Chicago: University of Chicago Press.

Midlarsky, Elizabeth. 1992. "Helping in Late Life." In P. M. Oliner et al. *Embracing the Other: Philosophical, Psychological, and Historical Perspectives on Altruism*. New York: New York University Press.

———. 1968. "Aiding Response: An Analysis and Review." *Merrill-Palmer Quarterly* 14:229–60.

Monroe, Kristen Renwick. 1995a. "Psychology and Rational Choice Theory." *Political Psychology* 16, no. 1:1–22.

———. 1995b. "The Psychology of Genocide." *Ethics and International Affairs* 9: 215–39.

———. 1994. "'But What Else Could I Do?'" A Cognitive-Perceptual Theory of Ethical Political Behavior." *Political Psychology* 15, no. 2:201–26.

————. 1991. *The Economic Approach to Politics: A Critical Reassessment of the Theory of Rational Action*. New York: HarperCollins.

————. 1990. "Altruism and the Theory of Rational Action: Rescuers of Jews in Nazi Europe." *Ethics* 101, no. 1:103–22.

————. 1989. "Thinking about Altruism." Manuscript. University of California, Irvine.

Monroe, Kristen Renwick, and Lina Haddad Kreidie. 1995. "Perspective on Islamic Fundamentalism." Paper presented at the Annual Meetings of the American Political Science Association.

Myers, Milton. 1983. *The Soul of Economic Man*. Chicago: University of Chicago Press.

Nagel, Thomas. 1987. *The View from Nowhere*. New York: Oxford University Press.

————. 1970. *The Possibility of Altruism*. Oxford: Clarendon Press.

Nietzsche, Friedrich. 1888/1967. "Ecce Homo." In *The Genealogy of Morals*, 200–333. Translated by Walter Kaufman. New York: Vintage Press.

Nisbett, Richard E., and Eugene Borgida. 1975. "Attribution and the Psychology of Prediction." *Journal of Personality and Social Psychology* 32, no. 5:932–43.

Nozick, Robert. 1974. *Anarchy, State, and Utopia*. New York: Basic Books.

Nussbaum, Martha C. 1986. *The Fragility of Goodness: Luck and Ethics in Greek Tragedy and Philosophy*. Cambridge and New York: Cambridge University Press.

Oliner, Pearl M., Samuel P. Oliner, Lawrence Baron, Lawrence A. Blum, Daniel L. Krebs, and M. Zuzanna Smolenska, eds. 1992. *Embracing the Other: Philosophical, Psychological, and Historical Perspectives on Altruism*. New York: New York University Press.

Oliner, Samuel P., and Pearl M. Oliner. 1988. *The Altruistic Personality: Rescuers of Jews in Nazi Europe*. New York: Free Press.

Olson, Mancur. 1971. *The Logic of Collective Action*. Cambridge: Harvard University Press.

Pankseep, Jack. 1986. "The Psychobiology of Prosocial Behaviors: Separation Distress, Play, and Altruism." In C. Zahn-Waxler, E. M. Cummings, and R. Iannotti, eds., *Altruism and Aggression: Biological and Social Origins*, 19–57. Cambridge: Cambridge University Press.

Parfit, Derek. 1984. *Reasons and Persons*. Oxford: Oxford University Press.

Parsons, Talcott. 1969. *Politics and Social Structure*. New York: Free Press.

Perry, John. 1975. "The Problem of Personal Identity." In J. Perry, ed., *Personal Identity*, 3–32. Berkeley: University of California Press.

Phelps, Edmund S., ed. 1975. *Altruism, Morality, and Economic Theory*. New York: Russell Sage Foundation.

Piaget, Jean. 1948. *The Moral Development of the Child*. Glencoe, Ill.: Free Press.

Piliavin, Jane A., John F. Dovidio, Samuel L. Gaertner, and Russel D. Clark, III. 1982. "Responsive Bystanders: The Process of Intervention." In V. J. Derlega and J. Grzelak, eds., *Cooperation and Helping Behavior: Theories and Research*, 279–304. New York: Academic Press.

Piliavin, Jane A., and I. M. Piliavin. 1973. "The Good Samaritan: Why Does He Help?" Manuscript. University of Wisconsin, Madison.

Psychological Inquiry. 1991. 2, no 2:107-58.

Quattrone, George A., and Amos Tversky. 1988. "Contrasting Rational and Psychological Analyses of Political Choice." *American Political Science Review* 82, no. 3: 719–37.

Quinn, Naomi, and Dorothy Holland. 1987. *Cultural Models in Language and Thought.* New York: Cambridge University Press.

Rapoport, Anatol. 1966. *Two-Person Game Theory: The Essential Ideas.* Ann Arbor: University of Michigan Press.

Rawls, John. 1973. *A Theory of Justice.* Cambridge: Harvard University Press.

Reykowski, Janusz. 1987. "Activation of Helping Motivation: The Role of Extensivity." Manuscript. Institute of Psychology, Polish Academy of Science, Warsaw.

———. 1984."Cognitive Development and Social Behavior." *Polish Psychology Bulletin* 8:35–43.

———. 1982. "Motivation of Pro-Social Behavior." In V. J. Derlaga and J. Grzelak, eds., *Cooperation and Helping Behavior: Theories and Research*, 357–76. New York: Academic Press.

Reykowski, Janusz, and M. Zuzanna Smolenska. 1992. "Motivations of People Who Helped Jews Survive the Nazi Occupation." In P. M. Oliner et al., *Embracing the Other: Philosophical, Psychological, and Historical Perspectives on Altruism*, 213–25. New York: New York University Press.

Rogers, Carl R. 1961. *On Becoming a Person.* Boston: Houghton-Mifflin.

Rosenberg, Shawn W. 1991. "Rationality, Markets, and Political Analysis: A Social Psychological Critique of Neoclassical Political Economy." In K. R. Monroe, ed., *The Economic Approach to Politics: A Critical Reassessment of the Theory of Rational Action*, 386–404. New York: HarperCollins.

———. 1988. *Reason, Politics, and Ideology.* Princeton: Princeton University Press.

Rosenberg, Shawn W., Shulamit Kahn, and Thuy Tran. 1991. "Creating a Political Image: Shaping Appearance and Manipulating the Vote." *Political Behavior* 13, no. 4: 345–67.

Rosenblum, Nancy. 1987. *Another Liberalism: Romanticism and the Reconstruction of Liberal Thought.* Cambridge: Harvard University Press.

Rosenhan, David. 1978. "Toward Resolving the Altruism Paradox." In L. Wispe, ed., *Altruism, Sympathy, and Helping: Psychological and Sociological Principles*, 101–13. New York: Academic Press.

———. 1970."The Natural Socialization of Altruistic Autonomy." In J. Macaulay and L. Berkowitz, eds., *Altruism and Helping Behavior*, 248–69. New York: Academic Press.

Rosenhan, D., P. Salovey, J. Karylowski, and K. Hargis. 1981. "Emotion and Altruism." In J. P. Rushton and R. M. Sorrentino, eds., *Altruism and Helping Behavior: Social, Personality, and Developmental Perspectives*, 233–48. Hillsdale, N.J.: Lawrence Erlbaum.

Rousseau, Jean-Jacques. 1755/1950. *The Social Contract; and, Discourses.* New York: E. P. Dutton.

Rummelhart, David E. 1986. *Parallel Distributed Processing: Explorations in the Microstructure of Cognition.* Cambridge: MIT Press.

Rushton, J. Phillipe. 1991. "Is Altruism Innate?" *Psychological Inquiry* 2, no. 2:141–43.

———. 1989. *Altruism, Socialization, and Society.* Engelwood Cliffs, N.J.: Prentice-Hall.

———. 1981. "The Altruistic Personality." In J. P. Rushton and R. M. Sorrentino, eds., *Altruism and Helping Behavior: Social, Personality, and Developmental Perspectives*, 271–90. Hillsdale, N.J.: Lawrence Erlbaum.

Rushton, J. Phillipe, David W. Fulker, Michael C. Neale, David K. B. Nias, and Hans J.

Eysenck. 1986. "Altruism and Aggression: The Heritability of Individual Differences." *Journal of Personality and Social Psychology* 50, no. 6: 1192–98.

Rushton, J. Phillipe, and Richard M. Sorrentino, eds. 1981. *Altruism and Helping Behavior: Social, Personality, and Developmental Perspectives*. Hillsdale, N.J.: Lawrence Erlbaum.

Sagi, A., and M. L. Hoffman. 1976. "Empathic Distress in Newborns." *Developmental Psychology* 12:175–76.

Sarbin, Theodore, and Karl Scheibe, eds. 1983. *Studies in Social Identity*. New York: Praeger.

Sauvage, Pierre (director). *Weapons of the Spirit*. Documentary film. Los Angeles: Friends of LeChambon.

Schelling, Thomas C. 1960. *The Strategy of Conflict*. Cambridge: Harvard University Press.

Schroeder, D. A., J. F. Dovidio, M. Bicky, and L. L. Matthews. 1988. "Empathy and Helping Behavior: Egoism or Altruism?" *Journal of Experimental Psychosocial Psychology* 24:333–53.

Schumpeter, Joseph. 1942. *Capitalism, Socialism, and Democracy*. New York: Harper and Row.

Schwartz, Barry. 1986. *The Battle for Human Nature*. New York: W. W. Norton.

Sellick, Mark P. 1994. "Cognition, Socialization, and Political Action: The Development of an Altruistic Perspective." Manuscript. University of California, Irvine.

Simner, M. L. 1971. "Newborn's Response to the Cry of Another Infant." *Developmental Psychology* 5:136–50.

Simon, Herbert A. 1985. "Human Nature in Politics: The Dialogue of Psychology with Political Science." *American Political Science Review* 79:293–304.

———. 1982. *Models of Bounded Rationality*. Vols. 1 and 2. Cambridge: MIT Press.

Smith, Adam. 1776/1937. *An Inquiry into the Nature and Causes of the Wealth of Nations*. Edited by Edwin Cannon. New York: Modern Library.

———. 1776/1902. *The Wealth of Nations*. New York: Collier.

———. 1759/1853. *The Theory of Moral Sentiments*. London: Henry G. Bohn.

Solomon, J. Fisher. 1988. *The Sign of Our Times: Semiotics, the Hidden Messages of Environments, Objects, and Cultural Images*. Los Angeles: J. P. Tarchner.

Solsow, E., ed. 1980. *Personality: Basic Aspects and Current Research*. Englewood Cliffs, N.J.: Prentice-Hall.

Sorokin, P. A. 1954. *The Ways and Power of Love: Types, Factors, and Techniques of Moral Transformation*. Boston: Beacon Press.

Spencer, Herbert. 1870/1872. *The Principles of Psychology*. Vols. 1 and 2. London: Williams and Norgate.

Spiegel, Henry. 1971. *The Growth of Economic Thought*. Durham, N.C.: Duke University Press.

Staub, Ervin. 1991. "Altruistic and Moral Motivations for Helping and Their Translation into Action." *Psychological Inquiry* 2, no. 2:150–53.

———. 1990. "Genocide and Mass Killing: Cultural-Societal and Psychological Origins." In H. T. Himmelweit and G. Gaskell, eds., *Societal Psychology*, 230–51. Newbury Park, Calif.: Sage Publications.

———. 1980. *Personality: Basic Aspects and Current Research*. Englewood Cliffs, N.J.: Prentice-Hall.

Staub, Ervin. 1979. *Positive Social Behavior and Morality: Socialization and Development.* Vol. 2. New York: Academic Press.

———. 1975. *The Development of Prosocial Behavior in Children.* Morristown, N.J.: General Learning Press.

Staub, Ervin, Daniel Bar-Tal, Jerzy Karylowski, and Janusz Reykowski, eds. 1982. *The Development and Maintenence of Prosocial Behavior.* New York and London: Plenum Press.

Styron, William. 1979. *Sophie's Choice.* New York: Random House.

Tannen, Deborah. 1990. *You Just Don't Understand: Women and Men in Conversation.* New York: Morrow.

———. 1986. *That's Not What I Meant! How Conversational Style Makes or Breaks Your Relations with Others.* New York: Morrow.

Taylor, Charles. 1989. *Sources of the Self: The Making of the Modern Identity.* Cambridge: Harvard University Press.

Taylor, Michael. 1987. *The Possibility of Cooperation.* Cambridge: Cambridge University Press.

Taylor, Shelley, and Susan Fiske. 1991. *Social Cognition.* New York: McGraw Hill.

Tetlock, Phillip, and Miren A. Gonzalez. 1980. *A Literature Review of Altruism and Helping Behavior.* New Haven: Institute for Social and Policy Studies, Yale University.

Titchener, Edward B. 1909. *A Text-Book of Psychology.* New York: MacMillan.

Titmuss, Richard Morris. 1971. *The Gift Relationship: From Human Blood to Social Policy.* New York: Pantheon Books.

Tocqueville, Alexis de. 1839/1955. *The Old Regime and the French Revolution.* Translated by S. Gilbert. Garden City, N.Y.: Doubleday Books.

Tönnies, Ferdinand. 1957. *Community and Association [Gemeinschaft und Gesellschaft].* Translated by Charles P. Loomis. East Lansing: Michigan State University Press.

Trivers, Robert. 1971. "The Evolution of Reciprocal Altruism." *Quarterly Review of Biology* 46:35–57.

Tullock, Gordon. 1975. In Edmund Phelps, ed., *Altruism, Morality, and Economic Theory,* 55–77. New York: Russell Sage Foundation.

Turner, John C. 1987. *Rediscovering the Social Group. A Self-Categorization Theory.* Oxford and New York: Basil Blackwell.

Tversky, Amos, and Daniel Kahneman. 1974. "Judgment under Uncertainty: Heuristics and Biases." *Science* 185: 1124–31.

Valavanis, S. 1958. "The Resolution of Conflict when Utilities Interact." *Journal of Conflict Resolution* 2:156–69.

Vine, I. 1992. "Altruism and Human Nature: Resolving the Evolutionary Paradox." In P. M. Oliner et al., *Embracing the Other: Philosophical, Psychological, and Historical Perspectives on Altruism,* 73–103. New York: New York University Press.

Vygotskii, Lev S. 1978. *Mind in Society: The Development of Higher Psychological Processes.* Edited by Michael Cole. Cambridge: Harvard University Press.

Wagner, Susan, Harvey A. Hornstein, and Stephan Holloway. 1982. "Willingness to Help a Stranger: The Effects of Social Context and Opinion." *Journal of Applied Social Psychology* 12, no. 6:429–43.

Wallach, Michael A., and Lise Wallach. 1990. *Rethinking Goodness.* Albany: State University of New York Press.

———. 1983. *Psychology's Sanction for Selfishness: The Error of Egoism in Theory and Therapy*. San Francisco: W. H. Freeman.

Whitehead, Jaan. 1991. "The Forgotten Limits: Reason and Regulation in Economic Theory." In K. R. Monroe, ed., *The Economic Approach to Political Behavior: A Critical Reassessment of the Theory of Rational Action*, 53–73. New York: HarperCollins.

Whiting, Beatrice. 1983. "The Genesis of Prosocial Behavior: Children in Six Cultures." In D. Bridgeman, ed., *The Nature of Prosocial Development*, 221–40. New York: Academic Press.

Williams, Bernard A. O. 1981. *Moral Luck: Philosophical Papers*. Cambridge and New York: Cambridge University Press.

Wilson, Edward O. 1975. *Sociobiology: The New Synthesis*. Cambridge: Harvard University Press.

Wintrobe, Ronald. 1981. "It Pays to Do Good, but Not More Good than It Pays." *Journal of Economic Behavior and Organization* 2, no. 3:201–13.

Wispe, Lauren G. 1991. *The Psychology of Sympathy*. New York: Plenum Press.

———. 1987. "History of the Concept of Empathy." In N. Eisenberg and J. Strayer, eds., *Empathy and Its Development*, 17–37. New York: Cambridge University Press.

———. 1986. "The Distinction between Sympathy and Empathy: To Call Forth a Concept, a Word is Needed." *Journal of Personality and Social Psychology* 50, no. 2:314–21.

———. 1978. *Altruism, Sympathy, and Helping: Psychological and Sociological Principles*. New York: Academic Press.

———. 1968. "Sympathy and Empathy." In D. L. Sills, ed., *International Encyclopedia of the Social Sciences*, 15:441–47. New York: Free Press.

Wuthnow, Robert. 1991. *Acts of Compassion*. Princeton: Princeton University Press.

Zahn-Waxler, Carol. 1991. "The Case for Empathy: A Developmental Perspective." *Psychological Inquiry* 2, no. 2:155–58.

Zahn-Waxler, Carol, E. M. Cummings, and R. Iannotti, eds. 1986. *Altruism and Aggression: Biological and Social Origins*. Cambridge: Cambridge University Press.

Zahn-Waxler, Carol, and M. Radke-Yarrow. 1982. "The Development of Altruism: Alternative Research Strategies." In N. Eisenberg, ed., *The Development of Prosocial Behavior*, 109–38. New York: Academic Press.

Zuckerman, M. 1975. "Belief in a Just World and Altruistic Behavior." *Journal of Personality and Social Psychology* 31:972–76.

Zuckert, Catherine H. 1995. "On the Rationality of Rational Choice." *Political Psychology* 16, no. 1:179–198.

Index

Abric, Jean-Claude, 242nn. 34 and 38

Ajzen, Icek, 257n.9

altruism: approval gained with, 149–51; archtypes of, 4–5; canonical expectations regarding, 11; cognitive frameworks and processing, 9–11, 240nn.20–22, 241nn.23–33; conceptual continuum and archetypes concerning, 16–18; costs and benefits of, 155–59; critical components of, 5; cross-disciplinary approaches to, 7–8; definitions of, 4, 6–8, 240n.11; empathy and, 12–13, 242n.47; empirical analysis of, 6; evolutionary biology and, 161–78; eyewitness accounts of, ix–x; familiarity as basis for, 190; guilt alleviated through, 149; interdisciplinary approaches to, 5; participation altruism, 151–52; perspectives on, 9–15; preference for, 147–49; as psychic good, 143–46; psychological aspects of, 6–9, 7, 179–94, 239n.5, 240n.22; reciprocity in, 151; research methodology concerning, 4–5, 15, 18–23; resource hypothesis regarding, 153–55; self-image and, 13–14; self-interest vs., 3; terminological complexity regarding, 6–7, 239n.8; traditional approaches to, 7–9; trigger mechanisms of, 214–16; world view and, 12

"altruistic personality": concept of, 148–49

anonymity, in altruism: entrepreneurs' preference for, 40, 246n.4; philanthropists' preference for, 59–62; rescuers' need for discretion and, 150–51, 251n.19

approval: altruism as means of winning, 149–51; networks and clusters hypotheses regarding, 170–76

archetypes of altruism, 16–18

attribution theory: altruism and, 239n.4

aversive-arousal theory: psychological aspects of altruism and, 256nn. 3 and 4, 259n.20

awareness: cognitive framework for altruism and, 10–11, 241n.32

Axelrod, Robert, 223, 228–29, 253n.12, 266n.4

Bartlett, F., 9, 241n.25

Batson, C. Daniel, 239n.5, 240nn. 11 and 13,

241n.22, 242nn. 38 and 46, 243nn. 48, 53, and 59, 248n.3, 256nn. 1 and 4, 257n.9, 259n.20, 263n.21

Bearman, Peter, 268n.27

Becker, Gary, 19, 162–64, 239n.3, 240n.12, 252n.27, 253nn. 9–11, 254nn. 15, 16, 18, and 19, 256n.3, 268n.31, 269n.2

behavior, altruistic: canonical expectations and, 11, 208–10; cognition linked to, 217–20; conceptual continuum and archetypes of, 16–18; conclusions regarding, 234–37; evolutionary biology theories of altruism and, 162–64, 254n.16; normalcy of, for rescuers, 104–18, 248n.10; reciprocity in, 151–52; world view and, 12

Berkowitz, Leonard, 245n.83, 256n.4

birth order: altruism and, 134–35

Blau, Peter M., 254n.14

Block, Gay, 251n.11

Boorman, Scott A., 252nn. 2 and 3

bounded rationality: perspectival approach to ethical political acts and, 226–27

brain structure: altruism and, 162, 252n.8

Bridgeman, Diane L., 257n.8

Browning, Christopher, 255n.28, 258n.19, 261n.40

Bruner, Jerome, 241n.29, 244nn. 72 and 73, 245n.82, 266n.4

Buchanan, James, 239n.3

bystander effect: altruism and, 193–94

Calabresi, Guido, 270n.11

Campbell, Donald, 239n.5, 256n.1

canonical expectations: altruism and, 11, 242nn.34–40; normal behavior and, 208–10, 264n.33

capitalist expansion: altruism and, 16, 244n.64

Carnegie Hero Fund Commission, 17, 21–22, 141, 170, 244n.68

charity: dual utilities of altruism and, 152–53, 251n.22; entrepreneurs' attitudes toward, 35–40; networks and clusters hypotheses regarding, 172–76; philanthropists' involvement in, 47–62, 247n.5

children: cognitive framework for altruism and, 11, 241n.33

choice: absence of, in altruism, 210–14, 234–
37; perspectival approach to ethical political
acts and, 224–28
Churchill, Sir Winston, xii
civic duty factor: perspectival theory and, 230–
31, 269n.50
civil rights: role of heroes and heroines in,
63–90. *See also* heroes and heroines
cluster hypothesis: altruism and, 170–76;
evolutionary biology theories of altruism
and, 162
cognitive framework: altruism in, 9–11,
240nn.20–22, 241nn.23–33; behavior
linked to, 217–20, 265n.4; empathy and,
12–13, 243n.47; narrative interview in, 20;
perspectival approach to ethical political
acts and, 226–28; rational choice theory
and, 220–23, 267nn. 19 and 20; world
views and, 198–202
community size: altruism and, 135–36, 170
Comte, Auguste, 137
conceptual continuum of altruism, 16–18
conscious acts: altruism and, 6, 239n.5
consequences: altruism and, vs. intentions, 6
core values: ethical political acts and, 218–19;
rational choice theory and, 20, 220–23,
267n.20
costs and benefits of altruism, 155–59
Courage to Care, The, 237, 270n.12
Crospey, Joseph, 269n.55
culture: altruism and, 9, 10–11; core values
and, 218–19; ethical political acts and,
218, 266n.11; kin selection hypothesis and,
176–78; perspectival approach to ethical
political acts and, 226–28; role of, for rescuers, 100–118
Czech underground: decimation of, xi–xii

Darwinism: altruism and, 6–9, 161–78,
239n.5, 254n.19; moral sense theory and,
266n.15
Dawkins, Richard, 253n.5
developmental psychology: categorization of
religion by, 248n.3; psychological aspects of
altruism and, 179–85, 256n.7
Devotions upon Emergent Occasions (Donne),
204
disabled people: entrepreneurs' attitude regarding, 30–42; philanthropists' attitudes
regarding, 57–62
discipline: psychological aspects of altruism
and, 180, 258n.18

Donne, John, 204
Downs, Anthony, 269n.48
dual utility functions of altruism, 152–53; evolutionary biology and, 254n.19
duty: heroines' and heroes' attitudes toward,
70–90
Dworkin, Ronald M., 242n.44

economic theory: altruism and, 3, 6–9, 136–
60, 239n.1, 251n.21, 252n.28; approval
won through altruism and, 149–51; costs
and benefits of altruism and, 155–59; dual
utilities of altruism, 152–53; evolutionary
biology and altruism linked with, 162–63,
253n.10; goods altruism (honors, praise,
and material rewards) and, 138–43; guilt alleviated through altruism and, 149; participation altruism, 146; perspectival approach
to altruism and, 231–32, 269n.54; and psychic good, altruism as, 143–46; psychological aspects of altruism and, 258n.19; reciprocity through altruism, 151–52; resource
hypothesis of altruism and, 153–55; taste for
altruism and, 147–49
Eisenberg, Nancy, 240n.13, 243nn. 48, 51,
and 55, 256n.4, 263n.22
Elster, Jon, 226, 252n.29, 266nn. 4 and 13
empathy: altruism and, 12–13, 234–37,
240n.22, 242n.47; heroines' and heroes'
attitudes toward, 70–90; perceptions of
shared humanity and, 25, 202–7, 263n.17,
265n.40; among philanthropists, 49–62;
role of, in rescuers, 95–118
empirical tests of perspectival theory, 228–
32; prisoner's dilemma approach, 228–30;
voting and civic duty, 230–31
endocentric altruism, 180–81, 259n.20
entrepreneurs: altruism and, 16, 64, 244n.62;
anonymity preferred by, 40, 246n.4; attitudes toward charity among, 35–40; case
study and interview with, 26–40; dual utility
of altruism for, 152–53, 251n.22; empathy
among, 203, 264n.26; family background,
wealth and occupation of, 131–32; family
position of, 132–34; group selection hypothesis, in-group/out-group distinctions,
168; heroines' and heroes' attitudes toward,
88–90; kin selection behavior among, 164–
65; networks and clusters hypotheses regarding, 172–73; philanthropists compared
with, 30–35, 58–62; psychic good of altruism for, 144–48, 251n.16; reciprocity in al-

truism of, 151–52; regard for person helped, altruism based on, 191–92; relations with parents and role models of, 181–82; self-images of, 202; subject selection among, 22; world view of, 199

Erikson, Erik, 266nn. 6 and 7

ethical political acts: core values and, 218–19; perspectival theory and, 224–28, 231–32, 269nn.51–55; unconsciousness of, 218

ethical values: deviation from, among altruists, 185–89, 260nn.29–34; political acts based on, altruism and, 217–32; standardized tests of, 262n.2; terminology of, 266n.9

Etzioni, Amitai, 239n.1

evolutionary biology: children caring for children, kin selection and, 176–78; community size and group selection, 170; economic theory and, 18–19, 162–64, 253nn.10–11, 254nn.16; group selection, in-group/out-group distinctions, 166–68; incentives and sanctions in group selection, 168–69, 255nn.29–31; kin selection and, 164–66; networks and clusters, 170–76, 255nn.33–35; personality of person helped as basis for altruism, 191–92, 261n.41; psychological aspects of altruism and, 259n.20; theories of, 8, 161–62, 252nn.2–3, 253n.6

Evolution of Cooperation, The, 228–29

exocentric altruism, 259n.20

expectations: altruism and, 11, 242nn.34–40

extensivity: theory of, 258n.19

external environment, altruists' interaction with, 189–92

familiarity: altruism based on, 190, 261n.35

family background: altruism and, 130–32; just world phenomenon and, 262n.13; psychological aspects of altruism and, 181–85. See also kin selection hypothesis

family position: altruism and, 132–34

family size: altruism and, 134–35

fear: heroines' and heroes' attitudes toward, 84–90

feminism: perspectival approach to ethical political acts and, 224–25, 269n.30; role of rescuers in, 70–90

Fitzgerald, Bruce D., 252n.28

Fitzgerald, Thomas, 252n.28

Fogelman, Eva, 264n.31

forgiveness: altruism and, 207, 264n.32

Foucault, Michel, 270n.6

Freudian theory: psychological aspects of altruism and, 256n.2, 260n.25

Frohlich, Norman, 252n.28

game theory: perspectival theory and, 228–30

Gardner, Howard, 270n.3

Geertz, Clifford, 268n.34

Gemeinschaft mentality: altruism and, 12, 198–99, 262n.4; role of, for rescuers, 103–4

genetics: altruism and, 161–63, 252n.8, 253nn. 10 and 11; kin selection theory and, 165–66; psychological aspects of altruism and, 259n.20

Gesellschaft mentality: altruism and, 12, 198–99, 262n.4; role of, for rescuers, 103–4

Gilligan, Carol, 240n.18, 257n.10, 260n.27, 263n.15

Goldberger, Leo, 251n.14, 257n.14, 262n.10

goods altruism, 138–43

Grafstein, Robert, 267n.17

group selection hypothesis: community size and, 170; evolutionary biology theories of altruism and, 166–78, 254n.19; incentives and sanctions, 168–69; in-group/out-group distinctions, 166–68; networks and clusters phenomena and, 170–76; role of, for rescuers, 103–18, 248n.9; theories of, 161–63; world view based on, 12, 198–99

guilt: altruism as alleviation of, 149

Haldane, J.B.S., 255n.24

Heidegger, Martin, 8, 270n.6

heroes and heroines: altruism and, 16–17, 67–68, 244n.62; anonymity of altruism and, 150–51, 251n.19; approval gained for, by altruism, 150–51; attitudes of, regarding religion, 124–30; bystander effect and, 193–94; case studies of, 63–90; costs and benefits of altruism and, 156–59; empathy among, 203–7, 234–35, 264n.27; family position of, 132–34; goods altruism among, 140–43; group selection hypothesis, in-group/out-group distinctions, 167–68; incentives and sanctions for altruism, 169; networks and clusters hypotheses regarding, 173–76; preference for altruism among, 147–49; psychic good of altruism and, 145–47; reciprocity in altruism of, 152; relations with parents and role models of, 183–84; rescuers compared with, 104–18; self-images of, 202; situational influences on, 193, 261n.44; world views of, 199, 262n.9

Heydrich, Reinhard, xi
Hirschman, Albert O., 270n.9
Hirshleifer, Jack, 253n.11
Hobbes, Thomas, 7, 143, 259n.20
Hoffman, Martin L., 241n.22, 243nn. 53
    and 59, 256n.4, 258n.18, 263nn. 13,
    21, and 22
Holocaust: altruism during, case studies of,
    90–118; deviation from ethical values
    during, 186–89, 260nn. 29 and 30; group
    selection hypothesis, in-group/out-group
    distinctions, 167–68, 255nn. 28 and 29; in-
    centives and sanctions for, 169, 255n.29;
    just world phenomenon, 200–201; kin
    selection hypothesis and, 165, 254n.22;
    networks and clusters hypotheses regarding,
    39, 172–76, 255nn.35; personality of Jews
    as basis for, 43, 191–92, 261n.41; psycho-
    logical aspects of altruism and, 180–81,
    257nn.15–17, 258n.19; world views of
    rescuers and, 199–202. See also rescuers:
    altruism among
Homans, George C., 254n.14
honors: as goods altruism, 138–43
human nature: cognitive framework for altru-
    ism and, 10
Hume, David, 12–13, 263n.17
Huneke, D. K., 240n.15, 248n.2

identity: decisions as recognition, not choice,
    220; discovery vs. creation of, 220, 267n.17;
    ethical political acts and, 217–18, 265n.4;
    moral values superseded by, 219, 266n.16;
    perspectival approach to ethical political
    acts and, 226–28, 269n.55; perspective in
    relation to others and, 217–18; perspectives
    on altruism more important than, 220; psy-
    chological aspects of altruism and, 179,
    256n.5; rational choice theory and, 220–23,
    267nn. 19 and 20; reflexivness of ethical
    political acts and, 218; shared humanity
    principle and, 206–7
incentives, effect of, on altruism: group selec-
    tion hypothesis and, 168–69, 255n.29; psy-
    chological aspects of altruism and, 179,
    256n.3
independent agency, identity and, 266n.16
information costs of altruism, 156, 252n.26
intentions: altruism and, vs. consequences, 6
interview techniques: in altruism research, 22,
    246n.89

James, William, 9
Johnson, James, 266n.4, 268nn. 34, 36, and
    38
Johnston, David, 266n.13
judgment: cognitive framework for altruism
    and, 10–11, 241n.32
just world phenomenon: altruism and, 200–
    201, 262n.13

Kahnemann, Daniel, 9, 241n.27, 268n.24
Kant, Immanuel, 268n.24
Karylowski, Jerzy, 256n.3, 259n.20
King Lear: altruism expressed in, 253n.11
kin selection hypothesis: children caring for
    children and, 176–78; evolutionary biology
    theories of altruism and, 164–66; theories
    of, 161–63, 252n.3
Klingemann, Ute, 261n.36
Kohut, Heinz, 203
Kolm, Serge-Christophe, 251n.21
Kohn, Alfie, 239n.1, 263nn. 18, 21, 23, and
    24, 264n.28, 270n.5
Kohut, Heinz, 203, 263n.19
Kolm, Serge-Christophe, 241n.28, 251n.21
Krebs, Dennis, 15, 239n.5, 240n.9, 241n.22,
    243nn.52 and 59, 256n.4
Kuhn, Thomas, 241n.32

Lakoff, George, 245n.79
Langer, Lawrence L., 243n.52, 245n.74
Latane, Bibb, 256n.4, 261n.45
Lerner, Melvin J., 241n.22, 254n.22, 262nn.7
    and 13
Lerner, Richard M., 241n.22
Losco, Joseph, 240n.11

Malfalda (WWII resistance fighter), xii–xiii, xv
Mansbridge, Jane, 239n.1, 224n.63
Margolis, Howard, 252n.23, 254nn.19,21,
    258n.19
marital relationships: perspectival approach to
    ethical political acts and, 225
Marxist theory: perspectival approach to ethi-
    cal political acts and, 224–25, 229–30,
    269n.30
Maslow, Abraham H., 257n.11
mass surveys: narrative interviews compared
    with, 20–21, 245n.77. 246n.86
material rewards: goods altruism as, 138–43
Mead, George H., 231
Midlarsky, Elizabeth, 239n.5, 259n.22

Monroe, Kristen, 244n.63, 247n.4, 248n.9, 258n.17, 266n.13, 267n.18, 268nn.41,46, 269n.49

moral reasoning: core values and, 219, 266n.15; deviation from ethical values in altruists and, 185–89; psychological aspects of altruism and, 180, 257n.12; rational choice theory and, 20, 220–23, 267n.20

Nagel, Thomas, 240n.11, 242n.44, 263n.23, 265n.36

narrative interviews: in altruism research, 18–20, 244n.73

network hypothesis: altruism and, 170–76

Nozick, Robert, 231, 269n.50

Nussbaum, Martha C., 266n.15, 269n.55, 270n.7

occupation: altruism and, 130–32

Oliner, Pearl M. and Samuel P., 180, 257n.15, 258nn. 18 and 19, 263n.25

Olson, Mancur, 268n.32

one-in-many selves paradox, 266n.12

opportunity costs of altruism, 156, 252n.26

outcome-oriented processes: evolutionary biology theories of altruism and, 163, 254n.16; perspectival approach to ethical political acts and, 227–28

parent-child relationships: developmental influences on altruism, 181–85; estrangement patterns in rescuers' families, 165–66, 175, 177–78, 255n.37

participation altruism, 146

perceptions: role of, in altruism, 215–16, 265n.42

personality of person helped: altruism based on, 191–92, 261nn. 37 and 38

perspectives theory of altruism, 14–15; conclusions regarding, 234–38; empathy and, 202–7, 263n.25; empirical tests of, 228–32; ethical political acts and, 217–32; identity superseded by, 220; prisoner's dilemma approach to, 228–30; research concerning, 197–98; role of, in rescuers and non-rescuers, 94–118, 247n.2; self in relation to others, for rescuers, 110–18; shared humanity perspective, 197–216

Phelps, Edmund S., 250n.3

philanthropists: altruism and, 16–17, 64–65, 244n.62; anonymity preferred by, 59–62;

attitudes regarding religion, 125–30; case study and interview from, 41–62; charitable activities of, 47–62, 247n.5; dual utility of altruism for, 153; empathy among, 203–4, 264n.27; entrepreneurs compared with, 30–35, 58–62; family background, wealth, and occupation of, 131; family position of, 132–34; goods altruism among, 140–43; group selection hypothesis, in-group/out-group distinctions, 168; guilt alleviated by altruism among, 149; heroines and heros' attitudes towards, 88–90; incentives and sanctions for, 168–69; kin selection behavior among, 165; networks and clusters hypotheses regarding, 172–76; preference for altruism among, 147–49; psychic good of altruism and, 144–51, 251n.16; reciprocity in altruism of, 151–52; regard for person helped, altruism based on, 191–92; relations with parents and role models of, 182–84; situational influences on, 261n.44; subject selection among, 22

Piaget, Jean, 257n.12

Piliavin, Jane A., 241n.22, 256n.3, 258n.17, 263n.22

political attitudes of altruists, xi

political theory: altruism and, 3, 6, 239n.1; cognitive framework for altruism and, 240n.20; terminology of, 266n.9

poverty: entrepreneurs' attitudes regarding, 30–42; philanthropists' attitudes regarding, 50–62

praise: as goods altruism, 138–43

preference for altruism, 147–49

prisoner's dilemma: perspectival theory and, 228–30

prosocial value orientation: psychological aspects of altruism and, 180, 257n.9

psychic good, altruism as: anonymity of altruism as contradiction to, 150–51; characteristics of, 143–51

psychic income theory: altruism and, 256n.3

psychic utility: of altruism, 7

psychology of altruism, 181–89; empathy and, 203–7, 263n.25; familiarity with person helped and, 190; interaction with external environment and, 189–92; overview, 6–9, 179–94, 239n.5, 240n.22; perspectival approach to ethical political acts and, 224–28, 268n.29; relations with parents and role models for altruists, 181–85; situational

psychology of altruism (cont.)
influences on, 192–94; stage theoretic approaches to, 185–89. See also cognitive framework; developmental psychology

rape: rescuers from, 66–90
Rapoport, Anatol, 268n.42
rational choice theory: deviation from ethical values and, 189, 260n.32; economists' view of altruism and, 159–60, 252n.28; ethical political acts and, 217, 220–23, 265n.1, 267nn. 19 and 20; evolutionary biology theories of altruism and, 163; norm of self-interest and, 239n.3; perspectival approach to ethical political acts and, 225–28; world view and, 12
Rawls, John, 242n.44, 262n.1, 265n.36
reciprocity: altruism and, 151–52; evolutionary biology theories of altruism and, 162–64
reflexive act: altruism as, 6, 210–13, 239n.5, 265n.39; ethical political acts as, 218, 266n.10
religion: altruism attributed to, 121–30, 248nn.2–5; categorization of, 248n.2; heroes' and heroines' attitudes regarding, 124–30; philanthropists' attitudes regarding, 125–30; psychological aspects of altruism and, 180–81, 257n.17; rescuers' attitudes regarding, 112–13, 122–32
rescuers: altruism among, 16–18, 70, 244n.62; altruism as normal behavior for, 106–18, 208–10, 248n.10; approval gained for, by altruism, 150–51; attitudes regarding religion, 112–13, 122–30; canonical expectations about normal behavior among, 208–10, 264n.33; caring and nurturing behavior among, 148–51, 251n.17; costs and benefits of altruism for, 156–59; deviation from ethical values in, 185–89, 260n.29; dual utility of altruism refuted by, 153; empathy among, 203–7, 234–35, 263n.25; estrangement from family of, 165–66, 175, 177–78, 255n.37; failures in child care of, 177–78; family background, wealth, and occupation of, 130–34; forgiveness among, 207, 264n.32; goods altruism among, 138–43; group selection hypothesis, in-group/out-group distinctions, 167–68; haphazard nature of activities of, 96–118; heroes and heroines compared with, 104–118; incen-

tives and sanctions for altruism, 169, 255n.29; kin selection behavior among, 165, 254n.22; networks and clusters hypotheses regarding, 172, 174–76, 255n.35; participation altruism of, 146–48; preference for altruism among, 147–49; psychic good of altruism and, 144–51; psychological aspects of altruism and, 180–81, 257n.17; reciprocity in altruism of, 152; reflexivness of altruism among, 210–13, 265n.39; relations with parents and role models of, 183–84, 260n.26; resource hypothesis regarding, 154–55; self-image of, 202, 243n.58; shared humanity perspective of, 215–16; situational influences on, 192–93, 261n.43; subject selection among, 21–22, 246n.89; world views of rescuers and, 199–202, 262n.11
research methodology regarding altruism, 4–5, 15, 18–23; narrative interviews, 18–20, 244n.73; psychological aspects of altruism and, 179, 256n.6; subject selection, 21–23; survey questionnaire combined with narrative, 20–21; world views, impact of, on altruism, 198, 262n.2
Resistance movement: rescuers' participation in, 175, 255n.39
resource hypothesis regarding altruism, 153–55
Reykowski, Janusz, 240n.21, 241n.22, 243n.56
risks of altruism, 156–59
Rogers, Carl R., 203, 263n.20
role models: altruism and, 150–51; prosocial behavior and, 15, 243n.59–60; psychological aspects of altruism and, 180–85, 257nn.15–17, 260n.25
Rosenberg, Shawn W., 241nn. 24 and 26
Rosenhan, David, 241n.22
Rummelhart, David E., 245nn. 78 and 79, 266n.4
Rushton, J. Phillipe, 253n.9

sanctions: altruism effected by, 168–69, 255n.29
Sauvage, Pierre, 237, 255n.37
Schelling, Thomas C., 268n.35
schema theory: altruism research using, 20, 245n.79, 269n.53
security in surroundings: altruism based on, 192–93

self-image: altruism and, 13–14, 243n.56; of entrepreneurs, 32–33; family position of altruists linked to, 134; of heroes and heroines, 68–90; moral values superseded by, 266n.16; of philanthropists, 61–62; psychic good of altruism and, 144–51, 251n.16; of rescuers, 110–18; world view and, 202

self-interest: altruism and, 3, 6, 13–14, 239n.1, 240n.22, 243nn. 56 and 57; conceptual continuum regarding, 16–18; conclusions regarding altruism and, 8, 235–37, 270n.6; costs and benefits of altruism and, 155–59, 252n.25; economic approaches to altruism and, 137–38; evolutionary biology theories of altruism and, 162–64, 253nn. 10 and 11, 254nn. 18 and 19; group selection hypothesis and, 166–68; narrative interviews and, 19–20; perspectival approach to ethical political acts and, 14–15, 213–16, 227–28; psychological aspects of altruism and, 4, 179, 256n.2, 258n.19

self-sacrifice: as attribute of altruism, 6–7, 239n.7

sexual harassment: rational choice theory and, 221–22

shared humanity perspective on altruism, 197–216, 236–37; altruism as reflex not choice, 210–13; canonical expectations of normal behavior, 208–10; empathy as part of, 202–7; just world phenomenon, 200–201; self-image and, 202; world views and, 198–200

Simon, Herbert A., 9, 227, 239n.3, 268nn.23,35

situational predictors of altruism, 192–94, 257n.17

Slovic, Paul, 9, 241n.27, 268n.24

Smith, Adam: on altruism, 137, 251n.21; on empathy, 12–13, 263n.17

social benefits of altruism, 170–76

social ostracism: of rescuers, 77–78, 140

social psychology of altruism, 179–81, 256n.7, 258n.19, 260n.25

sociocultural factors in altruism, 8–9, 121–36; birth order and size of family, 134–35; community closeness and, 135–36; conclusions regarding, 235–37; family background, wealth, and occupation, 130–32; family position, 132–34; religion, 121–30, 248nn.2–5

Sorokin, P. A., 242n.41

Spencer, Herbert, 240n.22

spontaneity in altruism, 212–13

Springer, Otto, ix–xv, 3–4

stage theoretic approach to altruism, 185–89

Staub, Ervin, 240n.10, 243n.59, 245n.83, 256n.2, 257nn.9,13, 258n.17

subject selection: in altruism research, 21–23

superego: psychological aspects of altruism and, 180, 256n.7

survey questionnaires: altruism research using, 20–21, 246n.86

Tannen, Deborah, 245n.80

tax incentives: altruism effected by, 168–69

Taylor, Charles, 242n.44, 266n.4, 269n.55

testing techniques: altruism research using, 20, 245nn.83–85

Tetlock, Phillip, 267n.20

theft: rational choice theory and, 222

Theory of Moral Sentiments, The (Smith), 251n.21

Thom, Gary, 266n.8

Titchener, Edward B., 202–3, 243n.47

Titmuss, Richard Morris, 137

Tocqueville, Alexis de, 242n.35

Tonnies, Ferdinand, 12, 242nn.41, 42, and 45, 262nn. 4 and 7

transcript editing and research of altruism interviews, 22–23, 246n.91

Trivers, Robert, 252n.2, 253nn. 7 and 13, 255n.32

Tullock, Gordon, 163, 253n.11

Turner, John C., 242n.43

Tversky, Amos, 9, 241n.27, 268n.24

utilitarianism: altruism and, 251n.21

Valvanis, S., 250n.1

volunteerism: altruism and, 244n.62; philanthropists' involvement in, 45–46

von Stauffenberg plot, xi–xii

voting: perspectival theory and, 230–31

Vygotskii, Lev S., 241n.22

wartime behavior: rational choice theory and, 222–23

wealth: altruism and, 130–32

Wealth of Nations, The (Smith), 251n.21

Weapons of the Spirit (film), 270n.13
welfare: as attribute of altruism, 6–7
Whitehead, Jaan, 268n.43, 270n.9
Whiting, Beatrice, 176–77
Williams, Bernard A. O., 263n.24, 266n.15, 269n.55
Wilson, Edward O., 252n.2, 253n.4, 254nn. 17 and 18, 255n.24
Wintrobe, Ronald, 253n.11, 254n.15
Wispe, Lauren G., 239n.5

world view: altruism and, 12, 142, 198–207, 244n.71, 262n.2; religious attitudes and, 129–30
Wuthnow, Robert, 244n.65, 247n.2, 251n.22

Yad Vashem medal winners, 21–22, 142, 244n.71

Zahn-Waxler, Carol, 256nn. 2 and 4
Zuckert, Catherine H., 270nn. 6, 8, and 11

About the Author

KRISTEN RENWICK MONROE is Professor of Politics and Associate Director of the Program in Political Psychology at the University of California, Irvine. She is the author of *Presidential Popularity and the Economy* and editor of *The Economic Approach to Politics: A Critical Reassessment of the Theory of Rational Action* and *The Political Process and Economic Change*.